Sheridan's Plays

NOW PRINTED AS HE WROTE THEM

AND HIS MOTHER'S UNPUBLISHED COMEDY

A Journey to Bath.

EDITED BY

W. FRASER RAE

(Author of 'Sheridan: a Biography,' &c.).

With an Introduction

BY

SHERIDAN'S GREAT-GRANDSON

THE MARQUESS OF DUFFERIN AND AVA.

LONDON: DAVID NUTT.
AT THE SIGN OF THE PHŒNIX, LONG ACRE.

1902.

This scarce antiquarian book is included in our special *Legacy Reprint Series*. In the interest of creating a more extensive selection of rare historical book reprints, we have chosen to reproduce this title even though it may possibly have occasional imperfections such as missing and blurred pages, missing text, poor pictures, markings, dark backgrounds and other reproduction issues beyond our control. Because this work is culturally important, we have made it available as a part of our commitment to protecting, preserving and promoting the world's literature. Thank you for your understanding.

The authentic version of Sheridan's Plays is

𝔇𝔢𝔡𝔦𝔠𝔞𝔱𝔢𝔡 𝔱𝔬

SIR HENRY IRVING

AND

SIR SQUIRE BANCROFT,

IN GRATEFUL ACKNOWLEDGMENT OF THE ARTISTIC AND CRITICAL COMMENTS ON SHERIDAN'S DRAMATIC CAPACITY AND ACHIEVEMENTS WHICH THEY KINDLY CONTRIBUTED TO MY "BIOGRAPHY" OF HIM.

CONTENTS.

	PAGE
INTRODUCTION	VII
PREFATORY NOTES	XIII
THE RIVALS	1
ST. PATRICK'S DAY; OR, THE SCHEMING LIEUTENANT	76
THE DUENNA	97
THE SCHOOL FOR SCANDAL	147
THE CRITIC	222
A JOURNEY TO BATH	263

INTRODUCTION.

AMONG the marvels of existence, nothing is more surprising than the birth of genius in unlooked-for places. Evolutionists can trace the development of species from stage to stage; but almost imperceptible progression seems to be the law of Nature, while all their science will not enable them to account for the "avatar" of Burns and Keats, or of many another star that has suddenly burst out of darkness into being. Neither can they explain with greater ease how it came about that Richard Brinsley Sheridan, a young man of four-and-twenty, without more experience of the world than a couple of seasons of Bath society could afford, should have produced several plays which at once raised him into the first rank of the world's lighter dramatists, and are now, after a century and a quarter, as universally popular as on the occasion when they were first applauded.

Pope has said, "What lasts a century can have no flaw," and henceforth 'The Rivals,' 'The School for Scandal,' 'The Duenna,' and 'The Critic' will continue to hold a foremost place in the living literature of England.

It is true Sheridan was descended from a family that had been intellectually remarkable for many generations; but, though his grandfather had wit, its playful flashes did not survive in his son, the actor and author of an English dictionary, who, though a man of exceptional parts, was, I apprehend, both tiresome and unamiable. Perhaps, however, it was from his mother that Sheridan inherited the subtle attribute which sublimates talent into genius, for the authoress who wrote 'Sidney Bidulph,' a novel which Charles James Fox, Lord North, and Richardson pronounced the best of the day, as well as 'The Discovery,' a comedy containing one of Garrick's favourite characters, must have had something of the divine essence.

I do not now intend to enter upon an examination of the relative merits of Sheridan's plays, or the causes of their enduring popularity. The impression produced by each depends a good deal upon the way in which it is acted. There are characters in two of them which it requires great delicacy and discernment to impersonate adequately. For instance, in 'The Rivals' there is always a danger of the innocent rusticity of Bob Acres becoming loutish vulgarity at the hands of a second-rate comedian, while perhaps even greater skill is required to prevent the fire-eating tendencies of Sir Lucius O'Trigger from dimming the charm of his high-bred and chivalrous demeanour.

I have always imagined that there must be few more difficult personages to represent than Joseph Surface in 'The School for Scandal,' for the success of the piece requires that the sympathy of the audience should remain with Lady Teazle, and the thought of her yielding to his wiles, were he a mere vulgar hypocrite, would lower her too much in their estimation. To maintain her, therefore, upon the plane she is intended to occupy, the presentment of her lover, both as regards his appearance and behaviour, ought to be rendered sufficiently attractive to account for the complaisance with which she seems to tolerate his advances.

Again, I have sometimes seen the effect of Mrs. Malaprop's charming eccentricities of diction marred by the actress showing her consciousness of their nature, and her expectation of the amusement they are intended to excite, whereas the real artist exhibits sublime ignorance of the mistakes she is making, and seems to ask, through the medium of that subtle telegraphy which is in perpetual action between those on either side of the footlights, "My good friends, what on earth are you laughing at?"

It might also prove interesting to speculate as to whether the remoteness of the time and fashion in which the scenes of these comedies are laid adds to or detracts from their pleasing effects. In the days when swords, powder, bag-wigs, and paniers were the fashion, the element of realism they contained might, perhaps, have proved an agreeable stimulus to the sympathies of the audience, while undoubtedly those portions of the dialogue which now appear somewhat stilted and artificial would have been tacitly accepted as consonant to what were then the current modes both of feeling and of expression. On the other hand, the shifting pictures of the personages now presented to our view in an unfamiliar garb, and the gay appointments which brightened the world a century and a quarter ago, have a tendency to involve the modern spectator in an atmosphere of illusion, which helps him to forget for the moment his own surroundings, and follow with more intense interest the varying fortunes of these representatives of a vanished age.

Owing to my residence abroad for so long a period, it has not been my good fortune to witness many representations either of 'The Rivals' or of 'The School for Scandal,' nor have I seen 'The Critic' played more than once, and that was many years ago; but I remember having had the satisfaction of admiring in a play, at Bologna, a remarkable achievement of Sheridan himself, who rescued Miss Linley, the beautiful "Maid of Bath," from the clutches of her persecutor by bringing a gondola under the windows of her house in Bond Street. I also assisted, in 1845, at a remarkable representation of 'The School for Scandal' at some private theatricals at our Embassy in Paris, when the part of Lady Teazle was taken by the late Countess

Granville, who had known Sheridan personally, that of Mrs. Candour being played by my mother, and that of Charles Surface by my uncle, Charles Sheridan. Lately, however, all the theatre-going world of London has had an opportunity of seeing both 'The Rivals' and 'The School for Scandal' admirably staged and acted at the Haymarket Theatre.

As to the circumstances which have led to the issue of the present edition of Sheridan's Plays, Mr. Fraser Rae, who edits them, has given full explanations in his prefatory remarks.

It has sometimes been objected that Sheridan took too much pains in polishing his work, as though the straining after perfection, which is an instinct innate in the breast of every true artist, were blameworthy. But, in his review of Moore's 'Memoirs of Sheridan,' Jeffrey admirably vindicated my great-grandfather's methods. Jeffrey wrote: "He, who was for thirty years the most brilliant talker — the greatest conversational wit of the splendid circle in which he moved — could not possibly have been a man to whom preparation was generally necessary in order to shine; and cannot be suspected of having had a cold or sluggish fancy, which did not give its golden harvests till it was diligently laboured and manured. Sheridan's conceptions, on the contrary, seem always to have flowed from him with great copiousness and rapidity. But he had taste as well as genius—and ambition as well as facility. He was not always satisfied with the first suggestions of his mind; but his labour was almost always employed, not in making what was bad, tolerable, but in making what was good, better and best."

In these circumstances, it seems highly desirable that the public should be enabled to judge of Sheridan's work exactly as it was when it first left his hands.

DUFFERIN AND AVA.

PREFATORY NOTES.

I.

IN the preface to my Biography of Sheridan I described how much information I had obtained from the library at Frampton Court, where many of Sheridan's manuscripts are very carefully preserved. Sheridan's grandfather gave much time and care to arranging the manuscripts of 'The Rivals,' 'The Duenna,' 'The School for Scandal,' and 'The Critic,' and he had them bound in handsome volumes. With the exception of 'The Rivals,' none of these plays was given to the world in print by Sheridan himself. All the other published copies were reproductions of those used on the stage. Many changes had been made in them for histrionic purposes.

The only important manuscript of which there is no trace is that of 'The Rivals,' which was acquired by Mr. Harris, the manager of Covent Garden Theatre, the manuscript being probably destroyed when that theatre was burnt to the ground. If it had been preserved we should have known the number and character of the alterations which were made between the first representation of the piece on the 17th January, 1775, and the second on the 28th. When the success of 'The Rivals' was assured, Sheridan prepared a copy for publication.

XIV   PREFATORY NOTES.

This is now a scarce book. It is a valuable one, however, because it contains Sheridan's own acting version of his comedy. The version which is now put on the stage differs from it.

The many reprints of Sheridan's plays are made from the edition in two volumes published by Murray in 1821. Tom Moore prefixed an introduction in which he disclaimed responsibility for the edition, and apologized for the delay in the appearance of 'Memoirs' which he had undertaken to write. I am indebted to Mr. John Murray for information gathered from the books of his firm to the effect that his grandfather paid Tom Moore and Mr. Wilkie for their labours with regard to preparing Sheridan's plays for the press. I assume, then, that Mr. Wilkie acted as editor.

The paramount duty of an editor is to exhibit strict loyalty to his author, and either to put the author's text before the public as its author would have done, or else to take the responsibility for alterations. Mr. Wilkie did not like some things in Sheridan's published version of 'The Rivals,' and he drew his pen through them without notice. The result is that readers of that play have now before them the truncated version which Mr. Wilkie prepared for Mr. Murray, and which subsequent editors have copied. Some of the alterations are trivial, yet none should have been concealed. In Sheridan's version of the *dramatis personæ* one of the men is styled "coachman," and the first act is headed with "coachman crosses the stage," while in that act Fag's conversation is carried on with the "coachman," but Thomas is substituted by Mr. Wilkie for the "coachman." He asks Fag what sort of place Bath is. Fag says in his reply, "at present we are, like other great assemblies, divided into parties — High-roomians and Low-roomians; however, for my part, I have resolved to stand neuter; and so I told Bob Brush at our last committee." Mr. Wilkie struck his pen through the words just quoted. Among several other passages which met the like fate is one in the conversation between Mrs. Malaprop and Sir Anthony Absolute. Sir Anthony having denounced circulating libraries, Mrs. Malaprop says: "Well, Sir Anthony, your wife, Lady Absolute, was fond of books." Sir Anthony. "Aye—and injury sufficient they were to her, Madam — But were I to chuse another helpmate, the extent of her erudition should consist in her knowing her simple letters, without their mischievous combinations;—and the summit of her science be—her ability to count as far as twenty. The first, Mrs. Malaprop, would enable her to work A. A. upon my linen;—and the latter quite sufficient to prevent her giving me a shirt No. 1 and a stock No. 2." The careful reader, who compares Sheridan's version, printed with absolute fidelity in this volume, with that commonly current, will wonder why Mr. Wilkie took so much trouble to so little purpose. I must add that he did not spare Mrs. Malaprop when she was writing to Sir Lucius O'Trigger. He cut out these words from her letter:—" As my motive is interested, you may be assured my love shall never be miscellaneous," and those which preceded her signature "Yours, while meretricious," Delia.

The fate of 'The Rivals' was very doubtful at the first performance. Had the comedy been damned, then there was an end to Sheridan as a playwright. But this piece having succeeded, his other plays had an easier ordeal. I have thought that the story of 'The Rivals' and its fate on the stage could not be told better than in the words of contemporary writers in newspapers, and the passages in chronological order which follow give a vivid account of what occurred. This critique (published on the morning after the first performance) is probably from the pen of William Woodfall:—

The Morning Chronicle, 18 Jan., 1775.
"In consideration of that plea [in the prologue, that the author is a novice], and in tenderness to a young bard, who betrays not, as is sometimes the case, any unbecoming forwardness, but rather discovers an ingenuous diffidence of his abilities,—in respect to such a situation, we should rather wish to abate the edge of public censure, than to animadvert with severity on the lapses of an inexperienced writer, in the midst of whose very imperfections we may trace the man of genius, the gentleman, and the scholar. His fable indeed is not happily chosen, nor skilfully conducted; nor are his characters faithfully copied from nature; but many parts of the dialogue, the graver scenes especially, are chaste and elegant; and the defects of the other parts of the drama do not appear to be the offspring of dulness or ignorance. A very little more acquaintance with the business of the stage would have instructed the author to curtail some of the scenes, which were last night insufferably tedious; and some of that stage art, much of which Cibber derived from his connexion with the theatre, would have taught our juvenile poet to give more *effect* to the part of Jack Absolute, who is, in some sort, a second Atall, *Double Galant*. The romantic vein of *Lydia Languish* is

not so well imagined, or so ably sustained as Steele's Lady (we forget her name*) in the *Accomplished Fools;* and the characters of Falkland and Julia are even beyond the pitch of *sentimental* comedy, and may be not improperly stiled *metaphysical*. We would wish, however, to make a particular exception to the scene between them in the beginning of the fifth act, in which we are at a loss to determine whether the author or the actress (Mrs. Bulkley) were most to be commended. What evil spirit could influence the writer and the managers to assign the part of *Sir Lucius O'Trigger to Mr. Lee,* or Mr. Lee himself to receive it? One would imagine they had intended, in Mr. Lee's person, to realize the unjust satire of Sir Charles Hanbury Williams on the whole Irish nation :—

> '*But nature, who denied them* sense
> *Has given them* legs *and* impudence,
> *Which beats all* understanding.'

This representation of Sir Lucius, is indeed an affront to the common sense of an audience, and is so far from giving the manners of our brave and worthy neighbours, that it scarce equals the picture of a *respectable Hotentot;* gabbling in an uncouth dialect, neither Welch, English, nor Irish. Shuter [Sir Anthony Absolute] was pleasant, but, as usual, shamefully imperfect. Woodward [Captain Absolute] has often appeared to more advantage. Mr. Lewis [Faulkland] struggled with a very difficult character, and acquitted himself creditably. Quick's character [Acres] betrayed him into farce ; and Lee-Lewes [Fag], and Dunstall [David], exhibited their accustomed pert valet and country bumpkin. The ladies, Mrs. Bulkley especially [Julia], did great justice to their parts, and we want words to express the satisfaction the last-mentioned lady gave by her just elegant manner of speaking one of the most excellent and poetical Epilogues we ever remember to have heard. The scenes and dresses were many of them new, but we think we remember

---

* The lady's name is Bridget Tipkin. She is far less attractive than Lydia Languish. Her most brilliant remark is, "It looks so ordinary, to go out of a door to be married. Indeed, I ought to be taken out of a window and run away with."

a better view of the North Parade at Bath in a play of Dr. Kenrick's exhibited some years ago at Drury Lane Theatre."

The Public Ledger, 18 Jan., 1775.

"The *Rivals*, as a Comedy, requires much castigation, and the pruning hand of judgment, before it can ever pass on the Town as even a tolerable Piece. In language it is defective to an extreme, in Plot outré and one of the *Characters* is an absolute exotic in the wilds of nature. The author seems to have considered puns, witticisms, similes and metaphors, as admirable substitutes for polished diction; hence they abound in every sentence; and hence it is that instead of the '*Metmorphosis*' of Ovid, one of the characters is made to talk of Ovid's 'Meat-for-Hopes,' a Lady is called the 'Pine Apple of beauty,' the Gentleman in return 'an Orange of perfection.' A Lover describes the sudden change of disposition in his Mistress by saying, that 'she flies off in a tangent born down by the current of disdain'; and a second Tony Lumkin, to describe how fast he rode, compares himself to a 'Comet with a tail of dust at his heels.'

"These are shameful absurdities in language, which can suit no character, how widely soever it may depart from common life and common manners.

"Whilst thus censure is freely passed, not to say that there are various sentiments in the Piece which demonstrate the Author's no stranger to the finer feelings, would be shameful partiality.

"Time will not permit a thorough investigation of this Comedy; but if the 'Rivals' rests its claim to public favour, solely on the basis of merit, the hisses of the auditors on the first night of representation, gives reason to suspect a most fatal disappointment. However, that it may be suffered to have the usual nine nights run, is what, on the Author's account, we most sincerely wish; but this we can assure him, that if the dulness of law writers have made him yawn, the dulness of the 'Rivals' lulled several of the middle gallery spectators into a profound sleep.

"The Prologue was delivered by Mr. Lee in the character of a Serjeant-at-Law who received the author's brief to plead his cause before the Jury of spectators.

"The Epilogue was spoken by Mrs. Bulkley.

"Many of the parts were improperly cast. Mr. Lee [Sir Lucius O'Trigger] is a most execrable Irishman. Miss Barsanti [Lydia Languish] is calculated only for a mimic; she has the archness of look and manner, that shrug of the shoulders, which must for ever unqualify her for genteel Comedy; and when she is represented as a girl of thirty thousand pounds fortune, we curse the blind Goddess for bestowing her favours so absurdly; then she has the agreeable lisp of Thomas Hull, and cannot be expected to articulate her words so as to be understood, unless her tongue first undergoes a cutting."

After a sketch of the piece, the critic says: "This Comedy said to be written by Mr. *Sheridan*, Jun., seems to be the hasty composition of a young man of more genius than present knowledge of the English drama; hence those defects in the main pillars, which are the only support of a dramatic composition. *The Morning Post, Jan., 1775.*

"The fable is not the most natural or intelligible, nor have the characters any great claim to novelty.—Sir *Lucius O'Trigger* and Sir *Anthony Absolute*, indifferent as they are, were most barbarously handled by the inattention of the performers, neither of the two being perfect in one sentence of their parts: Shameful! that the fame of an author should be thus sported with by persons, to whom he is under the necessity of intrusting it; for to their conduct we attribute a part of the bad reception which attended the representation.

"The dialogue, in many scenes, was natural and pleasing; in one or two, far superior to that of the modern race of comic writers;—the situation between Capt. *Absolute* and Mrs. *Malaprop* was well conceived and wrought up. We think the writer has here and there mistaken ribaldry for humour, at which the audience seemed displeased.—All the performers, the two already excepted, exerted themselves to the utmost.—A prologue by Mr. Lee, in the character of a Serjeant-at-Law, and Mr. Quick, as an Attorney, who brings the former a fee to plead for the bard, tho' novel, was not much relished. The Epilogue, however, made amends; for it struck us as one of the most harmonious, pretty pieces of the kind we have heard for some time.

"There were three new scenes upon the occasion, one of which, a perspective view through the South Parade at Bath, to the late Mr. Allen's delightful Villa, was universally admired."

SCORPION.

The Morning Chronicle, 19 Jan., 1775. "The modesty of the author of *The Rivals* is as commendable as the effrontery of some dramatic authors is censurable. The *Rivals* is presented for the first time; the town see its deficiencies; some displeasure is expressed in the Theatre at particular passages, and the next day the reprehensible parts are marked by the critics; the Author willing to show his obedience to the will of the town, withdraws his comedy that he may prune, correct, and alter it, till he thinks it worthy the public favour. ....The new comedy of the Rivals was, in the Green Room of Covent Garden Theatre, but last week, deemed the *ne plus ultra* of Comedy."

The Morning Post, 19 Jan., 1775. "The Comedy of the *Rivals*, at *Covent Garden*, is withdrawn for the present, to undergo some severe prunings, trimmings, and patchings, before its second appearance: the Author, we are informed, seeing the general disapprobation with which it was received, was very desirous of withdrawing it entirely, but the managers would not consent to it, determined to stand the event of a second embarcation, let the consequences be what they may."

The Morning Chronicle, 20 Jan., 1775. "To the Printer, Sir, There is certainly some evil genius attends the proceedings of Covent Garden Theatre. Our expectations have been some time raised with the hope that they were at last to produce us a truly good comedy; the hour of proof arrives, and we are presented with a piece got up with such flagrant inattention, that half the performers appear to know nothing of their parts, and the play itself is a *full hour* longer in the representation than any piece on the stage.—This last circumstance is an error of such a nature as shows either great obstinacy in the Author, or excessive ignorance in the managers; but the casting Mr. Lee for the part of *Sir Lucius O'Trigger*, is a blunder of the first brogue, which Mr. Lee plainly shewed as he was not *Irishman* enough to have committed for himself. If there had been no one in the theatre fit for the part, it should have been taken out of the piece which is full exuberant enough to spare it. As I find the further representation of it is put off for the present, I suppose this will be the case; for to attempt to continue him in the character will inevitably damn the play. There seemed to be a little malice from one corner of the gallery, which shewed itself too early to produce any effect; but it was absolutely impossible for the Author's warmest well wishers to over-rule the disapprobation that was shewn to Lee's horrid medley of discordant brogues. The character of Faulkland is touched with a delicate and masterly hand, yet Lewis was perfect enough to be at home in it: it is just such a part as Mr. Garrick twenty years ago would have marked among his first performances. There is as much true humour in *Acres* and *David* as in any character on the stage whatever. What the characters of *Sir Anthony* and *Sir Lucius ought* to have appeared I cannot take upon me to say, but Shuter, from being imperfect appeared to ruin some scenes, which, from the situations, seemed to promise noble effects from his *vis Comica*. The versification of the Prologue was sadly marred in the delivery, for we cannot suppose it to have been written by the Author of the Epilogue; which, after a vein of elegant humour, runs to the conclusion in some as beautiful lines as ever did credit to our language. Yours &c. *A Friend to Comedy.*

"Sir,—I cannot avoid taking the earliest opportunity of reprehending, in the severest manner, one of the performers of Covent Garden Theatre, for his shameful negligence, in not being perfect in a single sentence, at the representation of The *Rivals* on Tuesday last. Before I name the man, every lover of the drama, will, I am persuaded, point him out: for fear, however, the town should be wrong in their conjecture, and any other person should suffer by it, I will give you, Mr. Printer, his name in capitals. The person I allude to is MR. SHUTER. I will treat him like a gentleman in my appellation, though he probably may not deserve it. If his incorrectness arises from

The Morning Chronicle, 20 Jan., 1775.

XXII   PREFATORY NOTES.

his strong feelings, I really pity his condition, and a public declaration of this kind would do him service, but if it is the effect of *inattention*, I will be bold to tell him, that, in an equitable consideration, he is more immoral and unjust than a highwayman; for by this shameful usage, he, in all probability may rob the author of four or five hundred pounds, besides what is as dear to a man as his existence—his reputation.

"Mr. S. has often been admonished upon this subject; still he continues to insult his best friends, for surely it is an insult of the highest nature to the audience, for a man to be inattentive to the duties of his profession, when that profession obliges him to appear before that awful tribunal, the public.

"Before I conclude, Sir, I will take the liberty to observe, that the Rivals is a piece extremely irregular and inconsistent; it abounds with metaphors of the lowest kind; the miserable pun used by a footman to a coachman of *meat for horses*, instead of *metamorphosis*, is much too contemptible even for a postilion. Two or three pathetic scenes are however delicately touched; and the Epilogue as is asserted by your Theatrical Intelligencer, is very pleasing and poetical; but the characters, for the most part, are extremely *outré*. Mr. Lee Lewes, Mrs. Green, and Mrs. Bulkley, deserved the highest commendation for their several endeavours to please the town, and serve the author, and I could not help regretting the miserable situation of Messrs. Woodward and Lee, whose characters were injudiciously cast. I am, Sir, Your most obedient servant, *One of the Pitt.*

"Bedford Coffee house, January 18, 1775."

The Gazetteer.
20 Jan., 1775.

"Thursday morning, January 20 [19?]. Amidst the general inundation of criticisms on the new comedy of The Rivals, permit your correspondent to give his impartial opinion in as few words as possible. It appears to him, that the dramatic piece in question has more *beauties* in some scenes, and more *egregious deficiencies* in others, than any one modern production of a similar nature; and if the young Poet's genius sometimes breaks out unexpectedly like a flash of lightening, it seems to shine the brightest through the thick cloud of vapours that surroundeth it.

                                               Latonæ Filius."

"Sir, Next to the torment of sitting out a very dull Comedy, I know not a more uneasy situation than that of hearing an apparently good one mangled in the representation. I think I never saw a performance more disgraceful to a Theatre-Royal than the manner in which the *Rivals* was performed at Covent Garden; none of the performers seemed to be tolerably perfect except Mrs. Bulkley and Miss Barsanti; Shuter did not know any two lines together, and whenever he was out, he tried to fill the interval with oaths and buffoonery; in all his scenes with Woodward he put him out; and for the Irishman, of all the disgusting attempts that ever was damn'd in a strolling company, nothing ever came up to this. The audience shewed great partiality and lenity for the author, in making a distinction between the merit of the piece, and the excessive demerit of the representation of this character; which one would have thought must have damned the best play that ever was written: as it stands, it is absolutely impossible that the piece can go on; the others may get perfect, and do justice to their parts, but *Lee* never can be suffered in this character, and his deportment in it, is literally such, as will bully even the Author's friends into hissing. Yours, &c. Hibernicus." — The Morning Post, 20 Jan., 1775.

"Mr. Editor, I hold nothing more sacred than private character, but when anyone affects singularity in public, the public, I presume, have a right to animadvert on his conduct. — The Morning Post, 20 Jan., 1775.

"I am invited to this correspondence, by the intreaties of a large party of my friends, who were seated in the front-boxes at Covent Garden last night, for the purpose of seeing a new representation, which the town had been promised some days before. We met with a good deal of interruption in our design early in the evening, from a young man who had planted himself in our neighbourhood, and who seemed determined to create a prejudice against the performance, by every mode that malevolence could suggest. I do not mean to enter into a particular disquisition of the piece; if it had its objections, it is agreed even by connoisseurs to have its merits; consequently should have been allowed a candid hearing. With candour, Sir, it was received by

XXIV PREFATORY NOTES.

every part of the house, a few in one corner of the two shilling gallery, and this gentleman excepted. But what tended to inflame our indignation against this zealot for mischief, was a knowledge that he himself stands indebted to the emanations of a benevolent heart, and the dictates of a truly liberal mind, for his present situation, and every other advantage in life. For such is the nothingness of the man, that less than the fostering hand of the very best of Princes could never have raised him from his original obscurity.

"Should this awaken M. B—d to a recollection of his own good fortune, he may, perhaps, in future, instead of discovering a malicious and disgusting singularity, be induced to join the generous and quick-sighted public, who, dread as their tribunal may appear, never fail shewing indulgence, if genius be discerned,—though but in Embrio.

Yours, A LIBRARIAN."

Wednesday, January 18, 1775.

The Morning Post, 20 Jan., 1775. "We are assured that the part of the Hibernian Baronet, in the new Comedy of The Rivals, was undertaken by Mr. Lee, entirely as a matter of necessity, and at the instance of the author himself; and as it appears a walk not suited to him, we hear the Comedy will be deferred a few days till ANOTHER WILL BE ready in the character."

"Mr. Editor, Though poetry despises mediocrity, the critic that steers the middle course, like the most experienced pilot, is the likeliest to escape *the gulph of malevolence, or the rocks of partiality.* In this line, permit the present writer to convey to the public his weak, but unbiassed judgment, on the new Comedy of *The Rivals.* Short criticisms, if they are dull, are the least tedious.—To the point:—The fable is indifferent, but not bad; the characters, in general, partly in, and partly out of nature;—Faulkland, in most respects, a new, and a very good character, but badly sustained by Mr. Lewes;—Julia (considered in the line of elegant and sentimental Comedy) is an honour to the drama; and the representation is no less an honour to Mrs. Bulkley;— Sir Lucius O'Trigger is a very indifferent Irishman as drawn by the poet, and much worse so represented by the player;—Jack

Absolute, rather a little too unimportant, but in representation, sat very easy upon Mr. Woodward;—Sir Anthony Absolute, a strange kind of heterogeneous animal, though, perhaps, not badly conceived;—Shuter shamefully imperfect in his part, though he occasionally exerted his usual drollery;—the play, in general, received little or no advantage from the performers;— the author seems to be possessed of real genius, though his Muse is a very capricious kind of Lady; when in a good humour, she produces the most noble and refined sentiments, and at another time, she sinks unaccountably into ribaldry, and almost nonsense. The play was attempted to be damned in the most illiberal manner; the hisses were cruel, though sometimes not injudicious; —but as there are some scenes in this play that transcend any modern production, it is hoped their excellency will atone for the manifest deficiency of the rest. A little pruning very necessary. The Epilogue is so exceedingly refined, elegant, and classical, that it equals, if not exceeds, anything of the sort that Roscius [Garrick] himself hath ever produced; it breathes throughout, the elegant effusion of refined sentiments, and concludes with the noble ideas of 'lighting the lamp of wisdom with the torch of love.'—Mrs. Bulkley spoke the Epilogue exceedingly well.

IMPARTIALIST."

Wednesday morning, Jan. 18, 1775.

"I did not till this day see that you had declared me remiss and imperfect in my part in the new comedy of *The Rivals:* had you only blamed my incapacity to act the part, I should have remained silent; as the reason of my performing it will be made known to the public. But a tenderness for my reputation is what I hold the most material point, (I mean, that of *diligence* in my profession, in order to shew a proper respect to the patrons and encouragers of theatrical entertainments) induces me to acquaint you, that the author of the piece, the managers, and every person conversant with the rehearsals of it, will vouch for my being perfect in the words of the character, to a minute exactness, long before the representation of the play.

John Lee."

The Morning Chronicle, 21 Jan., 1775.

19 January, 1775.

PREFATORY NOTES.

The London Chronicle, 21-24 Jan., 1775.

"There never was so much crowding known as at the new Comedy of the Rivals on Tuesday last; and it was remarked that there had not been seen so many Ladies and people of fashion at a first night's representation for a long time. Several people in the galleries, who were evidently planted to disturb the performance, were turned out before the third act; and it is said a challenge was given in the boxes."

The Gazetteer, 21 Jan., 1775.

"Friday morning, 20 Jan. 1775 to my letter of yesterday, please to add the following postcript. The Epilogue to the Rivals, in the beginning, somewhat resembles the stile and humour of Roscius: but it is much more refined: the latter part runs a good deal into the diction and sentiment of Pope or Dryden; it is, perhaps, upon the whole, the best composition of the sort that the Theatre has been honoured with for some years.   LATONAE FILIUS."

Errata in my letter.—*For* the brightest, *read* the brighter.

The Morning Post, 21 Jan., 1725.

"MR. EDITOR, I am the last man in the world who would step forth to upbraid a degraded poet, but when I find a performer is execrated by the wretched puffs of the author's friends, in order to throw the principal part of the odium from his own shoulders on those of the player, I own I cannot help taking fire. I shall be acknowledged no partizan, either of Mr. *Lee* or Mr. *Shuter*, when I confess their performance was in every way reprehensible, nay shocking—but at the same time I will aver, that neither of them were invested with anything like a *character*: *Sir Lucius O'Trigger* was so ungenerous an attack upon a nation, that must justify any severity with which the piece will hereafter be treated: it is the first time I ever remember to have seen so villainous a portrait of an Irish Gentleman, permitted so openly to insult that country upon the boards of an English theatre. For the rest of the piece, the author has my pity; but for this unjustifiable attack, my warmest resentment.

Yours, &c.   A BRITON."

Pall Mall, Friday Noon.

Notice is given to the effect that the play will be performed, **The Gazetteer.** "for the second time," on Saturday next, with alterations, and **24 Jan., 1775,** that another performer will take the part which had been filled by Mr. Lee.

A paragraph runs thus :—" One of the pit advises Mr. Sheridan **The Morning** to proceed vigorously in the great work of castration, and **Post,** congratulates him on the present length of his piece. The **24 Jan., 1775.** representation must be shortened at least three quarters of an hour ;—surely so capital a mutilation must remove the objection of the coyest critic.

"The same friend takes the liberty to hint to the *celebrated* Hugh Kelly Esqre; that the motives of his generosity, in patronising this young author, are liable to misrepresentation; men so public as he is, are often injuriously accused of vanity and presumption."

"It was yesterday reported that overtures had been made to **The Morning** Mr. Sheridan, to give him one hundred pounds each night for **Chronicle,** his wife's singing at Drury Lane Oratorios, or for his having **25 Jan., 1775.** half the profits; and should he accept of either, the band need not be under the least apprehension of playing to empty benches."

"At the second representation of the new Comedy of the **The British** Rivals, it was received with the warmest bursts of approbation **Chronicle,** by a crowded, and apparently impartial audience. The Author **27-30 Jan.,** has very judiciously removed everything that could give offence **1775.** in the character of Sir Lucius O'Trigger; and Mr. Shuter exerted himself in a manner which entirely recovered his credit."

"Sir, I was present at Mr. Lee's performance in the Comedy **The Morning** of the Rivals, and said to my friend, I think Mr. Lee is very **Post,** imperfect in his part: Don't you hear the prompter very plain, **27 Jan., 1775.** replied I? Yes, I do, (we were next to the music) said my friend, and I am sorry for it, particularly on the author's account.

XXVIII   PREFATORY NOTES.

—But, however, Mr. Editor, had it been otherwise, I am very well persuaded, if he had continued this ill-adopted character, it would have been equally impossible for either the actor or author to have succeeded.   I am, your humble servant, Candour."

The Morning Post,
28 Jan., 1775.
"This evening we find the Comedy of the *Rivals*, having been taken into dock again, to undergo some repairs, and have a new keel, is to be re-launched in Covent-Garden bay: we wish she may run foul of nothing this tide, but quitting her stocks glibly, may sit like a duck on the water.

"We hear that the admired Epilogue to the Rivals is the composition of Mrs. Sheridan. There is a delicacy in the thoughts and in the expressions of this poem, that claim the warmest approbation, and leave us in doubt which we shall most applaud, Mrs. Sheridan's excellence in music, or in poetry."

Advertisement in *The British Chronicle* for 30 Jan. to 1 Feb.
"In a few days will be published price 1/6^d The Rivals, a Comedy. As it is now performing at the Theatre Royal Covent Garden. Printed for John Wilkie, No. 71, St. Paul's Church Yard."

The Gazetteer,
30 Jan., 1775.
"The new Comedy of The Rivals, which was performed for the second time on Saturday night, [the 28th] was received with very great applause, and will be repeated tomorrow for the benefit of the Author, with the new musical entertainment of The two Misers."

The Morning Post,
30 Jan., 1775.
"On Saturday evening last, Mr. Sheridan's Comedy of the *Rivals*, was performed for the second time with additions and alterations, at the theatre-royal, Covent Garden. It's present state is widely different from that, in which we found it on the first night's representation. Sir *Lucius O'Trigger* being retouched, has now the appearance of a character; and his assigning *Beverley's* reflection on his country, as the grounds for his desire to quarrel with him, is a reasonable pretence, and wipes off the former stigma undeservedly thrown on the sister kingdom:—it is due to the merit of Mr. Clinch to say, he did the strictest

justice to the part, and from his ease in this character we soon expect to see him fill more capital walks in genteel comedy with credit to himself, and pleasure to his audience:—we hope Mr. Lee was behind the scenes, and discovered the reward paid to modest merit, in opposition to that which occasioned his effusions of conceit.

"An alteration of a principal incident, gave a very favourable turn to the fable and the whole piece; viz. that where young *Acres* now delivers his challenge to his friend *Absolute*, begging to carry it to his rival *Beverley*, not knowing the two characters composed but one man; it's being at first given to Sir *Lucius*, the person who indited it, was highly inconsistent.—The cuttings have been everywhere judicious, except where they have deprived *Lydia* of that comic and picturesque description of her lover, standing like a *dripping-statue* in the garden, &c.—[this has been restored] the hiss that occasioned this cut, was that of party or ignorance, not of judgment.—We think the play still too long, and would recommend the total deprivation of the scene, where J. *Absolute* meets his father upon the parade, as he goes out to fight; it being an obvious obstruction to the business, and that to answer no purpose whatever.

"The performers were very attentive to the discharge of their duty; and though honest *Ned Shuter* was unfortunately reprehensible the first night, he has now wiped out the odium, and charmed as much as he had before displeased.—Mrs. Bulkley, though struggling with a violent cold, was excellent in the character of *Julia*.

"Upon the whole, if we could once bring ourselves to be reconciled to the extraordinary circumstance of Ensign *Beverley's* losing the affections of a woman who doated upon him, merely because she found him a Captain and a man of family and fortune, we should be induced from many evident traits of literary genius to pronounce the *Rivals*, a good Comedy S*******."

"We heartily wish it was a general custom for authors to withdraw their pieces after a first performance, in order to remove the objectionable passages, heighten the favourite characters, and

The Morning Chronicle, 30 Jan., 1775.

generally amend the play. The author of the RIVALS has made good use of his time; his comedy is altered much for the better since it was first acted. The cast of it is improved, and all the performers are now perfect, and better acquainted with their several parts. It comes within a reasonable compass as to the time taken up in the representation, and the sentiments thrown into the mouth of Sir Lucius O'Trigger produce a good effect, at the same time that they take away every possible idea of the character's being designed as an insult on our neighbours on the other side of St. George's Channel. In the room of the objectionable and heavy scenes which are cut out, two new ones of a very different turn are introduced, and we remarked more than one judicious alteration in the Prologue.—The RIVALS will now stand its ground; and although we cannot pronounce it, with all its amendments, a comic chef-d'ouvre, it certainly encourages us to hope for a very capital play from the same writer at a future season; he therefore, from motives of candour and encouragement, is entitled to the patronage and favour of a generous public."

The Morning Chronicle, 31 Jan., 1775.

"To Mr. S. on his Comedy of *The Rivals*.

"Dear D—k I often hear your friends declare
The merits of your 'Rivals' must prevail :
But I who know what rival poets are,
Sincerely wish your Rivals still to fail.
Your's, Fighting Bob."

The Morning Post, 31 Jan., 1775.

"A correspondent observes, that Mr. Clinch supported the part of O'Trigger, in the new play of The Rivals, beyond what could be expected, considering that he appeared to great disadvantage, after such a great man as Mr. Lee."

"Mr. Garrick was at the play of The Rivals last Saturday, and was very attentive; he told a gentleman who sat next to him, and a friend to the author, 'I see this play will creep'; the gentleman made no answer, but at the end of the play (after repeated peals of approbation) he told him 'I see this play will run.'"

"The literary plunderers, and sentimental blockheads, so much admired by the gaping multitude of our century, were not a little disappointed at the success of Mr. Sheridan. The first night of performing his Comedy, they took particular care to station the serpents of envy in every corner of the house, in order to nip the young adventurer in the bud, but Mr. Sheridan, Hercules-like, even *in the cradle of genius*, tore the serpents asunder by the vigour of his mind, and baulked the cankered malice of his foes."

"Advertisement extraordinary. Whereas a gentleman to produce a comedy at Covent Garden Theatre, without having ever been properly entered into the Company of Scribblers, and whereas he has endeavoured to support it by humour, spirited and elegant dialogue, and incident alone, without endeavouring to preach up the moral duties, and *benevolent feelings;* and whereas by such a conduct the stage will inevitably relapse into a *theatre*, and be no more regarded as a school for public lectures, and consequently the sentimental professors will lose their bread, and the Cardinal virtues receive no other support than from the pulpits.—We whose names are not for shame underwritten, in consequence of this alarming attempt, do severally covenant and agree, to labour to *the best of our abilities,* in aspersing and decrying the performance of the said author; and in order that this may be more effectually done, notice is hereby given, that a *duncial* committee will sit every day in some place appointed for the purpose, where we shall be able to *agree together;* where calumny and slander, post paid, will be thankfully received. Signed by order of the Chair, *Whalebone* Sec. N.B. The *ingenious* are desired not to trouble us with their Correspondence."

The Morning Chronicle, 1 Feb., 1775.

"Sir, I was one among many who attended both representations of The Rivals: and I cannot help congratulating the lovers of Comedy on the present success of a piece, which, from some levities and want of experience, was near being crushed the first night:—but now on the strength of its own merit, and an acquiescence to the taste of the public, will certainly stand foremost in the list of modern comedies.

The Morning Chronicle, 2 Feb., 1775.

XXXII   PREFATORY NOTES.

"There was a candour, at the same time a spirit, in the alterations in the *Prologue*, which had a happy effect—I need not say that the Serjeant was inimitably supported by Woodward. Mr. Clinch makes the genteelest Irishman we have on the stage, and there are some true Hibernian touches (which passed unnoticed before), but which now appeared admirably characteristic. All the most laboured portraits of Hibernian assurance, do not perhaps amount to so humourous an instance as Sir Lucius O'Trigger's forgetting the very name of modesty. Lucy tells him, her Mistress won't like him if he's so impudent. ' Faith she will, Lucy (says the Baronet) that same—pho—what's the name of it ? *Modesty*, &c.' The contrast between him and Acres in the duel scene, is finely pursued, and is particularly excellent, when he finds his *valour oozing away* at the approach of his antagonist; Shuter in Sir Anthony seemed piqued to exert himself, threw the house absolutely into a convulsion of laughter. It may be said that Woodward is too old for his character, but I will venture to assert that there is no man in England could *now* play it better, and that there never was one of his age could play half so well. The character of Faulkland will improve on the audience the more it is understood; and Mrs. Bulkeley never appeared to more advantage than in the amiable and elegant Julia. I am, Sir, yours &c.   *Aristarchus.*"

The Morning Post,
3 Feb., 1775.

"Mr. Editor, I desire you will inform the Author of the *Rivals* that his attack upon *Circulating Libraries* in his first act is unjust, and very impertinent: Besides his sentiments are so inconsistent—He pretends to make such fine speeches in his play about *love*, and to pay such a compliment in the Epilogue to the Ladies, yet would decry novels, which form the very food and sustenance of love. I should be glad to know what are most of the modern comedies but *dialogue novels?* Are the two Playhouses better than circulating libraries? Only that at Mr. *Noble's* we may chuse our entertainment, and there the managers chuse it for us ;—So, as our club consequently honour *your* paper with a place at our breakfast-table, I desire you will give this notice a place in it instantly, that the Author may expunge the malicious scene, or we will let him know that Ladies can *hiss* as well as smile. Yours &c. Sukey Saunter."

"I have not read all the theatrical squibs in your paper and others; therefore cannot know what may have been said for and against the new Comedy of the Rivals: I went however last Tuesday to the Representation, and confess I was much pleased; but the reason of my troubling you with this is to desire Mr. Sheridan to expunge the word *spunk* out of Sir Andrew [*sic*] Absolute's part; which, if taken in its literal meaning, is nonsense: and considered in any other light, conveys an indelicate idea.—It shocks the delicate ear, and hurts the feelings of the refined   SENSIBILITY."

The Morning Chronicle, 10 Feb., 1775.

"Three comic poets in three distant streets
All wrote at once;—a thing one seldom meets:
The first in liveliness of thought surpassed;
In sentiment the next;—in both the last:—
Thalia wished her credit to encrease,—
So bad the Rivals form one perfect piece."

The Morning Chronicle, 4 Feb., 1775.

II.

Two months after 'The Rivals' had become a favourite with London playgoers—which it continues to be though a century and a quarter have elapsed—it was represented at Bath. Mary Linley wrote to her sister, Mrs. Sheridan, an account of the proceedings, which I have printed elsewhere,* the most interesting piece of information being, " but, in my life, I never saw anything go off with such uncommon applause."

In the *Bath Chronicle* for 9 March, 1775, it is written: "Mr. Sheridan's comedy of 'The Rivals'

* 'Sheridan: a Biography,' vol. i. pp. 285-87.

was performed for the first time at our theatre last night; and we have the pleasure to say that it was received with every mark of approbation and applause from a numerous and polite audience." Unfortunately the file of Keene's *Bath Journal*, one of the oldest newspapers in the kingdom, having been founded in 1742, is imperfect, and the volume for the year 1775 is one of those missing; hence its verdict cannot be given. I may add, however, that when 'The Duenna' appeared, the *Bath Chronicle* wrote: " The piece is said to be written by Mr. Sheridan, author of ' The Rivals'; if that gentleman continues to improve as much as he has done in the course of the last year, he will shortly be one of the best comic writers for the stage in existence— he has by this opera given proof that he possesses those grand and essential requisites for dramatic authorship—a fertile imagination, great ability, and real genius."

In Bath, as in London, versifiers celebrated Sheridan's theatrical triumph. The following lines appeared in the *Bath Chronicle* with the heading, " On seeing the Comedy of ' The Rivals' on Tuesday evening ":—

" The comic muse Thalia droop'd her head,
Lamenting Wicherly and Congreve dead ;
Lamenting with a sigh her sad disgrace,
That few alas ! remain'd of all her race :—
Lo ! SHERIDAN a Candidate,—the name
Reviv'd at once the laughter-loving dame ;
On him she fix'd, her credit to regain,
His *Rivals* plac'd him foremost in her train.

Bath. *An admirer of Merit."*

III.

Four months after 'The Rivals' had been applauded by the public, a farce, 'The Scheming Lieutenant,' was performed at Drury Lane for the benefit of Mr. Clinch. The version taken from Sheridan's manuscript differs in a few unimportant particulars from that published in Murray's edition and succeeding ones. The only noteworthy point is that the handwriting of several pages towards the end is in that of Sheridan's wife.

His next piece was 'The Duenna,' of which the manuscript is incomplete, and I have had to fill up gaps from the current versions. It is noteworthy that Mrs. Sheridan wrote several parts of the manuscript. 'The Duenna' was first represented on 21 November, 1775, at Drury Lane. Moore happily characterized it as one of the very few English operas which combines the merits of legitimate comedy with the attractions of poetry and song. A printed version appeared in Sheridan's lifetime, but he had no hand in it. Whether Mr. Wilkie copied from it I do not know, neither can I tell whether the variations between the edition he edited for Murray and Sheridan's own words are due to him. Some specimens have already been published.* I shall now supplement them with a few more. The first four lines of the second song were written thus:—

> " The crimson dawn bids hence the night,
> Unveil those beauteous eyes my Fair
> For till the morn of Love is there,
> I feel no Day, I own no Light."

* 'Sheridan: a Biography,' vol. i. pp. 305-7.

The editor made these lines run :—
"The breath of morn bids forth the night,
Unveil those beauteous eyes my fair;
For till the dawn of love is there,
I feel no day, I own no light."

While many lines are altered for the worse, the prose is treated in as high-handed a manner. In scene third of the first act Sheridan made the Duenna utter the following words: " O rare effects of Passion and Obstinacy! *The first will blind him to the cheat—and the second will continue him in his Delusion.*" The sentence which I have italicized does not appear in all the printed copies. I must add that the omissions are many in number and seem to have been made at haphazard. At the beginning of the third scene of act second Don Jerome and Don Ferdinand are discovered in a library. In defending Don Anthonio, Ferdinand says that he never sullied his Honour which, with his Title, had outlived his means. Don Jerome replies: "Have they? More shame for them! What business have Honours or Titles to survive when his property is extinct? Nobility is but a help-mate to a good Fortune, and like a Japanese Wife, should perish on the funeral Pile of the Estate." Ferdinand answers: "Not with us, sir. Poverty here, can no more disgrace a Gentleman than Wealth can make one—for my part I think Anthonio's worth more evident since he lost the advantage of Fortune—it is well known that the costly setting of the Jewel more frequently serves to hide its Flaws than help its lustre." The foregoing paragraphs were cancelled. Those who have read 'The Duenna' before, will read the original version with increased pleasure. If put on the stage again, it would probably be quite as successful as Sheridan's other plays.

IV.

On 8 May, 1777, 'The School for Scandal' was performed for the first time; as an attractive acting Comedy it has held the stage ever since. The detractors by whom Sheridan was followed during life, and who were reinforced after his death by others as spiteful and prejudiced, could not deny that the comedy was fine, but they affirmed that it was the work of a young lady, from whom it was stolen and who died soon after its production. However, the manuscript of it in Sheridan's own handwriting is preserved at Frampton Court and is now printed in this volume. This version differs in many respects from that which is generally known, and I think it is even better than that which has hitherto been read and acted. As I have endeavoured to reproduce the works of Sheridan as he wrote them, I may be told that he was a bad hand at punctuating and very bad at spelling. Very little good punctuation is due to an author, because but few understand it, and the compositor generally deserves what praise may be merited for rightly placing commas, colons, semicolons, and full stops. The compositor, also, deserves much credit where the spelling is correct. But Sheridan's shortcomings as a speller have been exaggerated. When a boy at Harrow he wrote frequently to his uncle, the word "uncle" being spelt as is now done. In the 'School for Scandal' and other plays he repeatedly writes "Unkle." This is not a sign of ignorance, but it is a proof that he followed the fashion. Writing to his niece Mary White in 1781, the Rev. Gilbert White, of Selborne ends his letter, "With all due respects I remain Y^r loving Un*k*le" (for that is the modish way of spelling the relationship).*

The lines with which, according to Moore, the manuscript of the comedy ends are not in the original manuscript. When Sheridan's grandson prepared the manuscript for binding, he noticed that the last leaf had been abstracted, on which it is said to have been written: "Finished at last, Thank God, R. B. Sheridan. Amen! W. Hopkins, the Prompter."

'The Critic,' Sheridan's last original play, was first represented on 30 October, 1779. There are several additions in the manuscript to the current version, but they are unimportant. However, the reader of the plays in this volume will have the satisfaction of perusing Sheridan's original words. At a future time an edition may appear with various readings.

---

v.

Some writers who were both ill-informed and ill-intentioned have stated that Sheridan could not have produced 'The Rivals' if his mother had not

* 'Life and Letters of Gilbert White,' vol. ii. p. 74.

first penned 'A Journey to Bath.' The readers of that comedy, at the end of this volume, can decide this matter for themselves. It may be questionable whether the fragment now printed from the manuscript in the British Museum represents all that was composed. It is true that Mr. Thomas Sheridan wrote to Samuel Whyte from Blois on 23 December, 1764, that his wife had finished a comedy which was "spick and span new throughout." It appears to have been submitted to Garrick through Mrs. Victor as an intermediary. Garrick objected to the piece, urging, among other drawbacks, that all the scenes were detached. Mrs. Sheridan made a long defence, saying that all the scenes contribute to the main purpose of the play, which is divulged in the last lines, adding that the fate of two innocent young people "is not decided till the very last scene." Now, if the piece had been before Garrick in a finished form, what need was there of telling him the nature of the conclusion?*

After Sheridan's death his elder sister, Mrs. Joseph Lefanu, wrote as follows to Lady Morgan: "My mother's sketch of a comedy, unfinished, was put into my brother Richard's hands by my father at Bath, when we were resident there; but my father never hinted that he had made any use of it in 'The Rivals.' Of my own knowledge I can say nothing, for I never read it."† It is a mistake to say that Sheridan made no use of his mother's

---

* 'Private Correspondence of David Garrick,' vol. i. pp. 17 18.
† 'Lady Morgan's Memoirs,' vol. ii. p. 61.

handiwork, though it is true his indebtedness is but slight. He took a few phrases out of Mrs. Tryfort's mouth and put them into Mrs. Malaprop's. The name of Savage, given by his mother to the keeper of a lodging-house, he applied to two of the chief characters in 'The School for Scandal.'

THE RIVALS.

A COMEDY.

PREFACE.

A PREFACE to a play seems generally to be considered as a kind of Closet-prologue, in which—if his Piece has been successful the Author solicits that indulgence from the Reader which he had before experienced from the Audience: But as the scope and immediate object of a Play is to please a mixed assembly in *Representation* (whose judgment in the Theatre at least is decisive), its degree of reputation is usually as determined by the public, before it can be prepared for the cooler tribunal of the Study. Thus any farther solicitude on the part of the Writer becomes unnecessary at least, if not an intrusion; and if the Piece has been condemned in the Performance, I fear an Address to the Closet, like an Appeal to posterity, is constantly regarded as the procrastination of a suit, from a consciousness of the weakness of the cause. From these considerations, the following Comedy would certainly have been submitted to the Reader, without any further introduction than what it had in the Representation, but that its success has probably been founded on a circumstance which the Author is informed has not before attended a theatrical trial, and which consequently ought not to pass unnoticed.

I need scarcely add, that the circumstance alluded to was the withdrawing of the Piece, to remove those imperfections in the first Representation which were too obvious to escape reprehension, and too numerous to admit of a hasty correction. There are few writers, I believe, who, even in the fullest consciousness of error, do not wish to palliate the faults which they acknowledge; and, however trifling the performance, to second their confession of its deficiencies, by whatever plea seems least disgraceful to their ability. In the present instance, it cannot be said to amount either to candour or modesty in me, to acknowledge an extreme inexperience and want of judgment on matters, in which, without guidance from practice, or spur from success, a young man should scarcely boast of being an adept. If it be said that under such disadvantages no one should attempt to write a play—I must beg leave to dissent from the position, while the first point of experience that I have gained on the subject is, a knowledge of the candour and judgment with which an impartial Public distinguishes between the errors of inexperience and incapacity, and the indulgence which it shews even to a disposition to remedy the defects of either.

It were unnecessary to enter into any farther extenuation of what was thought exceptionable in this Play, but that it has been said, that the Managers should have prevented some of the defects before its appearance to the public—and in particular the uncommon length of the piece as represented the first night.—It were an ill return for the most liberal and gentlemanly conduct on their side, to suffer any censure to rest where none was deserved. Hurry in writing has long been exploded as an excuse for an author;—however, in the dramatic line, it may happen, that both an Author and a Manager may wish to fill a chasm in the entertainment of the Public with a hastiness not altogether culpable. The season was advanced when I first put the play into Mr. Harris's hands:—it was at that time at least double the length of any acting comedy.—I profited by his judgment and experience in the curtailing of it—'till, I believe, his feeling for the vanity of a young Author got the better of his desire for correctness, and he left many excrescences remaining, because he had assisted in pruning so many more. Hence, though I was not uninformed that the Acts were still too long, I flattered myself that, after the first trial, I might with safer judgment proceed to remove what should appear to have been most dissatisfactory. Many other errors there were, which might in part have arisen from my being by no means conversant with plays in general, either in reading or at the theatre.—Yet I own that, in one respect, I did not regret my ignorance: for as my first wish in attempting a Play was to avoid every appearance of plagiary, I thought I should stand a better chance of effecting this from being in a walk which I had not frequented, and where consequently the progress of invention was less likely to be interrupted by starts of recollection: for on subjects on which the mind has been much informed, invention is slow of exerting itself.—Faded ideas float in the fancy like half-forgotten dreams; and the imagination in its fullest enjoyments becomes suspicious of its offspring, and doubts whether it has created or adopted.

With regard to some particular passages which on the First Night's Representation seemed generally disliked, I confess, that if I felt any emotion of surprise at the disapprobation, it was not that they were disapproved of, but that I had not before perceived that they deserved it. As some part of the attack on the Piece was begun too early to pass for the sentence of *Judgment*, which is ever tardy in condemning, it has been suggested to me, that much of the disapprobation must have arisen from virulence of Malice, rather than severity of Criticism: but as I was more apprehensive of there being just grounds to excite the latter, than conscious of having deserved the former, I continue not to believe that probable, which I am sure must have been unprovoked. However, if it was so, and I could even mark the quarter from whence it came, it would be ungenerous to retort; for no passion suffers more than malice from disappointment. For my own part, I see no reason why the Author of a Play should not regard a First Night's Audience as a candid and judicious friend attending, in behalf of the Public, at his last Rehearsal. If he can dispense with flattery, he is sure at least of sincerity, and even though the annotation be rude, he may rely upon the justness of the comment. Considered in this light, that Audience, whose *fiat* is essential to the Poet's claim, whether his object be Fame or Profit, has surely a right to expect some deference to its opinion, from principles of Politeness at least, if not from Gratitude.

As for the little puny Critics, who scatter their peevish strictures in private circles, and scribble at every Author who has the eminence of being unconnected with them, as they are usually spleen-swoln from a vain idea of increasing their consequence, there will always be found a petulance and illiberality in their remarks, which should place them as far beneath the notice of a Gentleman, as their original dulness had sunk them from the level of the most unsuccessful Author.

It is not without pleasure that I catch at an opportunity of justifying myself from the charge of intending any national reflection in the character of Sir *Lucius O'Trigger*. If any Gentlemen opposed the Piece from that idea, I thank them sincerely for their opposition; and if the condemnation of this Comedy (however misconceived the provocation) could have added one spark to the decaying flame of national attachment to the country supposed to be reflected on, I should have been happy in its fate; and might with truth have boasted, that it had done more real service in its failure, than the successful morality of a thousand stage-novels will ever effect.

It is usual, I believe, to thank the Performers in a new Play, for the exertion of their several abilities. But where (as in this instance) their merit has been so striking and uncontroverted, as to call for the warmest and truest applause from a number of judicious Audiences, the Poet's after-praise comes like the feeble acclamation of a child to close the shouts of a multitude. The conduct, however, of the Principals in a theatre cannot be so apparent to the Public.—I think it therefore but justice to declare, that from this Theatre (the only one I can speak of from experience) those Writers who wish to try the Dramatic Line will meet with that candour and liberal attention, which are generally allowed to be better calculated to lead genius into excellence, than either the precepts of judgment, or the guidance of experience.

THE AUTHOR.

THE RIVALS.

DRAMATIS PERSONÆ.

AS ORIGINALLY ACTED AT COVENT GARDEN THEATRE IN 1775.

SIR ANTHONY ABSOLUTE . . . *Mr. Shuter.*	DAVID . . . . *Mr. Dunstal.*
CAPTAIN ABSOLUTE *Mr. Woodward.*	THOMAS . . . *Mr. Fearon.*
FAULKLAND . . *Mr. Lewis.*	MRS. MALAPROP. *Mrs. Green.*
ACRES . . . . *Mr. Quick.*	LYDIA LANGUISH *Miss Barsanti.*
SIR LUCIUS O'TRIGGER . . *Mr. Lee.*	JULIA . . . . *Mrs. Bulkley.*
FAG . . . . . *Mr. Lee Lewes.*	LUCY . . . . *Mrs. Lessingham.*

Maid, Boy, Servants, &c.

SCENE.—BATH.

Time of Action—Five Hours.

PROLOGUE.

By the Author.

SPOKEN BY MR. WOODWARD AND MR. QUICK.

Enter SERJEANT-AT-LAW, *and* ATTORNEY *following, and giving a paper.*

Serj. What's here !—a vile cramp hand ! I cannot see
Without my spectacles.
    Att.   He means his fee.
Nay, Mr. Serjeant, good sir, try again.   [*Gives money.*
    Serj. The scrawl improves ! [*more*] O come, 'tis pretty plain.
Hey ! how's this ? The Poet's Brief *again.* O ho !
A poet's brief ! a poet and a fee !
    Att. Yes, sir ! though you without reward, I know,
Would gladly plead the Muse's cause.
    Serj.   So !—so !
    Att. And if the fee offends your wrath should fall
On me.
    Serj. Dear Dibble, no offence at all.
    Att. Some sons of Phœbus in the courts we meet,
    Serj. And fifty sons of Phœbus in the Fleet !
    Att. Nor pleads he worse, who with a decent sprig
Of bays adorns his legal waste of wig.
    Serj. Full-bottomed heroes thus, on signs, unfurl
A leaf of laurel in a grove of curl !
Yet tell your client, that, in adverse days,
This wig is warmer than a bush of bays.
    Att. Do you, then, sir, my client's place supply,
Profuse of robe, and prodigal of tie——
Do you, with all those blushing powers of face,

And wonted bashful hesitating grace,
Rise in the court and flourish on the case. [*Exit.*

Serj. For practice then suppose—this brief will show it,—
Me, Serjeant *Woodward*,—Council for the Poet.
Us'd to the ground—I know 'tis hard to deal
With this dread *Court*, from whence there's *no appeal;*
No *Tricking* here, to blunt the edge of *Law,*
Or, damn'd in *Equity,* escape by *Flaw:*
But *Judgment* given—*your Sentence* must remain ;
No *Writ of Error* lies—to *Drury Lane!*

Yet when so kind you seem—'tis past dispute
We gain some favour, if not *Costs of Suit.*
No spleen is here ! I see no hoarded fury ;—
I think I never faced a milder Jury !
Sad else our plight ! where frowns are transportation,
A hiss the gallows, and a groan, damnation !
But such the public candour, without fear
My Client waives all *right of challenge* here.
No Newsman from *our* Session is dismiss'd,
Nor Wit nor Critic *we* scratch off the list ;
His faults can never hurt another's ease,
His crime at worst—a *bad attempt* to please :
Thus, all respecting, he appeals to all,
And by the general voice will *stand* or *fall.*

PROLOGUE.

By the Author.

SPOKEN ON THE TENTH NIGHT, BY MRS. BULKLEY.

GRANTED our cause, our suit and trial o'er,
The worthy serjeant need appear no more :
In pleasing I a different client choose,
He served the Poet—I would serve the Muse.
Like him, I'll try to merit your applause,
A female counsel in a female's cause.

Look on this form,*—where humour, quaint and sly,
Dimples the cheek, and points the beaming eye ;
Where gay invention seems to boast its wiles
In amourous hint, and half-triumphant smiles ;

* Pointing to the figure of Comedy.

While her light mask or covers satire's strokes,
Or hides the conscious blush her wit provokes.
Look on her well—does she seem'd form'd to teach?
Should you expect to hear this lady preach?
Is grey experience suited to her youth?
Do solemn sentiments become that mouth?
Bid her be grave, those lips should rebel prove
To every theme that slanders mirth or love.

  Yet, thus adorn'd with every graceful art
To charm the fancy and yet reach the heart——
Must we displace her, and instead advance
The goddess of the woful countenance—
The sentimental Muse?—Her emblems view,
The Pilgrim's Progress, and a sprig of rue!
View her—too chaste to look like flesh and blood—
Primly portray'd on emblematic wood!
There, fix'd in usurpation, should she stand,
She 'll snatch the dagger from her sister's hand:
And having made her votaries weep a flood,
Good heaven! she 'll end her comedies in blood—
Bid Harry Woodward break poor Dunstal's crown!
Imprison Quick, and knock Ned Shuter down;
While sad Barsanti, weeping o'er the scene,
Shall stab herself—or poison Mrs. Green.

  Such dire encroachments to prevent in time,
Demands the critic's voice—the poet's rhyme.
Can our light scenes add strength to holy laws
Such puny patronage but hurts the cause:
Fair virtue scorns our feeble aid to ask;
And moral truth disdains the trickster's mask
For here their favourite stands,* whose brow severe
And sad, claims youth's respect, and pity's tear;
Who, when oppress'd by foes her worth creates,
Can point a poniard at the guilt she hates.

       * Pointing to Tragedy.

ACT I.

Scene I.—*A Street in Bath.*

Coachman crosses the Stage; enter FAG, *looking after him.*

Fag. What! Thomas! sure 'tis he?—What! Thomas! Thomas!

Coach. Hay!—Odd's life! Mr. Fag!—give us your hand, my old fellow-servant.

Fag. Excuse my glove, Thomas:—I'm devilish glad to see you, my lad. Why, my prince of charioteers, you look as hearty!—but who the deuce thought of seeing you in Bath?

Coach. Sure, master, Madam Julia, Harry, Mrs. Kate, and the postilion be all come.

Fag. Indeed!

Coach. Ay, master thought another fit of the gout was coming to make him a visit; so he'd a mind to gi't the slip, and whip! we were all off at an hour's warning.

Fag. Aye, aye, hasty in everything, or it would not be Sir Anthony Absolute!

Coach. But tell us, Mr. Fag, how does young Master? Odd! Sir Anthony will stare to see the Captain here!

Fag. I do not serve Captain Absolute now.

Coach. Why sure!

Fag. At present I am employ'd by Ensign Beverley.

Coach. I doubt, Mr. Fag, you ha'n't changed for the better.

Fag. I have not changed, Thomas.

Coach. No! Why didn't you say you had left young Master?

Fag. No.—Well, honest Thomas, I must puzzle you no farther briefly then—Captain Absolute and Ensign Beverley are one and the same person.

Coach. The devil they are!

Fag. So it is indeed, Thomas; and the *Ensign* half of my master being on guard at present—the *Captain* has nothing to do with me.

Coach. So, so!—What, this is some freak, I warrant!—Do, tell us, Mr. Fag, the meaning o't—you know I ha' trusted you.

Fag. You'll be secret, Thomas?

Coach. As a coach-horse.

Fag. Why then the cause of all this is—Love,—Love, Thomas, who (as you may get read to you) has been a masquerader ever since the days of Jupiter.

Coach. Aye, aye ;—I guessed there was a lady in the case :—but pray, why does your Master pass only for *Ensign ?*—Now if he had shamm'd *General* indeed——

Fag. Ah! Thomas, there lies the mystery o' the matter. Hark'ee, Thomas, my Master is in love with a lady of a very singular taste : a lady who likes him better as a *half-pay Ensign* than if she knew he was son and heir to Sir Anthony Absolute, a baronet with three thousand a year.

Coach. That is an odd taste indeed!—But has she got the stuff, Mr. Fag? Is she rich, hey?

Fag. Rich!—Why, I believe she owns half the stocks! Z—ds! Thomas, she could pay the national debt as easily as I could my washerwoman! She has a lapdog that eats out of gold,—she feeds her parrot with small pearls,—and all her thread-papers are made of bank-notes!

Coach. Bravo! faith!—Odd! I warrant she has a set of thousands at least :—but does she draw kindly with the Captain?

Fag. As fond as pigeons.

Coach. May one hear her name?

Fag. Miss Lydia Languish.—But there is an old tough aunt in the way ; though, by-the-by, she has never seen my Master—for we got acquainted with Miss while on a visit in Gloucestershire.

Coach. Well—I wish they were once harnessed together in matrimony.—But pray, Mr. Fag, what kind of a place is this Bath?—I ha' heard a deal of it—here's a mort o' merry-making, hey?

Fag. Pretty well, Thomas, pretty well—'tis a good lounge. Though present we are, like other great assemblies, divided into parties—High-roomians and Low-roomians; however for my part, I have resolved to stand neuter, and so I told Bob Brush at our last committee.

Coach. But what do the folks do here?

Fag. Oh! there are little amusements enough; in the morning we go to the pump-room (though neither my Master nor I drink the waters); after breakfast we saunter on the parades or play a game at billiards; at night we dance; but d—n the place, I'm tired of it: their regular hours stupefy me—not a fiddle nor a card after eleven!—However Mr. Faulkland's gentleman and I keep it up a little in private parties ;—I'll introduce you there, Thomas—you'll like him much.

Coach. Sure I know Mr. Du-Peigne—you know his Master is to marry Madam Julia.

Fag. I had forgot.—But, Thomas, you must polish a little—indeed you must.—Here now—this wig! What the devil do you do with a *wig*, Thomas ?—None of the London whips of any degree of Ton wear *wigs* now.

Coach. More's the pity ! more's the pity ! I say.—Odd's life ! when I heard how the lawyers and doctors had took to their own hair, I thought how 'twould go next :—odd rabbit it ! when the fashion had got foot on the Bar, I guessed 'twould mount to the Box !—but 'tis all out of character, believe me, Mr. Fag : and look'ee, I'll never gi' up mine—the lawyers and doctors may do as they will.

Fag. Well, Thomas, we'll not quarrel about that.

Coach. Why, bless you, the gentlemen of they professions ben't all of a mind—for in our village now thoff *Jack Gauge*, the *exciseman*, has ta'en to his carrots, there's little Dick the farrier swears he'll never forsake his *bob*, tho' all the college should appear with their own heads !

Fag. Indeed ! well said, Dick !—but hold—mark ! mark ! Thomas.

Coach. Zooks ! 'tis the captain.—Is that the lady with him ?

Fag. No ! no ! that is Madam Lucy, my Master's mistress's maid. They lodge at that house--but I must after him to tell him the news.

Coach. Odd ! he's giving her money !—Well, Mr. Fag——

Fag. Good-bye, Thomas. I have an appointment in Gydes' Porch this evening at eight ; meet me there, and we'll make a little party.

[*Exeunt severally.*

SCENE II.—*A Dressing-room in* MRS. MALAPROP'S *Lodgings.*

LYDIA *sitting on a sofa, with a book in her hand.* LUCY, *as just returned from a message.*

Luc. Indeed, Ma'am, I transferr'd half the town in search of it ! I don't believe there's a circulating library in Bath I han't been at.

Lyd. And could not you get *The Reward of Constancy ?*

Lucy. No, indeed, Ma'am.

Lyd. Nor *The Fatal Connection ?*

Lucy. No, indeed, Ma'am.

Lyd. Nor *The Mistakes of the Heart ?*

Lucy. Ma'am, as ill luck would have it, Mr. Bull said Miss Sukey Saunter had just fetched it away.

Lyd. Heigh-ho ! Did you inquire for *The Delicate Distress ?*

Lucy. Or, *The Memoirs of Lady Woodford ?* Yes, indeed, Ma'am. I asked everywhere for it ; and I might have brought it from Mr. Frederick's, but Lady Slattern Lounger, who had just sent it home, had so soiled and dog's-eared it, it wa'n't fit for a christian to read.

Lyd. Heigh-ho ! Yes, I always know when Lady Slattern has been before me. She has a most observing thumb ; and I believe cherishes her nails for the convenience of making marginal notes.—Well, child, what *have* you brought me?

Lucy. Oh! here, ma'am.—[*Taking books from under her cloke, and from her pockets.*] This is *The Gordian Knot,*—and this *Peregrine Pickle.* Here are *The Tears of Sensibility,* and *Humphry Clinker.* This is *The Memoirs of a Lady of Quality, written by herself,* and here the second volume of *The Sentimental Journey.*

Lyd. Heigh-ho!—What are those books by the glass?

Lucy. The great one is only *The Whole Duty of Man,* where I press a few blonds, Ma'am.

Lyd. Very well—give me the *sal volatile.*

Lucy. Is it in a blue cover, Ma'am?

Lyd. My smelling-bottle, you simpleton!

Lucy. Oh, the drops!—here, Ma'am.

Lyd. No note, Lucy?

Lucy No, indeed, Ma'am—but I have seen a certain person—

Lyd. What, my Beverley! Well Lucy?

Lucy. O Ma'am he looks so desponding and melancholic!

Lyd. Hold! Lucy—here's some one coming—quick! see who it is. (*Exit* LUCY.)—Surely I heard my cousin Julia's voice.

Re-enter LUCY.

Lucy. Lud! Ma'am, here is Miss Melville.

Lyd. Is it possible!—

Enter JULIA.

Lyd. My dearest Julia, how delighted am I!—[*Embrace.*] How unexpected was this happiness!

Jul. True, Lydia—and our pleasure is the greater.—But what has been the matter?—you were denied to me at first!

Lyd. Ah, Julia, I have a thousand things to tell you!—But first inform me what has conjur'd you to Bath?—Is Sir Anthony here?

Jul. He is—we are arrived within this hour—and I suppose he will be here to wait on Mrs. Malaprop as soon as he is dress'd.

Lyd. Then before we are interrupted, let me impart to you some of my distress! I know your gentle nature will sympathize with me, tho' your prudence may condemn me! My letters have informed you of my whole connexion with Beverley; but I have lost him, Julia! My aunt has discovered our intercourse by a note she intercepted, and has confin'd me ever since! Yet, would you believe it? she has absolutely fallen in love with a tall Irish baronet she met one night since she has been here, at Lady Macshuffle's rout.

Jul. You jest, Lydia !

Lyd. No, upon my word.—She really carries on a kind of correspondence with him, under a feigned name though, till she chooses to be known to him ;—but it is a *Delia* or a *Celia*, I assure you.

Jul. Then, surely, she is now more indulgent to her niece.

Lyd. Quite the contrary. Since she has discovered her own frailty, she is become more suspicious of mine. Then I must inform you of another plague !—That odious Acres is to be in Bath to-day ; so that I protest I shall be teased out of all spirits !

Jul. Come, come, Lydia, hope the best—Sir Anthony shall use his interest with Mrs. Malaprop.

Lyd. But you have not heard the worst. Unfortunately I had quarrelled with my poor Beverley, just before my aunt made the discovery, and I have not seen him since, to make it up.

Jul. What was his offence ?

Lyd. Nothing at all !—But, I don't know how it was, as often as we had been together, we had never had a quarrel ! And, somehow I was afraid he would never give me an opportunity.—So, last Thursday, I wrote a letter to myself, to inform myself that Beverley was at that time paying his addresses to another woman.—I sign'd it *your Friend unknown*, showed it to Beverley, charg'd him with his falsehood, put myself in a violent passion, and vow'd I'd never see him more.

Jul. And you let him depart so, and have not seen him since ?

Lyd. 'Twas the next day my aunt found the matter out. I intended only to have teased him three days and a half, and now I've lost him for ever.

Jul. If he is as deserving and sincere as you have represented him to me, he will never give you up so. Yet, consider, Lydia, you tell me he is but an ensign, and you have thirty thousand pounds !

Lyd. But you know I lose most of my fortune, if I marry without my aunt's consent, till of age ; and that is what I have determin'd to do, ever since I knew the penalty. Nor could I love the man, who would wish to wait a day for the alternative.

Jul. Nay, this is caprice !

Lyd. What, does Julia tax me with caprice ?—I thought her lover Faulkland had enured her to it.

Jul. I do not love even *his* faults.

Lyd. But a-propos—you have sent to him, I suppose ?

Jul. Not yet, upon my word—nor has he the least idea of my being in Bath.—Sir Anthony's resolution was so sudden, I could not inform him of it.

Lyd. Well, Julia, you are your own mistress (though under the protection of Sir Anthony), yet have you, for this long year, been the slave to the caprice, the whim, the jealousy of this ungrateful Faulkland, who will ever delay assuming the right of a husband, while you suffer him to be equally imperious as a lover.

Jul. Nay, you are wrong entirely. We were contracted before my father's death.—*That,* and some consequent embarrassments, have delay'd what I know to be my Faulkland's most ardent wish.—He is too generous to trifle on such a point—and for his character, you wrong him there, too.—No, Lydia, he is too proud, too noble to be jealous; if he is captious, 'tis without dissembling; if fretful, without rudeness.—Unus'd to the foppery of love, he is negligent of the little duties expected from a lover—but being unhackney'd in the passion, his love is ardent and sincere; and as it engrosses his whole soul, he expects every thought and emotion of his mistress to move in unison with his.—Yet, though his pride calls for this full return—his humility makes him undervalue those qualities in him, which should entitle him to it; and not feeling why he should be lov'd to the degree he wishes, he still suspects that he is not lov'd enough.—This temper, I must own, has cost me many unhappy hours; but I have learned to think myself his debtor, for those imperfections which arise from the ardour of his love.

Lyd. Well, I cannot blame you for defending him.—But tell me candidly, Julia, had he never sav'd your life, do you think you should have been attach'd to him as you are?—Believe me, the rude blast that overset your boat was a prosperous gale of love to him.

Jul. Gratitude may have strengthened my attachment to Mr. Faulkland, but I loved him before he had preserv'd me; yet surely that alone were an obligation sufficient.

Lyd. Obligation!—why a water spaniel would have done as much! —Well, I should never think of giving my heart to a man because he could swim!

Jul. Come, Lydia, you are too inconsiderate.

Lyd. Nay, I do but jest—What's here?

Enter LUCY *in a hurry.*

Lucy. O Ma'am, here is Sir Anthony Absolute just come home with your aunt.

Lyd. They'll not come here.—Lucy do you watch. [*Exit* LUCY.

Jul. Yet I must go.—Sir Anthony does not know I am here, and if we meet, he'll detain me, to show me the town. I'll take another opportunity of paying my respects to Mrs. Malaprop, when she shall treat me, as long as she chooses, with her select words so ingeniously *misapplied,* without being *mispronounced.*

Re-enter LUCY.

Lucy. O Lud! Ma'am, they are both coming upstairs.

Lyd. Well, I'll not detain you, Coz.—Adieu, my dear Julia, I'm sure you are in haste to send to Faulkland.—There—through my room you'll find another staircase.

Jul. Adieu! [*Embrace.*] [*Exit* JULIA.

Lyd. Here, my dear Lucy, hide these books. Quick, quick!—Fling *Peregrine Pickle* under the toilet—throw *Roderick Random* into the closet—put *The Innocent Adultery* into *The Whole Duty of Man*—thrust *Lord Aimworth* under the sofa—cram *Ovid* behind the bolster—there—put *The Man of Feeling* into your pocket—so, so—now lay *Mrs. Chapone* in sight, and leave *Fordyce's Sermons* open on the table.

Lucy. O burn it, Ma'am! the hair-dresser has torn away as far as *Proper Pride.*

Lyd. Never mind—open at *Sobriety.*—Fling me *Lord Chesterfield's Letters.*—Now for 'em. [*Exit* LUCY.

Enter MRS. MALAPROP, *and* SIR ANTHONY ABSOLUTE.

Mrs. Mal. There, Sir Anthony, there sits the deliberate Simpleton who wants to disgrace her family, and lavish herself on a fellow not worth a shilling.

Lyd. Madam, I thought you once——

Mrs. Mal. You thought, Miss!—I don't know any business you have to think at all—thought does not become a young woman; the point we would request of you is, that you will promise to forget this fellow—to illiterate him, I say, quite from your memory.

Lyd. Ah, Madam! our memories are independent of our wills. It is not so easy to forget.

Mrs. Mal. But I say it is, Miss; there is nothing on earth so easy as to *forget*, if a person chooses to set about it.—I'm sure I have as much forgot your poor dear uncle as if he had never existed—and I thought it my duty so to do; and let me tell you, Lydia, these violent memories don't become a young woman.

Sir Anth. Why sure she won't pretend to remember what she's ordered not!—aye, this comes of her reading!

Lyd. What crime, Madam, have I committed, to be treated thus?

Mrs. Mal. Now don't attempt to extirpate yourself from the matter; you know I have proof controvertible of it.—But tell me, will you promise to do as you're bid?—Will you take a husband of your friends choosing?

Lyd. Madam, I must tell you plainly, that had I no preference for any one else, the choice you have made would be my aversion.

Mrs. Mal. What business have you, Miss, with *preference* and *aversion?* They don't become a young woman; and you ought to know, that as both always wear off, 'tis safest in matrimony to begin with a little *aversion.* I am sure I hated your poor dear uncle before marriage as if he'd been a black-a-moor—and yet, Miss, you are sensible what a wife I made!—and when it pleas'd Heaven to release me from him, 'tis unknown what tears I shed!—But suppose we were going to give you another choice, will you promise us to give up this Beverley?

Lyd. Could I belie my thoughts so far, as to give that promise, my actions would certainly as far belie my words.

Mrs. Mal. Take yourself to your room.—You are fit company for nothing but your own ill-humours.

Lyd. Willingly, Ma'am—I cannot change for the worse. [*Exit* LYDIA.

Mrs. Mal. There's a little intricate hussy for you!

Sir Anth. It is not to be wondered at, Ma'am,—all this is the natural consequence of teaching girls to read. Had I a thousand daughters, by Heavens! I'd as soon have them taught the black art as their alphabet!

Mrs. Mal. Nay, nay, Sir Anthony, you are an absolute misanthropy.

Sir Anth. In my way hither, Mrs. Malaprop, I observed your niece's maid coming forth from a circulating library!—She had a book in each hand—they were half-bound volumes, with marbled covers!—From that moment I guess'd how full of duty I should see her mistress!

Mrs. Mal. Those are vile places, indeed!

Sir Anth. Madam, a circulating library in a town is, as an evergreen tree, of diabolical knowledge!—It blossoms through the year!—And depend on it, Mrs. Malaprop, that they who are so fond of handling the leaves, will long for the fruit at last.

Mrs. Mal. Well, but Sir Anthony, your wife, Lady Absolute, was fond of books.

Sir Anth. Aye—and injury sufficient they were to her, Madam—But were I to chuse another helpmate, the extent of her erudition should consist in knowing her simple letters, without their mischievous combinations;—and the summit of her science be—her ability to count as far as twenty.—The first, Mrs. Malaprop, would enable her to work *A. A.* upon my linen;—and the latter would be quite sufficient to prevent her giving me a Shirt, No. 1, and a Stock No. 2.

Mrs. Mal. Fie, fie, Sir Anthony! you surely speak laconically!

Sir Anth. Why, Mrs. Malaprop, in moderation now, what would you have a woman know?

Mrs. Mal. Observe me, Sir Anthony. I would by no means wish a daughter of mine to be a progeny of learning; I don't think so much learning becomes a young woman; for instance, I would never let her meddle with Greek, or Hebrew, or Algebra, or Simony, or Fluxions, or Paradoxes, or such inflammatory branches of learning—neither would it be necessary for her to handle any of your mathematical, astronomical, diabolical instruments.—But, Sir Anthony, I would send her, at nine years old, to a boarding-school, in order to learn a little ingenuity and artifice. Then, Sir, she should have a supercilious knowledge in accounts;—and as she grew up, I would have her instructed in geometry, that she might know something of the contagious countries;—but above all, Sir Anthony, she should be mistress of orthodoxy, that she might not mis-spell, and mis-pronounce words so shamefully as girls usually do; and likewise that she might reprehend the true meaning of what she is saying.—This, Sir Anthony, is what I would have a woman know;—and I don't think there is a superstitious article in it.

Sir Anth. Well, well, Mrs. Malaprop, I will dispute the point no further with you; though I must confess, that you are a truly moderate and polite arguer, for almost every third word you say is on my side of the question.—But, Mrs. Malaprop, to the more important point in debate—you say, you have no objection to my proposal?

Mrs. Mal. None, I assure you.—I am under no positive engagement with Mr. Acres, and as Lydia is so obstinate against him, perhaps your son may have better success.

Sir Anth. Well, Madam, I will write for the boy directly.—He knows not a syllable of this yet, though I have for some time had the proposal in my head. He is at present with his regiment.

Mrs. Mal. We have never seen your son, Sir Anthony; but I hope no objection on his side.

Sir Anth. Objection!—let him object if he dare!—No, no, Mrs. Malaprop, Jack knows that the least demur puts me in a frenzy directly.—My process was always very simple—in their younger days, 'twas "Jack do this";—if he demurred, I knocked him down—and if he grumbled at that, I always sent him out of the room.

Mrs. Mal. Aye, and the properest way, o' my conscience!—nothing is so conciliating to young people as severity.—Well, Sir Anthony, I shall give Mr. Acres his discharge, and prepare Lydia to receive your son's invocations;—and I hope you will represent *her* to the Captain as an object not altogether illegible.

Sir Anth. Madam, I will handle the subject prudently.—Well, I must leave you; and let me beg you, Mrs. Malaprop, to enforce this matter roundly to the girl.—Take my advice—keep a tight hand; if she rejects this proposal, clap her under lock and key; and if you were just to let the servants forget to bring her dinner for three or four days, you can't conceive how she'd come about. [*Exit* SIR ANTH.

Mrs. Mal. Well, at any rate, I shall be glad to get her from under my intuition.—She has somehow discovered my partiality for Sir Lucius O'Trigger—sure, Lucy can't have betray'd me!—No, the girl is such a simpleton, I should have made her confess it.—Lucy!—Lucy!—[*Calls.*] Had she been one of your artificial ones, I should never have trusted her.

Enter LUCY.

Lucy. Did you call, Ma'am?

Mrs. Mal. Yes, girl.—Did you see Sir Lucius while you was out?

Lucy. No, indeed, Ma'am, not a glimpse of him.

Mrs. Mal. You are sure, Lucy, that you never mention'd——

Lucy. O Gemini! I'd sooner cut my tongue out.

Mrs. Mal. Well, don't let your simplicity be imposed on.

Lucy. No, Ma'am.

Mrs. Mal. So, come to me presently, and I'll give you another letter to Sir Lucius;—but mind, Lucy—if ever you betray what you are entrusted with—(unless it be other people's secrets to me) you forfeit my malevolence for ever:—and your being a simpleton shall be no excuse for your locality. [*Exit* MRS. MALAPROP.

Lucy. Ha! ha! ha!—So, my dear *simplicity*, let me give you a little respite.—[*Altering her manner.*] Let girls in my station be as fond as they please of appearing expert, and knowing in their trusts;—commend me to a mask of *silliness*, and a pair of sharp eyes for my own interest under it!—Let me see to what account have I turn'd my simplicity lately.—[*Looks at a paper.*] For *abetting Miss Lydia Languish in a design of running away with an Ensign!—in money sundry times, twelve pound twelve; gowns, five; hats, ruffles, caps, &c., &c., numberless!—From the said Ensign, within this last month, six guineas and a half.*—About a quarter's pay!—Item, *from Mrs. Malaprop, for betraying the young people to her*—when I found matters were likely to be discovered—*two guineas, and a black paduasoy.*—Item, *from Mr. Acres, for carrying divers letters*—which I never deliver'd—*two guineas, and a pair of buckles*—Item, *from Sir Lucius O'Trigger, three crowns, two gold pocket-pieces, and a silver snuff-box!*—Well done, simplicity!—Yet I was forced to make my Hibernian believe that he was corresponding, not with the *Aunt*, but with the *Niece*: for though not over rich, I found he had too much pride and delicacy to sacrifice the feelings of a gentleman to the necessities of his fortune. [*Exit.*

END OF THE FIRST ACT.

ACT II.

Scene I.—*Captain Absolute's Lodgings.*

Captain Absolute and Fag.

Fag. Sir, while I was there, Sir Anthony came in : I told him you had sent me to inquire after his health, and to know if he was at leisure to see you.

Abs. And what did he say, on hearing I was at Bath?

Fag. Sir, in my life I never saw an elderly gentleman more astonished! He started back two or three paces, rapt out a dozen interjectoral oaths, and asked what the devil had brought you here!

Abs. Well, sir, and what did you say?

Fag. Oh, I lied, Sir—I forgot the precise lie; but you may depend on't, he got no truth from me. Yet, with submission, for fear of blunders in future, I should be glad to fix what *has* brought us to Bath : in order that we may lie a little consistently. Sir Anthony's servants were curious, Sir, very curious indeed.

Abs. You have said nothing to them——?

Fag. Oh, not a word, Sir,—not a word! Mr. Thomas, indeed, the coachman (whom I take to be the discreetest of whips)——

Abs. 'Sdeath!—you rascal! you have not trusted him!

Fag. Oh, *no*, sir—no—no—not a syllable, upon my veracity!—He was, indeed, a little inquisitive; but I was sly, sir—devilish sly! My Master (said I), honest Thomas (you know, Sir, one says *honest* to one's inferiors), is come to Bath to *recruit*.—Yes, sir, I said to *recruit*—and whether for men, money, or constitution, you know, Sir, is nothing to him, nor any one else.

Abs. Well, *recruit* will do—let it be so.

Fag. Oh, Sir, recruit will do surprisingly—indeed, to give the thing an air, I told Thomas that your honour had already inlisted five disbanded chairmen, seven minority waiters, and thirteen billiard-markers.

Abs. You blockhead, never say more than is necessary.

Fag. I beg pardon, Sir—I beg pardon—But, with submission, a lie is nothing unless one supports it. Sir, whenever I draw on my invention for a good current lie, I always forge *indorsements* as well as the bill.

Abs. Well, take care you don't hurt your credit by offering too much security.—Is Mr. Faulkland returned?

Fag. He is above, Sir, changing his dress.

Abs. Can you tell whether he has been informed of Sir Anthony's and Miss Melville's arrival?

Fag. I fancy not, Sir; he has seen no one since he came in, but his gentleman, who was with him at Bristol.—I think, Sir, I hear Mr. Faulkland coming down——

Abs. Go, tell him, I am here.

Fag. Yes, Sir.—[*Going.*] I beg pardon, Sir, but should Sir Anthony call, you will do me the favour to remember that we are *recruiting*, if you please.

Abs. Well, well.

Fag. And, in tenderness to my character, if your Honour could bring in the chairmen and waiters, I should esteem it as an obligation; for though I never scruple a lie to serve my Master, yet it *hurts* one's conscience to be found out. [*Exit.*

Abs. Now for my whimsical friend—if he does not know that his mistress is here, I'll tease him a little before I tell him——

Enter FAULKLAND.

Faulkland, you're welcome to Bath again; you are punctual in your return.

Faulk. Yes; I had nothing to detain me when I had finished the business I went on. Well, what news since I left you? how stand matters between you and Lydia?

Abs. Faith, much as they were; I have not seen her since our quarrel; however, I expect to be recalled every hour.

Faulk. Why don't you persuade her to go off with you at once?

Abs. What, and lose two-thirds of her fortune? You forget that, my friend.—No, no, I could have brought her to that long ago.

Faulk. Nay, then, you trifle too long—if you are sure of *her*, propose to the aunt *in your own character*, and write to Sir Anthony for his consent.

Abs. Softly, softly; for though I am convinced my little Lydia would elope with me as Ensign Beverley, yet am I by no means certain that she would take me with the impediment of our friends' consent, a regular humdrum wedding, and a reversion of a good fortune on my side; no, no; I must prepare her gradually for the discovery, and make myself necessary to her, before I risk it.—Well, but Faulkland, you'll dine with us to-day at the Hotel?

Faulk. Indeed, I cannot: I am not in spirits to be of such a party.

Abs. By Heavens! I shall forswear your company. You are the most teasing, captious, incorrigible lover!—Do, love like a man.

Faulk. I own I am unfit for company.

Abs. Am *I* not a lover; ay, and a romantic one too? Yet do I carry everywhere with me such a confounded farrago of doubts, fears, hopes, wishes, and all the flimsy furniture of a country Miss's brain!

Faulk. Ah! Jack, your heart and soul are not, like mine, fixed immutably on one only object.—You throw for a large stake, but losing—you could stake, and throw again:—but I have set my sum of happiness on this cast, and not to succeed, were to be stript of all.

Abs. But, for Heaven's sake! what grounds for apprehension can your whimsical brain conjure up at present? Has Julia missed writing this last post? or was her last too tender, or too cool; or too grave, or too gay; or—

Faulk. Nay, nay, Jack.

Abs. Why, her love—her honour—her prudence, you cannot doubt.

Faulk. O! upon my soul, I never have;—but what grounds for apprehension, did you say? Heavens! are there not a thousand! I fear for her spirits—her health—her life.—My absence may fret her; her anxiety for my return, her fears for me, may oppress her gentle temper. And for her health—does not every hour bring me cause to be alarmed? If it rains, some shower may even then have chilled her delicate frame!—If the wind be keen, some rude blast may have affected her! The heat of noon, the dews of the evening, may endanger the life of her, for whom only I value mine. O! Jack! when delicate and feeling souls are separated, there is not a feature in the sky, not a movement of the elements; not an aspiration of the breeze, but hints some cause for a lover's apprehension!

Abs. Aye, but we may choose whether we will take the hint or no. —Well then, Faulkland, if you were convinced that Julia was well and in spirits, you would be entirely content.

Faulk. I should be happy beyond measure—I am anxious only for that.

Abs. Then to cure your anxiety at once—Miss Melville is in perfect health, and is at this moment in Bath.

Faulk. Nay, Jack—don't trifle with me.

Abs. She is arrived here with my father within this hour.

Faulk. Can you be serious?

Abs. I thought you knew Sir Anthony better than to be surprised at a sudden whim of this kind.—Seriously, then, it is as I tell you—upon my honour.

Faulk. My dear friend!—Hollo, Du-Peigne! my hat—my dear Jack—*now nothing on earth can give me a moment's uneasiness.*

Enter FAG.

Fag. Sir, Mr. Acres just arrived is below.

Abs. Stay, Faulkland, this Acres lives within a mile of Sir Anthony, and he shall tell you how your mistress has been ever since you left her.—Fag, show the gentleman up.   [*Exit* FAG.

Faulk. What, is he much acquainted in the family?

Abs. Oh, very intimate: I insist on your not going: besides, his character will divert you.

Faulk. Well, I should like to ask him a few questions.

Abs. He is likewise a rival of mine—that is of my *other self's*, for he does not think his friend Captain Absolute ever saw the lady in question;—and it is ridiculous enough to hear him complain to me of one *Beverley*, a concealed skulking rival, who——

Faulk. Hush!—He's here.

Enter ACRES.

Acres. Hah! my dear friend, noble captain, and honest Jack, how do'st thou? just arrived faith, as you see.—Sir, your humble servant. Warm work on the roads, Jack!—Odds, whips and wheels, I've travelled like a Comet, with a tail of dust all the way as long as the Mall.

Abs. Ah! Bob, you are indeed an excentric planet, but we know your attraction hither—give me leave to introduce Mr. Faulkland to you; Mr. Faulkland, Mr. Acres.

Acres. Sir, I am most heartily glad to see you: Sir, I solicit your connections.—Hey, Jack—what, this is Mr. Faulkland, who——

Abs. Aye, Bob, Miss Melville's Mr. Faulkland.

Acres. Od'so! she and your father can be but just arrived before me—I suppose you have seen them.—Ah! Mr. Faulkland, you are indeed a happy man.

Faulk. I have not seen Miss Melville yet, Sir;—I hope she enjoyed full health and spirits in Devonshire?

Acres. Never knew her better in my life, Sir,—never better. Odds Blushes and Blooms! she has been as healthy as the German Spa.

Faulk. Indeed!—I did hear that she had been a little indisposed.

Acres. False, false, Sir—only said to vex you: quite the reverse, I assure you.

Faulk. There, Jack, you see she has the advantage of me; I had almost fretted myself ill.

Abs. Now are you angry with your mistress for not having been sick.

Faulk. No, no, you misunderstand me:—yet surely a little trifling indisposition is not an unnatural consequence of absence from those we love.—Now confess—isn't there something unkind in this violent, robust, unfeeling health?

Abs. Oh, it was very unkind of her to be well in your absence to be sure!

Acres. Good apartments, Jack.

Faulk. Well, Sir, but you were saying that Miss Melville has been so *exceedingly* well—what then she has been merry and gay I suppose?—Always in spirits—hey?

Acres. Merry, Odds Crickets! she has been the belle and spirit of the company wherever she has been—so lively and entertaining! so full of wit and humour!

Faulk. There, Jack, there.—O, by my soul! there is an innate levity in woman, that nothing can overcome.—What! happy and I away!

Abs. Have done: How foolish this is! just now you were only apprehensive for your mistress' *spirits*.

Faulk. Why, Jack, have I been the joy and spirit of the company?

Abs. No, indeed, you have not.

Faulk. Have I been lively and entertaining?

Abs. O, upon my word, I acquit you.

Faulk. Have I been full of wit and humour?

Abs. No, faith, to do you justice, you have been confoundedly stupid indeed.

Acres. What's the matter with the gentleman?

Abs. He is only expressing his great satisfaction at hearing that Julia has been so well and happy—that's all—hey, Faulkland?

Faulk. Oh! I am rejoiced to hear it—yes, yes, she has a *happy* disposition!

Acres. That she has indeed—then she is so accomplished—so sweet a voice—so expert at her Harpsichord—such a mistress of flat and sharp, squallante, rumblante, and quiverante!—There was this time month —Odds Minims and Crotchets! how she did chirrup at Mrs. Piano's Concert!

Faulk. There again, what say you to this? you see she has been all mirth and song—not a thought of me!

Abs. Pho! man, is not music the food of love?

Faulk. Well, well, it may be so.—Pray, Mr. ——, what's his d—d name?—Do you remember what Songs Miss Melville sung?

Acres. Not I indeed.

Abs. Stay, now, they were some pretty melancholy, purling-stream airs, I warrant; perhaps you may recollect;—did she sing, *When absent from my soul's delight?*

Acres. No, that wa'n't it.

Abs. Or—*Go, gentle Gales!* "*Go, gentle Gales!*" [*Sings.*

Acres. O no! nothing like it. Odds slips? now I recollect one of them—"*My heart's my own, my will is free.*" [*Sings.*

Faulk. Fool! fool that I am! to fix all my happiness upon such a trifler! 'Sdeath! to make herself the pipe and ballad-monger of a circle! to sooth her light heart with catches and glees!—What can you say to this, Sir?

Abs. Why, that I should be glad to hear my mistress had been so merry, *Sir.*

Faulk. Nay, nay, nay—I'm not sorry that she has been happy—no, no, I am glad of that—I would not have had her sad or sick—yet surely a sympathetic heart would have shown itself even in the choice of a song—she might have been temperately healthy, and somehow, plaintively gay;—but she has been dancing too, I doubt not!

Acres. What does the gentleman say about dancing?

Abs. He says the lady we speak of dances as well as she sings.

Acres. Ay, truly, does she—there was at our last race ball——

Faulk. Hell and the devil!—There!—there—I told you so! Oh! she thrives in my absence!—Dancing! But her whole feelings have been in opposition with mine!—I have been anxious, silent, pensive, sedentary—my days have been hours of care, my nights of watchfulness.—She has been all health! Spirit! Laugh! Song! Dance!—Oh! d—nd, d—e'd levity!

Abs. For Heaven's sake, Faulkland, don't expose yourself so!—Suppose she has danced, what then?—does not the ceremony of society often oblige——

Faulk. Well, well, I'll contain myself—perhaps as you say—for form sake.—What, Mr. Acres, you were praising Miss Melville's manner of dancing a *minuet*—hey?

Acres. O, I dare insure her for that—but what I was going to speak of was her *country dancing*. Odds swimmings! she has such an air with her!

Faulk. Now disappointment on her!—Defend this, Absolute; why don't you defend this?—Country-dances! jiggs and reels! am I to blame now? A Minuet I could have forgiven—I should not have minded that — I say I should not have regarded a Minuet—but *Country-dances!*—Z—ds! had she made one in a *Cotillon*—I believe I could have forgiven even that—but to be monkey-led for a night!—to run the gauntlet thro' a string of amorous palming puppies!—to show paces like a managed filly!—Oh, Jack, there never can be but *one* man in the world, whom a truly modest and delicate woman ought to pair with in a *country-dance;* and, even then, the rest of the couples should be her great-uncles and aunts!

Abs. Aye, to be sure!—grandfathers and grandmothers!

Faulk. If there be but one vicious mind in the Set, 'twill spread like a contagion—the action of their pulse beats to the lascivious movement of the jigg—their quivering, warm-breathed sighs impregnate the very air—the atmosphere becomes electrical to love, and each amorous spark darts thro' every link of the chain!—I must leave you—I own I am somewhat flurried—and that confounded looby has perceived it. [*Going.*

Abs. Aye, aye, you are in a hurry to throw yourself at Julia's feet.

Faulk. I'm not in a humour to be trifled with—I shall see her only to upbraid her.

Abs. Nay, but stay, Faulkland, and thank Mr. Acres for his good news.

Faulk. D—n his news! [*Exit* FAULKLAND.

Abs. Ha! ha! ha! poor Faulkland five minutes since—"nothing on earth could give him a moment's uneasiness!"

Acres. The gentleman wa'n't angry at my praising his mistress, was he?

Abs. A little jealous, I believe, Bob.

Acres. You don't say so? Ha! ha! jealous of me—that's a good joke.

Abs. There's nothing strange in that, Bob: let me tell you, that sprightly grace and insinuating manner of your's will do some mischief among the girls here.

Acres. Ah! you joke—ha! ha! mischief—ha! ha! but you know I am not my own property, my dear Lydia has forestalled me. She could never abide me in the country, because I used to dress so badly—but odds frogs and tambours! I shan't take matters so here, now ancient Madam has no voice in it—I'll make my old clothes know who's master. I shall straitway cashier the hunting-frock—and render my leather breeches incapable. My hair has been in training some time.

Abs. Indeed!

Acres. Ay—and tho'ff the side curls are a little restive, my hind-part takes to it very kindly.

Abs. O, you'll polish, I doubt not.

Acres. Absolutely I propose so—then if I can find out this Ensign Beverley, odds triggers and flints! I'll make him know the difference o't.

Abs. Spoke like a man! But pray, Bob, I observe you have got an odd kind of a new method of swearing——

Acres. Ha! ha! you've taken notice of it—'tis genteel, isn't it?—I didn't invent it myself though; but a commander in our militia—a great scholar, I assure you—says that there is no meaning in the common oaths, and that nothing but their antiquity makes them respectable; because, he says, the ancients would never stick to an oath or two, but would say, by Jove! or by Bacchus! or by Mars! or by Venus! or by Pallus, according to the sentiment—so that to swear with propriety, says my little Major, the 'oath should be an echo to the sense'; and this we call the *oath referential*, or *sentimental swearing*—ha! ha! ha! 'tis genteel, isn't it.

Abs. Very genteel, and very new, indeed—and I dare say will supplant all other figures of imprecation.

Acres. Aye, aye, the best terms will grow obsolete.—D—ns have had their day.

Enter FAG.

Fag. Sir, there is a gentleman below desires to see you.—Shall I show him into the parlour?

Abs. Aye—you may.

Acres. Well, I must be gone——

Abs. Stay; who is it, Fag?

Fag. Your father, sir.

Abs. You puppy, why didn't you show him up directly?

[*Exit* FAG.

Acres. You have business with Sir Anthony.—I expect a message from Mrs. Malaprop at my lodgings. I have sent also to my dear friend, Sir Lucius O'Trigger. Adieu, Jack! we must meet at night. Odds bottles and glasses! you shall give me a dozen bumpers to little Lydia.

Abs. That I will with all my heart.—[*Exit* ACRES.] Now for a parental lecture—I hope he has heard nothing of the business that brought me here—I wish the gout had held him fast in Devonshire, with all my soul!

Enter SIR ANTHONY.

Abs. Sir I am delighted to see you here; looking so well! your sudden arrival at Bath made me apprehensive for your health.

Sir Anth. Very apprehensive, I dare say, Jack.—What, you are recruiting here, hey?

Abs. Yes, Sir, I am on duty.

Sir Anth. Well, Jack, I am glad to see you, tho' I did not expect it, for I was going to write to you on a little matter of business.—Jack, I have been considering that I grow old and infirm, and shall probably not trouble you long.

Abs. Pardon me, Sir, I never saw you look more strong and hearty; and I pray frequently that you may continue so.

Sir Anth. I hope your prayers may be heard with all my heart. Well, then, Jack, I have been considering that I am so strong and hearty, I may continue to plague you a long time. Now, Jack, I am sensible that the income of your commission, and what I have hitherto allowed you, is but a small pittance for a lad of your spirit.

Abs. Sir, you are very good.

Sir Anth. And it is my wish, while yet I live, to have my Boy make some figure in the world.—I have resolved, therefore, to fix you at once in a noble independence.

Abs. Sir, your kindness overpowers me—such generosity makes the gratitude of reason more lively than the sensations even of filial affection.

Sir Anth. I am glad you are so sensible of my attention—and you shall be master of a large estate in a few weeks.

Abs. Let my future life, Sir, speak my gratitude: I cannot express the sense I have of your munificence.—Yet, sir, I presume you would not wish me to quit the army?

Sir Anth. Oh, that shall be as your wife chooses.

Abs. My wife, Sir!

Sir Anth. Aye, aye, settle that between you—settle that between you.

Abs. A *wife*, Sir, did you say?

Sir Anth. Aye, a wife—why; did not I mention her before?

Abs. Not a word of it, Sir.

Sir Anth. Odd so!—I mus'n't forget *her* tho'.—Yes, Jack, the independence I was talking of is by a marriage—the fortune is saddled with a wife—but I suppose that makes no difference.

Abs. Sir! Sir!—you amaze me!

Sir Anth. Why, what the d—l's the matter with the fool? Just now you were all gratitude and duty.

Abs. I was, Sir—you talked to me of independence and a fortune, but not a word of a wife.

Sir Anth. Why—what difference does that make? Odds life, Sir! if you have the estate, you must take it with the live stock on it, as it stands.

Abs. If my happiness is to be the price, I must beg leave to decline the purchase.—Pray, Sir, who is the lady?

Sir Anth. What's that to you, Sir?—Come, give me your promise to love, and to marry her directly.

Abs. Sure, Sir, this is not very reasonable, to summon my affections for a lady I know nothing of!

Sir Anth. I am sure, Sir, 'tis more unreasonable in you *to object* to a lady you know nothing of.

Abs. Then, Sir, I must tell you plainly that my inclinations are fix'd on another.

Sir Anth. They are, are they ? Well that's lucky—because you will have more merit in your obedience to me.

Abs. Sir, my heart is engaged to an Angel.

Sir Anth. Then pray let it send an excuse. It is very sorry—but *business* prevents its waiting on her.

Abs. But my vows are pledged to her.

Sir Anth. Let her foreclose, Jack ; let her foreclose ; they are not worth redeeming : besides, you have the Angel's vows in exchange, I suppose ; so there can be no loss there.

Abs. You must excuse me, Sir, if I tell you, once for all, that in this point I cannot obey you.

Sir Anth. Hark 'ee, Jack ;—I have heard you for some time with patience—I have been cool—quite cool ; but take care—you know I am compliance itself—when I am not thwarted ;—no one more easily led—when I have my own way ;—but don't put me in a frenzy.

Abs. Sir, I must repeat—in this I cannot obey you.

Sir Anth. Now d—n me ! if ever I call you *Jack* again while I live !

Abs. Nay, Sir, but hear me.

Sir Anth. Sir, I won't hear a word—not a word ! not one word ! so give me your promise by a nod—and I'll tell you what, Jack—I mean, you Dog—if you don't, by——

Abs. What, Sir, promise to link myself to some mass of ugliness ! to——

Sir Anth. Zounds ! sirrah ! the lady shall be as ugly as I choose : she shall have a hump on each shoulder ; she shall be as crooked as the Crescent ; her one eye shall roll like the Bull's in Cox's Museum ; she shall have a skin like a mummy, and the beard of a Jew—she shall be all this, sirrah !—yet I'll make you ogle her all day, and sit up all night to write sonnets on her beauty.

Abs. This is reason and moderation indeed !

Sir Anth. None of your sneering, puppy ! no grinning, jackanapes !

Abs. Indeed, Sir, I never was in a worse humour for mirth in my life.

Sir Anth. 'Tis false, Sir ! I know you are laughing in your sleeve : I know you will grin when I am gone, sirrah !

Abs. Sir, I hope I know my duty better.

Sir Anth. None of your passion, Sir ! none of your violence, if you please !—It won't do with me, I promise you.

Abs. Indeed, Sir, I never was cooler in my life.

Sir Anth. 'Tis a confounded lie!—I know you are in a passion in your heart; I know you are, you hypocritical young dog! but it won't do.

Abs. Nay, Sir, upon my word.

Sir Anth. So you will fly out! can't you be cool, like me? What the devil good can *Passion* do?—*Passion* is of no service, you impudent, insolent, overbearing Reprobate!—There, you sneer again! don't provoke me!—but you rely upon the mildness of my temper—you do, you Dog! you play upon the weakness of my disposition!—Yet take care—the patience of a saint may be overcome at last!—but mark! I give you six hours and a half to consider of this: if you then agree, without any condition, to do everything on earth that I choose, why—confound you! I may in time forgive you.—If not, z—ds! don't enter the same hemisphere with me! don't dare to breathe the same air, or use the same light with me; but get an atmosphere and a sun of your own! I'll strip you of your commission; I'll lodge a five-and-threepence in the hands of trustees, and you shall live on the interest.—I'll disown you, I'll disinherit you, I'll unget you! and d—n me, if ever I call you Jack again! [*Exit* SIR ANTHONY.

ABSOLUTE *solus*.

Abs. Mild, gentle, considerate father—I kiss your hands!—What a tender method of giving his opinion in these matters Sir Anthony has! I dare not trust him with the truth.—I wonder what old wealthy Hag it is that he wants to bestow on me!—Yet he married himself for love! and was in his youth a bold Intriguer, and a gay Companion!

Enter FAG.

Fag. Assuredly, Sir, our Father is wrath to a degree; he comes down stairs eight or ten steps at a time—muttering, growling, and thumping the bannisters all the way: I, and the Cook's dog stand bowing at the door—rap! he gives me a stroke on the head with his cane; bids me carry that to my master, then kicking the poor Turnspit into the area, d—ns us all, for a puppy triumvirate!—Upon my credit, Sir, were I in your place, and found my father such very bad company, I should certainly drop his acquaintance.

Abs. Cease your impertinence, Sir, at present.—Did you come in for nothing more?—Stand out of the way!

[*Pushes him aside, and Exit.*

FAG, *solus*.

Fag. Soh! Sir Anthony trims my Master; He is afraid to reply to his Father—then vents his spleen on poor Fag!—When one is vexed by one person, to revenge one's self on another, who happens to come in the way, is the vilest injustice! Ah! it shows the worst temper—the basest——

Enter ERRAND-BOY.

Boy. Mr. Fag! Mr. Fag! your Master calls you.

Fag. Well, you little dirty puppy, you need not baul so!—The meanest disposition! the——

Boy. Quick, quick, Mr. Fag!

Fag. Quick! quick! you impudent Jackanapes! am I to be commanded by you too? you little, impertinent, insolent, kitchenbred——
[*Exit, kicking and beating him.*

SCENE II.—*The* North Parade.

Enter LUCY.

Lucy. So—I shall have another Rival to add to my mistress's list—Captain Absolute. However, I shall not enter his name till my purse has received notice in form. Poor Acres is dismissed!—Well, I have done him a last friendly office, in letting him know that Beverley was here before him.—Sir Lucius is generally more punctual, when he expects to hear from his *dear Dalia*, as he calls her: I wonder he's not here!—I have a little scruple of conscience from this deceit; tho' I should not be paid so well, if my hero knew that Delia was near fifty, and her own mistress.—I could not have thought he would have been so nice, when there's a golden egg in the case, as to care whether he has it from a pullet or an old hen.

Enter SIR LUCIUS O'TRIGGER.

Sir Luc. Hah! my little ambassadress—upon my conscience, I have been looking for you; I have been on the South Parade this half hour.

Lucy. [*Speaking simply.*] O gemini! and I have been waiting for your worship here on the North.

Sir Luc. Faith!—may be, that was the reason we did not meet; and it is very comical too, how you could go out and I not see you—for I was only taking a nap at the Parade Coffee-house, and I chose the *window* on purpose that I might not miss you.

Lucy. My stars! Now I'd wager a sixpence I went by while you were asleep.

Sir Luc. Sure enough it must have been so—and I never dreamt it was so late, till I waked. Well, but my little girl, have you got nothing for me?

Lucy. Yes, but I have:—I've got a letter for you in my pocket.

30   THE RIVALS.

Sir Luc. O faith! I guessed you weren't come empty-handed.—Well —let me see what the dear creature says.

Lucy. There, Sir Lucius.   [*Gives him a letter.*

Sir Luc. [Reads.] *Sir—there is often a sudden incentive impulse in love, that has a greater induction than years of domestic combination: such was the commotion I felt at the first superfluous view of Sir Lucius O'Trigger.*—Very pretty, upon my word.—*As my motive is interested, you may be assured my love shall never be miscellaneous.* Very well.

Female punctuation forbids me to say more; yet let me add, that it will give me joy infallible to find Sir Lucius worthy the last criterion of my affections. Yours, while meretricious.—DELIA. Upon my conscience! Lucy, your lady is a great mistress of language.—Faith, she's quite the queen of the dictionary!—for the devil a word dare refuse coming at her call—though one would think it was quite out of hearing.

Lucy. Aye, Sir, a lady of her experience——

Sir Luc. Experience! what, at seventeen?

Lucy. O true, Sir—but then she reads so—my stars! how she will read off-hand!

Sir Luc. Faith, she must be very deep read to write this way— tho' she is rather an arbitrary writer too—for here are a great many poor words pressed into the service of this note, that would get their *habeas corpus* from any court in Christendom.—However, when affection guides the pen, Lucy, he must be a brute who finds fault with the style.

Lucy. Ah! Sir Lucius, if you were to hear how she talks of you!

Sir Luc. Oh, tell her, I'll make her the best husband in the world, and Lady O'Trigger into the bargain!—But we must get the old gentlewoman's consent—and do everything fairly.

Lucy. Nay, Sir Lucius, I thought you wa'n't rich enough to be so nice.

Sir Luc. Upon my word, young woman, you have hit it:—I am so poor, that I can't afford to do a dirty action.—If I did not want money, I'd steal your mistress and her fortune with a great deal of pleasure.— However, my pretty girl, [*gives her money,*] here's a little something to buy you a ribband; and meet me in the evening, and I'll give you an answer to this. So, hussy, take a kiss beforehand to put you in mind.   [*Kisses her.*

Lucy. O lud! Sir Lucius—I never seed such a gemman! My lady won't like you if you're so impudent.

Sir Luc. Faith she will, Lucy!—That same—pho! what's the name of it?—*Modesty*—is a quality in a lover more praised by the women than liked ; so, if your mistress asks you whether Sir Lucius ever gave you a kiss, tell her *fifty*—my dear.

Lucy. What, would you have me tell her a lie ?

Sir Luc. Ah, then, you baggage ! I 'll make it a truth presently.

Lucy. For shame now ; here is some one coming.

Sir Luc. Oh, faith, I 'll quiet your conscience !

[*Sees* FAG.—*Exit, humming a tune.*

Enter FAG.

Fag. So, so, Ma'am ! I humbly beg pardon.

Lucy. O lud ! now, Mr. Fag, you flurry one so.

Fag. Come, come, Lucy, here 's no one bye—so a little less simplicity, with a grain or two more sincerity, if you please.—You play false with us, Madam.—I saw you give the baronet a letter.—My master shall know this—and if he don't call him out, I will.

Lucy. Ha ! ha ! ha ! you gentlemen's gentlemen are so hasty.—That letter was from Mrs. Malaprop, simpleton.—She is taken with Sir Lucius's address.

Fag. What tastes some people have !—Why, I suppose I have walked by her window an hundred times.—But what says our young lady ? any message to my master ?

Lucy. Sad news. Mr. Fag.—A worse Rival than Acres ! Sir Anthony Absolute has proposed his son.

Fag. What, Captain Absolute ?

Lucy. Even so—I overheard it all.

Fag. Ha ! ha ! ha ! very good, faith. Good bye, Lucy, I must away with this news.

Lucy. Well,...you may laugh...but it is true, I assure you.—[*Going.*] But...Mr. Fag...tell your master not to be cast down by this.

Fag. O he 'll be so disconsolate !

Lucy. And charge him not to think of quarrelling with young Absolute.

Fag. Never fear !...never fear !

Lucy. Be sure...bid him keep up his spirits.

Fag. We will...we will. [*Exeunt severally.*

END OF THE SECOND ACT.

ACT III.

SCENE I.—*The* North Parade.

Enter ABSOLUTE.

'Tis just as Fag told me, indeed....Whimsical enough, faith! My Father wants to *force* me to marry the very girl I am plotting to run away with!—He must not know of my connection with her yet a-while.—He has too summary a method of proceeding in these matters...and Lydia shall not yet lose her hopes of an elopement.—However, I'll read my recantation instantly.—My conversion is something sudden, indeed...but I can assure him it is very *sincere*. So, so...here he comes. He looks plaguy gruff. [*Steps aside.*

Enter SIR ANTHONY.

No...I'll die sooner than forgive him....*Die*, did I say! I'll live these fifty years to plague him.—At our last meeting, his impudence had almost put me out of temper....An obstinate, passionate, self-willed boy!...Who can he take after? This is my return for getting him before all his brothers and sisters!...for putting him at twelve years old, into a marching regiment, and allowing him fifty pounds a year, beside his pay, ever since!...But I have done with him;...he's anybody's son for me.—I never will see him more, never...never...never...never.

Abs. Now for a penitential face.

Sir Anth. Fellow, get out of my way.

Abs. Sir, you see a penitent before you.

Sir Anth. I see an impudent scoundrel before me.

Abs. A sincere penitent.—I am come, Sir, to acknowledge my error, and to submit entirely to your will.

Sir Anth. What's that?

Abs. I have been revolving, and reflecting, and considering on your past goodness, and kindness, and condescension to me.

Sir Anth. Well, sir?

Abs. I have been likewise weighing and balancing what you were pleased to mention concerning duty, and obedience, and authority.

Sir Anth. Well, Puppy?

Abs. Why then, Sir, the result of my reflections is...a resolution to sacrifice every inclination of my own to your satisfaction.

Sir Anth. Why now you talk sense...absolute sense....I never heard anything more sensible in my life....Confound you; you shall be *Jack* again.

Abs. I am happy in the appellation.

Sir Anth. Why, then, Jack, my dear Jack, I will now inform you... who the lady really is.—Nothing but your passion and violence, you silly fellow, prevented my telling you at first. Prepare, Jack, for wonder and rapture—prepare. —What think you of Miss Lydia Languish?

Abs. Languish! What, the Languishes of Worcestershire?

Sir Anth. Worcestershire! no. Did you never meet Mrs. Malaprop and her Niece, Miss Languish, who came into our country just before you were last ordered to your regiment?

Abs. Malaprop! Languish! I don't remember ever to have heard the names before. Yet, stay—I think I do recollect something.— *Languish! Languish!* She squints, don't she?—A little, red-haired girl?

Sir Anth. Squints?—A red-haired girl!—Z—ds! no.

Abs. Then I must have forgot; it can't be the same person.

Sir Anth. Jack! Jack! what think you of blooming, love-breathing seventeen?

Abs. As to that, Sir, I am quite indifferent.—If I can please you in the matter, 'tis all I desire.

Sir Anth. Nay, but Jack, such eyes! such eyes! so innocently wild! so bashfully irresolute! not a glance but speaks and kindles some thought of love! Then, Jack, her cheeks! her cheeks, Jack! so deeply blushing at the insinuations of her tell-tale eyes! Then, Jack, her lips!—O, Jack, lips smiling at their own discretion; and if not smiling, more sweetly pouting; more lovely in sullenness.

Abs. That's she, indeed....Well done, old gentleman.

Sir Anth. Then, Jack, her neck!—O Jack! Jack!

Abs. And which is to be mine, Sir; the Niece or the Aunt?

Sir Anth. Why, you unfeeling, insensible Puppy, I despise you! When I was of your age, such a description would have made me fly like a rocket! The *Aunt*, indeed! Odds life! when I ran away with your mother, I would not have touched anything old or ugly to gain an empire.

Abs. Not to please your father, sir?

Sir Anth. To please my father! z—ds! not to please—Oh, my father—odd so!—yes—yes; if my father indeed had desired—that's quite another matter. Tho' he wa'n't the indulgent father that I am, Jack.

Abs. I dare say not, Sir.

Sir Anth. But, Jack, you are not sorry to find your mistress is so beautiful?

Abs. Sir, I repeat it; if I please you in this affair, 'tis all I desire.

D

Not that I think a woman the worse for being handsome ; but, Sir, if you please to recollect, you before hinted something about a hump or two, one eye, and a few more graces of that kind—now, without being very nice, I own I should rather chuse a wife of mine to have the usual number of limbs, and a limited quantity of back : and tho' *one* eye may be very agreeable, yet as the prejudice has always run in favour of *two*, I would not wish to affect a singularity in that article.

Sir Anth. What a phlegmatic sot it is ! Why, sirrah, you're an anchorite !—a vile, insensible stock. You a soldier !—you're a walking block, fit only to dust the company's regimentals on !—Odds life ! I have a great mind to marry the girl myself !

Abs. I am entirely at your disposal, sir : if you should think of addressing Miss Languish yourself, I suppose you would have me marry the *Aunt* ; or if you should change your mind, and take the old lady—'tis the same to me—I'll marry the *Niece*.

Sir Anth. Upon my word, Jack, thou 'rt either a very great hypocrite, or—but, come, I know your indifference on such a subject must be all a lie—I'm sure it must—come, now—d—n your demure face ! —come, confess Jack—you have been lying, ha'n't you ? You have been lying, hey !—I'll never forgive you, if you ha'n't :—So now, own, my dear Jack, you have been playing the hypocrite, hey ! I'll never forgive you, if you ha'n't been lying and playing the hypocrite.

Abs. I'm sorry, sir, that the respect and duty which I bear to you should be so mistaken.

Sir Anth. Hang your respect and duty ! But come along with me, I'll write a note to Mrs. Malaprop, and you shall visit the lady directly.

Abs. Where does she lodge, Sir ?

Sir Anth. What a dull question ! Only on the Grove here.

Abs. O ! then I can call on her in my way to the coffee-house.

Sir Anth. In your way to the coffee-house ! You'll set your heart down in your way to the coffee-house, hey ? Ah ! you leaden-nerv'd, wooden-hearted dolt ! But come along, you shall see her directly ; her eyes shall be the Promethean torch to you—come along, I'll never forgive you, if you don't come back, stark mad with rapture and impatience—if you don't, egad, I'll marry the girl myself ! [*Exeunt.*

Scene II.

Julia's *Dressing-room.*

Faulkland *solus.*

Faulk. They told me Julia would return directly ; I wonder she is not yet come !—How mean does this captious, unsatisfied temper of mine appear to my cooler judgment! Yet I know not that I indulge it in any other point: but on this one subject, and to this one object, whom I think I love beyond my life, I am ever ungenerously fretful, and madly capricious! I am conscious of it—yet I cannot correct myself! What tender, honest joy sparkled in her eyes when we met! How delicate was the warmth of her expression!—I was ashamed to appear less happy—though I had come resolved to wear a face of coolness and upbraiding. Sir Anthony's presence prevented my proposed expostulations; yet I must be satisfied that she has not been so *very* happy in my absence. She is coming! Yes!—I know the nimbleness of her tread, when she thinks her impatient Faulkland counts the moments of her stay.

Enter JULIA.

Jul. I had not hop'd to see you again so soon.

Faulk. Could I, Julia, be contented with my first welcome—restrained as we were by the presence of a third person?

Jul. O Faulkland, when your kindness can make me thus happy, let me not think that I discovered more coolness in your first salutation than my long-hoarded joy could have presaged.

Faulk. 'Twas but your fancy, Julia. I *was* rejoiced to see you—to see you in such health. Sure I had no cause for coldness?

Jul. Nay then, I see you have taken something ill. You must not conceal from me what it is.

Faulk. Well, then—shall I own to you—but you will despise me, Julia—nay, I despise myself for it.—Yet I *will* own that my joy at hearing of your health and arrival here, by your neighbour Acres, was somewhat damped by his dwelling much on the high spirits you had enjoyed in Devonshire—on your mirth—your singing—dancing, and I know not what! For such is my temper, Julia, that I should regard every mirthful moment in your absence as a treason to constancy:— The mutual tear that steals down the cheek of parting lovers is a compact, that no smile shall live there till they meet again.

Jul. Must I never cease to tax my Faulkland with this teasing minute caprice? Can the idle reports of a silly boor weigh in your breast against my tried affection?

Faulk. They have no weight with me, Julia: No, no—I am happy if you have been so—yet only say, that you did not sing with *mirth*—say that you *thought* of Faulkland in the dance.

Jul. I never can be happy in your absence.—If I wear a countenance of content, it is to shew that my mind holds no doubt of my Faulkland's truth. If I seemed sad, it were to make malice triumph; and say, that I fixed my heart on one, who left me to lament his roving, and my own credulity.—Believe me, Faulkland, I mean not to upbraid you, when I say, that I have often dressed sorrow in smiles, lest my friends should guess whose unkindness had caused my tears.

Faulk. You were ever all goodness to me. O, I am a brute, when I but admit a doubt of your true constancy!

Jul. If ever, without such cause from you, as I will not suppose possible, you find my affections veering but a point, may I become a proverbial scoff for levity, and base ingratitude.

Faulk. Ah! Julia, that *last* word is grating to me. I would I had no title to your *gratitude!* Search your heart, Julia; perhaps what you have mistaken for Love, is but the warm effusion of a too thankful heart.

Jul. For what quality must I love you?

Faulk. For no quality! To regard me for any quality of mind or understanding, were only to *esteem* me. And for person—I have often wish'd myself deformed, to be convinced that I owed no obligation *there* for any part of your affection.

Jul. Where Nature has bestowed a shew of nice attention in the features of a man, he should laugh at it, as misplaced. I have seen men, who in this vain article perhaps might rank above you; but my heart has never asked my eyes if it were so or not.

Faulk. Now this is not well from *you*, Julia—I despise person in a man—yet if you loved me as I wish, though I were an Æthiop, you'd think none so fair.

Jul. I see you are determined to be unkind! The *contract* which my poor father bound us in gives you more than a lover's privilege.

Faulk. Again, Julia, you raise ideas that feed and justify my doubts. I would not have been more free—no—I am proud of my restraint. Yet—yet—perhaps your high respect alone for this solemn compact has fettered your inclinations, which else had made a worthier choice. How shall I be sure, had you remained unbound in thought and promise, that I should still have been the object of your persevering love?

Jul. Then try me now. Let us be free as strangers as to what is past:—*my* heart will not feel more liberty!

Faulk. There now! so hasty, Julia! so anxious to be free! If your love for me were fixed and ardent, you would not lose your hold, even tho' I wish'd it!

Jul. Oh! you torture me to the heart! I cannot bear it.

Faulk. I do not mean to distress you. If I loved you less I should never give you an uneasy moment.—But hear me.—All my fretful doubts arise from this—Women are not used to weigh, and separate the motives of their affections :—the cold dictates of prudence, gratitude, or filial duty, may sometimes be mistaken for the pleadings of the heart. I would not boast—yet let me say, that I have neither age, person, or character, to found dislike on; my fortune such as few ladies could be charged with *indiscretion* in the match. O Julia! when *Love* receives such countenance from *Prudence*, nice minds will be suspicious of its *birth*.

Jul. I know not whither your insinuations would tend :—but as they seem pressing to insult me, I will spare you the regret of having done so.—I have given you no cause for this ! [*Exit in tears.*

Faulk. In Tears! stay, Julia: stay but for a moment.—The door is fastened ! — Julia ! — my soul—but for one moment ! — I hear her sobbing !—'Sdeath ! what a brute am I to use her thus ! Yet stay ! Aye—she is coming now :—how little resolution there is in women !—how a few soft words can turn them !—No, faith !—she is *not* coming either.—Why, Julia—my love—say but that you forgive me—come but to tell me that—now this is being *too* resentful. Stay ! she *is* coming too—I thought she would—no *steadiness* in anything ! her going away must have been a mere trick then—she sha'n't see that I was hurt by it.—I'll affect indifference—[*Hums a tune; then listens.*] No z—ds ! she's *not* coming !—nor don't intend it, I suppose.—This is not *steadiness*, but *obstinacy!* Yet I deserve it.—What, after so long an absence to quarrel with her tenderness !—'twas barbarous and unmanly !—I should be ashamed to see her now.—I'll wait till her just resentment is abated—and when I distress her so again, may I lose her for ever ! and be linked instead to some antique virago, whose gnawing passions, and long-hoarded spleen, shall make me curse my folly half the day, and all the night. [*Exit.*

SCENE III.

MRS. MALAPROP'S *Lodgings.*

MRS. MALAPROP *and Captain* ABSOLUTE.

Mrs. Mal. Your being Sir Anthony's son, Captain, would itself be a sufficient accommodation; but from the ingenuity of your appearance, I am convinced you deserve the character here given of you.

Abs. Permit me to say, madam, that as I never yet have had the pleasure of seeing Miss Languish, my principal inducement in this affair at present is the honour of being allied to Mrs. Malaprop; of whose intellectual accomplishments, elegant manners, and unaffected learning, no tongue is silent.

Mrs. Mal. Sir, you do me infinite honour ! I beg, Captain, you'll be seated.—[*Sit.*] Ah! few gentlemen, now a days, know how to value the ineffectual qualities in a woman!—few think how a little knowledge become a gentlewoman.—Men have no sense now but for the worthless flower, beauty!

Abs. It is but too true, indeed, Ma'am;—yet I fear our ladies should share the blame—they think our admiration of *beauty* so great, that *knowledge* in *them* would be superfluous. Thus, like garden-trees, they seldom show fruits till time has robb'd them of more specious blossom.—Few, like Mrs. Malaprop and the Orange-tree, are rich in both at once!

Mrs. Mal. Sir, you overpower me with good-breeding.—He is the very Pine-apple of politeness!—You are not ignorant, Captain, that this giddy girl has somehow contrived to fix her affections on a beggarly, strolling, eves-dropping ensign, whom none of us have seen, and nobody knows anything of.

Abs. Oh, I have heard the silly affair before.—I'm not at all prejudiced against her on *that* account.

Mrs. Mal. You are very good and very considerate, Captain. I am sure I have done everything in my power since I exploded the affair; long ago I laid my positive conjunction on her, never to think on the fellow again;—I have since laid Sir Anthony's preposition before her; but, I am sorry to say, she seems resolved to decline every particle that I enjoin her.

Abs. It must be very distressing, indeed, Ma'am.

Mrs. Mal. Oh! it gives me the hydrostatics to such a degree.—I thought she had persisted from corresponding with him; but behold this very day, I have interceded another letter from the fellow! I believe I have it in my pocket.

Abs. Oh, the devil! my last note.   [*Aside.*

Mrs. Mal. Ay, here it is.

Abs. Ay, my note indeed! Oh, the little traitress Lucy. [*Aside.*

Mrs. Mal. There, perhaps you may know the writing.

[*Gives him the letter.*

Abs. I think I have seen the hand before—yes, I *certainly must* have seen this hand before:—

Mrs. Mal. Nay, but read it, Captain.

Abs. [*Reads*] "*My soul's idol, my adored Lydia!*"—Very tender, indeed!

Mrs. Mal. Tender! aye, and prophane too, o' my conscience.

Abs. [*Reads*] "*I am excessively alarmed at the intelligence you send me, the more so as my new rival*"——

Mrs. Mal. That's *you*, sir.

Abs. "*Has universally the character of being an accomplished gentl-man, and a man of honour.*"—Well, that's handsome enough.

Mrs. Mal. Oh, the fellow has some design in writing so.

Abs. That he had, I'll answer for him, Ma'am.

Mrs. Mal. But go on, Sir—you'll see presently.

Abs. "*As for the old weather-beaten she-dragon who guards you.*"—Who can he mean by that?

Mrs. Mal. Me, Sir!—*me!*—he means *me* there—what do you think now?—but go on a little further.

Abs. Impudent scoundrel!—"*it shall go hard but I will elude her vigilance, as I am told that the same ridiculous vanity, which makes her dress up her coarse features, and deck her dull chat with hard words which she don't understand*"——

Mrs. Mal. There, Sir! an attack upon my language! what do you think of that?—an aspersion upon my parts of speech! was ever such a brute! save if I reprehend any thing in this world, it is the use of my oracular tongue, and a nice derangement of epitaphs!

Abs. He deserves to be hang'd and quartered! let me see—"*same ridiculous vanity*"——

Mrs. Mal. You need not read it again, Sir.

Abs. I beg pardon, Ma'am—"*does also lay her open to the grossest deceptions from flattery and pretended admiration*"—an impudent coxcomb!—"*so that I have a scheme to see you shortly with the old Harridan's consent, and even to make her a go-between in our interviews.*"—Was ever such assurance!

Mrs. Mal. Did you ever hear anything like it?—he'll elude my vigilance, will he?—Yes, yes! ha! ha! he's very likely to enter these floors;—we'll try who can plot best!

Abs. Ha! ha! ha! a conceited puppy, ha! ha! ha!—Well, but Mrs. Malaprop, as the girl seems so infatuated by this fellow, suppose you were to wink at her corresponding with him for a little time—let her even plot an elopement with him—then do you connive at her escape—while *I*, just in the nick, will have the fellow laid by the heels, and fairly contrive to carry her off in his stead.

Mrs. Mal. I am delighted with the scheme; never was anything better perpetrated!

Abs. But, pray, could not I see the lady for a few minutes now?—I should like to try her temper a little.

Mrs. Mal. Why, I don't know—I doubt she is not prepared for a first visit of this kind. There is a decorum in these matters.

Abs. O Lord! she won't mind *me*—only tell her Beverley——

Mrs. Mal. Sir!

Abs. Gently, good tongue. [*Aside.*

Mrs. Mal. What did you say of Beverley?

Abs. Oh, I was going to propose that you should tell her, by way of jest, that it was Beverley who was below; she'd come down fast enough then—ha! ha! ha!

Mrs. Mal. 'Twould be a trick she well deserves; besides, you know the fellow tells her he'll get my consent to see her—ha! ha! Let him if he can, I say again. Lydia, come down here!—[*Calling.*] He'll make me a *go-between in their interviews!*—ha! ha! ha! Come down, I say, Lydia! I don't wonder at your laughing, ha! ha! ha! his impudence is truly ridiculous.

Abs. 'Tis very ridiculous, upon my soul, Ma'am, ha! ha! ha!

Mrs. Mal. The little hussy won't hear. Well, I'll go and tell her at once who it is—she shall know that Captain Absolute is come to wait on her. And I'll make her behave as becomes a young woman.

Abs. As you please, Ma'am.

Mrs. Mal. For the present, captain, your servant. Ah! you've not done laughing yet, I see—*elude my vigilance*; yes, yes; ha! ha! ha! [*Exit.*

Abs. Ha! ha! ha! one would think now that I might throw off all disguise at once, and seize my prize with security; but such is Lydia's caprice, that to undeceive were probably to lose her. I'll see whether she knows me.

[*Walks aside, and seems engaged in looking at the pictures.*

Enter LYDIA.

Lyd. What a scene am I now to go through! surely nothing can be more dreadful than to be obliged to listen to the loathsome addresses of a stranger to one's heart. I have heard of girls persecuted as I am, who have appealed in behalf of their favoured lover to the generosity of his rival: suppose I were to try it—there stands the hated rival—an officer too!—but O, how unlike my Beverley! I wonder he don't begin—truly he seems a very negligent wooer!—quite at his ease, upon my word!—I'll speak first—Mr. Absolute.

Abs. Madam. [*Turns round.*

Lyd. O Heav'ns! Beverley!

Abs. Hush!—hush, my life! softly! be not surprised!

Lyd. I am so astonished! and so terrified! and so overjoy'd!—for Heav'n's sake! how came you here?

Abs. Briefly, I have deceived your Aunt—I was informed that my new rival was to visit here this evening, and contriving to have him kept away, have passed myself on *her* for Capt. Absolute.

Lyd. O, charming ! And she really takes you for young Absolute.

Abs. O, she's convinced of it.

Lyd. Ha ! ha ! ha ! I can't forbear laughing to think how her sagacity is overreached !

Abs. But we trifle with our precious moments—such another opportunity may not occur ; then let me conjure my kind, my condescending angel, to fix the time when I may rescue her from undeserved persecution, and with a licensed warmth plead for my reward.

Lyd. Will you then, Beverley, consent to forfeit that portion of my paltry wealth ?—that burden on the wings of love ?

Abs. Oh, come to me—rich only thus—in loveliness ! Bring no portion to me but thy love—'twill be generous in you, Lydia,—for well you know it is the only dower your poor Beverley can repay.

Lyd. How persuasive are his words !—how charming will poverty be with him !

Abs. Ah ! my soul, what a life will we then live ! Love shall be our idol and support ! we will worship him with a monastic strictness ; abjuring all worldly toys, to center every thought and action there.—Proud of calamity, we will enjoy the wreck of wealth ; while the surrounding gloom of adversity shall make the flame of our pure love show doubly bright. By Heav'ns ! I would fling all goods of fortune from me with a prodigal hand, to enjoy the scene where I might clasp my Lydia to my bosom, and say, the world affords no smile to me— but here — [*Embracing her.*] If she holds out now, the devil is in it ! [*Aside.*

Lyd. Now could I fly with him to the Antipodes ! but my persecution is not yet come to a crisis. [*Aside.*

Re-enter MRS. MALAPROP, *listening.*

Mrs. Mal. I am impatient to know how the little huzzy deports herself. [*Aside.*

Abs. So pensive, Lydia !—is then your warmth abated ?

Mrs. Mal. Warmth abated !—so !—she has been in a passion, I suppose. [*Aside.*

Lyd. No—nor ever can while I have life.

Mrs. Mal. An ill-temper'd little devil ! She'll be *in a passion all her life*—will she ? [*Aside.*

Lyd. Think not the idle threats of my ridiculous aunt can ever have any weight with me.

Mrs. Mal. Very dutiful, upon my word ! [*Aside.*

Lyd. Let her choice be *Capt. Absolute*, but Beverley is mine.

Mrs. Mal. I am astonished at her assurance!—*to his face—this to his face!* [*Aside.*

Abs. Thus then let me enforce my suit. [*Kneeling.*

Mrs. Mal. [*Aside*] Aye, poor young man!—down on his knees entreating for pity!—I can contain no longer.—Why, huzzy! huzzy!—I have overheard you.

Abs. Oh, confound her vigilance! [*Aside.*

Mrs. Mal. Capt. Absolute,—I know not how to apologize for her shocking rudeness.

Abs. [*Aside*] So—all's safe, I find.—[*Aside*] I have hopes, Madam, that time will bring the young lady——

Mrs. Mal. Oh, there's nothing to be hoped for from her! she's as headstrong as an allegory on the banks of Nile.

Lyd. Nay, Madam, what do you charge me with now?

Mrs. Mal. Why, thou unblushing rebel—didn't you tell this gentleman to his face that you loved another better?—didn't you say you never would be his?

Lyd. No, Madam—I did not.

Mrs. Mal. Good Heav'ns! what assurance!—Lydia, Lydia, you ought to know that lying don't become a young woman!—Didn't you boast that Beverley, that stroller Beverley, possessed your heart?—Tell me that, I say.

Lyd. 'Tis true, Ma'am, and none but Beverley——

Mrs. Mal. Hold;—hold, Assurance!—you shall not be so rude.

Abs. Nay, pray, Mrs. Malaprop, don't stop the young lady's speech: she's very welcome to talk thus—it does not hurt *me* in the least, I assure you.

Mrs. Mal. You are *too* good, captain—*too* amiably patient—but come with me, Miss.—Let us see you again soon, Captain—remember what we have fixed.

Abs. I shall, Ma'am.

Mrs. Mal. Come, take a graceful leave of the gentleman.

Lyd. May every blessing wait on my Beverley, my lov'd Bev——

Mrs. Mal. Huzzy! I'll choke the word in your throat!—come along—come along.

[*Exeunt severally;* CAPTAIN ABSOLUTE *kissing his hand to* LYDIA— MRS. MALAPROP *stopping her from speaking.*]

Scene IV.

Acres' *Lodgings.*

Acres *and* David.

Acres, *as just dress'd.*

Acres. Indeed, David—do you think I become it so?

Dav. You are quite another creature, believe me, Master, by the Mass! an' we've any luck we shall see the Devon monkeyrony in all the print-shops in Bath!

Acres. Dress *does* make a difference, David.

Dav. 'Tis all in all, I think—difference! why, an' you were to go now to Clod Hall, I am certain the old lady wouldn't know you: Master Butler wouldn't believe his own eyes, and Mrs. Pickle would cry, "Lard presarve me!" our dairy-maid would come giggling to the door, and I warrant Dolly Tester, your Honour's favourite, would blush like my waistcoat.—Oons! I'll hold a gallon, there an't a dog in the house but would bark, and I question whether *Phillis* would wag a hair of her tail!

Acres. Aye, David, there's nothing like *polishing.*

Dav. So I says of your Honour's boots; but the boy never heeds me!

Acres. But, David, has Mr. De-la-Grace been here? I must rub up my balancing, and chasing, and boring.

Dav. I'll call again, Sir.

Acres. Do—and see if there are any letters for me at the post-office.

Dav. I will.—By the Mass, I can't help looking at your head!—if I hadn't been by at the cooking, I wish I may die if I should have known the dish again myself. [*Exit.*

[*Acres comes forward, practising a dancing-step.*] *Acres.* Sink, slide —coupee.—Confound the first inventors of cotillons! say I—they are as bad as algebra to us country gentlemen.—I can walk a Minuet easy enough when I am forced!—and I have been accounted a good stick in a Country-dance.—Odds jigs and tabors! I never valued your cross-over two couple—figure in—right and left—and I'd foot it with e'er a captain in the county!—but these outlandish heathen Allemandes and Cotillons are quite beyond me!—I shall never prosper at 'em, that's sure—mine are true-born English legs—they don't understand their curst French lingo!—their *Pas* this, and *Pas* that, and *Pas* t'other!—d—n me! my feet don't like to be called Paws! no, 'tis certain I have most Antigallican Toes!

Enter Servant.

Serv. Here is Sir Lucius O'Trigger to wait on you, Sir.

Acres. Show him in.

Enter SIR LUCIUS.

Sir Luc. Mr. Acres, I am delighted to embrace you.

Acres. My dear Sir Lucius, I kiss your hands.

Sir Luc. Pray, my friend, what has brought you so suddenly to Bath?

Acres. Faith! I have followed Cupid's Jack-a-lantern, and find myself in a quagmire at last.—In short, I have been very ill used, Sir Lucius.—I don't choose to mention names, but look on me as on a very ill-used gentleman.

Sir Luc. Pray what is the case?—I ask no names.

Acres. Mark me, Sir Lucius, I falls as deep as need be in love with a young lady—her friends take my part—I follow her to Bath—send word of my arrival; and receive answer, that the lady is to be otherwise disposed of.—This, Sir Lucius, I call being ill-used.

Sir Luc. Very ill, upon my conscience.—Pray, can you divine the cause of it?

Acres. Why, there's the matter; she has another lover, *one* Beverley, who, I am told, is now in Bath.—Odds slanders and lies! he must be at the bottom of it.

Sir Luc. A rival in the case, is there?—and you think he has supplanted you unfairly?

Acres. Unfairly! to be sure he has.—He never could have done it fairly.

Sir Luc. Then sure you know what is to be done!

Acres. Not I, upon my soul!

Sir Luc. We wear no swords here, but you understand me.

Acres. What! fight him.

Sir Luc. Aye, to be sure : what can I mean else?

Acres. But he has given me no provocation.

Sir Luc. Now, I think he has given you the greatest provocation in the world.—Can a man commit a more heinous offence against another than to fall in love with the same woman? O, by my soul! it is the most unpardonable breach of friendship.

Acres. Breach of *friendship!* aye, aye ; but I have no acquaintance with this man. I never saw him in my life.

Sir Luc. That's no argument at all—he has the less right then to take such a liberty.

Acres. 'Gad, that's true—I grow full of anger, Sir Lucius!—I fire apace! Odds hilts and blades! I find a man may have a deal of valour in him, and not know it! But couldn't I contrive to have a little right of my side?

Sir Luc. What the d—l signifies *right*, when your *honour* is concerned? Do you think *Achilles*, or my little *Alexander the Great*, ever inquired where the right lay? No, by my soul, they drew their broad-swords, and left the lazy sons of peace to settle the justice of it.

Acres. Your words are a grenadier's march to my heart! I believe courage must be catching!—I certainly do feel a kind of valour rising as it were—a kind of courage, as I may say.—Odds flints, pans, and triggers! I'll challenge him directly.

Sir Luc. Ah, my little friend, if I had *Blunderbuss Hall* here, I could show you a range of ancestry, in the old O'Trigger line, that would furnish the new room; every one of whom had killed his man!—For though the mansion-house and dirty acres have slipt through my fingers, I thank God our honour and the family-pictures are as fresh as ever.

Acres. O, Sir Lucius! I have had ancestors too!—every man of 'em colonel or captain in the militia!—Odds balls and barrels! say no more—I'm brac'd for it—my nerves are become catgut! my sinews wire! and my heart Pinchbeck! The thunder of your words has soured the milk of human kindness in my breast:—Z—ds! as the man in the play says, "I could do such deeds!"

Sir Luc. Come, come, there must be no passion at all in the case—these things should always be done civilly.

Acres. I must be in a passion, Sir Lucius—I must be in a rage.—Dear Sir Lucius, let me be in a rage, if you love me. Come, here's pen and paper.—[*Sits down to write.*] I would the ink were red!—Indite, I say, indite!—How shall I begin? Odds bullets and blades! I'll write a good *bold hand*, however.

Sir Luc. Pray compose yourself.

Acres. Come—now shall I begin with an oath? Do, Sir Lucius, let me begin with a damme.

Sir Luc. Pho! pho! do the thing *decently*, and like a Christian. Begin now—"*Sir*"——

Acres. That's too civil by half.

Sir Luc. "*To prevent the confusion that might arise.*"

Acres. Well——

Sir Luc. "*From our both addressing the same lady.*"

Acres. Aye, there's the reason—"*same lady*"—Well——

Sir Luc. "*I shall expect the honour of your company.*"

Acres. Z—ds! I'm not asking him to dinner.

Sir Luc. Pray be easy.

Acres. Well, then, " honour of your company."

Sir Luc. " To settle our pretensions."

Acres. Well.

Sir Luc. Let me see, aye, *King's-Mead-fields* will do—" *In King's-Mead fields.*"

Acres. So, that's done—Well, I'll fold it up presently; my own crest—a hand and dagger—shall be the seal.

Sir Luc. You see now this little explanation will put a stop at once to all confusion or misunderstanding that might arise between you.

Acres. Aye, we fight to prevent any misunderstanding.

Sir Luc. Now, I'll leave you to fix your own time.—Take my advice, and you'll decide it this evening if you can; then let the worst come of it, 'twill be off your mind to-morrow.

Acres. Very true.

Sir Luc. So I shall see nothing of you, unless it be by letter, till the evening.—I would do myself the honour to carry your message; but, to tell you a secret, I believe I shall have just such another affair on my own hands. There is a gay captain here, who put a jest on me lately, at the expence of my country, and I only want to fall in with the gentleman, to call him out.

Acres. By my valour, I should like to see you fight first! Odds life! I should like to see you kill him, if it was only to get a little lesson.

Sir Luc. I shall be very proud of instructing you.—Well for the present—but remember now, when you meet your antagonist, do every thing in a mild and agreeable manner.—Let your courage be as keen, but at the same time as polished as your sword.

[*Exeunt severally.*

END OF THE THIRD ACT.

ACT IV.

Scene I.

Acres' *Lodgings*.

Acres *and* David.

David. Then, by the Mass, Sir! I would do no such thing—ne'er a St. Lucius O'Trigger in the kingdom should make me fight, when I wa'n't so minded. Oons! what will the old lady say, when she hears o't?

Acres. Ah! David, if you had heard Sir Lucius!—Odds sparks and flames! he would have roused your valour.

David. Not he, indeed. I hates such bloodthirsty cormorants. Look'ee, Master, if you'd wanted a bout at boxing, quarter-staff, or short-staff, I should never be the man to bid you cry off: but for your curst sharps and snaps, I never knew any good come of 'em.

Acres. But my *honour*, David, my *honour!* I must be very careful of my honour.

David. Aye, by the Mass! and I would be very careful of it; and I think in return my *honour* couldn't do less than to be very careful of *me*.

Acres. Odds blades! David, no gentleman will ever risk the loss of his honour!

David. I say then, it would be but civil in *honour* never to risk the loss of the *gentleman*—Look'ee, Master, this *honour* seems to me to be a marvellous false friend: aye, truly, a very courtier-like servant.—Put the case, I was a gentleman (which, thank God, no one can say of me;) well—my honour makes me quarrel with another gentleman of my acquaintance.—So—we fight. (Pleasant enough that!) Boh;—I kill him—(the more's my luck!) now, pray who gets the profit of it?—Why, my *honour*. But put the case that he kills me!—by the Mass! I go to the worms, and my honour whips over to my enemy.

Acres. No, David—in that case!—odds crowns and laurels! your honour follows you to the grave.

David. Now, that's just the place where I could make a shift to do without it.

Acres. Z—ds! David, you are a coward!—It doesn't become my valour to listen to you.—What, shall I disgrace my ancestors?—Think of that, David—think what it would be to disgrace my ancestors!

David. Under favour, the surest way of not disgracing them, is to keep as long as you can out of their company. Look'ee now, Master, to go to them in such haste—with an ounce of lead in your brains—I should think might as well be let alone. Our ancestors are very good kind of folks; but they are the last people I should choose to have a visiting acquaintance with.

Acres. But, David, now, you don't think there is such very, very, very great danger, hey?—Odds life! people often fight without any mischief done!

David. By the Mass, I think 'tis ten to one against you!—Oons! here to meet some lion-headed fellow, I warrant, with his d—n'd double-barrelled swords, and cut-and-thrust pistols! Lord bless us! it makes me tremble to think o't—Those be such desperate bloody-minded weapons! Well, I never could abide 'em!—from a child I never could fancy 'em!—I suppose there an't so merciless a beast in the world as your loaded pistol!

Acres. Z—ds! I *won't* be afraid!—Odds fire and fury! you shan't make me afraid.—Here is the challenge, and I have sent for my dear friend Jack Absolute to carry it for me.

David. Aye, i' the name of michief, let *him* be the messenger.— For my part, I wouldn't lend a hand to it for the best horse in your stable. By the Mass! it don't look like another letter! It is, as I may say, a designing and malicious-looking letter! and I warrant smells of gunpowder like a soldier's pouch!—Oons! I wouldn't swear it mayn't go off!

Acres. Out, you poltroon! you han't the valour of a grasshopper.

David. Well, I say no more—'twill be sad news, to be sure, at Clod Hall! but I ha' done. How Phillis will howl when she hears of it!— Aye, poor bitch, she little thinks what shooting her Master's going after! And I warrant old Crop, who has carried your honour, field and road, these ten years, will curse the hour he was born.

[*Whimpering.*

Acres. It won't do, David—I am determined to fight—so get along, you Coward, while I'm in the mind.

Enter SERVANT.

Ser. Captain Absolute, Sir.

Acres. O! show him up. [*Exit* SERVANT.

David. Well, Heaven send we be all alive this time to-morrow.

Acres. What's that!—Don't provoke me, David!

David. Good-bye, Master. [*Whimpering.*

Acres. Get along, you cowardly, dastardly, croaking raven!

[*Exit* DAVID.

Enter CAPTAIN ABSOLUTE.

Abs. What's the matter, Bob?

Acres. A vile, sheep-hearted blockhead! If I hadn't the valour of St. George and the dragon to boot——

Abs. But what did you want with me, Bob?

Acres. Oh!—There—— [*Gives him the challenge.*

Abs. To Ensign Beverley.—So—what's going on now? [*Aside*]—[*Aloud.*] Well, what's this?

Acres. A challenge!

Abs. Indeed! Why, you won't fight him; will you, Bob?

Acres. 'Egad, but I will, Jack. Sir Lucius has wrought me to it. He has left me full of rage—and I'll fight this evening, that so much good passion mayn't be wasted.

Abs. But what have I to do with this?

Acres. Why, as I think you know something of this fellow, I want you to find him out for me, and give him this mortal *defiance.*

Abs. Well, give it to me, and trust me he gets it.

Acres. Thank you, my dear friend, my dear Jack; but it is giving you a great deal of trouble.

Abs. Not in the least—I beg you won't mention it.—No trouble in the world, I assure you.

Acres. You are very kind.—What it is to have a friend!—You couldn't be my second, could you, Jack?

Abs. Why no, Bob—not in *this* affair—it would not be quite so proper.

Acres. Well, then, I must fix on my friend Sir Lucius. I shall have your good wishes, however, Jack?

Abs. Whenever he meets you, believe me.

Enter SERVANT.

Ser. Sir Anthony Absolute is below, inquiring for the Captain.

Abs. I'll come instantly.—Well, my little hero, success attend you.
[*Going.*

Acres. Stay—stay, Jack.—If Beverley should ask you what kind of a man your friend Acres is, do tell him I am a devil of a fellow—will you, Jack?

Abs. To be sure I shall. I'll say you are a determined dog—hey, Bob?

Acres. Aye, do, do—and if that frightens him, 'egad, perhaps he mayn't come. So tell him I generally kill a man a week; will you, Jack?

Abs. I will, I will; I'll say you are called in the country "*Fighting Bob.*"

Acres. Right—right—'tis all to prevent mischief; for I don't want to take his life if I clear my honour.

Abs. No!—that's very kind of you.

Acres. Why, you don't wish me to kill him—do you, Jack?

Abs. No, upon my soul, I do not. But a devil of a fellow, hey?

[*Going.*

Acres. True, true—but stay—stay Jack,—you may add, that you never saw me in such a rage before—a most devouring rage!

Abs. I will, I will.

Acres. Remember, Jack—a determined dog!

Abs. Aye, aye, "*Fighting Bob!*" [*Exeunt severally.*

SCENE II.

Mrs. MALAPROP's *Lodgings.*

Mrs. MALAPROP *and* LYDIA.

Mrs. Mal. Why, thou perverse one!—tell me what you can object to him? Isn't he a handsome man?—tell me that. A genteel man? a pretty figure of a man?

Lyd. [*Aside*] She little thinks whom she is praising!—[*Aloud.*] So is Beverley, Ma'am.

Mrs. Mal. No caparisons, Miss, if you please. Caparisons don't become a young woman. No! Captain Absolute is indeed a fine gentleman!

Lyd. Aye, the Captain Absolute *you* have seen. [*Aside.*

Mrs. Mal. Then he's *so* well bred;—*so* full of alacrity, and adulation! —and has *so much* to say for himself:—in such good language, too! His physiognomy so grammatical! Then his presence is so noble! I protest, when I saw him, I thought of what Hamlet says in the play:—" Hesperian curls—the front of *Job* himself!—An eye, like March, to threaten at command!—A Station, like Harry Mercury, new—" Something about kissing—on a hill—however, the similitude struck me directly.

Lyd. How enraged she'll be presently, when she discovers her mistake! [*Aside.*

Enter SERVANT.

Ser. Sir Anthony, and Captain Absolute are below, Ma'am.

Mrs. Mal. Show them up here.—[*Exit* SERV.] Now, Lydia, I insist on your behaving as becomes a young woman. Shew your good breeding, at least, though you have forgot your duty.

Lyd. Madam, I have told you my resolution ;—I shall not only give him no encouragement, but I won't even speak to, or look at him.
[*Flings herself into a chair, with her face from the door.*

Enter SIR ANTHONY *and* ABSOLUTE.

Sir Anth. Here we are, Mrs. Malaprop ; come to mitigate the frowns of unrelenting beauty, — and difficulty enough I had to bring this fellow.—I don't know what's the matter ; but if I hadn't held him by force, he'd have given me the slip.

Mrs. Mal. You have infinite trouble, Sir Anthony, in the affair. I am ashamed for the cause ! Lydia, Lydia, rise, I beseech you !— pay your respects ! [*Aside to her*]

Sir Anth. I hope, madam, that Miss Languish has reflected on the worth of this gentleman, and the regard due to her aunt's choice, and my alliance.—Now, Jack, speak to her ! [*Aside to him.*]

Abs. What the d—l shall I do ! [*Aside.*]—[*Aside*] You see, Sir, she won't even look at me, whilst you are here. I knew she wouldn't ! I told you so. Let me entreat you, Sir, to leave us together !
[ABSOLUTE *seems to expostulate with his father.*

Lyd. [*Aside.*] I wonder I han't heard my Aunt exclaim yet ! sure she can't have looked at him !—perhaps their regimentals are alike, and she is something blind.

Sir Anth. I say, Sir, I won't stir a foot yet !

Mrs. Mal. I am sorry to say, Sir Anthony, that my affluence over my Niece is very small.—Turn round, Lydia : I blush for you ! [*Aside to her.*]

Sir Anth. May I not flatter myself that Miss Languish will assign what cause of dislike she can have to my son !—Why don't you begin, Jack ?—Speak, you puppy—speak ! [*Aside to him.*]

Mrs. Mal. It is impossible, Sir Anthony, she can have any. She will not *say* she has.—Answer, hussy ! why don't you answer ? [*Aside to her.*]

Sir Anth. Then, Madam, I trust that a childish and hasty predilection will be no bar to Jack's happiness.—Z—ds ! sirrah ! why don't you speak ? [*Aside to him.*]

Lyd. [*Aside.*] I think my lover seems as little inclined to conversation as myself.—How strangely blind my Aunt must be !

Abs. Hem ! hem ! **Madam**—hem !—[ABSOLUTE *attempts to speak, then returns to* SIR ANTHONY.] Faith ! Sir, I am so confounded !—and—so —so—confused !—I told you I should be so, Sir—I knew it.—The —the—tremor of my passion entirely takes away my presence of mind.

E 2

Sir Anth. But it don't take away your voice, fool, does it?—Go up, and speak to her directly!

[ABSOLUTE *makes signs to* MRS. MAL. *to leave them together.*

Mrs. Mal. Sir Anthony, shall we leave them together?—Ah! you stubborn, little vixen! [*Aside to her.*]

Sir Anth. Not yet, Ma'am, not yet!—What the d—l are you at? unlock your jaws, sirrah, or—— [*Aside to him.*] [ABSOLUTE *draws near* LYDIA.]

Abs. Now Heav'n send she may be too sullen to look round!—I must disguise my voice.—[*Speaks in a low hoarse tone.*] Will not Miss Languish lend an ear to the mild accents of true love? Will not——

Sir Anth. What the d—l ails the fellow? why don't you speak out?—not stand croaking like a frog in a quinsey!

Abs. The—the—excess of my awe, and my—my—modesty quite choak me!

Sir Anth. Ah! your *modesty* again!—I'll tell you what, Jack, if you don't speak out directly, and glibly too, I shall be in such a rage!—Mrs. Malaprop, I wish the lady would favour us with something more than a side-front.

[MRS. MALAPROP *seems to chide* LYDIA.

Abs. So!—all will out, I see!—[*Goes up to* LYDIA, *speaks softly.*] Be not surprised, my Lydia, suppress all surprise at present.

Lyd. [*Aside.*] Heav'ns! 'tis Beverley's voice! Sure he can't have imposed on Sir Anthony too!—[*Looks round by degrees, then starts up.*] Is this possible!—my Beverley!—how can this be?—my Beverley?

Abs. Ah! 'tis all over. [*Aside.*

Sir Anth. Beverley!—the devil—Beverley!—What can the girl mean?—this is my son, Jack Absolute.

Mrs. Mal. For shame, hussy! for shame! your head runs so on that fellow, that you have him always in your eyes!—beg Captain Absolute's pardon directly.

Lyd. I see no Captain Absolute, but my loved Beverley!

Sir Anth. Z—ds! the girl's mad!—her brain's turned by reading.

Mrs. Mal. O' my conscience, I believe so!—What do you mean by Beverley, hussey?—You saw Captain Absolute before to-day; there he is—your husband that shall be.

Lyd. With all my soul, Ma'am—when I refuse my Beverley——

Sir Anth. Oh! she's as mad as Bedlam!—or has this fellow been playing us a rogue's trick!—Come here, sirrah, who the d—l are you!

Abs. Faith, Sir, I am not quite clear myself; but I'll endeavour to recollect.

THE RIVALS.

Sir Anth. Are you my son or not?—answer for your mother, you dog, if you won't for me.

Mrs. Mal. Aye, Sir, who are you? O mercy! I begin to suspect!——

Abs. Ye Powers of Impudence, befriend me!—[*Aside.*] Sir Anthony, most assuredly I am your wife's son; and that I sincerely believe myself to be *your's* also, I hope my duty has always shewn.—Mrs. Malaprop, I am your most respectful admirer, and shall be proud to add *affectionate nephew.*—I need not tell my Lydia, that she sees her faithful Beverley, who, knowing the singular generosity of her temper, assum'd that name, and a station, which has proved a test of the most disinterested love, which he now hopes to enjoy in a more elevated character.

Lyd. So!—there will be no elopement after all! [*Sullenly.*

Sir Anth. Upon my soul, Jack, thou art a very impudent fellow! to do you justice, I think I never saw a piece of more consummate assurance!

Abs. Oh, you flatter me, sir—you compliment—'tis my *modesty*, you know, sir—my *modesty* that has stood in my way.

Sir Anth. Well, I am glad you are not the dull, insensible varlet you pretended to be, however!—I'm glad you have made a fool of your father, you dog—I am. So this was your *penitence*, your *duty* and *obedience!*—I thought it was d—n'd sudden!—*You never heard their names before,* not you!—*what, Languishes of Worcestershire,* hey?—*if you could please me in the affair, 'twas all you desired!*—Ah! you dissembling villain!—What!—[*pointing to* LYDIA] *she squints don't she?—a little red-haired girl!*—hey?—Why, you hypocritical young rascal!—I wonder you a'n't ashamed to hold up your head!

Abs. 'Tis with difficulty, Sir.—I *am* confus'd—very much confus'd, as you must perceive.

Mrs. Mal. O Lud! Sir Anthony!—a new light breaks in upon me! —hey!—how! what! Captain, did *you* write the Letters then?— What—I am to thank *you* for the elegant compilation of '*an old weather-beaten she-dragon*'—hey?—O mercy!—was it *you* that reflected on my parts of speech?

Abs. Dear Sir! my modesty will be overpower'd at last, if you don't assist me.—I shall certainly not be able to stand it!

Sir Anth. Come, come, Mrs. Malaprop, we must forget and forgive;—odds life! matters have taken so clever a turn all of a sudden, that I could find in my heart to be so good-humoured! and so gallant! hey! Mrs. Malaprop!

Mrs. Mal. Well, Sir Anthony, since *you* desire it, we will not anticipate the past;—so mind, young people—our retrospection will be all to the future.

Sir Anth. Come, we must leave them together; Mrs. Malaprop, they long to fly into each other's arms, I warrant!—Jack, isn't the *cheek* as I said, hey?—and the eye, you dog?—and the lip—hey? Come, Mrs. Malaprop, we'll not disturb their tenderness—theirs is the time of life for happiness!—" *Youth's the season made for joy* "— [*Sings*]—hey!—Odds life! I'm in such spirits,—I don't know what I couldn't do!—Permit me, Ma'am—[*Gives his hand to* Mrs. Malaprop.] (*Sings*) Tol-de-rol—'gad, I should like to have a little fooling myself—Tol-de-rol! de-rol.

[*Exit singing, and handing* Mrs. Mal.

Lydia *sits sullenly in her chair.*

Abs. So much thought bodes me no good.—[*Aside.*] So grave, Lydia!

Lyd. Sir!

Abs. So!—egad! I thought as much!—that d—n'd monosyllable has froze me!—[*Aside.*] What, Lydia, now that we are as happy in our *friends consent*, as in our *mutual vows*——

Lyd. Friends consent, indeed! [*Peevishly.*

Abs. Come, come, we must lay aside some of our romance—a little *wealth* and *comfort* may be endur'd after all. And for your fortune, the lawyers shall make such settlements as——

Lyd. Lawyers! I *hate* lawyers!

Abs. Nay then, we will not wait for their lingering forms, but instantly procure the licence, and——

Lyd. The *licence!*—I *hate* licence!

Abs. Oh my Love! *be* not so unkind!—thus let me intreat——
[*Kneeling.*

Lyd Pshaw!—what signifies kneeling, when you know I *must* have you?

Abs. [*Rising.*] Nay, Madam, there shall be no constraint upon your inclinations, I promise you.—If I have lost your *heart*—I resign the rest—'Gad, I must try what a little *spirit* will do. [*Aside.*]

Lyd. [*Rising.*] Then, Sir, let me tell you, the interest you had there was acquired by a mean, unmanly imposition, and deserves the punishment of fraud.—What, you have been treating *me* like a *child!* —humouring my romance! and laughing, I suppose, at your success!

Abs. You wrong me, Lydia, you wrong me—only hear——

Lyd. So, while *I* fondly imagined we were deceiving my relations, and flatter'd myself that I should outwit and incense them *all*— behold! my hopes are to be crush'd at once, by my Aunt's consent and approbation—and *I* am *myself* the only dupe at last!—[*Walking about in heat.*]

Abs Nay, but hear me——

Lyd. No, Sir, you could not think that such paltry artifices could please me, when the mask was thrown off! But I suppose since your tricks have made you secure of my *fortune*, you are little solicitous about my *affections*.—But here, Sir, here is the picture—Beverley's picture! [*taking a miniature from her bosom*] which I have worn, night and day, in spite of threats and entreaties!—There, Sir; [*flings it to him*] and be assured I throw the original from my heart as easily!

Abs. Nay, nay, Ma'am, we will not differ as to that.—Here [*taking out a picture*] here is Miss Lydia Languish.—What a difference!—aye, *there* is the heav'nly assenting smile, that first gave soul and spirit to my hopes!—those are the lips which seal'd a vow, as yet scarce dry in Cupid's calendar! and *there* the *half* resentful blush, that *would* have check'd the ardour of my thanks!—Well, all that's past?—all over indeed!—There, Madam—in *beauty*, that copy is not equal to you, but in my mind it's merit over the original, in being still the same, is such—that—I cannot find in my heart to *part with it*.

[*Puts it up again.*

Lyd [*Softening.*] 'Tis *your own* doing, Sir—I, I, I suppose you are perfectly satisfied.

Abs. O, most certainly—sure, now this is much better than being in love!—ha! ha! ha!—there's some spirit in *this!*—What signifies breaking some scores of solemn promises, half an hundred vows, under one's hand, with the marks of a dozen or two angels to witness—all that's of no consequence, you know. To be sure people will say, that Miss don't know her own mind—but never mind that :—Or, perhaps, they may be ill-natured enough to hint, that the gentleman grew tired of the lady and forsook her—but don't let that fret you.

Lyd. There is no bearing his insolence.   [*Bursts into tears.*

Enter Mrs Malaprop *and* Sir Anthony.

Mrs. Mal. [*Entering.*] Come, we must interrupt your billing and cooing a while.

Lyd. This is *worse* than your treachery and deceit, you base ingrate!
[*Sobbing.*

Sir Anth. What the devil's the matter now?—Z—ds! Mrs. Malaprop, this is the *oddest billing* and *cooing* I ever heard!—but what the deuce is the meaning of it?—I am quite astonished!

Abs. Ask the lady, Sir.

Mrs. Mal. O mercy!—I'm quite analyzed for my part!—Why, Lydia, what is the reason of this?

Lyd. Ask the *gentleman*, Ma'am.

Sir Anth. Z—ds! I shall be in a phrenzy!—Why, Jack, you scoundrel, you are not come out to be any one else, are you?

Mrs. Mal. Aye, Sir, there's no more *trick*, is there?—you are not like Cerberus, *three* Gentlemen at once, are you?

Abs. You'll not let me speak—I say the *lady* can account for *this* much better than I can.

Lyd. Ma'am, you once commanded me never to think of Beverley again—*there* is the man—I now obey you: for, from this moment, I renounce him for ever. [*Exit* LYDIA.

Mrs. Mal. O mercy! and miracles! what a turn here is—why, sure, Captain, you haven't behaved disrespectfully to my Niece?

Sir Anth. Ha! ha! ha!—ha! ha! ha!—now I see it. Ha! ha! ha!—now I see it—you have been too lively, Jack.

Abs. Nay, sir, upon my word——

Sir Anth. Come, no lying, Jack—I'm sure 'twas so.

Mrs. Mal. O Lud! Sir Anthony!—O fie, Captain!

Abs. Upon my soul, Ma'am——

Sir Anth. Come, no excuse, Jack; why, your father, you rogue, was so before you!—the blood of the Absolutes was always impatient.—Ha! ha! ha! poor little Lydia! why, you've frightened her, you Dog, you have.

Abs. By all that's good, sir——

Sir Anth. Z—ds! say no more, I tell you. Mrs. Malaprop shall make your peace. You must make his peace, Mrs. Malaprop:—you must tell her 'tis Jack's way—tell her 'tis all our ways—it runs in the blood of our family! Come, get on, Jack. Ha! ha! ha!—Mrs. Malaprop—a young villain! [*Pushing him out.*

Mrs. Mal. O! Sir Anthony!—O fie, Captain! [*Exeunt severally.*

SCENE III.

The North Parade.

Enter SIR LUCIUS O'TRIGGER.

Sir Luc. wonder where this Capt. Absolute hides himself! Upon my conscience! these officers are always in one's way in love affairs:—I remember I might have married Lady Dorothy Carmine, if it had not been for a little rogue of a major, who ran away with her before she could get a sight of me! And I wonder too what it is the ladies can see in them to be so fond of them—unless it be a touch of the old serpent in 'em, that makes the little creatures be caught, like vipers with a bit of red cloth. Hah ! isn't this the Captain coming ?—faith it is !—There is a probability of succeeding about that fellow, that is mighty provoking ! Who the devil is he talking to ? [*Steps aside.*

Enter CAPT. ABSOLUTE.

Abs. To what fine purpose I have been plotting ! a noble reward for all my schemes, upon my soul !—a little gypsey !—I did not think her romance could have made her so d—n'd absurd either. 'Sdeath, I never was in a worse humour in my life !—I could cut my own throat, or any other person's with the greatest pleasure in the world !

Sir Luc. O, faith ! I'm in the luck of it. I never could have found him in a sweeter temper for my purpose—to be sure I'm just come in the nick ! Now to enter into conversation with him, and so quarrel genteelly.—[SIR LUCIUS *goes up to* ABSOLUTE. With regard to that matter, Captain, I must beg leave to differ in opinion with you.

Abs. Upon my word, then, you must be a very subtle disputant :—because, Sir, I happened just then to be giving no opinion at all.

Sir Luc. That's no reason. For give me leave to tell you, a man may *think* an untruth as well as *speak* one.

Abs. Very true, Sir ; but if a man never utters his thoughts, I should think they *might* stand a *chance* of escaping controversy.

Sir Luc. Then, sir, you differ in opinion with me, which amounts to the same thing.

Abs. Hark'ee, Sir Lucius ; if I had not before known you to be a gentleman, upon my soul, I should not have discovered it at this interview : for what you can drive at, unless you mean to quarrel with me, I cannot conceive !

Sir Luc. I humbly thank you, Sir, for the quickness of your apprehension.—[*Bowing.*]—you have named the very thing I would be at.

Abs. Very well, Sir ; I shall certainly not baulk your inclinations.—But I should be glad you would please to explain your motives.

Sir Luc. Pray, Sir, be easy—the quarrel is a very pretty quarrel as it stands—we should only spoil it, by trying to explain it.—However, your memory is very short, or you could not have forgot an affront you pass'd on me within this week. So no more, but name your time and place.

Abs. Well, Sir, since you are so bent on it, the sooner the better ; let it be this evening—here, by the Spring Gardens.—We shall scarcely be interrupted.

Sir Luc. Faith ! that same interruption in affairs of this nature shows very great ill-breeding. I don't know what's the reason, but in England, if a thing of this kind gets wind, people make such a pother, that a gentleman can never fight in peace and quietness. However, if it's the same to you, Captain, I should take it as a particular kindness, if you'd let us meet in King's-Mead-Fields, as a little business will call me there about six o'clock, and I may despatch both matters at once.

Abs. 'Tis the same to me exactly. A little after six, then we will discuss this matter more seriously.

Sir Luc. If you please, Sir; there will be very pretty small-sword light, though it won't do for a long shot. So that matter's settled, and my mind's at ease! [*Exit.*

Enter FAULKLAND *meeting* ABSOLUTE.

Abs. Well met—I was going to look for you. O Faulkland! all the Dæmons of spite and disappointment have conspired against me! I'm so vex'd, that if I had not the prospect of a resource in being knock'd o' the head by and bye, I should scarce have spirits to tell you the cause.

Faulk. What can you mean?—Has Lydia changed her mind?—I should have thought her duty and inclination would now have pointed to the same object.

Abs. Aye, just as the eyes do of a person who squints: when her *love-eye* was fixed on *me*, t'other, her *eye* of *duty*, was finely obliqued: but when duty bid her point *that* the same way, off t'other turned on a swivel, and secured its retreat with a frown!

Faulk. But what's the resource you——

Abs. O, to wind up the whole, a good-natured Irishman here has—[*Mimicking* SIR LUCIUS] beg'd leave to have the pleasure of cutting my throat—and I mean to indulge him—that's all.

Faulk. Prithee, be serious!

Abs. 'Tis fact, upon my soul! Sir Lucius O'Trigger—you know him by sight—for some affront, which I am sure I never intended, has obliged me to meet him this evening at six o'clock: 'tis on that account I wished to see you—you must go with me.

Faulk. Nay, there must be some mistake, sure.—Sir Lucius shall explain himself—and I dare say matters may be accommodated: but this evening did you say? I wish it had been any other time.

Abs. Why? there will be light enough:—there will (as Sir Lucius says) "be very pretty small-sword light, tho' it won't do for a long shot." Confound his long shots!

Faulk. But I am myself a good deal ruffled by a difference I have had with Julia—my vile tormenting temper has made me treat her so cruelly, that I shall not be myself till we are reconciled.

Abs. By Heav'ns! Faulkland, you don't deserve her!

Enter Servant, gives FAULKLAND *a letter.*

Faulk. Oh, Jack! this is from Julia—I dread to open it—I fear it may be to take a last leave—perhaps to bid me return her letters—and restore——O, how I suffer for my folly!

Abs. Here, let me see.—[*Takes the letter and opens it.*] Ay, a final sentence, indeed!—'tis all over with you, faith!

Faulk. Nay, Jack, don't keep me in suspense!

Abs. Hear then—As "*I am convinced that my dear Faulkland's own reflections have already upbraided him for his last unkindness to me, I will not add a word on the subject. I wish to speak with you as soon as possible. Your's ever and truly,* JULIA." There's stubbornness and resentment for you!—[*Gives him the letter.*] Why, man, you don't seem one whit happier at this!

Faulk. O yes, I am; but—but——

Abs. Confound your *buts.*—You never hear anything that would make another man bless himself, but you immediately d—n it with a *but.*

Faulk. Now, Jack, as you are my friend, own honestly—don't you think there is something forward—something indelicate in this haste to forgive? Women should never sue for reconciliation: *that* should *always* come from us. *They* should retain their coldness till *woo'd* to kindness; and their *pardon*, like their love, should "not unsought be won."

Abs. I have not patience to listen to you:—thou 'rt incorrigible! so say no more on the subject.—I must go to settle a few matters. Let me see you before six—remember—at my lodgings.—A poor industrious devil like me, who have toil'd, and drudg'd, and plotted to gain my ends, and am at last disappointed by other people's folly—may in pity be allowed to swear and grumble a little;—but a captious sceptic in love—a slave to fretfulness and whim—who has no difficulties but of *his own* creating—is a subject more fit for ridicule than compassion! [*Exit* ABSOLUTE.

Faulk. I feel his reproaches!—yet I would not change this too exquisite nicety for the gross content with which *he* tramples on the thorns of love.—His engaging me in this duel, has started an idea in my head, which I will instantly pursue.—I'll use it as the touchstone of Julia's sincerity and disinterestedness—if her love prove pure and sterling ore—my name will rest on it with honour! and once I've stamped it there, I lay aside my doubts for ever:—but if the dross of selfishness, the allay of pride predominate, 'twill be best to leave her as a toy for some less cautious Fool to sigh for! [*Exit* FAULKLAND.

END OF THE FOURTH ACT.

ACT V.

Scene I.

JULIA'S *Dressing-Room.*

JULIA, *sola.*

How this message has alarmed me! what dreadful accident can he mean! why such charge to be alone?—O Faulkland!—how many unhappy moments!—how many tears have you cost me!

Enter FAULKLAND, *muffled up in a Riding-coat.*

Jul. What means this?—why this caution, Faulkland?

Faulk. Alas! Julia, I am come to take a long farewell.

Jul. Heav'ns! what do you mean?

Faulk. You see before you a wretch, whose life is forfeited. Nay, start not!—the infirmity of my temper has drawn all this misery on me.—I left you fretful and passionate—an untoward accident drew me into a quarrel—the event is, that I must fly this kingdom instantly. O Julia, had I been so fortunate as to have called you mine intirely, before this mischance had fallen on me, I should not so deeply dread my banishment!—But no more of that—your heart and promise were given to one happy in friends, character and station! They are not bound to wait upon a solitary, guilty exile.

Jul. My soul is opprest with sorrow at the *nature* of your misfortune: had these adverse circumstances arisen from a less fatal cause I should have felt strong comfort in the thought that I could *now* chase from your bosom every doubt of the warm sincerity of my love.—My heart has long known no other guardian—I now entrust my person to your honour—we will fly together.—When safe from pursuit, my Father's will may be fulfilled—and I receive a legal claim to be the partner of your sorrows, and tenderest comforter. Then on the bosom of your wedded Julia, you may lull your keen regret to slumbering; while virtuous love, with a Cherub's hand, shall smooth the brow of upbraiding thought, and pluck the thorn from compunction.

Faulk. O Julia! I am bankrupt in gratitude! but the time is so pressing, it calls on you for so hasty a resolution.—Would you not wish some hours to weigh the advantages you forego, and what little compensation poor Faulkland can make you beside his solitary love?

Jul. I ask not a moment. No, Faulkland, I have lov'd you for yourself: and if I now, more than ever, prize the solemn engagement which so long has pledged us to each other, it is because it leaves no room for hard aspersions on my fame, and puts the seal of duty to an act of love.—But let us not linger.—Perhaps this delay——

Faulk. 'Twill be better I should not venture out again till dark.—Yet am I grieved to think what numberless distresses will press heavy on your gentle disposition!

Jul. Perhaps your fortune may be forfeited by this unhappy act.—I know not whether 'tis so; but sure that alone can never make us unhappy. The little I have will be sufficient to *support* us; and *exile* never should be splendid.

Faulk. Aye, but in such an abject state of life, my wounded pride perhaps may increase the natural fretfulness of my temper, till I become a rude, morose companion, beyond your patience to endure. Perhaps the recollection of a deed, my conscience cannot justify, may haunt me in such gloomy and unsocial fits, that I shall hate the tenderness that would relieve me, break from your arms, and quarrel with your fondness!

Jul. If your thoughts should assume so unhappy a bent, you will the more want some mild and affectionate spirit to watch over and console you! one who can, by bearing *your* infirmities with gentleness and resignation, may teach you *so* to bear the evils of your fortune.

Faulk. O Julia, I have proved you to the quick! and with this useless device I throw away all my doubts. How shall I plead to be forgiven this last unworthy effect of my restless, unsatisfied disposition?

Jul. Has no such disaster happened as you related?

Faulk. I am ashamed to own that it was pretended; yet in pity, Julia, do not kill me with resenting a fault which never can be repeated: But sealing, this once, my pardon, let me to-morrow, in the face of Heaven, receive my future guide and monitress, and expiate my past folly, by years of tender adoration.

Jul. Hold, Faulkland!—that you are free from a crime, which I before feared to name, Heaven knows how sincerely I rejoice!—These are tears of thankfulness for that! But that your cruel doubts should have urged you to an imposition that has wrung my heart, gives me now a pang more keen than I can express.

Faulk. By Heav'ns! Julia——

Jul. Yet hear me,—My Father loved you, Faulkland! and you preserv'd the life that tender parent gave me; in his presence I pledged my hand—*joyfully* pledged it—where before I had given my heart. When, soon after, I lost that parent, it seemed to me that Providence had, in Faulkland, shown me whither to transfer without a pause, my grateful duty, as well as my affection : hence I have been content to bear from you what pride and delicacy would have forbid me from another. I will not upbraid you, by repeating how you have trifled with my sincerity——

Faulk. I confess it all ! yet hear——

Jul. After such a year of trial—I might have flattered myself that I should not have been insulted with a new probation of my sincerity, as cruel as unnecessary ! A trick of such a nature, as to shew me plainly, that when I thought you lov'd me best, you even then regarded me as a mean dissembler ; an artful, prudent hypocrite.

Faulk. Never ! never !

Jul. I now see it is not in your nature to be content or confident in love. With this conviction—I never will be yours. While I had hopes that my persevering attention, and unreproaching kindness might in time reform your temper, I should have been happy to have gain'd a dearer influence over you ; but I will not furnish you with a licensed power to keep alive an incorrigible fault, at the expense of one who never would contend with you.

Faulk. Nay, but, Julia, by my soul and honour, if after this——

Jul. But one word more.—As my faith has once been given to you, I never will barter it with another.—I shall pray for your happiness with the truest sincerity ; and the dearest blessing I can ask of Heaven to send you, will be to charm you from that unhappy temper, which alone has prevented the performance of our solemn engagement.—All I request of *you* is, that you will yourself reflect upon this infirmity, and when you number up the many true delights it has deprived you of, let it not be your *least* regret, that it lost you the love of one who would have follow'd you in beggary through the world ! [*Exit.*

Faulk. She's gone !—for ever !—There was an awful resolution in her manner, that rivetted me to my place.—O Fool !—Dolt !—Barbarian ! Cursed as I am, with more imperfections than my fellow-wretches, kind Fortune sent a heaven-gifted cherub to my aid, and, like a ruffian, I have driven her from my side !—I must now haste to my appointment. Well my mind is tuned for such a scene. I shall wish only to become a principal in it, and reverse the tale my cursed folly put me upon forging here.—O Love !—Tormenter !—Fiend !—whose influence, like the Moon's, acting on men of dull souls, makes idiots of them, but meeting subtler spirits, betrays their course, and urges sensibility to madness ! [*Exit.*

Enter MAID *and* LYDIA.

Maid. My Mistress, Ma'am, I know, was here just now—perhaps she is only in the next room. [*Exit* MAID.

Lyd. Heigh ho! Though he has used me so, this fellow runs strangely in my head. I believe one lecture from my grave Cousin will make me recall him.

Enter JULIA.

Lyd. O Julia, I have come to you with such an appetite for consolation.—Lud! Child, what's the matter with you? You have been crying!—I 'll be hanged, if that Faulkland has not been tormenting you.

Jul. You mistake the cause of my uneasiness!—Something *has* flurried me a little. Nothing that you can guess at.—I would not accuse Faulkland to a Sister! [*Aside.*]

Lyd. Ah! whatever vexations you may have, I can assure you mine surpass them. You know who Beverley proves to be?

Jul. I will now own to you, Lydia, that Mr. Faulkland had before informed me of the whole affair. Had young Absolute been the person you took him for, I should not have accepted your confidence on the subject, without a serious endeavour to counteract your caprice.

Lyd. So, then, I see I have been deceived by every one! But I don't care—I 'll never have him.

Jul. Nay, Lydia——

Lyd. Why, is it not provoking; when I thought we were coming to the prettiest distress imaginable, to find myself made a mere Smithfield bargain of at last! There had I projected one of the most sentimental elopements!—so becoming a disguise!—so amiable a ladder of Ropes!—Conscious Moon—four horses—Scotch parson—with such surprise to Mrs. Malaprop—and such paragraphs in the News-papers!—Oh, I shall die with disappointment!

Jul. I don't wonder at it?

Lyd. Now—sad reverse!—what have I to expect, but, after a deal of flimsy preparation with a bishop's licence, and my Aunt's blessing, to go simpering up to the Altar; or perhaps be cried three times in a country-church, and have an unmannerly fat clerk ask the consent of every butcher in the parish to join John Absolute and Lydia Languish, *Spinster!* O, that I should live to hear myself called Spinster!

Jul. Melancholy, indeed!

Lyd. How mortifying, to remember the dear delicious shifts I used to be put to, to gain half a minute's conversation with this fellow!—How often have I stole forth, in the coldest night in January, and found him in the garden, stuck like a dripping statue! There would he kneel to me in the snow, and sneeze and cough so pathetically! he shivering with cold, and I with apprehension! and while the freezing blast numb'd our joints, how warmly would he press me to pity his flame, and glow with mutual ardour!—Ah, Julia, that was something like being in love.

Jul. If I were in spirits, Lydia, I should chide you only by laughing heartily at you: but it suits more the situation of my mind, at present, earnestly to entreat you not to let a man, who loves you with sincerity, suffer that unhappiness from your *caprice*, which I know too well caprice can inflict.

Lyd. O Lud! what has brought my Aunt here?

Enter MRS. MALAPROP, FAG, *and* DAVID.

Mrs. Mal. So! so! here's fine work!—here's fine suicide, paracide, and salivation going on in the fields! and Sir Anthony not to be found to prevent the antistrophe!

Jul. For Heaven's sake, Madam, what's the meaning of this?

Mrs. Mal. That gentleman can tell you—'twas he enveloped the affair to me.

Lyd. Do, Sir, will you, inform us? [*To* FAG.

Fag. Ma'am, I should hold myself very deficient in every requisite that forms the man of breeding, if I delay'd a moment to give all the information in my power to a lady so deeply interested in the affair as you are.

Lyd. But quick! quick, sir!

Fag. True, Ma'am, as you say, one should be quick in divulging matters of this nature; for should we be tedious, perhaps while we are flourishing on the subject, two or three lives may be lost!

Lyd. O patience!—do, Ma'am, for Heaven's sake! tell us what is the matter?

Mrs. Mal. Why, murder's the matter! slaughter's the matter! killing's the matter!—but he can tell you the perpendiculars.

Lyd. Then, prythee, Sir, be brief.

Fag. Why, then, Ma'am, as to murder—I cannot take upon me to say—and as to slaughter, or man-slaughter, that will be as the jury finds it.

Lyd. But who, Sir—who are engaged in this?

Fag. Faith, Ma'am, one is a young gentleman whom I should be very sorry anything was to happen to—a very pretty behaved gentleman! We have lived much together, and always on terms.

Lyd. But who is this? who? who? who?

Fag. My Master, Ma'am—my Master—I speak of my Master.

Lyd. Heavens! What, Captain Absolute!

Mrs. Mal. Oh, to be sure, you are frightened now!

Jul. But who are with him, Sir?

Fag As to the rest, Ma'am, his gentleman can inform you better than I?

Jul. Do speak, friend. [*To* DAVID.

Dav. Look'ee, my Lady—by the Mass! there's mischief going on. Folks don't use to meet for amusement with firearms, firelocks, fire-engines, fire-screens, fire-office, and the devil knows what other crackers beside!—This, my Lady, I say, has an angry savour.

Jul. But who is there beside Captain Absolute, friend?

Dav. My poor Master—under favour for mentioning him first. You know me, my Lady—I am David—and my Master of course is, or was, Squire Acres.—Then comes Squire Faulkland.

Jul. Do, Ma'am, let us instantly endeavour to prevent mischief.

Mrs. Mal. O fie! it would be very inelegant in us:—we should only participate things.

Dav. Ah! do, Mrs. Aunt, save a few lives—they are desperately given, believe me.—Above all, there is that bloodthirsty Philistine, Sir Lucius O'Trigger.

Mrs. Mal. Sir Lucius O'Trigger? O mercy! have they drawn poor little dear Sir Lucius into the scrape?—Why, how you stand, girl! you have no more feeling than one of the Derbyshire Putrifactions!

Lyd. What are we to do, Madam?

Mrs. Mal. Why, fly with the utmost felicity, to be sure, to prevent mischief!—Here, friend, you can show us the place?

Fag. If you please, Ma'am, I will conduct you.—David, do you look for Sir Anthony. [*Exit* DAVID.

Mrs. Mal. Come, girls! this gentleman will exhort us.—Come, Sir, you're our envoy—lead the way, and we'll precede.

Fag. Not a step before the ladies for the world!

Mrs. Mal. You're sure you know the spot?

Fag. I think I can find it, Ma'am; and one good thing is, we shall hear the report of the pistols as we draw near, so we can't well miss them;—never fear, Ma'am, never fear. [*Exeunt, he talking.*

SCENE II.

South-Parade.

Enter ABSOLUTE, *putting his sword under his great-coat.*

Abs. A sword seen in the streets of Bath would raise as great an alarm as a mad-dog.—How provoking this is in Faulkland!—never punctual! I shall be obliged to go without him at last.—O, the devil! here's Sir Anthony! how shall I escape him?

[*Muffles up his face, and takes a circle to go off.*

Enter SIR ANTHONY.

Sir Anth. How one may be deceived at a little distance! Only that I see he don't know me, I could have sworn that was Jack!—Hey! 'Gad's life! it is.—Why, Jack, you Dog!—what are you afraid of? hey—sure I'm right. Why Jack, Jack Absolute!

[*Goes up to him.*

Abs. Really, sir, you have the advantage of me :—I don't remember ever to have had the honour—my name is Saunderson, at your service.

Sir Anth. Sir, I beg your pardon—I took you—hey!—why, z—ds! it is—Stay—[*Looks up to his face.*] So, so—your humble servant, Mr. Saunderson! Why, you scoundrel, what tricks are you after now?

Abs. Oh, a joke, Sir, a joke! I came here on purpose to look for you, Sir.

Sir Anth. You did! well, I am glad you were so lucky :—but what are you muffled up so for?—what's this for?—hey?

Abs. 'Tis cool, Sir, isn't it?—rather chilly somehow :—but I shall be late—I have a particular engagement.

Sir Anth. Stay!—Why, I thought you were looking for me?—Pray, Jack, where is't you are going?

Abs. Going, sir?

Sir Anth. Ay, where are you going?

Abs. Where am I going?

Sir Anth. You unmannerly puppy!

Abs. I was going, sir, to—to—to—to Lydia—Sir, to Lydia—to make matters up if I could ;—and I was looking for you, Sir, to—to—

Sir Anth. To go with you, I suppose.—Well, come along.

Abs. Oh! z—ds! no, Sir, not for the world!—I wished to meet with you, Sir,—to—to—to—You find it cool, I'm sure, Sir—you'd better not stay out.

Sir Anth. Cool!—not at all.—Well, Jack—and what will you say to Lydia?

Abs. Oh, Sir, beg her pardon, humour her—promise and vow : but I detain you, Sir—consider the cold air on your gout.

Sir Anth. Oh, not at all!—not at all! I'm in no hurry.—Ah! Jack, you youngsters, when once you are wounded here [*Putting his hand to* ABSOLUTE's *breast.*] Hey! what the deuce have you got here?

Abs. Nothing, Sir—nothing.

Sir Anth. What's this?—here's something d—d hard.

Abs. Oh, trinkets, Sir! trinkets!—a bauble for Lydia.

Sir Anth. Nay, let me see your taste.—[*Pulls his coat open, the sword falls.*] Trinkets! a bauble for Lydia!—z—ds! sirrah, you are not going to cut her throat, are you?

Abs. Ha! ha! ha!—I thought it would divert you, Sir, tho' I didn't mean to tell you till afterwards.

Sir Anth. You didn't?—Yes, this is a very diverting trinket, truly!

Abs. Sir, I'll explain to you.—You know, Sir, Lydia is romantic, dev'lish romantic, and very absurd of course:—now, Sir, I intend, if she refuses to forgive me, to unsheath this sword, and swear—I'll fall upon its point, and expire at her feet!

Sir Anth. Fall upon fiddlestick's end!—why, I suppose it is the very thing that would please her.—Get along, you Fool!

Abs. Well, Sir, you shall hear of my success—you shall hear.—"O Lydia!—forgive me, or this pointed steel"—says I.

Sir Anth. "O, booby! stab away and welcome"—says she.—Get along! and damn your trinkets! [*Exit* ABSOLUTE.

Enter DAVID, *running.*

Dav. Stop him! stop him! Murder! Thief! Fire!—Stop fire! Stop fire!—O Sir Anthony—call! call! bid 'em stop! Murder! Fire!

Sir Anth. Fire! Murder!—Where?

Dav. Oons! he's out of sight, and I'm out of breath for my part, O Sir Anthony, why didn't you stop him? why didn't you stop him?

Sir Anth. Z—ds! the fellow's mad!—Stop whom? stop Jack?

Dav. Ay, the Captain, Sir!—there's murder and slaughter——

Sir Anth. Murder!

Dav. Ay, please you, Sir Anthony, there's all kinds of murder, all sorts of slaughter to be seen in the fields: there's fighting going on, Sir—bloody sword-and-gun fighting!

Sir Anth. Who are going to fight, Dunce?

Dav. Everybody that I know of, Sir Anthony:—everybody is going to fight, my poor Master, Sir Lucius O'Trigger, your son, the Captain——

Sir Anth. Oh, the Dog! I see his tricks.—Do you know the place?

Dav. King's-Mead-Fields.

Sir Anth. You know the way?

Dav. Not an inch; but I'll call the mayor—aldermen—constables—churchwardens—and beadles—we can't be too many to part them.

Sir Anth. Come along—give me your shoulder! we'll get assistance as we go—the lying villain!—Well, I shall be in such a frenzy!—So—this was the history of his d—d trinkets! I'll bauble him! [*Exeunt.*

Scene III.

King's-Mead-Fields.

Enter Sir Lucius *and* Acres, *with pistols.*

Acres. By my valour! then, Sir Lucius, forty yards is a good distance. Odds levels and aims!—I say it is a good distance.

Sir Luc. Is it for muskets or small field-pieces? Upon my conscience, Mr. Acres, you must leave those things to me.—Stay now—I'll show you.—[*Measures paces along the stage.*] There now, that is a very pretty distance—a pretty gentleman's distance.

Acres. Z—ds! we might as well fight in a centry-box! I tell you Sir Lucius, the farther he is off, the cooler I shall take my aim.

Sir Luc. Faith! then I suppose you would aim at him best of all if he was out of sight!

Acres. No, Sir Lucius; but I should think forty or eight and thirty yards——

Sir Luc. Pho! pho! nonsense! three or four feet between the mouths of your pistols is as good as a mile.

Acres. Odds bullets, no!—by my valour! there is no merit in killing him so near: do, my dear Sir Lucius, let me bring him down at a long shot:—a long shot, Sir Lucius, if you love me!

Sir Luc. Well—the gentleman's friend and I must settle that.—But tell me now, Mr. Acres, in case of an accident, is there any little will or commission I could execute for you?

Acres. I am much obliged to you, Sir Lucius, but I don't understand——

Sir Luc. Why, you may think there's no being shot at without a little risk—and if an unlucky bullet should carry a *Quietus* with it—I say it will be no time then to be bothering you about family matters.

Acres. A *Quietus!*

Sir Luc. For instance, now—if that should be the case—would you chuse to be pickled and sent home?—or would it be the same to you to lie here in the Abbey? I'm told there is very snug lying in the Abbey.

Acres. Pickled!—Snug lying in the Abbey!—Odds tremors! Sir Lucius, don't talk so!

Sir Luc. I suppose, Mr. Acres, you never were engaged in an affair of this kind before?

Acres. No, Sir Lucius, never before.

Sir Luc. Ah! that's a pity!—there's nothing like being used to a thing. Pray now, how would you receive the gentleman's shot?

Acres. Odds files!—I've practised that—there, Sir Lucius—there. [*Puts himself in an attitude.*] A side-front, hey? Odd! I'll make myself small enough? I'll stand edgeways.

Sir Luc. Now—you're quite out—for if you stand so when I take my aim—— [*Levelling at him.*

Acres. Z—ds! Sir Lucius—are you sure it is not cocked?

Sir Luc. Never fear.

Acres. But—but—you don't know—it may go off of its own head!

Sir Luc. Pho! be easy.—Well, now if I hit you in the body, my bullet has a double chance—for if it misses a vital part of your right side—'twill be very hard if it don't succeed on the left!

Acres. A vital part! O, my poor vitals!

Sir Luc. But, there—fix yourself so—[*Placing him*]—let him see the broad-side of your full front—there—now a ball or two may pass clean through your body, and never do any harm at all.

Acres. Clean through me!—a ball or two clean through me!

Sir Luc. Aye—may they—and it is much the genteelest attitude into the bargain.

Acres. Look'ee! Sir Lucius—I'd just as lieve be shot in an awkward posture as a genteel one; so, by my valour! I will stand edge-ways.

Sir Luc. [*Looking at his watch.*] Sure they don't mean to disappoint us—Hah?—no faith—I think I see them coming.

Acres. Hey!—what!—coming!——

Sir Luc. Aye.—Who are those yonder getting over the stile?

Acres. There are two of them indeed!—well—let them come—hey, Sir Lucius!—we—we—we—we—won't run.

Sir Luc. Run!

Acres. No—I say—we *won't* run, by my valour!

Sir Luc. What the devil's the matter with you?

Acres. Nothing—nothing—my dear friend—my dear Sir Lucius—but I—I—I don't feel quite so bold, somehow, as I did.

Sir Luc. O fie!—consider your honour.

Acres. Aye—true—my honour. Do, Sir Lucius, hedge in a word or two every now and then about my honour.

Sir Luc. Well, here they're coming. [*Looking.*

Acres. Sir Lucius—if I wa'n't with you, I should almost think I was afraid.—If my valour should leave me!—Valour will come and go.

Sir Luc. Then pray keep it fast, while you have it.

Acres. Sir Lucius—I doubt it is going—yes—my valour is certainly going!—it is sneaking off!—I feel it oozing out as it were at the palms of my hands!

Sir Luc. Your honour—your honour.—Here they are.

Acres. O mercy!—now—that I was safe at Clod-Hall! or could be shot before I was aware!

Enter FAULKLAND *and* ABSOLUTE.

Sir Luc. Gentlemen, your most obedient.—Hah!—what, Captain Absolute!—So, I suppose, sir, you are come here, just like myself—to do a kind office, first for your friend—then to proceed to business on your own account.

Acres. What, Jack!—my dear Jack!—my dear friend!

Abs. Hark'ee, Bob, Beverley's at hand.

Sir Luc. Well, Mr. Acres—I don't blame your saluting the gentleman civilly.—So, Mr. Beverley, [*To* FAULKLAND] if you'll chuse your weapons, the Captain and I will measure the ground.

Faulk. My weapons, Sir!

Acres. Odds life! Sir Lucius, I'm not going to fight Mr. Faulkland; these are my particular friends.

Sir Luc. What, Sir, did you not come here to fight Mr. Acres?

Faulk. Not I, upon my word, Sir.

Sir Luc. Well, now, that's mighty provoking! But I hope, Mr. Faulkland, as there are three of us come on purpose for the game—you won't be so cantanckerous as to spoil the party by sitting out.

Abs. O pray, Faulkland, fight to oblige Sir Lucius.

Faulk. Nay, if Mr. Acres is so bent on the matter——

Acres. No, no, Mr. Faulkland; I'll bear my disappointment like a Christian.—Look'ee, Sir Lucius, there's no occasion at all for me to fight; and if it is the same to you, I'd as lieve let it alone.

Sir Luc. Observe me, Mr. Acres—I must not be trifled with. You have certainly challenged somebody—and you came here to fight him. Now, if that gentleman is willing to represent him—I can't see, for my soul, why it isn't just the same thing.

Acres. Z—nds,—Sir Lucius—I tell you, 'tis one Beverley I've challenged—a fellow, you see, that dare not show his face!—if *he* were here, I'd make him give up his pretensions directly!

Abs. Hold, Bob—let me set you right—there is no such man as Beverley in the case.—The person who assumed that name is before you; and as his pretensions are the same in both characters, he is ready to support them in whatever way you please.

Sir Luc. Well, this is lucky.—Now you have an opportunity——

Acres. What, quarrel with my dear friend, Jack Absolute?—not if he were fifty Beverleys! Z—ds! Sir Lucius, you would not have me be so unnatural.

Sir Luc. Upon my conscience, Mr. Acres, your valour has *oozed* away with a vengeance!

Acres. Not in the least! Odds Backs and Abettors! I'll be your second with all my heart—and if you should get a *Quietus*, you may command me entirely. I'll get you a *snug lying* in the *Abbey here;* or *pickle* you, and send you over to Blunderbuss-hall, or any of the kind, with the greatest pleasure.

Sir Luc. Pho! pho! you are little better than a coward.

Acres. Mind, gentlemen, he calls me a *Coward;* Coward was the word, by my valour!

Sir Luc. Well, Sir?

Acres. Look'ee, Sir Lucius, 'tisn't that I mind the word Coward—*Coward* may be said in joke—But if you had called me a *Poltroon*, odds Daggers and Balls——

Sir Luc. Well, sir?

Acres.—I should have thought you a very ill-bred man.

Sir Luc. Pho! you are beneath my notice.

Abs. Nay, Sir Lucius, you can't have a better second than my friend Acres.—He is a most *determined dog*—called in the country, *Fighting Bob.*—He generally *kills a man a week* - don't you Bob?

Acres. Aye—at home!

Sir Luc. Well, then, Captain, 'tis we must begin—so come out, my little counsellor—[*Draws his sword*]—and ask the gentleman, whether he will resign the lady, without forcing you to proceed against him?

Abs. Come on then, sir—[*Draws*]; since you won't let it be an amicable suit, here's *my reply.*

Enter SIR ANTHONY, DAVID, *and the* WOMEN.

David. Knock 'em all down, sweet Sir Anthony; knock down my Master in particular; and bind his hands over to their good behav i our

Sir Anth. Put up, Jack, put up, or I shall be in a frenzy—how came you in a duel, Sir?

Abs. Faith, Sir, that gentleman can tell you better than I; 'twas he call'd on me, and you know, Sir, I serve his Majesty.

Sir Anth. Here's a pretty fellow; I catch him going to cut a man's throat, and he tells me he serves his Majesty!—Zounds! sirrah, then how durst you draw the King's sword against one of his subjects?

Abs. Sir! I tell you, that gentleman called me out, without exp lain ing his reasons.

Sir Anth. Gad! Sir, how came you to call my son out, without explaining your reasons!

Sir Luc. Your son, Sir, insulted me in a manner which my honour could not brook.

Sir Anth. Zounds! Jack, how durst you insult the gentleman in a manner which his honour could not brook?

Mrs. Mal. Come, come, let's have no Honour before ladies—Captain Absolute, come here—How could you intimidate us so?—Here's Lydia has been terrified to death for you.

Abs. For fear I should be kill'd, or escape, Ma'am?

Mrs. Mal. Nay, no delusions to the past—Lydia is convinc'd; speak, child.

Sir Luc. With your leave, Ma'am, I must put in a word here—I believe I could interpret the young lady's silence—Now mark——

Lyd. What is it you mean, Sir?

Sir Luc. Come, come, Delia, we must be serious now—this is no time for trifling.

Lyd. 'Tis true, Sir; and your reproof bids me offer this gentleman my hand, and solicit the return of his affections.

Abs. O! my little angel, say you so?—Sir Lucius—I perceive there must be some mistake here—with regard to the affront which you affirm I have given you—I can only say, that it could not have been intentional. And as you must be convinced, that I should not fear to support a real injury—you shall now see that I am not ashamed to atone for an inadvertency—I ask your pardon.—But for this lady, while honour'd with her approbation, I will support my claim against any man whatever.

Sir Anth. Well said, Jack, and I'll stand by you, my Boy.

Acres. Mind, I give up all my claim—I make no pretensions to any-thing in the world; and if I can't get a wife, without fighting for her, by my Valour! I'll live a bachelor.

Sir Luc. Captain, give me your hand—an affront handsomely acknowledged becomes an obligation—and as for the Lady, if she chuses to deny her own handwriting here——[*Takes out letters.*

Mrs. Mal. O, he will disolve my mystery!—Sir Lucius, perhaps there's some mistake—perhaps, I can illuminate——

Sir Luc. Pray, old gentlewoman, don't interfere where you have no business.—Miss Languish, are you my Delia, or not?

Lyd. Indeed, Sir Lucius, I am not.

[LYDIA *and* ABSOLUTE *walk aside.*

Mrs. Mal. Sir Lucius O'Trigger—ungrateful as you are—I own the soft impeachment—pardon my blushes, I am Delia.

Sir Luc. You Delia—pho! pho! be easy.

Mrs. Mal. Why, thou barbarous Vandyke—those letters are mine.—When you are more sensible of my benignity—perhaps I may be brought to encourage your addresses.

Sir Luc. Mrs. Malaprop, I am extremely sensible of your condescension; and whether you or Lucy have put this trick on me, I am equally beholden to you.—And to show you I am not ungrateful, Captain Absolute! since you have taken that lady from me, I'll give you my Delia into the bargain.

Abs. I am much obliged to you, Sir Lucius; but here's our friend, fighting Bob, unprovided for.

Sir Luc. Hah! little Valour—here, will you make your fortune?

Acres. Odds Wrinkles! No.—But give me your hand, Sir Lucius, forget and forgive; but if ever I give you a chance of pickling me again, say Bob Acres is a Dunce, that's all.

Sir Anth. Come, Mrs. Malaprop, don't be cast down—you are in your bloom yet.

Mrs. Mal. O Sir Anthony—men are all barbarians.

[*All retire but* JULIA *and* FAULKLAND.

Jul. [*Aside.*] He seems dejected and unhappy—not sullen; there was some foundation, however, for the tale he told me—O woman! how true should be your judgment, when your resolution is so weak!

Faulk.—Julia!—how can I sue for what I so little deserve? I dare not presume—yet Hope is the child of Penitence.

Jul. Oh! Faulkland, you have not been more faulty in your unkind treatment of me, than I am now in wanting inclination to resent it. As my heart honestly bids me place my weakness to the account of love, I should be ungenerous not to admit the same plea for yours.

Faulk. Now I shall be blest indeed! (*Sir Anthony comes forward.*)

Sir Anth. What's going on here?—So you have been quarrelling too, I warrant? Come, Julia, I never interfered before; but let me have a hand in the matter at last.—All the faults I have ever seen in my friend Faulkland, seemed to proceed from what he calls the *delicacy* and *warmth* of his affection for you.—There, marry him directly, Julia, you'll find he'll mend surprisingly! [*The rest come forward.*

Sir Luc. Come, now, I hope there is no dissatisfied person, but what is content; for as I have been disappointed myself, it will be very hard if I have not the satisfaction of seeing other people succeed better——

Acres. You are right, Sir Lucius.—So Jack, I wish you joy.—Mr. Faulkland the same.—Ladies,—come now, to show you I'm neither vex'd nor angry, Odds Tabors and Pipes! I'll order the fiddles in half an hour to the New Rooms—and I insist on your all meeting me there.

Sir Anth. 'Gad! Sir, I like your spirit; and at night we single lads will drink a health to the young couples, and a husband to Mrs. Malaprop.

Faulk. Our partners are stolen from us, Jack—I hope to be congratulated by each other—yours for having checked in time the errors of an ill-directed Imagination, which might have betray'd an innocent heart; and mine, for having, by her gentleness and candour, reformed the unhappy temper of one, who by it made wretched whom he loved most, and tortured the heart he ought to have ador'd.

Abs. Well, Jack, [Faulkland?] we have both tasted the Bitters, as well as the Sweets of Love; with this difference only, that *you* always prepared the bitter cup for yourself, while I——

Lyd. Was always obliged to *me* for it, hey! Mr. Modesty?——But come, no more of that—our happiness is now as unallay'd as general.

Jul. Then let us study to preserve it so: and while Hope pictures to us a flattering scene of future Bliss, let us deny its pencil those colours which are too bright to be lasting.—When Hearts deserving Happiness would unite their fortunes, Virtue would crown them with an unfading garland of modest, hurtless flowers; but ill-judging Passion will force the gaudier Rose into the wreath, whose thorn offends them, when its Leaves are dropped! [*Exeunt omnes.*

EPILOGUE.

BY THE AUTHOR.

SPOKEN BY MRS. BULKLEY.

LADIES, for *You*—I heard our Poet say—
He'd try to coax some *Moral* from his Play:
'One moral's plain—cried I—without more fuss;
Man's social happiness all rests on Us—
Thro' all the Drama—whether d—n'd or not—
Love gilds the *Scene*, and *Women* guide the *plot*.
From every rank—obedience is our due—
D'ye doubt?—The world's great stage shall prove it true.'
 The Cit—well skill'd to shun domestic strife—
Will sup abroad;—but first—he'll ask his *wife:*
John Trot, his friend—for once, will do the same,
But then—he'll just *step home to tell my dame.*
 The *surly Squire*—at noon resolves to rule,
And half the day—zounds! Madam is a fool!
Convinced at night, the vanquish'd Victor says,
Ah, Kate! *you women have such coaxing ways.*

THE RIVALS.

The *jolly Toper* chides each tardy blade,—
Till reeling Bacchus calls on Love for aid :
Then with each Toast he sees fair bumpers swim,
And kisses Chloe on the sparkling Brim !

Nay, I have heard that Statesmen—great and wise—
Will *sometimes* counsel with a Lady's eyes !
The servile suitors—watch her various face,
She smiles preferment—or she frowns disgrace,
Curtsies a pension here—there nods a place.

Nor with less awe, in scenes of humbler life,
Is *view'd* the *mistress*, or is *heard* the *wife*.
The poorest Peasant of the poorest soil,
The child of Poverty, and heir to Toil,
Early from radiant Love's impartial light
Steals one small spark, to cheer his world of night :
Dear spark !—that oft through winter's chilling woes
Is all the warmth his little cottage knows !

The wandering *Tar*—who, not for *years* has press'd,
The widow'd Partner of his *day* of rest,
On the cold deck—far from her arms remov'd,—
Still hums the ditty which his Susan loved :
And while around the cadence rude is blown,
The Boatswain whistles in a softer tone.

The *Soldier*, fairly proud of wounds and toil,
Pants for the *triumph* of his Nancy's smile !
But ere the battle should he list' her cries,
The Lover trembles—and the Hero dies !
That heart, by war and honour steel'd to fear,
Droops on a sigh, and sickens at a tear !

But ye more cautious—ye nice judging few,
Who give to Beauty only Beauty's due,
Tho' friends to Love—*Ye* view with deep regret
Our conquests marr'd—our triumphs incomplete,
'Till polish'd wit more lasting charms disclose,
And Judgment fix the darts which Beauty throws !
In female breasts did Sense and Merit rule,
The Lover's mind would ask no other school ;
Sham'd into sense—the Scholars of our eyes,
Our Beaux from *Gallantry* would soon be wise ;
Would gladly light, their homage to improve,
The Lamp of Knowledge at the Torch of Love !

ST. PATRICK'S DAY;

OR, THE SCHEMING LIEUTENANT.

A FARCE.

DRAMATIS PERSONÆ.

AS ORIGINALLY ACTED AT COVENT GARDEN THEATRE IN 1775.

LIEUTENANT O'CONNOR . . } *Mr. Clinch.*
DR. ROSY . . . *Mr Quick.*
JUSTICE CREDULOUS *Mr. Lee Lewes.*
SERJEANT TROUNCE *Mr. Booth.*
CORPORAL FLINT.

LAURETTA . . . *Mrs. Cargill.*
MRS. BRIDGET CREDULOUS . . } *Mrs. Pitt.*

Drummer, Soldiers, Countrymen, *and* Servant.

SCENE—A TOWN IN ENGLAND.

ACT I.

SCENE I.—LIEUTENANT O'CONNOR'S *Lodgings.*

Enter SERJEANT TROUNCE, CORPORAL FLINT, *and four* SOLDIERS.

1 *Sol.* I say you are wrong; we should all speak together, each for himself and all at once, that we may be heard the better.

2 *Sol.* Right, Jack, we'll argue in platoons.

3 *Sol.* Ay, ay, let him have our grievances in a volley, and if we be to have a spokesman, there's the corporal is the lieutenant's countryman, and knows his humour.

Flint. Let me alone for that. I served three years, within a bit, under his honour, in the Royal Inniskillions, and I never will see a sweeter tempered gentleman, nor one more free with his purse. I put a great shammock in his hat this morning, and I'll be bound for him he'll wear it, was it as big as Steven's Green.

4 *Sol.* I say again then you talk like youngsters, like militia striplings: there's a discipline, look'ee in all things, whereof the serjeant must be our guide; he's a gentleman of words; he understands your foreign lingo, your figures, and such like auxiliaries in scoring. Confess now for a reckoning, whether in chalk or writing, ben't he your only man?

Flint. Why the serjeant is a scholar to be sure, and has the gift of reading.

Trounce. Good soldiers, and fellow-gentlemen, if you make me your spokesman, you will show the more judgment; and let me alone for the argument. I'll be as loud as a drum, and point blank from the purpose.

All. Agreed, agreed.

Flint. Oh, faith! here comes the lieutenant.—Now, Serjeant.

Trounce. So then, to order.—Put on your mutiny looks; every man grumble a little to himself, and some of you hum the Deserter's March.

Enter LIEUTENANT O'CONNOR.

O'Con. Well, honest lads, what is it you have to complain of?

Sol. Ahem! hem!

Trounce. So please your honour, the very grievance of the matter is this:—ever since your honour differed with Justice Credulous, our inn-keepers use us most scurvily. By my halbert, their treatment is such, that if your spirit was willing to put up with it, flesh and blood could by no means agree; so we humbly petition that your honour would make an end of the matter at once, by running away with the justice's daughter, or else get us fresh quarters,—hem! hem!

O'Con. Indeed! Pray which of the houses use you ill?

1 *Sol.* There's the Red Lion an't half the civility of the old Red Lion.

2 *Sol.* There's the White Horse, if he wasn't casehardened, ought to be ashamed to show his face.

O'Con. Very well; the Horse and the Lion shall answer for it at the quarter sessions.

Trounce. The two Magpies are civil enough; but the Angel uses us like devils, and the Rising Sun refuses us light to go to bed by.

O'Con. Then, upon my word, I'll have the Rising Sun put down, and the Angel shall give security for his good behaviour; but are you sure you do nothing to quit scores with them?

Flint. Nothing at all, your honour, unless now and then we happen to fling a cartridge into the kitchen fire, or put a spatterdash or so into the soup; and sometimes Ned drums up and down stairs a little of a night.

O'Con. Oh, all that's fair; but hark'ee, lads, I must have no grumbling on St. Patrick's day; so here, take this, and divide it amongst you. But observe me now,—show yourselves men of spirit, and don't spend sixpence of it in drink.

Trounce. Nay, hang it, your honour, soldiers should never bear malice; we must drink St. Patrick's and your honour's health.

All. Oh, damn malice! St. Patrick's and his honour's by all means.

Flint. Come away, then, lads, and first we'll parade round the Market-cross, for the honour of King George.

1 Sol. Thank your honour.—Come along; St. Patrick, his honour, and strong beer for ever! [*Exeunt* SOLDIERS.

O'Con. Get along, you thoughtless vagabonds! yet, upon my conscience, 'tis very hard these poor fellows should scarcely have bread from the soil they would die to defend.

Enter DOCTOR ROSY.

Ah, my little Dr. Rosy, my Galen a-bridge, what's the news?

Rosy. All things are as they were, my Alexander; the justice is as violent as ever: I felt his pulse on the matter again, and, thinking his rage began to intermit, I wanted to throw in the bark of good advice, but it would not do. He says you and your cut-throats have a plot upon his life, and swears he had rather see his daughter in a scarlet fever than in the arms of a soldier.

O'Con. Upon my word the army is very much obliged to him. Well, then, I must marry the girl first, and ask his consent afterwards.

Rosy. So, then, the case of her fortune is desperate, hey?

O'Con. Oh, hang fortune,—let that take its chance; there is a beauty in Lauretta's simplicity, so pure a bloom upon her charms.

Rosy. So there is, so there is. You are for beauty as nature made her, hey! No artificial graces, no cosmetic varnish, no beauty in grey, hey!

O'Con. Upon my word, doctor, you are right; the London ladies were always too handsome for me; then they are so defended, such a circumvallation of hoop, with a breastwork of whale-bone that would turn a pistol-bullet, much less Cupid's arrows,—then turret on turret on top, with stores of concealed weapons, under pretence of black pins, —and above all, a standard of feathers that would do honour to a knight of the Bath. Upon my conscience, I could as soon embrace an Amazon, armed at all points.

Rosy. Right, right, my Alexander! my taste to a tittle.

O'Con. Then, doctor, though I admire modesty in women, I like to see their faces. I am for the changeable rose; but with one of these quality Amazons, if their midnight dissipations had left them blood enough to raise a blush, they have not room enough in their cheeks to show it. To be sure, bashfulness is a very pretty thing; but, in my mind, there is nothing on earth so impudent as an everlasting blush.

Rosy. My taste, my taste!—Well, Lauretta is none of these. Ah! I never see her but she puts me in mind of my poor dear wife.

O'Con. Ay, faith; in my opinion she can't do a worse thing. Now he is going to bother me about an old hag that has been dead these six years. [*Aside.*

Rosy. Oh, poor Dolly! I never shall see her like again; such an arm for a bandage—veins that seemed to invite the lancet. Then her skin, smooth and white as a gallipot; her mouth as large and not larger than the mouth of a penny phial; her lips conserve of roses; and then her teeth—none of your sturdy fixtures—ache as they would, it was but a small pull, and out they came. I believe I have drawn half a score of her poor dear pearls—[*weeps*]—But what avails her beauty? Death has no consideration—one must die as well as another.

O'Con. [*Aside.*] Oh, if he begins to moralize——

[*Takes out his snuff-box.*

Rosy. Fair and ugly, crooked or straight, rich or poor—flesh is grass—flowers fade!

O'Con. Here, doctor, take a pinch, and keep up your spirits.

Rosy. True, true, my friend; grief can't mend the matter—all's for the best; but such a woman was a great loss, lieutenant.

O'Con. To be sure, for doubtless she had mental accomplishments equal to her beauty.

Rosy. Mental accomplishments! she would have stuffed an alligator, or pickled a lizard, with any apothecary's wife in the kingdom. Why, she could decipher a prescription, and invent the ingredients, almost as well as myself: then she was such a hand at making foreign waters!—for Seltzer, Pyrmont, Islington, or Chalybeate, she never had her equal; and her Bath and Bristol springs exceeded the originals.—Ah, poor Dolly! she fell a martyr to her own discoveries.

O'Con. How so, pray?

Rosy. Poor soul! her illness was occasioned by her zeal in trying an improvement on the Spa-water, by an infusion of rum and acid.

O'Con. Ay, ay, spirits never agree with water-drinkers.

Rosy. No, no, you mistake. Rum agreed with her well enough; it was not the rum that killed the poor dear creature, for she died of a dropsy. Well, she is gone, never to return, and has left no pledge of our loves behind. No little babe, to hang like a label round papa's neck. Well, well, we are all mortal—sooner or later—flesh is grass—flowers fade.

O'Con. Oh, the devil!—again! [*Aside.*

Rosy. Life's a shadow—the world a stage—we strut an hour.

O'Con. Here, doctor. [*Offers snuff.*

Rosy. True, true, my friend: well, high grief can't cure it. All's for the best, hey! my little Alexander?

O'Con. Right, right; an apothecary should never be out of spirits. But come, faith, 'tis time honest Humphrey should wait on the justice; that must be our first scheme.

Rosy. True, true; you should be ready: the clothes are at my house, and I have given you such a character, that he is impatient to have you: he swears you shall be his body-guard. Well, I honour the army, or I should never do so much to serve you.

O'Con. Indeed I am bound to you for ever, doctor; and when once I'm possessed of my dear Lauretta, I will endeavour to make work for you as fast as possible.

Rosy Now you put me in mind of my poor wife again.

O'Con. Ah, pray forget her a little: we shall be too late.

Rosy. Poor Dolly!

O'Con. 'Tis past twelve.

Rosy. Inhuman dropsy!

O'Con. The justice will wait.

Rosy. Cropped in her prime!

O'Con. For heaven's sake, come!

Rosy. Well, flesh is grass.

O'Con. O, the devil!

Rosy. We must all die——

O'Con. Doctor!

Rosy. Kings, lords, and common whores——

[*Exeunt* LIEUTENANT O'CONNOR *forcing* ROSY *off.*

SCENE II.—*A Room in* JUSTICE CREDULOUS' *House.*

Enter LAURETTA *and* MRS. BRIDGET CREDULOUS.

Lau. I repeat it again, mamma, officers are the prettiest men in the world, and Lieutenant O'Connor is the prettiest officer I ever saw.

Mrs. Bri. For shame, Laura! how can you talk so?—or if you must have a military man, there's Lieutenant Plow, or Captain Haycock, or Major Dray, the brewer, are all your admirers; and though they are peaceable, good kind of men, they have as large cockades, and become scarlet, as well as the fighting folks.

Lau. Psha! you know, mamma, I hate militia officers; a set of dunghill cocks with spurs on—heroes scratched off a church door—clowns in military masquerade, wearing the dress without supporting the character. No, give me the bold upright youth, who makes love to-day, and his head shot off to-morrow. Dear! to think how the sweet fellows sleep on the ground, and fight in silk stockings and lace ruffles.

ST. PATRICK'S DAY.

Mrs. Bri. Oh, barbarous! to want a husband that may wed you to-day, and be sent the Lord knows where before night; then in a twelvemonth perhaps to have him come like a Colossus, with one leg at New York, and the other at Chelsea Hospital.

Lau. Then I'll be his crutch, mamma.

Mrs. Bri. No, give me a husband that knows where his limbs are, though he want the use of them:—and if he should take you with him, to sleep in a baggage-cart, and stroll about the camp like a gipsy, with a knapsack and two children at your back; then, by way of entertainment in the evening, to make a party with the sergeant's wife to drink bohea tea, and play at all-fours on a drumhead:—'tis a precious life, to be sure!

Lau. Nay, mamma, you shouldn't be against my lieutenant, for I heard him say you were the best natured and best looking woman in the world.

Mrs. Bri. Why, child, I never said but that Lieutenant O'Connor was a very well-bred and discerning young man; 'tis your papa is so violent against him.

Lau. Why, Cousin Sophy married an officer. .

Mrs. Bri. Ay, Laura, an officer of the militia.

Lau. No, indeed, ma'am, a marching regiment.

Mrs. Bri. No, child, I tell you he was a major of militia.

Lau. Indeed, mamma, it wasn't.

Enter JUSTICE CREDULOUS.

Just. Bridget, my love, I have had a message.

Lau. It was Cousin Sophy told me so.

Just. I have had a message, love——

Mrs. Bri. No, child, she would say no such thing.

Just. A message, I say.

Lau. How could he be in the militia when he was ordered abroad?

Mrs. Bri. Ay, girl, hold your tongue!—Well, my dear.

Just. I have had a message from Doctor Rosy.

Mrs. Bri. He ordered abroad! He went abroad for his health.

Just. Why, Bridget!——

Mrs. Bri. Well, deary.—Now hold your tongue, miss.

Just. A message from Dr. Rosy, and Dr. Rosy says——

Lau. I'm sure, mamma, his regimentals——

Just. Damn his regimentals!—Why don't you listen?

Mrs. Bri. Ay, girl, how durst you interrupt your papa?

Lau. Well, papa.

Just. Dr. Rosy says he'll bring——

G

Lau. Were blue turned up with red, mamma.

Just. Laury !—says he will bring the young man——

Mrs. Bri. Red ! yellow, if you please, miss.

Just. Bridget !—the young man that is to be hired——

Mrs. Bri. Besides, miss, it is very unbecoming in you to want to have the last word with your mamma ; you should know——

Just. Why, zounds ! will you hear me or no ?

Mrs. Bri. I am listening, my love, I am listening !—But what signifies my silence, what good is my not speaking a word, if this girl will interrupt and let nobody speak but herself ?—Ay, I don't wonder, my life, at your impatience ; your poor dear lips quiver to speak ; but I suppose she'll run on, and not let you put in a word.—You may very well be angry ; there is nothing, sure, so provoking as a chattering, talking——

Lau. Nay, I'm sure, mamma, it is you will not let papa speak now.

Mrs. Bri. Why, you little provoking minx——

Just. Get out of the room directly, both of you—get out !

Mrs. Bri. Ay, go, girl.

Just. Go, Bridget, you are worse than she, you old hag. I wish you were both up to the neck in the canal, to argue there till I took you out.

Enter SERVANT.

Ser. Doctor Rosy, sir.

Just. Show him up. [*Exit* SERVANT.

Lau. Then you own, mamma, it was a marching regiment ?

Mrs. Bri. You're an obstinate fool, I tell you ; for if that had been the case——

Just. You won't go ?

Mrs. Bri. We are going, Mr. Surly.—If that had been the case, I say, how could——

Lau. Nay, mamma, one proof——

Mrs. Bri. How could Major——

Lau. And a full proof—— [JUSTICE CREDULOUS *drives them off.*

Just. There they go, ding dong in for the day. Good lack ! a fluent tongue is the only thing a mother don't like her daughter to resemble her in.

Enter DOCTOR ROSY.

Well, doctor, where's the lad—where's Trusty ?

Rosy. At hand ; he'll be here in a minute, I'll answer for't. He's such a one as you an't met with,—brave as a lion, gentle as a saline draught.

Just. Ah, he comes in the place of a rogue, a dog that was corrupted by the lieutenant. But this is a sturdy fellow, is he, doctor?

Rosy. As Hercules; and the best back-sword in the country. Egad, he'll make the red coats keep their distance.

Just. O the villains; this is St. Patrick's day, and the rascals have been parading my house all the morning. I know they have a design upon me; but I have taken all precautions: I have magazines of arms, and if this fellow does but prove faithful, I shall be more at ease.

Rosy. Doubtless he'll be a comfort to you.

Re-enter SERVANT.

Ser. There is a man below, inquires for Doctor Rosy.

Rosy. Show him up.

Just. Hold! a little caution—how does he look?

Ser. A country-looking fellow, your worship.

Just. Oh, well, well, for Doctor Rosy; these rascals try all ways to get in here.

Ser. Yes, please your worship; there was one here this morning wanted to speak to you; he said his name was Corporal Breakbones.

Just. Corporal Breakbones!

Ser. And drummer Crackskull came again.

Just. Ay, did you ever hear of such a damned confounded crew? Well, show the lad in here! [*Exit* SERVANT.

Rosy. Ay, he'll be your porter; he'll give the rogues an answer.

Enter LIEUTENANT O'CONNOR, *disguised.*

Just. So, a tall—Efacks! what! has lost an eye?

Rosy. Only a bruise he got in taking seven or eight highwaymen.

Just. He has a damned wicked leer somehow with the other.

Rosy. Oh, no, he's bashful—a sheepish look——

Just. Well, my lad, what's your name?

O'Con. Humphrey Hum.

Just. Hum—I don't like Hum!

O'Con. But I be mostly called honest Humphrey——

Rosy. There, I told you so, of noted honesty.

Just. Well, honest Humphrey, the doctor has told you my terms, and you are willing to serve, hey?

O'Con. And please your worship I shall be well content.

Just. Well, then, hark'ye, honest Humphrey,—you are sure now, you will never be a rogue—never take a bribe, hey, honest Humphrey?

O'Con. A bribe! what's that?

Just. A very ignorant fellow indeed!

Rosy. His worship hopes you will not part with your honesty for money.

O'Con. Noa, noa.

Just. Well said, Humphrey—my chief business with you is to watch the motions of a rake-helly fellow here, one Lieutenant O'Connor.

Rosy. Ay, you don't value the soldiers, do you, Humphrey?

O'Con. Not I; they are but zwaggerers, and you'll see they'll be as much afraid of me as they would of their captain.

Just. And i' faith, Humphrey, you have a pretty cudgel there!

O'Con. Ay, the zwitch is better than nothing, but I should be glad of a stouter: ha' you got such a thing in the house as an old coach-pole, or a spare bed-post?

Just. Oons! what a dragon it is!—Well, Humphrey, come with me. —I'll just show him to Bridget, doctor, and we'll agree.—Come along, honest Humphrey. [*Exit.*

O'Con. My dear doctor, now remember to bring the justice presently to the walk: I have a scheme to get into his confidence at once.

Rosy. I will, I will. [*They shake hands.*

Re-enter JUSTICE CREDULOUS.

Just. Why, honest Humphrey, hey! what the devil are you at?

Rosy. I was just giving him a little advice.—Well, I must go for the present.—Good-morning to your worship—you need not fear the lieutenant while he is in your house.

Just. Well, get in, Humphrey. Good-morning to you doctor.— [*Exit* DOCTOR ROSY.] Come along, Humphrey.—Now I think I am a match for the lieutenant and all his gang. [*Exeunt.*

ACT II.

Scene I.—*A Street.*

Enter Serjeant Trounce, Drummer *and* Soldiers.

Trounce. Come, silence your drum—there is no valour stirring to-day. I thought St. Patrick would have given us a recruit or two to-day.

Sol. Mark, serjeant!

Enter two Countrymen.

Trounce. Oh! these are the lads I was looking for; they have the look of gentlemen.—An't you single, my lads?

1 *Coun.* Yes, an please you, I be quite single: my relations be all dead, thank heavens, more or less. I have but one poor mother left in the world, and she's an helpless woman.

Trounce. Indeed! a very extraordinary case—quite your own master then—the fitter to serve his Majesty.—Can you read?

1 *Coun.* Noa, I was always too lively to take to learning; but John here is main clever at it.

Trounce. So, what you're a scholar, friend?

2 *Coun.* I was born so, measter. Feyther kept grammar-school.

Trounce. Lucky man—in a campaign or two put yourself down chaplain to the regiment. And I warrant you have read of warriors and heroes?

2 *Coun.* Yes, that I have: I have read of Jack the Giant Killer, and the Dragon of Wantly, and the—Noa, I believe that's all in the hero way, except once about a comet.

Trounce. Wonderful knowledge!—Well, my heroes, I'll write word to the king of your good intentions, and meet me half an hour hence at the Two Magpies.

Coun. We will, your honour, we will.

Trounce. But stay; for fear I shouldn't see you again in the crowd, clap these little bits of ribbon into your hats.

1 *Coun.* Our hats are none of the best.

Trounce. Well, meet me at the Magpies, and I'll give you money to buy new ones.

Coun. Bless your honour, thank your honour. [*Exeunt.*

Trounce. [*Winking at* Soldiers.] Jack! [*Exeunt* Soldiers.

Enter LIEUTENANT O'CONNOR.

So, here comes one would make a grenadier—Stop, friend, will you list?

O'Con. Who shall I serve under?

Trounce. Under me, to be sure.

O'Con. Isn't Lieutenant O'Connor your officer?

Trounce. He is, and I am commander over him.

O'Con. What! be your serjeants greater than your captains?

Trounce. To be sure we are; 'tis our business to keep them in order. For instance, now, the general writes to me, dear Serjeant, or dear Trounce, or dear Serjeant Trounce, according to his hurry, if your lieutenant does not demean himself accordingly, let me know.—Yours, General Deluge.

O'Con. And do you complain of him often?

Trounce. No, hang him, the lad is good-natured at the bottom, so I pass over small things. But hark'ee, between ourselves, he is most confoundedly given to wenching.

Enter CORPORAL FLINT.

Flint. Please your honour, the doctor is coming this way with his worship—We are all ready, and have our cues. [*Exit.*

O'Con. Then, my dear Trounce, or my dear Serjeant, or my dear Serjeant Trounce, take yourself away.

Trounce. Zounds! the lieutenant—I smell of the black hole already.
[*Exit.*

Enter JUSTICE CREDULOUS *and* DOCTOR ROSY.

Just. I thought I saw some of the cut-throats.

Rosy. I fancy not; there's no one but honest Humphrey. Ha! Odds life, here comes some of them—we'll stay by these trees, and let them pass.

Just. Oh, the bloody-looking dogs!
[*Walks aside with* DOCTOR ROSY.

Re-enter CORPORAL FLINT *and two* SOLDIERS.

Flint. Halloa, friend! do you serve Justice Credulous?

O'Con. I do.

Flint. Are you rich?

O'Con. Noa.

Flint. Nor ever will be with that old stingy booby. Look here—take it. [*Gives him a purse.*

O'Con. What must I do for this?

Flint. Mark me, our lieutenant is in love with the old rogue's daughter: help us to break his worship's bones, and carry off the girl, and you are a made man.

O'Con. I'll see you hanged first, you pack of skurry villains!

[*Throws away the purse.*

Flint. What, sirrah, do you mutiny? Lay hold of him.

O'Con. Nay, then, I'll try your armour for you. [*Beats them.*

All. Oh! oh!—quarter! quarter!

[*Exeunt* CORPORAL FLINT *and* SOLDIERS.

Just. [*Coming forward.*] Trim them, trounce them, break their bones, honest Humphrey—What a spirit he has!

Rosy. Aquafortis.

O'Con. Betray your master!

Rosy. What a miracle of fidelity!

Just. Ay, and it shall not go unrewarded—I'll give him sixpence on the spot. Here, honest Humphrey, there's for yourself: as for this bribe, [*takes up the purse,*] such trash is best in the hands of justice. Now, then, doctor, I think I may trust him to guard the women: while he is with them I may go out with safety.

Rosy. Doubtless you may—I'll answer for the lieutenant's behaviour whilst honest Humphrey is with your daughter.

Just. Ay, ay, she shall go nowhere without him. Come along, honest Humphrey. How rare it is to meet with such a servant!

[*Exeunt.*

SCENE II.—*A Garden.*

LAURETTA *discovered. Enter* JUSTICE CREDULOUS *and*
LIEUTENANT O'CONNOR.

Just. Why, you little truant, how durst you wander so far from the house without my leave? Do you want to invite that scoundrel lieutenant to scale the walls and carry you off.

Lau. Lud, papa, you are so apprehensive for nothing.

Just. Why, hussy——

Lau. Well, then, I can't bear to be shut up all day so like a nun. I am sure it is enough to make one wish to be run away with—and I wish I was run away with—I do—and I wish the lieutenant knew it.

Just. You do, do you, hussy? Well, I think I'll take pretty good care of you. Here, Humphrey, I leave this lady in your care. Now you may walk about the garden, Miss Pert; but Humphrey shall go with you wherever you go. So mind, honest Humphrey, I am obliged to go abroad for a little while; let no one but yourself come near her;

don't be shame-faced, you booby, but keep close to her. And now, miss, let your lieutenant or any of his crew come near you if they can. [*Exit.*

Lau. How this booby stares after him! [*Sits down and sings.*
O'Con. Lauretta!
Lau. Not so free, fellow! [*Sings.*
O'Con. Lauretta! look on me.
Lau. Not so free, fellow!
O'Con. No recollection!
Lau. Honest Humphrey, be quiet.
O'Con. Have you forgot your faithful soldier?
Lau. Ah! Oh preserve me!
O'Con. 'Tis, my soul! your truest slave, passing on your father in this disguise.
Lau. Well now, I declare this is charming—you are so disguised, my dear lieutenant, and you look so delightfully ugly. I am sure no one will find you out, ha! ha! ha!—You know I am under your protection; papa charged you to keep close to me.
O'Con. True, my angel, and thus let me fulfil——
Lau. O pray now, dear Humphrey——
O'Con. Nay, 'tis but what old Mittimus commanded.
[*Offers to kiss her.*

Re-enter JUSTICE CREDULOUS.

Just. Laury, my—hey! what the devil's here?
Lau. Well now, one kiss, and be quiet.
Just. Your very humble servant, honest Humphrey! Don't let me—pray don't let me interrupt you!
Lau. Lud, papa! Now that's so good-natured—indeed there's no harm. You did not mean any rudeness, did you, Humphrey?
O'Con. No, indeed, miss; his worship knows it is not in me.
Just. I know that you are a lying, canting, hypocritical scoundrel; and if you don't take yourself out of my sight——
Lau. Indeed, papa, now I'll tell you how it was. I was sometime taken with a sudden giddiness, and Humphrey seeing me beginning to totter, ran to my assistance, quite frightened, poor fellow, and took me in his arms.
Just. Oh! was that all—nothing but a little giddiness, hey!
O'Con. That's all, indeed, your worship; for seeing miss change colour, I ran up instantly.
Just. Oh, 'twas very kind in you!
O'Con. And luckily recovered her.

ST. PATRICK'S DAY.

Just. And who made you a doctor, you impudent rascal, hey? Get out of my sight, I say, this instant, or by all the statutes——

Lau. Oh now, papa, you frighten me, and I am giddy again!—Oh, help!

O'Con. O dear lady, she'll fall!   [*Takes her into his arms.*

Just. Zounds! what before my face—why then, thou miracle of impudence!—[*Lays hold of him and discovers him.*]—Mercy on me, who have we here?—Murder! Robbery! Fire! Rape! Gunpowder! Soldiers! John! Susan! Bridget!

O'Con. Good sir, don't be alarmed; I mean you no harm.

Just. Thieves! Robbers! Soldiers!

O'Con. You know my love for your daughter——

Just. Fire! Cut-throats!

O'Con. And that alone——

Just. Treason! Gunpowder!

Enter a SERVANT *with a blunderbuss.*

Now, scoundrel! let her go this instant.

Lau. O papa, you'll kill me!

Just. Honest Humphrey, be advised. Ay, miss, this way, if you please.

O'Con. Nay, sir, but hear me——

Just. I'll shoot.

O'Con. How injurious——

Just. I'll shoot—and so your very humble servant, honest Humphrey Hum.   [*Exeunt separately.*

SCENE 3d.—The Walk.*

DR. ROSY.

Rosy. Well—I think my Friend is now in a fair way of succeeding. Ah!—I warrant He's full of hope—and Doubt—and Fear—and Anxiety—Truly he has the Fever of Love strong upon him—Faint Peevish—Languishing all Day—with burning—restless Nights.—Ah! just my Case—when first I pined for my poor dear Dolly—when she used to have daily Cholics and her little Doctor be sent for, then would I interpret the language of her Pulse—declare my own suffering in my recipes for hers—send her a pearl Necklace in a Pill-box—or a cordial Draught with an acrostic on the Label! well those Days are over! No happiness lasting! all's Vanity! now sunshine, now cloud!—we are as we were made King and Peasant—then what avails!—

---

* The sheets of manuscript which have been preserved begin here.

Enter LIEUTENANT.

Lieu. O Doctor ruined and undone——
Dr. The Pride of Beauty——
Lieu. I am discovered and——
Dr. The gaudy Palace——
Lieu. The Justice is——
Dr. The pompous Wig!
Lieu. More enraged than ever
Dr. The gilded cane——!
Lieu. Why Doctor! (*loud.*)
Dr. Hey?
Lieu. Confound your morals! I tell you I am discovered! discomfited! disappointed! ruined!
Dr. Indeed! Good Lack—to think of the Instability of human Affairs!—Nothing certain in this world!—most deceived when most confident!—Fools of Fortune all!
Lieu. My dear Doctor, I want at present a little practical Wisdom—I am resolved this instant to try the Scheme we were going to put into execution last week. The present event will give probability to the Plan—I have the letter ready written—and only want your assistance to recover my Ground——
Dr. With all my Heart—I warrant I'll bear my Part in it: but how the Deuce were you discover'd?
Lieu. I'll tell you as we go—There's not a Moment to be lost.
Dr. Well, Heaven send we succeed better at present—but there's no knowing.
Lieu. Very true——
Dr. We may and we may not.
Lieu. Right——
Dr. Time must show——
Lieu. Certainly——
Dr. We are but blind Guessers——
Lieu. Nothing more——
Dr. Short-sighted Mortals.
Lieu. Remarkably!
Dr. Wandr'ing in Error.
Lieut. Even so
Dr. Futurity is Dark.
Lieut. As a Cellar.
Dr. Men are moles. [*Exe.* DR. *moralizing.*

ST. PATRICK'S DAY.

SCENE 4th.—*The* JUSTICE'S *House.*

JUSTICE *and* BRIDGET.

Just. Odds life Bridget, you are enough to make one mad—I tell you He would have deceived a Chief Justice—The Dog seem'd as ignorant as my Clerk—and talked of Honesty as if he had been a Church-warden——

Bri. Pho! Nonsense, Honesty indeed—what had you to do pray with Honesty? a fine Business you have made of it with your Humphrey Hum: and miss too—She must have been privy to it—Lauretta! indeed—aye you *would* have her call'd so—but for my Part I never knew any good come of giving girls these Heathen Christian Names—if you had called her Deborah—or Tabitha—or Ruth—or Rebecca—nothing of this would have happened—but I always knew *Lauretta* was a Runaway Name.

Just. Pshaw, you're a Fool——

Bri. No Mr. Credulous 'tis you are a Fool—and no one but such a simpleton would have been so imposed on——

Just. Why, z—ds! Madam, how durst you talk so—If you have no Respect for your Husband—I should think unus Quorum might command a little Deference.

Bri. Don't tell me—Unus Fiddlestick—you ought to be ashamed to show your Face at the Sessions—you'll be the Laughing-stock of the Bench and byeword with all the pig-tailed Lawyers and bob-wig Attorneys.

Just. Is this Language to his Majesty's Representative? By the statutes! 'tis high Treason and petty Treason, both at once!

Enter SERVANT.

Ser. A Letter for your Worship.
Just. Who brought it?
Ser. A Soldier—your Worship.
Just. Take it away and bury it.—Combustible stuff I warrant it—A threatening Letter—put ten Pound under Stone—with d—d infammatory spelling—and the bloody Hands of a Dozen Rogues at Bottom——

Bri. Stay now—you're in such a Hurry—'tis some canting Scrawl from the Lieutenant I suppose—here—(takes the letter) let me see—ay, 'tis sign'd Lieutenant O'Connor.

Just. Well—come—read it out.
Bri. (reads) Sir, Revenge is sweet.

Just. It begins so, does it? I'm glad of that—I'll let the Dog [know] I am of his Opinion.

Mrs. Bri. And though disappointed of my Designs upon your Daughter—I have still the satisfaction of knowing I am revenged on her unnatural Father—for this morning, in your Chocolate, I had the pleasure of administering to you a Dose of Poison!—Mercy—on us!

Just. No Tricks, Bridget—come now you know 'tis not so! you know 'tis a lie.

Bri. Read it yourself—(crying)

Just. Pleasure of Administering a Dose of Poison!—Oh, horrible—Cut-throat Villain!—Bridget!

Bri. Lovee!—stay here's a Postscript—N.B. 'tis not in the power of medicine to save you!—Oh! Oh!

Just. Odds Life, Bridget why don't you call for help—I've lost my Voice.—My Brain's Giddy—I shall burst, and no assistance—John!—Laury!—John!

Bri. Oh!—you see, my Lovee, what you have brought on yourself!

Enter JOHN.

John. Your Worship——

Just. Stay John—did you perceive anything in my Chocolate Cup this morning——

Ser. Nothing your Worship—unless it was a little Grounds—

Just. Aye Arsenick—Arsenic—'tis plain enough—Why don't you run for Dr. Rosy you Rascal?

Ser. Now your Worship.—

Bri. Oh Lovee—you may be sure 'tis in vain—let him go for the Lawyer to witness your will my Life——

Just. Z—ds! go for the Dr. you scoundrel—you are all confederate murderers.

Ser. O here he is your Worship——

Just. Now Bridget—hold your tongue—let me see if my horrid situation is apparent.

Enter DR.

Dr. I have but just call'd in to inform—hey! bless me what's the matter with your Worship?

Just. There—He sees it already—Poison in my Face, in Capitals—Yes—yes, I'm a sure Job—for the Undertakers indeed——

Mrs. Bri. Oh! oh! alas, Doctor!

Just. Peace—Bridget—why Doctor—my dear old Friend—do—you really—see—any change in me—hey?——

ST. PATRICK'S DAY. 93

Dr. Change—never was man so alter'd! How came these black spots on your Nose?

Just. Spots on my Nose!

Dr. And that wild Stare in your right Eye!

Just. In my right eye? O look!——

Dr. Ay, and, alack, Efack! how you are swell'd.

Just. Swell'd!

Dr. Aye don't you think He is Madam?

Bri. O 'tis in vain to conceal it!—indeed, Lovee, you are as big again as you were in the morning?

Just. Yes—I feel it now—I'm poisoned Dr.—help me for the love of Justice—Give me Life to see my murderer hang'd.

Dr. What?

Just. I'm poison'd—I say——

Dr. Speak out——

Just. What—can't you hear me?

Dr. Your voice is so low and Hollow as it were I can't hear a word you say——

Just. I am gone then—Hic jacet—many years one of his Majesty's Justices!

Bri. Read that Dr.—Ah! Lovee the Will—consider my Life, how soon you'll be dead.

Just. No—Bridget I shall die by Inches——

Bri. Well Lovee—and at twelve inches a Day and that's good slow Dying—you'll be gone, in five days and a half——

Just.—'Tis false—Cocatrice—I'm five foot eight.

Dr. I never heard such monstrous Iniquity—Ah! you are gone indeed my Friend—The Mortgage of your little bit of clay is up—and the sexton has nothing to do but foreclose—Well all's for the Best—we must all go, sooner or Later—High or Low—Death's a Debt—his mandamus binds all alike—to bail—no demurrer.

Just. Silence—Dr. Croaker—will you cure me or will you not?

Dr. Alas my Friend, it isn't in my Power—but I'll certainly see Justice done on your Murderer.

Just. I thank you my dear Friend—but I had rather see it myself.

Dr. Aye but if you recover, the Villain will escape——

Bri. Will He? then indeed Lovee 'twould be a Pity you should recover—I'm so enraged against the Villain—that I can't bear the thought of his escaping the Halter——

Just. That's very kind my Dear—but if it is the same thing to you I had as lieve recover notwithstanding. Doctor—No assistance!

Dr. Efacks—I can do nothing—but here is the German Quack,

whom you wanted to send from the town—I met him at the next Door—I know he has Antidotes for all Poisons.

Just. Fetch him, my dear Friend, fetch him! I'll get him a Diploma if he cures me.

Dr. Well there's no time to be lost—you continue to swell immensely. [*Exit* DR.

Bri. What my Dear, will you submit to be cured by a Quack—a Nostrum-Monger?—there's something creditable in being kill'd in a regular way—For my Part—as much as I love you—I had rather follow you to the Grave—than see you owe your Life to any one but a regular-Bred Physician.

Just. I'm sensible of your Affection, Dearest — and believe me nothing consoles me in my present melancholy situation—so much as the Thought of leaving you behind my Angel!—

(Enter Dr. and the Lieut. dressed with Wig and Cloak as a Physician.)

Dr. Great luck—I met him passing by the door. (They salute.)

Lieu. Metto dowsin Pulsum.

Dr. He desires to feel your Pulse.

Just. Can't He speak English?

Dr. Not a word.

Lieu. Palio vivem mortem soonem.

Dr. He says you haven't six hours to live.

Just. O mercy—does he know my Distemper?

Dr. I believe not.

Just. Tell him 'tis Arsenic they have given me.—

Dr. Geneable illi arsnecca.

Lieu. Poisonatus.

Just. What does He say?

Dr. He says that you are poisoned.

Just. We know that—but what will be the Effect?

Dr. Quid effectum.—

Lieu. Diable tutellum.

Dr. He says you'll die presently.

Just. O Horrible! What no Antidote?

Lieu. Curum benakere bono fullum.

Rosy. He says He'll undertake to cure you for three thousand Pounds.

Bri. Three thousand Halters—No Lovee, you shall never submit to such an imposition. Die at once, my Life, and be a customer obliged to None of them.

Just. I will *not* die, Bridget!—I don't like death.

Bri. Pshaw! there's nothing in it—a moment and it is over.

Just. Aye, but it leaves a Numbness behind that lasts for a Plaguy long time.

Enter LAURETTA.

Lau. O my Father! what is it I hear?

Lieu. Quiddam seomriam deos tollam rosam.

Dr. The Doctor is astonish'd at the sight of your Daughter.

Just. How so!

Lieu. Damsellum livivum suvum rislibani.

Dr. He says that He has lost his heart to her—and that if you will give him leave to pay his addresses to the young Lady, and promise your consent to the Union if he should gain her Affections, He will on those conditions cure you instantly without Fee or Reward.

Just. The Devil! did he say all that in so few Words?—What a fine Language it is! Well I agree if he can prevail on the Girl.—And that I'm sure He never will (aside).

Dr. Great——

Lieu. Writhum Bothum.

Dr. He says you must give this under your hand while he writes you a miraculous Recipe.   [*Both write at the Table.*

Lau. Do mama tell me the meaning of all this.

Bri. Don't speak to me Girl, unnatural Parasite!

Just. There Doctor; that's what he requires.—

Dr. And here's your Recipe—read it yourself.

Just. Hey—what's here? plain English?

Dr. Read it out; a wondrous Nostrum I'll answer for't.

(While the *Just.* reads, *Lieu.* throws off his Disguise and kneels with *Laura*.)

(*Just.* reads.) On reading this you are cured, by your affectionate Son-in-law, O'CONNOR.—Who in the name of Beelzebub, sirrah, who are you?

Just. What the Deuce is the meaning of all this?—

Bri. Oh monstrous imposition.

Just. In the name of Beelzebub, who have we here?

Lieu. Lieutenant O'Connor at your service and your faithful Servant honest Humphrey.

Bri. So, so another Trick.

Jus. Out of my sight Varlet, I'll be off the Bargain—I'll be poison'd again, and you shall be hang'd.—

Dr. Come, come my dear friend don't put yourself in a passion—a Man just escaped from the Jaws of Death should'nt be so violent.—Come make a merit of Necessity and let your Blessing join those, whom nothing on Earth can keep asunder.

Jus. I'll not do it—I'd sooner die and leave my fortune to Bridget.

Bri. To be sure. O' my conscience I'd rather you should Die and leave me ten Estates than consent to such a thing.

Jus. You had, had you? Hearkee Bridget, you behav'd so affectionately just now that I'll never follow your advice again while I live.— So Mr. Lieutenant——

Lieu. Sir——

Jus. You're an Irishman and an Officer arn't you?

Lieu. I am, and proud of both.

Jus. The two things in the World I hate most—so mark me—forswear your Country and quit the Army and I'll receive you as my Son-in-Law—

Lieu. You Mr. Justice, if you were not the Father of your Daughter there, I'd pull your Nose for mentioning the first, and break your bones for proposing the latter.—

Dr. You're right Lieutenant——

Jus. Is he? Why then I must be wrong—here Lauretta—you're a sly tricking little Baggage, and I believe no one so fit for managing you as my honest friend here who is the most impudent Dog I ever saw——

Lieu. With such a gift every word is a Compliment.

Bri. Come then, since everything's settled I give my Consent and this Days adventure Lovee, will be a good scolding subject for you and me this ten years.

Jus. So it will my Dear—tho' we are never much at a loss——

Dr. Come I insist on one Day without wrangling—the Capt. shall give us a Dinner at the two Magpies, and your Worship shall put every man in the Stocks who is sober at eight o'clock—so joy to you my little favourite (to Laur.) I wish you may make just such a Wife as my poor Dear Dolly——

&c. &c.*

FINIS.

* The manuscript from "Enter LAURETTA" is in Mrs. Sheridan's handwriting, and an L. is written between "&c." and "Finis."

THE DUENNA.

DRAMATIS PERSONÆ.

DON JEROME.
FERDINAND, his Son.
ANTHONIO.
ISAAC.
MANUEL, Ferdinand's Servant.
3 Friars. { PAUL. FRANCIS. AUGUSTIN.

LUISA, Don Jerome's Daughter.
CLARA, Daughter Don Pedro, Cousin to Clara.
CATHERINE, The Duenna.
LISETTE, Luisa's Maid.
Masks and Servants.

SCENE.—SEVILLE.

ACT 1st. Scene 1st.

A Piaza before DON JEROME'S House.

The Morning breaking—Clock strikes 3.

Enter MANUEL from the House with a Dark Lantern in his Hand.

Man. (*listening*). Past 3 o'clock!—Soh! a notable hour for one of my regular Disposition to be strolling like a Bravo through the Streets of Seville! Well of all services to serve a Young Lover is the hardest—! truly a prudent Domestick would do well to make a Clause in favour of double Wages when his Master shall think proper to fall in Love.— Don Ferdinand is much too gallant to eat, drink, or Sleep :—now for my part Love gives me an appetite—then I am fond of dreaming of my mistress, and I like dearly to toast her—neither this can't be done without good sleep and good Liquor : hence my partiality to a Feather-bed and a Bottle! But a Plague on these haughty Damsels say I— when they play their airs on their whining gallants—they ought to consider that we are the chief sufferers.—we have all their ill-humours at second-hand—Donna Luisa's cruelty to my master usually con- verts itself into Blows by the time it gets to me—she can frown me black and blue at any time, and I shall carry the marks of the last box on the Ear she gave him—to my Grave—nay if she smiles on any one else—I'm the sufferer for it. If she says a civil word to a Rival—I am a Rogue and a Scoundrel—and if she sends him a Letter my Back is sure to pay the Postage! What a pity, now, that I have not further time for Reflections! but my master expects thee, honest Manuel, to secure his Retreat from Donna Luisa's window! Hey! sure, I heard music! So! so! Who have we here? Oh! Don Anthonio, my master's Friend, come from the masquerade, to serenade my young mistress, I suppose—soh! we shall have the old gentleman up presently.—Lest He should miss his [son] I had best lose no time in getting to my Post. [*Exit.*

Enter ANTHONIO and MASKS with Music.

ANTH sings—Song—soft symphony.

Tell me, my Lute, can thy fond strain
So gently speak thy master's Pain?
So sweetly sing, so humbly sigh,
   That tho' my sleeping Love shall know
   Who sings—who sighs below,
Her rosy slumbers shall not fly?
   Thus may some vision whisper more
   Than ever I dare speak before.

1 *Mask.* Anthonio—your mistress will never wake while you sing so dolefully:—Love, like a cradled Infant, is lulled by a sad melody.

Ant. I do not wish to disturb her rest.

2d *Mas.* The reason is because you know She does not regard you enough to appear if you wak'd her.

Ant. Nay then I'll convince you. [*Sings.*

SONG.

Anth. Sings.)   The crimson Dawn bids hence the Night—
   Unveil those beauteous eyes my Fair;
   For till the morn of Love is there,
     I feel no Day, I own no Light.

(Clara replies from ye window.)

   Waking I heard thy Numbers chide,
   Waking the dawn did bless my sight;
   'Tis *Phœbus* sure that woos, I cried,
     Who speaks in song—who moves in Light.

(Don Jerome appears at another window.)

TRIO.

Don Jer.   What Vagabonds are these I hear,
   Fiddling—fluting—rhyming ranting
   Piping scraping—whining, canting—
     Hence scurvy Minstrels, fly!

TRIO.

Clara   Prithee Father why so rough—
Anth.   An humble Lover I.
Don Jer.   Daughter how durst you lend an ear
   To such deceitful stuff—
     Quick from the window fly!

Clara	Adieu, Anthonio ! (*Anth.*)—must you go ?
Anth.	We soon perhaps may meet again.
	For though hard Fortune is our Foe,
	The God of Love will fight for us
Don Jer.	Get me the Blunderbuss.
Anth. and Clara	The God of Love who knows our Pain—
Don Jer.	Hence ! or these are slugs thro' your Brain.

(*Exe. Anth. and Masks and Don Jer. and Clara from the window.*)

SCENE 2ᵈ   A Street—

Enter FERDINAND and MANUEL.

Man. Truly, sir, I think a little sleep once in week or so——

Ferd. Peace Fool ! don't mention sleep to me—

Man. No—no—Sir—I don't recommend your lowbred vulgar sound sleep—but I can't help thinking that a genteel slumber or half an hour's dozing—if it were only for the novelty of the thing——

Ferd. Peace Booby, I say—Oh Luisa dear cruel disturber of my Rest—

Man. And of mine too !

Ferd. 'Sdeath to trifle with me at such a juncture as this !—now to stand on Punctilios !—love me ! I don't believe she ever did.

Man. Nor I either.

Ferd. Or is [it] that her Sex never know their Desires for an hour together !

Man. Ah ! they know them oftener than they 'll own them.

Don Ferd. Is there in the world so inconsistent a creature as Luisa.

Man. I could name one.

Ferd. Yes—the Tame Fool that submits to her Caprice.

Man. I thought he couldn't miss it.

Fer. By my Life now it were justice to renounce her for ever !

Man. I was always of that Opinion—

Don. Ferd. Is she not capricious—teasing, tyrannical—obstinate—perverse—absurd ?

Man. Yes—yes—a very wilderness of Faults and Follies—

Fer. Her looks are scorn, and her very smiles—'Sdeath ! I wish I hadn't mention'd her smiles—for when she *does*—such beaming Loveliness—such fascinating Brightness—O Death madness I shall die if I lose her—

Man. Ah ! those damn'd smiles have undone all !

Song

Ferd. Could I her Faults remember
Forgetting every charm—
Soon would impartial Reason
The Tyrant Love disarm:
But while enraged I number
Each Failing of her mind
Love still suggests her Beauty,
And *sees* while Reason's *blind*.

Man. Here comes Don Anthonio, Sir.
Don Ferd. Well go you home—I shall be there presently.
Man. Ah! those curst smiles! [*Exit.*

Enter ANTHONIO.

Anth. Ferdinand—! Soh! another troubled spirit come from hovering round the walls that entomb his mistress and sculking from Daybreak—

Ferd. A troubled Spirit indeed—of one inhumanly murder'd by— a barbarous Disapointment!—but Manuel tells me he left you chanting before our door—was my father waked?

Anth. Yes yes—He has a singular affection for music—so I left him roaring at his barr'd [window] like the print of Bajazet in the cage— but what! no festal Disapointment I hope!

Ferd. Worse than ever was outlived by a Lover before—I am just returned from Luisa's Bedchamber—

Anth. What then 'tis *she* that's Disapointed——

Ferd. I believe I told you, that to-morrow was the Day fixed by Don Gusman and Luisa's unnatural stepmother for her to enter a Convent—in order that her brat might possess her fortune: made desperate by this, I procured a Key to the Door, and bribed Luisa's maid to leave it unbolted—at two this morning I enter'd unperceived and stole to Luisa's chamber!—I found her waking and weeping.

Anth. Aye—aye this was at first—

Ferd. No such thing I tell you—she call'd her maid—who Slep'd in the next room—I urged every argument—to persuade her to elope with me, but all in vain! She vow'd to die in a convent sooner—and threatened to raise her Father if I did not instantly leave her.

Anth. Well, but at last?

Ferd. At last!—why I was forced to leave the House as I came in.

Anth. And did you do nothing to offend her?

Ferd. Nothing as I hope to be saved—I believe I might snatch a dozen or two kisses.

Anth. Was that all—and you were really forced to decamp?

Ferd. Aye—and treated like a Dog—

Anth. Well I think—I never heard of such assurance—Lord ! I don't mean you, but in her—

Ferd. Aye—did you ever hear anything equal—to it ?

Anth. Never ! Well the confidence of some women is amazing— ! and the curst maid too—what business had she to hear— ?

Ferd. Aye a treacherous confounded Huzzy that came with my Ducats clinking in her Pocket——

Anth. But hearken Ferdinand did you leave your Key with them ?

Ferd. Yes ; the maid who saw me out, took it from the door.

Anth. Then my life for it, her mistress elopes after you.

Ferd. Aye to bless some Rival perhaps—I am in a humour to suspect everybody.—You, Anthonio, loved her once and thought her an Angel, as I do now—

Ant. Yes, I loved her till I found she wouldn't love me—and then I discovered that she hadn't a good Feature in her Face.

AIR.

I ne'er could any Lustre see
In eyes that would not look on me ;
I ne'er saw Nectar on a Lip,
But where my own did hope to sip.
Has the Nymph who seeks my Heart
Cheeks of Rose, untouch'd by Art?
I will own the coulour **true**,
When yielding Blushes aid their hue.

Is her Hand so soft and pure?
I must press it to be sure;
Nor can I e'en be certain then,
Till it grateful press again.
Must I, with attentive eye,
Watch her heaving bosom sigh?
I will do so, when [I] see
That heaving Bosom sigh for me !

Besides, Ferdinand, you have full security in my Love for your Sister —help me there and I can never disturb you with Luisa.

Ferd. As far as I can, consistently with the Honour of our Family —you know I will—but there must be no Eloping.

Anth. And yet, now, you would carry off Luisa ?

Ferd. Aye that's a different case—we never mean that others should act to our sisters or wives as we do to theirs.—but to-morrow Luisa is to be forced into a convent.

Anth. Well am not I as unfortunately circumstanced ?—to-morrow your Father forces Clara to marry Isaac the Portuguese !—but come with me—and we'll devise something I warrant.

Ferd. I must go home first—

Anth. And I to lay aside these Trappings, adieu—let us meet presently.

Don Ferd. But Anthonio, if you did not love my sister you have too much honour—Friendship and Honour—to think of supplanting me with Luisa—

Song.

Anth. Friendship is the Bond of Reason;
    But if Beauty disapprove—
Heaven absolves all other Treason
    In the Heart that's true to Love.
The Faith which to my Friend I swore,
    As a civil oath I view;
But to the Charms which I adore,
    'Tis religion to be true.
And if to one I false must be
    Can I doubt which to prefer?
A Breach of social Faith with thee
    Or sacrilege to Love and Her.
                          [*Exit.*

Ferd. There is always a Levity in Anthonio's manner of replying to me on this subject that is very alarming.—'Sdeath, if Luisa should love him after all.

Song.

Tho' cause for suspicion appears,
    Yet Proofs of her Love too are strong
—I'm a wretch if I'm right in my Fears,
    And unworthy of Bliss if I'm wrong.
What heart-breaking Torments from jealousy flow,
Ah None but the Jealous, the Jealous can know!
    When blest with the smiles of my Fair,
    I know not how much I adore
    Those smiles let another but share,
    And I wonder I priz'd them no more!
Then whence can I hope a relief from my woe,
When the falser she seems still the fonder I grow?
                          [*Exit.*

Scene 3d.

A Room in Don Jerome's House.

Luisa and the Duenna.

Luisa. But, my dear Margaret, my charming Duenna, do you think we shall succeed?

Duen. I tell you again—have no doubt on't—but it must be instantly put to the Trial. Everything is prepared in your Room—and for the rest we must trust to Fortune.

THE DUENNA. 103

Luisa. My Father's oath was never to see me till I had consented to——

Duen. 'Twas thus I overheard him say to his confident—Don Guzman,—' I will demand of her to-morrow morning, once for all whether she will consent to marry Isaac if she hesitates I will make a solemn oath never to see or speak to her from that hour till she returns to her duty.'—Those were his very words.

Luisa. And on his known obstinate adherence to what he has once said—you have formed this plan for my escape——but have you secured my maid in our Interests?

Duen. She is a Party in the whole—but remember if we succeed you resign all right and tittle in this little Jew over to me.

Don. Luisa. That I do with all my soul—get him if you can, and I shall wish you joy most heartily—

AIR.*

Thou canst not boast of fortune's store,
My love, while me they wealthy call:
But I was glad to find thee poor—
For with my heart I 'd give thee all.
And then the grateful youth shall own
I loved him for himself alone.
But when his worth my hand shall gain,
No word or look of mine shall show
That I the smallest thought retain
Of what my bounty did bestow;
Yet still his grateful heart shall own
I loved him for himself alone.

Duen. I hear don Jerome coming—quick give me the last Letter I brought you from Anthonio—you know that is to be the ground of my dismission.—I must slip out to seal it up, as undelivered—
Exit.

Enter DON JEROME and FERDINAND.

Don Jer. What I suppose you have been serenading too! disturbing some peaceable Neighbourhood with villanous catgut and lascivious piping!—Out on 't! you set your Sister here a vile example—But I'm come to tell you Madam—that I 'll suffer no more of these midnight incantations—these amorous orgies that steal the senses in the hearing: as they say, Egyptian embalmers serve mummies—extracting the brain thro' their ears.

Luisa. If young men will divert themselves at my window can I

* "Song" was written here and the pen was drawn through it. The words were not added; these now given are taken from the printed version.

help it? and if the music is pleasing my ears have a will of their own, and yield attention in spite of Duty!

Don Jer. No—nor you can't help rising and opening the window and replying the Rakes I suppose? What, I warrant your legs and your Tongue have a will of their own too?*

Luisa. Never, while I have life!

Ferd. Indeed, sir, I wonder how you can think of such a man for a son-in-law.

Don Jer. Sir, you are very kind to favour me with your sentiments—and pray, what is your objection to him?

Don Ferd. He is a Portuguese, in the first place.

Don Jer. No such thing, boy; he has forsworn his country.

Don. Luisa. He is a Jew.

Don Jer. Another mistake: he has been a Christian these six weeks.

Don Ferd. Ay, he left his old religion for an estate, and has not had time to get a new one.

Don. Luisa. But stands like a dead wall between church and synagogue, or like the blank leaves between the Old and New Testament.

Don Jer. Anything more?

Don Ferd. But the most remarkable part of his character is his passion for deceit and tricks of cunning.

Don. Luisa. Though at the same time the fool predominates so much over the knave, that I am told he is generally the dupe of his own art.

Don Ferd. True; like an unskilful gunner, he usually misses his aim, and is hurt by the recoil of his own piece.

Don Jer. Anything more?

Don. Luisa. To sum up all, he has the worst fault a husband can have—he's not my choice.

Don Jer. But you are his; and choice on one side is sufficient—two lovers should never meet in marriage—be you sour as you please, he is sweet-tempered; and for your good fruit, there's nothing like ingrafting on a crab.

Don. Luisa. I detest him as a lover, and shall ten times more as a husband.

Don. Jer. I don't know that—marriage generally makes a great change—but, to cut the matter short, will you have him or not?

---

* The following words, which do not appear in the manuscript, are in be printed version, and they are required to make the context intelligible: "However, there's an end of your frolics. Isaac Mendoza will be here presently, and to-morrow you shall marry him."

Don Luisa. There is nothing else I could disobey you in.

Don Jer. Do you value your father's peace?

Don. Luisa. So much, that I will not fasten on him the regret of making an only daughter wretched.

Don. Jer. Very well, ma'am, then mark me—never more will I see or converse with you till you return to your duty—no reply—this and your chamber shall be your apartments; I never will stir out without leaving you under lock and key, and when I'm at home no creature can approach you but through my library: we'll try who can be most obstinate. Out of my sight!—there remain till you know your duty.

[*Pushes her out.*

Don Ferd. Surely, sir, my sister's inclinations should be consulted in a matter of this kind, and some regard paid to Don Antonio, being my particular friend

Don Jer. That, doubtless, is a very great recommendation!—I certainly have not paid sufficient respect to it.

Don Ferd. There is not a man living I would sooner choose for a brother-in-law

Don Jer. Very possible; and if you happen to have e'er a sister, who is not at the same time a daughter of mine, I'm sure I shall have no objection to the relationship; but at present, if you please, we'll drop the subject.

Don Ferd. Nay, sir, 'tis only my regard for my sister makes me speak.

Don Jer. Then, pray sir, in future, let your regard for your father make you hold your tongue.

Don Ferd. I have done, sir. I shall only add a wish that you would reflect what at our age you would have felt, had you been crossed in your affection for the mother of her you are so severe to.

Don Jer. Why, I must confess I had a great affection for your mother's ducats, but that was all, boy. I married her for her fortune, and she took me in obedience to her father, and a very happy couple we were. We never expected any love from one another, and so we were never disappointed. If we grumbled a little now and then, it was soon over, for we were never fond enough to quarrel; and when the good woman died, why, why,—I had as lieve she had lived, and I wish every widower in Seville could say the same. I shall now go and get the key of this dressing room—so, good son, if you have any lecture in support of disobedience to give your sister, it must be brief; so make the best of your time d'ye hear? [*Exit.*

Don Ferd. I fear, indeed, my friend Anthonio has little to hope for; however, Louisa has firmness, and my father's anger will probably only increase her affection.—In our intercourse with the world, it is natural for us to dislike those who are innocently the cause of our distress; but in the heart's attachment a woman never likes a man with ardour till she has suffered for his sake.—[*Noise.*] So! what bustle is here—between my father and the Duenna too I'll e'en get out of the way. [*Exit.*]

Re-enter DON JEROME *with a letter, pulling in* DUENNA.

Don Jer. I'm astonished! I'm thunderstruck! here's treachery with a vengeance! You, Antonio's creature, and chief manager of this plot for my daughter's eloping!—you, that I placed here as a scarecrow?

Duen. What?

Don Jer. A scarecrow—to prove a decoy-duck! What have you to say for yourself?

Duen. Well Sir, since you have forced that letter from me, and discovered my real sentiments, I scorn to renounce them.—I am Anthonio's Friend—and it was my intention that your Daughter should have served you as all such old tyrannical Sots should be served—I delight in the tender Passions and would befriend all under their influence.

Don Jer. The tender passions! yes, they would become those impenetrable features! Why, thou deceitful hag! I placed thee as a guard to the rich blossoms of my daughter's beauty. I thought that dragon's front of thine would cry aloof to the sons of gallantry: steel traps and spring guns seemed writ in every wrinkle of it.—But you shall quit my house this instant. The tender passions, indeed! go, thou wanton sibyl, thou amorous woman of Endor, go!

Duen. You base, scurrilous, old—but I won't demean myself by naming what you are.—Yes, savage, I'll leave your den; but I suppose you don't mean to detain my apparel—I may have my things, I presume?

Don Jer. I took you, mistress, with your wardrobe on—what have you pilfered, eh?

Duen. Sir, I must take leave of my mistress; she has valuables of mine: besides, my cardinal and veil are in her room.

Don Jer. Your veil, forsooth! what, do you dread being gazed at? or are you afraid of your complexion? Well, go take your leave, and get your veil and cardinal! so! you quit the house within these five minutes.—In—in—quick!—[*Exit* DUENNA.] Here was a precious plot of mischief!—these are the comforts daughters bring us!

AIR.

If a daughter you have, she's the plague of your Life—
No Peace shall you know—tho you've buried your Wife!
At twenty she mocks at the Duty you taught her—
Oh what a plague is an obstinate Daughter!
      Sighing and whining,
      Dying and pining,
Oh, what a plague is an obstinate daughter!

When scarce in their teens they have wit to perplex us,
With letters and lovers for ever they vex us;
While each still rejects the fair suitor you've brought her;
Oh, what a plague is an obstinate daughter!
      Wrangling and jangling,
      Flouting and pouting,
Oh, what a plague is an obstinate daughter!

Reenter DUENNA—*her veil on seeming to cry*—

This way, mistress, this way.—What, I warrant a tender Parting; soh! tears of turpentine down those deal cheeks.—aye you may well hide your head—yes whine till your heart breaks—but I'll not hear one word of excuse—so you are right to be dumb. This way, this way. [*Exeunt.*

Enter DUENNA.

Duen. So—speed you well, sagacious Don Jerome! O rare effects of Passion and Obstinacy! The first will blind him to the cheat—and the second will continue him in his Delusion—now shall I try whether I can't play the fine Lady as well as my mistress—and if I succeed I may be a fine Lady for the rest of my Life—I'll lose no time to equip myself. [*Exit.*

SCENE IV.—*The Court Yard before* DON JEROME'S *House.*

Enter DON JEROME and DUENNA.

He unlocks the Gate.

Don Jer. Come—mistress—there lies your way—the world lies before you, so troop thou antiquated Eve, thou original Sin—hold yonder is some fellow skulking—perhaps it is Anthonio—go to him, d'ye hear, and tell him to make you amends d'ye hear—as he has got you turn'd away, tell him I say it is but just he should take you himself; go—[*Exit* DONNA LOUISA.] Soh! I am rid of *her* thank Heaven! and now I shall be able to keep my Oath—and confine my Daughter with better security! (Reenters the House.)

Scene V.—*The Piazza.*

Enter Donna Clara *and* Maid.

Maid. But where, madam, is it you intend to go?

Don. Clara. Anywhere to avoid the selfish violence of my mother-in-law, and Ferdinand's insolent importunity.

Maid. Indeed, ma'am, since we have profited by Don Ferdinand's key, in making our escape, I think we had best find him, if it were only to thank him.

Don. Clara. No—he has offended me exceedingly. [*Retires.*

Enter Donna Louisa.

Don. Louisa. So I have succeeded in being turned out of doors—but how shall I find Antonio? I dare not inquire for him, for fear of being discovered; I would send to my friend Clara, but then I doubt her prudery would condemn me.

Maid. Then suppose, ma'am, you were to try if your friend Donna Clara would not receive you?

Don. Louisa. No, her notions of filial piety are so severe, she would certainly betray me. Clara is of a cold temper, and would think this step of mine highly forward. Her respect for her father is so great, she would not credit the unkindness of mine.

[Donna Louisa *turns, and sees* Donna Clara *and* Maid.

Don. Louisa. Ha! who are those? sure one is Clara—if it be, I'll trust her. Clara! [*Advances.*

Don. Clara. Louisa! and in masquerade too!

Don. Louisa. You will be more surprised when I tell you, that I have run away from my father.

Don. Clara. Surprised indeed! and I should certainly chide you most horridly, only that I have just run away from mine.

Don. Louisa. My dear Clara! [*Embrace.*

Don. Clara. Dear sister truant! and whither are you going?

Don. Louisa. To find the man I love, to be sure; and, I presume, you would have no aversion to meet with my brother?

Don. Clara. Indeed I should: he has behaved so ill to me, I don't believe I shall ever forgive him.

Air.

When sable night, each drooping plant restoring,
    Wept o'er the flowers her breath did cheer,
As some sad widow o'er her babe deploring,
    Wakes its beauty with a tear;

When all did sleep whose weary hearts did borrow
　　　　One hour from love and care to rest,
　　　Lo! as I press'd my couch in silent sorrow,
　　　My lover caught me to his breast!
　　　　He vow'd he came to save me
　　　　From those who would enslave me!
　　　　　　Then kneeling,
　　　　　　Kisses stealing,
　　　Endless faith he swore;
　　　　But soon I chid him thence,
　　　　For had his fond pretence
　　　　Obtain'd one favour then,
　　　　And he had press'd again,
　　　I fear'd my treacherous heart might grant him more.

Don. Louisa. Well, for all this, I would have sent him to plead his pardon, but that I would not yet awhile have him know of my flight. And where do you hope to find protection?

Don. Clara. The Lady Abbess of the convent of St. Catherine is a relation and kind friend of mine—I shall be secure with her, and you had best go thither with me.

Don. Louisa. No; I am determined to find Antonio first; and, as I live, here comes the very man I will employ to seek him for me.

Don. Clara. Who is he? he's a strange figure.

Don. Louisa. Yes; that sweet creature is the man whom my father has fixed on for my husband.

Don. Clara. And will you speak to him? are you mad?

Don. Louisa. He is the fittest man in the world for my purpose; for, though I was to have married him to-morrow, he is the only man in Seville who, I am sure, never saw me in his life.

Don. Clara. And how do you know him?

Don. Louisa. He arrived but yesterday, and he was shown to me from the window, as he visited my father.

Don. Clara. Well, I'll begone.

Don. Louisa. Hold, my dear Clara—a thought has struck me: will you give me leave to borrow your name, as I see occasion?

Don. Clara. It will but disgrace you; but use it as you please: I dare not stay.—[*Going.*]—But, Louisa, if you should see your brother, be sure you don't inform him that I have taken refuge with the Dame Prior of the convent of St. Catherine, on the left hand side of the piazza which leads to the church of St. Anthony.

Don. Louisa. Ha! ha! ha! I'll be very particular in my directions where he may not find you.—[*Exeunt* DONNA CLARA *and* MAID.
—So! my swain, yonder, has done admiring himself, and draws nearer. [*Retires.*

Enter ISAAC *and* DON CARLOS.

Isaac. [*Looking in a pocket-glass.*] I tell you, friend Carlos, I will please myself in the habit of my chin.

Don Car. But, my dear friend, how can you think to please a lady with such a face?

Isaac. Why, what's the matter with the face! I think it is a very engaging face; and, I am sure, a lady must have very little taste who could dislike my beard.—[*Sees* DONNA LOUISA.]—See now! I'll die if here is not a little damsel struck with it already.

Don. Louisa. Signor, are you disposed to oblige a lady who greatly wants your assistance. [*Unveils.*

Isaac. Egad, a very pretty black-eyed girl! she has certainly taken a fancy to me, Carlos. First, ma'am, I must beg the favour of your name.

Don. Louisa. [*Aside.*] So! it's well I am provided.—[*Aloud.*]—My name, sir, is Donna Clara d'Almanza.

Isaac. What? Don Guzman's daughter? I' faith, I just now heard she was missing.

Don. Louisa. But sure, sir, you have too much gallantry and honour to betray me, whose fault is love?

Isaac. So! a passion for me! poor girl! Why, ma'am, as for betraying you, I don't see how I could get anything by it; so, you may rely on my honour; but as for your love, I am sorry your case is so desperate.

Don. Louisa. Why so, signor?

Isaac. Because I am positively engaged to another—an't I, Carlos?

Don. Louisa. Nay, but hear me.

Isaac. No, no; what should I hear for? It is impossible for me to court you in an honourable way; and for anything else, if I were to comply now, I suppose you have some ungrateful brother, or cousin, who would want to cut my throat for my civility—so, truly, you had best go home again.

Don. Louisa. [*Aside.*] Odious wretch!—[*Aloud.*]—But, good signor, it is Antonio d'Ercilla, on whose account I have eloped.

Isaac. How! what! it is not with me, then, that you are in love?

Don. Louisa. No, indeed, it is not.

Isaac. Then you are a forward, impertinent simpleton! and I shall certainly acquaint your father.

Don. Louisa. Is this your gallantry?

Isaac. Yet hold—Antonio d'Ercilla, did you say? egad, I may make something of this—Antonio d'Ercilla?

Don. Louisa. Yes; and if ever you wish to prosper in love, you will bring me to him.

Isaac. By St. Iago and I will too!—Carlos, this Antonio is one who rivals me (as I have heard) with Louisa—now, if I could hamper him with this girl, I should have the field to myself; hey, Carlos! A lucky thought, isn't it?

Don. Car. Yes, very good—very good!

Isaac. Ah! this little brain is never at a loss—cunning Isaac! cunning rogue! Donna Clara, will you trust yourself awhile to my friend's direction?

Don. Louisa. May I rely on you, good signor?

Don. Car. Lady, it is impossible I should deceive you.

AIR.

Had I a heart for falsehood framed,
　　I ne'er could injure you;
For though your tongue no promise claim'd,
　　Your charms would make me true.
To you no soul shall bear deceit,
　　No stranger offer wrong;
But friends in all the aged you'll meet,
　　And lovers in the young.

But when they learn that you have blest
　　Another with your heart,
They'll bid aspiring passion rest,
　　And act a brother's part:
Then, lady, dread not here deceit,
　　Nor fear to suffer wrong;
For friends in all the aged you'll meet,
　　And brothers in the young.

Isaac. Conduct the lady to my lodgings, Carlos; I must haste to Don Jerome. Perhaps you know Louisa, ma'am. She's divinely handsome, isn't she?

Don. Louisa. You must excuse me not joining with you.

Isaac. Why I have heard it on all hands.

Don. Louisa. Her father is uncommonly partial to her; but I believe you will find she has rather a matronly air.

Isaac. Carlos, this is all envy.—You pretty girls never speak well of one another.—[*To* DON CARLOS.] Hark ye, find out Antonio, and I'll saddle him with this scrape, I warrant. Oh, 'twas the luckiest thought! Donna Clara, your very obedient. Carlos to your post.

DUET.

Isaac . . My mistress expects me, and I must go to her,
　　Or how can I hope for a smile?

Don. Louisa.	Soon may you return a prosperous wooer,
	But think what I suffer the while?
	Alone, and away from the man whom I love,
	In strangers I'm forced to confide.
Isaac . . .	Dear lady, my friend you may trust, and he'll prove
	Your servant, protector, and guide.

AIR.

Don Car. .	Gentle maid, ah! why suspect me?
	Let me serve thee—then reject me.
	Canst thou trust, and I deceive thee?
	Art thou sad, and shall I grieve thee?
	Gentle maid, ah! why suspect me?
	Let me serve thee—then reject me.

TRIO.

Don. Louisa . .	Never mayst thou happy be,
	If in aught thou 'rt false to me.
Isaac.	Never may he happy be,
	If in aught he's false to thee.
Don Car. . . .	Never may I happy be,
	If in aught I'm false to thee.
Don. Louisa . .	Never mayst thou, &c.
Isaac	Never may he, &c.
Don Car. . . .	Never may I, &c. [*Exeunt.*

ACT 2nd.*

Scene 1st.

A Library in Don Jerome's *House*.

Enter Don Jerome and Isaac.

Don Jer. Ha! ha! ha! run away from her Father has she? given him the slip, hey? Ha! ha! poor Don Guzman!

Isaac. Aye and I am to conduct her to Anthonio—by which means you see I shall hamper him so that he can give me no disturbance with your daughter—this is a Trap, isn't it? a nice stroke of cunning —hey?

Don Jer. Excellent! excellent! yes, yes, carry her to him, hamper him by all means, ha! ha! ha! Poor Don Guzman! an old fool!— imposed on by a Girl!

Isaac. Nay they have the cunning of Serpents, that's the truth of it.

Don Jer. Pshaw! they are cunning only when they have fools to deal with.—why don't my Girl play me such a Trick? let her cunning over-reach my caution, I say, hey little Isaac?—

Isaac. True—true—or let me see any of the Sex make a Fool of me—no—no—egad! little Solomon (as my Aunt used to call me) understands tricking a little too well.

Don Jer. Aye, but such a Driveller as Don Guzman!

Isaac. And such a dupe as Anthonio!

Don Jer. True—Sure never were seen such a couple of credulous Simpletons! But come, 'tis time you should see my Daughter—you must carry on the Siege by yourself friend Isaac—

Isaac. Sure, you'll introduce me?

Don Jer. No—I have sworn a solemn Oath not to see or to speak to her till she renounces her Disobedience; win her to that, and she gains a Father and a Husband at once.

Isaac. Gad! I shall never be able to deal with her alone.—nothing keeps me in such awe as perfect Beauty—now there is something consoling and encouraging in Ugliness.

Song.

 Give Isaac the Nymph who no Beauty can boast
 But health and good Humour to make her my Toast;
 If straight I don't mind whether slender or Fat,
 And six Foot or four—I'll ne'er quarrel for that.

* Several sheets of the manuscript from this part onwards are in Mrs. Sheridan's handwriting.

Whate'er her complexion—I vow I don't care
If Brown—it is lasting—more pleasing if fair :
And tho' in her Cheeks I no Dimples should see,
Let her smile—and each Dell is a Dimple to me.

Let her Locks be the reddest that ever were seen,
And her Eyes may be—e'en any Colour but Green;
For in Eyes, th'o so various in lustre and hue,
I swear I 've no choice—only let her have two.

'Tis true I 'd dispense with a Throne on her Back,
And white Teeth, I own, are *genteeler* than black;
A little round Chin too's a Beauty, I 've heard;
But I only desire she mayn't have a Beard.

To one thus accomplish'd I durst speak my Mind
And flattery doubtless would soon make her kind
For the Man who should praise her she needs must adore
Who ne'er in her Life received praises before.

But the frowns of a Beauty in hopes to remove
Should I prate of her Charms and tell of my Love
No thanks wait the praise which she knows to be true
Nor smiles for the Homage she takes as her due.

Don Jer. You will change your Note, my Friend, when you've seen Louisa.

Isaac. Oh, Don Jerome the Honour of your Alliance——

Don Jer. Aye but her Beauty will affect you—she is, tho' I say it, who am her Father, a very prodigy—There you will see Features— with an Eye—like mine—yes, e'faith, there is a kind of wicked sparkling—sometimes of a roguish brightness, that shows her to be my own.

Isaac. Pretty rogue!

Don Jer. Then when she smiles, you'll see a little Dimple in one Cheek only—a Beauty it is certainly—yet you shall not say which is prettiest, the cheek with the Dimple, or the Cheek without.

Isaac. Pretty rogue!

Don Jer. Then the Roses on those Cheeks are shaded with a sort of velvet Down, that gives a Delicacy to the Glow of Health.

Isaac. Pretty rogue!

Don Jer. Her skin pure Dimity—yet more fair being spangled here and there with a golden Freckle.

Isaac. Charming pretty rogue!

Duet.

Don Je. Dominion was given
To Beauty from Heav'n
—Pleasing Bondage to the Mind!—
Will *you* then alone
Its Worship disown?—

Isaac   Never!—could I favour find
            But when for my Pain
            I meet with Disdain
Don Je: Coax her, kiss her, till she's kind.

Come courage Man—you must not be dismay'd if you find Louisa a little haughty at first—

Isaac. Pray how is the Tone of her Voice?

Don Jer. Remarkably pleasing—but if you could prevail on her to sing, you would be enchanted — She is a Nightingale — a Virginia Nightingale—but come—come—her Maid shall conduct you to her antichamber.

Isaac. Well egad I'll pluck up Resolution, and meet her frowns intrepidly.

Don Jer. Aye—woo her briskly—win her—and give me a proof of your address, my little Solomon.

Isaac. But hold—I expect my friend Carlos to call on me here—if he comes, will you send him to me?

Don Jer. I will—I will Lisetta!—Come—she'll show you to the Room—what! do you droop? here's a mournful Face to make Love with!   [*Exeunt.*

Don Jer.   SONG.

              When the Maid whom we love
              No entreaties can move,
              Who'd lead a Life of pining?
              If her charms will excuse
              The fond rashness we use
              —Away with idle whining!

              Never stand like a Fool
              With looks sheepish and cool—
              Such bashful Love is tiezing:
              But with Spirit address
              And your sure of success
              —For honest warmth is pleasing.

              Nay tho' Wedlock's your view
              Like a Rake if you'll woo
              Girls sooner quit their coldness
              They know Beauty inspires
              Less Respect than Desires
              —Hence Love is prov'd by boldness.

              So ne'er stand like a Fool, &c.   [Ex.ᵗ

THE DUENNA.

Scene 2ᵈ :—Louisa's Dressing-Room.

(Maid crosses the Stage and goes to the Door in the back Scene—Enter Isaac.)

Maid. Sir my mistress will wait on you presently.

Isaac. When she's at leisure—don't hurry her.—[Exit Maid.]—I wish I had ever practised a Love Scene—I doubt I shall make a poor Figure here—I could'nt be more afraid if I was going before the Inquisition. Soh! the Door opens—yes—she's coming—the very rustling of her silks has a disdainful sound.

Enter Duenna, *dress'd as* Louisa.

Isaac. Now darn't I look round for the Soul of me—her Beauty will certainly strike me dumb if I do.—I wish she'd speak first.

Duen. Sir, I attend your Pleasure.

Isaac. So—the ice is broke—and a pretty civil beginning too!—Hem—Madam—Miss—Madam—I'm all attention.

Duen. Nay Sir, 'tis I who should listen, and you propose.

Isaac. Egad! this isn't so disdainful neither.—I believe I may venture to look.—No—I dar'n't—one Glance of those roguish sparklers would fix me again.

Duen. You seem thoughtful Sir. Let me persuade you to sit down.

Isaac. So, so; she mollifies apace—she's struck with my Figure—this attitude has had its effect.

Duen. Come Sir—here's a Chair.—

Isaac. Madam—the greatness of your Goodness overpowers me—that a lady so lovely should deign to turn her beauteous Eyes on one so. (She takes his hand, he turns and sees her.)

Duen. You seem surprised at my Condescension.

Isaac. Why yes Ma'am, I am a little surprised at—at—Z—ds! this can never be Louisa!—she's as old as my Mother. (Aside.)

Duen. But former prepossessions give way to my Father's commands.

Isaac. Her Father!—Yes, 'tis she then.—Lord, Lord? how blind Parents are!— (Aside)

Duen. Signor Isaac!

Isaac. Truly the little Damsel was right.—She has rather a Matronly air indeed!—ah! 'tis well my Affections are fixed on her Fortune, and not her Person.

Duen. Signor Isaac won't you sit?   She sits.

Isaac. Pardon me Madam—I have scarce recover'd my astonishment at—your Condescension Madam.—She has the Devil's own Dimples, to be sure! (Aside.)

Duen. Signor Mendoza!

Isaac. Yes Madam.—her Roguish sparklers too! by St. Jago I believe she has but one eye. (Aside.)

Duenn. Nay, you shall stand. (Both sit.)

Duen. I do not wonder Sir that you are surprised at my affability— I own Signor—I was vastly prepossessed against you, and, being tiesed by my Father, I did give some encouragement to Anthonio —but then Sir you were described to me as a quite different Person.

Isaac. Aye—and so you were to me, upon my soul Ma'am—

Duen. But when I saw you I was never more struck in my Life.

Isaac. That was just my case, too, Ma'am—I was struck all of a heap for my part.—

Duen. Well Sir, I see our Misapprehension has been mutual—you expected to find me haughty and averse, and I was taught to believe you a little black, snub-nosed fellow without Person, Manners or address.

Isaac. Egad!—I wish she had answer'd her picture as well!

Duen. But Sir, your air is so noble — something so liberal in your Carriage, with so penetrating an Eye, and so bewitching a Smile!——

Isaac. E'faith, now I look at her again, I don't think she is so ugly!

Duen. So little like a Jew, and so much like a gentleman!

Isaac. Well there certainly *is* something pleasing in the Tone of her Voice.

Duen. You will pardon this breach of Decorum in my praising you thus—but my joy at being so agreeably deceived has given me such a flow of Spirits!

Isaac. O Dear Lady may I thank those sweet Lips for this goodness?—[*Kisses her.*] Why she has a pretty sort of Velvet Down, that's the truth on't. (Aside.)

Duen. O sir you have the most insinuating manner—but indeed you should get rid of that odious Beard—one might as well kiss a Hedge Hog.

Isaac. [*Aside.*] Yes—yes Ma'am, the Razor wouldn't be amiss— for either of us.—[*Aside*]. Pray Madam could you favour me with a Song?

Duen. Willingly Sir.—tho' I'm rather hoarse—ahem!

[*Begins to sing.*]

Isaac. [*Aside.*] Very like a Virginia nightingale!—[*Aloud.*] Ma'am, I perceive you're hoarse—I beg you will not distress——

Duen. O, not in the least Distress! Now sir.

Song.*

When a tender maid
Is first assay'd
By some admiring swain.
    How her blushes rise—if she meets his eyes
While He unfolds his Pain—
If he takes her Hand, she trembles quite!
Touch her lip and she swoons outright!
    While a pit-a-pat, &c.
    Her Heart avows her Fright.

But in time appear Fewer signs of Fear—
The Youth she boldly views:
    If her Hand he grasp—or her Bosom clasp
No mantling blush ensues!
Then to Church well pleased the Lovers move,
While her smiles her Contentment prove;
    And a pit-a-pat, &c.
    Her heart avows her love.

Isaac. Charming, ma'am! enchanting! and, truly, your notes put me in mind of one that's very dear to me—a Lady indeed whom you greatly resemble!

Duen. How—is there then another so dear to you?

Isaac. No, Ma'am, you mistake me——

Duen.† No—no you offer me your hand—then another has your Heart—

Isaac. Oh Lud! no ma'am—'twas my Mother I meant as I hop'd to be saved.

Duen. What—Sir—am I like your Mother?

Isaac. Stay, dear ma'am, I meant that you put me in mind of what my mother was when a Girl!—Yes—yes—ma'am my Mother was formerly a great Beauty I assure you—and when she married my Father about thirty years ago—as you may perhaps remember Ma'am—

Duen. I Sir—I remember thirty years ago?

Isaac. O good lack—no ma'am—thirty years! No—no Ma'am it was thirty months I said—yes—yes Ma'am thirty months ago on her marriage with my Father who was as I was saying a great Beauty—but catching cold the year afterwards in Child Bed of your humble Servant.

Duen. Of *you* Sir—and married within these thirty months?

Isaac. O the Devil I've made myself out but a year old!

Duen. Come, sir, I see you are amazed and confounded at my condescension, and know not what to say.

---

* This song is in the handwriting of Sheridan.

† From " No—no " down to "a year old " the handwriting is Sheridan's.

Isaac. 'Tis very true indeed Ma'am ; but I look on it as a Judgment, for delaying to urge the time when you 'll permit me to compleat my happiness, by acquainting Don Jerome with your Condescension.

Duen. Sir I must frankly own to you that I can never be yours with my Father's Consent.

Isaac. Good lack ! how so ?

Duen. When my Father in his Passion swore he would not see me again till I acquiesced in his will, I also made a vow that I would never take a Husband from his Hand—nothing shall make me break that Oath : but if you have Spirit and Contrivance enough to carry me off without his knowledge, I'm yours.—

Isaac. Humph !—

Duen. Nay Sir if you hesitate——

Isaac. E'faith no bad whim this—If I take her at her word I shall secure her fortune, and avoid making any Settlement in return—thus I shall not only cheat the Lover, but the Father too. Oh cunning rogue, Isaac! aye aye let this little Brain alone ! Egad, I'll take her in the mind !

Duen. Well Sir—what's your Determination ?

Isaac. Madam I was dumb only from Rapture—I applaud your spirit, and joyfully close with your Proposal—for which thus let me on this Lilly Hand express my Gratitude. (Kisses he hand.)

Duen. Well Sir, you must get my Father's Consent to walk with me in the Garden.—but by no means inform him of my kindness to you.

Isaac. No, to be sure—that would spoil all—but trust me—when tricking is the word—let me alone for a piece of Cunning ; this very Day you shall be out of his Power.

Duen. Well—I leave the management of it all to you ; I perceive plainly that you are not one that can be easily outwitted.

Isaac. Egad ! you 're right, ma'am—you are right, e'faith.

Enter MAID.

Maid. Here is a gentleman at the Door—who begs permission to speak with Signor Isaac.

Isaac. O a friend of mine, Madam—and a trusty Friend—let him come in—[*Exit* MAID.] He is one to be depended on, Ma'am.

Enter DON CARLOS.

Isaac. So coz. (Aside to him.)

Don Car. I have left Donna Clara safe at your lodgings, but can nowhere find Don Anthonio.

Isaac. Well—I will search him out myself anon. Carlos, you rogue, I thrive, I prosper !

Don Car. Where is your Mistress?

Isaac. There you Booby there she stands.

Don Car. Why, she's D——d ugly!

Isaac. Hush! [*Stops his mouth.*

Duen. What is your friend saying, Signor?

Isaac. O Ma'am, he is expressing his Raptures at such Charms as he never saw before, hey, Carlos?

Don Car. Aye such as I never saw before indeed!

Duen. You are a very obliging gentleman. Well, Signor Isaac I believe we had better part for the present.—remember our Plan.

Isaac. O, Madam—it is written in my Heart—fixed as the Image of those divine Beauties. Adieu—Idol of my Soul!—yet once more permit me—— [*Kisses her.*

Duen. Sweet—Courteous Sir—adieu!—

Isaac. Your slave eternally! Come Carlos, say something civil at taking leave.

Don Car. E'faith, Isaac—she is the hardest woman to compliment I ever saw—however I'll try something I had studied for the occasion.

SONG.

Ah! sure a Pair was never seen
 So justly form'd to meet by Nature!
The Youth excelling so in mien,
 The Maid in ev'ry grace of Feature.
 O how happy are such Lovers—
 When kindred Beauties each discovers;
  For surely she
  Was made for thee,
 And Thou to bless this lovely Creature!

So mild your looks—your Children thence
 Will early learn the Task of Duty!
The Boys with all their Father's Sense,
 The Girls with all their Mother's Beauty!
 Oh, how Charming to inherit
 At once such Graces and such Spirit!
  Thus while you live
  May Fortune give
 Each Blessing equal to your Merit! [*Exeunt.*

SCENE 3ᵈ.—A Library.

DON JEROME & FERDINAND *discovered.*

Don Jer. Object to Anthonio!—I have said it—his Poverty can you acquit him of that?

Ferd. Sir, I own he is not over rich—but he is of as ancient and as reputable a Family as any in the Kingdom.—

Don Jer. Yes—I know the Beggars are a very ancient Family in most kingdoms—but never in any great repute, Boy.

Ferd. Anthonio Sir, has many amiable qualities.—

Don Jer. But he is poor—can you clear him of that I say?—is he not a gay, dissipated Rake, that has squandered his Patrimony?

Ferd. Sir, he inherited but little—and that, his Generosity, more than his Profuseness has stripped him of—but he has never sullied his Honour, which, with his Title, has outliv'd his Means.

Don Jer. Have they? More shame for them!—What business have Honours or Titles to survive when his Property is extinct? Nobility is but a help-mate to a good Fortune, and like a Japanese Wife should Perish on the funeral Pile of the Estate!—

Fer. Not with us, Sir.—Poverty here, can no more disgrace a Gentleman than Wealth can make one—for my part I think Anthonio's worth more evident since he has lost the advantage of Fortune—it is well known that the costly setting of the Jewel more frequently serves to hide its Flaws than help its Lustre.

Don Jer. Pshaw! you talk like a Blockhead! Nobility without an Estate is as ridiculous as Gold Lace on a Frize Coat.

Ferd. This Language Sir, would better become a Dutch or English trader than a Spaniard.—

Don Jer. Yes—and those Dutch, and English Traders, as you call them, are the wiser People.—Why, Booby,—in England they were formerly as nice as to Birth and Family as we are—but they have long discovered what a wonderful purifier Gold is—and now—no one there regards Pedigree in anything but a Horse.

Fer. True Sir, and the Consequence is, that a Nobleman there is surer of the Breed of his Poney than the Legitimacy of his Heir.

Don Jer. Ferdinand—I insist on it that this subject be dropt once for all. O, here comes Isaac. I hope he has prospered in his suit.

Ferd. Doubtless that agreeable Figure of his must have helped his Cause surprisingly——

Don Jer. How now? [FERDINAND *walks aside.*

Enter ISAAC.

Well my Friend—have you softened her?

Isaac. O yes—I have softened her.

Don Jer. What—does she come to?

Isaac. Why truly she was kinder than I expected to find her.

Don Jer. And the dear pretty little Angel was civil, hey?

Isaac. Yes, the pretty little Angel was very civil.

Don Jer. I'm transported to hear it! Well—and you were astonished at her Beauty hey?

Isaac. I was astonished, indeed!—pray, how old is Miss!

Don Jer. How old? let me see—eight and twelve—She is just twenty.

Isaac. Twenty!

Don Jer. Aye to a month.

Isaac. Then, upon my Soul she is the oldest-looking Girl of her age in Christendom!

Don Jer. Do you think so? But I believe you will not see a prettier girl——

Isaac. Here and there one—

Don Jer. Louisa has the family face.

Isaac. Yes, egad I should have taken it for a family Face, and one that has been in the family some time too. (Half aside.)

Don Jer. She has her Father's Eyes.

Isaac. Truly I should have guessed them to have been so—and if she had her Mother's Spectacles I believe she would not see the worse. (*Aside.*)

Don Jer. Her aunt Ursula's Nose—and her Grandmother's Forehead to a Hair.

Isaac. Aye, faith and her Grandfather's Chin to a hair I think.

(*Aside.*)

Don Jer. Well—if She was but as Dutiful as She's handsome!—and harkee, friend Isaac, she is none of your made-up Beauties—her charms are of the lasting kind.

Isaac. E'faith so they should—for if she be but Twenty now, She may double her age before her years will overtake her Face.

Don Jer. Why Z—ds! Master Isaac, you are not sneering, are you?

Isaac. Why now—seriously Don Jerome, do you think your Daughter handsome?

Don Jer. By this Light She is as handsome a Girl as any in Seville.

Isaac. Then by these Eyes I think her as plain a Woman as ever I beheld.

Don Jer. By St. Jago! you must be blind!

Isaac. No, no; 'tis you are partial.

Don Jer. How! have I neither Sense [n]or Taste?—if a fair Skin—fine eyes—Teeth of Ivory—with a lovely Bloom—and a delicate Shape—if these—with a heavenly Voice and a world of Grace, are not Charms—I know not what you call beautiful.

Isaac. Good lack, with what Eyes a Father sees! as I have Life she is the very reverse of all this—as for the Dimity Skin you told one of, I swear 'tis a thorough Nankeen as ever I saw—for her Eyes—their utmost merit is in not squinting—for her Teeth—where there is one of Ivory, its Neighbour is pure Ebony—black and white alternately, just like the keys of a Harpsichord.—then, as to her singing and heavenly Voice—by this hand—she has a shrill cracked Pipe, that sounds for all the world like a Child's Trumpet.

Don Jer. Why you little Hebrew scoundrel—do you mean to insult me? Out of my house out I say!

Ferd. Dear Sir what's the matter?

Don Jer. Why—this Israelite here has the impudence to say your Sister's ugly.

Ferd. He must be either blind or insolent.

Isaac. So—I find they are all in a Story! egad, I believe I have gone too far—

Ferd. Or sure Sir, there must be some mistake—it can't be my Sister whom he has seen.

Don Jer. 'Sdeath! you are as great a fool as he!—what mistake can there be?—did not I lock up Louisa myself and haven't I the Key in my own Pocket? and didn't her maid show him into the Dressing Room? and yet you talk of a Mistake! No—the Portuguese meant to insult me—and, but that this roof protects him—old as I am—this Sword should do me justice.—

Isaac. I must get off as well as I can—her Fortune is not the less handsome. (*Aside.*)

Duet.

Isaac.	Believe me, good Sir, I ne'er meant to offend;
	My Mistress I love and I value my Friend:
	To win her and wed her is still my request,
	For better for worse—I swear I don't jest.
Don Jer.	Z—ds! you'd best not provoke me—my Rage is so high!
Isaac.	Hold him fast I beseech you his Rage is so high?
	Good Sir, you're too hot and this place I must fly.
Don Jer.	You're a Knave and a Sot, and this place you'd best fly.

Isaac. Don Jerome—come now—yet let us lay aside all joking—and be serious.

Don Jer. Joking!

Isaac. Aye—why sure you did not think I was in earnest?

Don Jer. How!

Isaac. Ha! ha! ha! I'll be hanged if you haven't taken my abuse of your Daughter seriously.

Don Jer. You meant it so didn't you?

Isaac. O mercy! no! a Joke—a Joke—just to try how angry it would make you.

Don Jer. Was that all, efaith? I didn't know you had been such a wag. Ha! ha! ha! By St. Jago! you made me very angry, tho'—well—and you *do* think Louisa handsome?

Isaac. Handsome! Venus de Medicis was a Sibil to her!

Don Jer. Give me your hand you little jocose Rogue!—egad, I thought we had been all off.

Ferd. Soh! I did hope this would have been a Quarrel—but I find the Jew is too cunning.

Don Jer. As I live—that little gust of Passion has made me dry—I am but seldom ruffled. Boy—bring some wine—let us drink the Girl's Health. Poor Louisa! ugly, hey! ha! ha! it was a very good joke indeed.

Isaac. And a very true one for all that. (*Aside.*)

Don Jer. And here Ferdinand—I insist upon your drinking Success to my Friend.

Ferd. Sir—I will drink Success to my Friend with all my heart.

Don Jer. Come—little Solomon—if any sparks of Anger had remain'd this would be the only way to quench them.

TRIO.

A Bumper of good Liquor
Will end a Contest quicker
Than Justice, Judge, or Vicar;
  So fill a chearful Glass,
  And let good humour pass.
But if more deep the Quarrel,
Why, sooner drain the Barrel
Than be the hateful Fellow
That's crabbed when he's Mellow.   [*Exeunt.*

SCENE 4th—ISAAC's Lodgings.

LOUISA alone.*

Louisa. Was ever Truant Daughter so whimsically circumstanced as I am? I have sent my intended husband to look after my Lover—The Man of my father's choice is gone to bring me the Man of my own! but how dispiriting is this interval of Expectation!

* Here the handwriting is Sheridan's and the ink is red.

SONG.

 What Bard—O Time, discover—
  With Wings first made thee move?
 Ah! sure He was some Lover
  Who ne'er had left his Love!
 For who that once did prove
 The Pangs which *absence* brings,
  Tho' but one Day
  He were away.
 Could picture thee with wings?
  What bard, &c.

Enter DON CARLOS.

Lou. So Friend, is Anthonio found?

Don Car. I could not meet with him Lady—but I doubt not Isaac will be here with him presently.

Louisa. O Shame! ye have used no Diligence!—Is this your courtesy to a Lady, who has trusted herself to your Protection?

Don Car. Indeed Ma'am—I have not been remiss.

Louisa. Well, well—but if either of you had known how each Moment of Delay weighs upon the Heart of her who loves, and waits the Object of her Love—o ye would not then have trifled thus!

Don Car. Alas! I know it well—

Louisa. Were you ever in Love then?

Don Car. I was Lady; but while I've Life will never be again.

Louisa. Was your Mistress so cruel?

Don Car. If she had always been so—I should have been happier.

SONG.

 O had my Love ne'er smiled on me,
  I ne'er had known such Anguish;
 But think how false, how cruel she
  To bid me cease to Languish;
 To bid me hope her hand to gain,
  Breathe on a Flame half perish'd;
 And then with cold, and fix'd Disdain,
  To kill the Hope she cherish'd.

 Not worse his fate—who on a Wreck,
  That drove as Winds did blow it,
 Silent had left the shatter'd Deck,
  To find a Grave below it,
 Then Land was cried—no more resign'd,
  He glow'd with joy to hear it;
 Not worse his Fate—his Woe, to find
  The wreck must sink ere near it!

Louisa. As I live—here is your friend coming with Anthonio! I'll retire for a moment to surprise him.   [*Exit.*

Enter ISAAC *and* ANTHONIO.

Anth. Indeed, my Friend Isaac you must be mistaken—Clara de Almanza in love with *me*, and employ you to bring me here to meet her! it is impossible!

Isaac. That you shall see in an instant. Carlos, where is the Lady?—[DON CARLOS *points to the closet.*] In the next Room is she?

Anth. Nay—if that Lady is really here—she certainly wants me to conduct her to a Dear Friend of mine who has long been her Lover.

Isaac. Pshaw! I tell you 'tis no such thing—you are the man she wants, and nobody but you—here's ado indeed to persuade you to take a pretty Girl that's dying for you!

Anth. But I have no affection for this Lady.

Isaac. And you have for Louisa, hey? but take my word for it Anthonio, you have no chance there – so you may as well secure the good that offers itself to you.

Anth. And could you reconcile it to your Conscience to supplant your Friend?

Isaac. Pish! Conscience has no more to do with Gallantry than it has with Politicks. why you are no honest Fellow, if Love can't make a Rogue of you—so come—do go in and speak to her at least.

Anth. Well, I have no objection to that.

Isaac. [*Opens the door.*] There – there she is—yonder by the window —get in do.—[*he pushes him in and half shuts the Door.*) Now Carlos now I shall hamper him, I warrant! stay, I'll peep how they go on. (*looks thro' the Door*) egad—he looks confoundedly posed.—now She's coaxing him. See Carlos—he begins to come to—aye, aye, he'll soon forget his Conscience!

Car. Look—now they are both laughing—

Isaac. Aye—so they are—both laughing—yes, yes, they are laughing at that dear Friend he talked of—aye, poor Devil they've outwitted him.

Don Car. Now he's kissing her hand.

Isaac. Yes!—yes! faith they're agreed—he's caught, he's entangled! My dear Carlos—we have brought it about! Oh, this little cunning Head! I'm a Machiavel!—a very Machiavel!

Don Car. I hear somebody inquiring for you—I'll see who it is.

[*Exit.*

Enter ANTH. *and* DONNA LOU.

Anth. Well—my good Friend—this Lady has so entirely convinced me of the certainty of your success at Don Jerome's—that I now resign my pretensions there.

Isaac. You never did a wiser thing, believe me—and as for deceiving your friend—that's nothing at all. Tricking is all fair in Love, isn't it Ma'am?

Louisa. Certainly Sir,—and I am particularly glad to find you are of that opinion.

Isaac. O Lud! yes, Ma'am—let any one outwit me that can, I say—but here—let me join your hands.—There, you lucky Rogue I wish you happily married from the bottom of my Soul!

Louisa. And I am sure if you wish it—no one else should prevent it.

Isaac. Now, Anthonio—we are rivals no more, so let us be Friends—will you?

Anth. With all my heart Isaac.

Isaac. It isn't every Man let me tell you would have taken such pains, or been so generous to a Rival.

Anth. No faith—I don't believe there's another beside yourself in Spain.

Isaac. Well—but you resign all pretensions to the other Lady?

Anth. That I do most sincerely.

Isaac. I doubt you have a little hankering there still.

Anth. None in the least upon my Soul.

Isaac. I mean after her Fortune.

Anth. No—believe me you are heartily welcome to every thing she has.

Isaac. Well—efaith, you have the best of the Bargain as to beauty, twenty to one—but now I'll tell you a Secret—I am to carry off Louisa this very Evening.

Louisa. Indeed!

Isaac. Yes, she has sworn not to take a Husband from her Father's hand—so I've persuaded him to trust her to walk with me in the Garden and then we shall give him the Slip.

Louisa. And is Don Jerome to know nothing of this?

Isaac. O Lud, no! there lies the jest—don't you see that, by this step, I over-reach him—and shall be entitled to the girl's fortune, without settling a Ducat on her. Ha! ha! I'm a cunning Dog, an't I? a sly little villain? hey?

Anth. Ha! ha! you are indeed!

Isaac. Roguish, you'll say, but keen, hey? devilish keen.

Anth. So you are indeed—keen, very keen.

Isaac. And what a laugh we shall have at Don Jerome's when the truth comes out—hey?

Louisa. Yes—yes I'll answer for't, we shall have a good Laugh, when the truth comes out. Ha! ha!

Enter Don Carlos.

Don Car. Here are the dancers come to practice the fandango you intended to have honoured Donna Louisa with.

Isaac. O I shan't want them—but, as I must pay 'em, I'll see a Caper for my Money. Will you excuse me?

Louisa. Willingly.

Isaac. Here's my Friend — whom you may command for any Services—Madam—your most obedient—Anthonio, I wish you all happiness—O the easy Blockhead! what a Fool I have made of him! —This was a masterpiece! [*Exit.*

Louisa. Carlos, will you be my Guard again, and conduct me to the convent of St. Catharine?

Anth. Why, Louisa—why should you go thither?

Louisa. I have my Reasons—and you must not be seen to go with me—I shall write from thence to my Father—perhaps, when he finds what he has driven me to, he may relent.

Anth. I have no hope from him. O Louisa in these Arms should be your Sanctuary.

Louisa. Be patient but for a little while—my Father cannot force me thence—but let me see you there before Evening, and I will explain myself.

Anth. I shall obey.

Louisa. Come Friend. Anthonio, Carlos has been a lover himself.

Anth. Then he knows the value of his trust.

Car. You shall not find me unfaithful.

Trio.

> Soft pity never leaves the gentle breast
> Where Love has been receiv'd a welcome Guest;
> As wandering Saints poor Huts have sacred made,
> He hallows every Heart he once has sway'd,
> And when obliged to quit the kind Abode
> Still leaves a Relick that bespeaks the God. [*Exeunt.*

End of Act 2ᵈ

ACT III.*

Scene I.—*A Library in* Don Jerome's *House.*

Enter Don Jerome *and* Servant.

Don Jer. Why, I never was so amazed in my life! Louisa gone off with Isaac Mendoza! What! steal away with the very man whom I wanted her to marry—elope with her own husband, as it were—it is impossible!

Ser. Her maid says, sir, they had your leave to walk in the garden, while you were abroad. The door by the shrubbery was found open, and they have not been heard of since. [*Exit.*

Don Jer. Well, it is the most unaccountable affair! 'sdeath! there is certainly some infernal mystery in it I can't comprehend!

Enter Second Servant, *with a letter.*

Ser. Here is a letter, sir, from Signor Isaac. [*Exit.*

Don Jer. So, so, this will explain—ay, Isaac Mendoza—let me see—— [*Reads.*

"Dearest Sir,

You must, doubtless, be much surprised at my flight with your daughter!—yes, 'faith, and well I may—I had the happiness to gain her heart at our first interview—The devil you had!—But, she having unfortunately made a vow not to receive a husband from your hands, I was obliged to comply with her whim!—So, so!—We shall shortly throw ourselves at your feet, and I hope you will have a blessing ready for one, who will then be your son-in-law. Isaac Mendoza."

A whim, hey? Why, the devil's in the girl, I think! This morning, she would die sooner than have him, and before evening she runs away with him! Well, well, my will's accomplished—let the motive be what it will—and the Portuguese, sure, will never deny to fulfil the rest of the article.

Re-enter Servant, *with another letter.*

Ser. Sir, here's a man below, who says he brought this from my young lady, Donna Louisa. [*Exit.*

Don Jer. How! yes, it's my daughter's hand, indeed! Lord, there was no occasion for them both to write; well, let's see what she says—— [*Reads.*

---

* Several sheets of the manuscript are missing from the beginning of this Act to the duet at the end of scene vi.

My dearest father,

How shall I entreat your pardon for the rash step I have taken—how confess the motive?—Pish! hasn't Isaac just told me the motive?—one would think they weren't together when they wrote.—*If I have a spirit too resentful of ill usage, I have also a heart as easily affected by kindness.*—So, so, here the whole matter comes out; her resentment for Antonio's ill usage has made her sensible of Isaac's kindness—yes, yes, it is all plain enough. Well. *I am not married yet, though with a man who, I am convinced, adores me.*—Yes, yes, I dare say Isaac is very fond of her. *But I shall anxiously expect your answer, in which, should I be so fortunate as to receive your consent, you will make completely happy your ever affectionate daughter,* LOUISA.

My consent! to be sure she shall have it! Egad, I was never better pleased—I have fulfilled my resolution—I knew I should. Oh, there's nothing like obstinacy! Lewis! [*Calls.*

Re-enter SERVANT.

Let the man who brought the last letter, wait; and get me a pen and ink below.—[*Exit* SERVANT.] I am impatient to set poor Louisa's heart at rest. Holloa! Lewis! Sancho! [*Calls.*

Enter SERVANTS.

See that there be a noble supper provided in the saloon to-night; serve up my best wines, and let me have music, d' ye hear?

Ser. Yes, sir.

Don Jer. And order all my doors to be thrown open; admit all guests, with masks or without masks.—[*Exeunt* SERVANTS.] I' faith, we'll have a night of it! and I'll let them see how merry an old man can be.

SONG.

Oh, the days when I was young,
  When I laugh'd in fortune's spite;
Talk'd of love the whole day long,
  And with nectar crown'd the night!
Then it was, old Father Care,
  Little reck'd I of thy frown;
Half thy malice youth could bear,
  And the rest a bumper drown.

Truth, they say, lies in a well,
  Why, I vow I ne'er could see;
Let the water-drinkers tell,
  There it always lay for me.
For when sparkling wine went round,
  Never saw I falsehood's mask;
But still honest truth I found
  In the bottom of each flask.

> True, at length my vigour's flown,
>   I have years to bring decay;
> Few the locks that now I own,
>   And the few I have are grey.
> Yet, old Jerome, thou mayst boast,
>   While thy spirits do not tire;
> Still beneath thy age's frost
>   Glows a spark of youthful fire. *Exit.*

SCENE II.—*The New Piazza.*

Enter DON FERDINAND *and* LOPEZ.

Don Ferd. What, could you gather no tidings of her? nor guess where she was gone? O Clara! Clara!

Lop. In truth, sir, I could not. That she was run away from her father, was in everybody's mouth; and that Don Guzman was in pursuit of her, was also a very common report. Where she was gone, or what was become of her, no one could take upon them to say.

Don Ferd. 'Sdeath and fury, you blockhead! she can't be out of Seville.

Lop. So I said to myself, sir. 'Sdeath and fury, you blockhead, says I, she can't be out of Seville. Then some said, she had hanged herself for love; and others have it, Don Antonio had carried her off.

Don Ferd. 'Tis, false, scoundrel! no one said that.

Lop. Then I misunderstood them, sir.

Don Ferd. Go, fool, get home! and never let me see you again till you bring me news of her.—[*Exit* LOPEZ.] Oh, how my fondness for this ungrateful girl has hurt my disposition.

Enter ISAAC.

Isaac. So, I have her safe, and have only to find a priest to marry us. Antonio now may marry Clara, or not, if he pleases.

Don Ferd. What! what was that you said of Clara?

Isaac. Oh, Ferdinand! my brother-in-law that shall be, who thought of meeting you?

Don Ferd. But what of Clara?

Isaac. I' faith, you shall hear. This morning, as I was coming down, I met a pretty damsel, who told me her name was Clara d'Almanza, and begged my protection.

Don Ferd. How!

Isaac. She said she had eloped from her father, Don Guzman, but that love for a young gentleman in Seville was the cause.

Don Ferd. Oh, Heavens! did she confess it?

Isaac. Oh, yes, she confessed at once. But then, says she, my lover is not informed of my flight, nor suspects my intention.

Don Ferd. [*Aside.*] Dear creature! no more I did indeed! Oh, I am the happiest fellow!—[*Aloud.*] Well, Isaac?

Isaac. Why then she entreated me to find him out for her, and bring him to her.

Don Ferd. Good Heavens, how lucky! Well, come along, let's lose no time. [*Pulling him.*

Isaac. Zooks! where are we to go?

Don Ferd. Why, did anything more pass?

Isaac. Anything more! yes; the end on't was, that I was moved with her speeches, and complied with her desires.

Don Ferd. Well, and where is she?

Isaac. Where is she? why, don't I tell you? I complied with her request, and left her safe in the arms of her lover.

Don Ferd. 'Sdeath, you trifle with me!—I have never seen her.

Isaac. You! O Lud, no! how the devil should you? 'Twas Antonio she wanted; and with Antonio I left her.

Don Ferd. [*Aside.*] Hell and madness!—[*Aloud.*] What, Antonio d'Ercilla?

Isaac. Ay, ay, the very man; and the best part of it was, he was shy of taking her at first. He talked a good deal about honour, and conscience, and deceiving some dear friend; but, Lord, we soon overruled that!

Don Ferd. You did!

Isaac. Oh, yes, presently.—Such deceit! says he.—Pish! says the lady, tricking is all fair in love. But then, my friend, says he.—Psha! damn your friend, says I. So, poor wretch, he has no chance. —No, no; he may hang himself as soon as he pleases.

Don Ferd. I must go, or I shall betray myself. [*Aside.*

Isaac. But stay, Ferdinand, you han't heard the best of the joke.

Don Ferd. Curse on your joke!

Isaac. Good lack! what's the matter now? I thought to have diverted you.

Don Ferd. Be racked! tortured! damned!

Isaac. Why, sure you are not the poor devil of a lover, are you?— I' faith, as sure as can be, he is! This is a better joke than t'other. Ha! ha! ha!

Don Ferd. What! do you laugh? you vile, mischievous varlet!— [*Collars him.*] But that you're beneath my anger, I'd tear your heart out. [*Throws him from him.*

Isaac. O mercy! here's usage for a brother-in-law!

Don Ferd. But, hark ye, rascal ! tell me directly where these false friends are gone, or, by my soul—— [*Draws.*

Isaac. For Heaven's sake, now, my dear brother-in-law, don't be in a rage ! I'll recollect as well as I can.

Don Ferd. Be quick, then !

Isaac. I will, I will !—but people's memories differ ; some have a treacherous memory : now mine is a cowardly memory—it takes to its heels at sight of a drawn sword—it does i' faith ; and I could as soon fight as recollect.

Don Ferd. Zounds ! tell me the truth, and I won't hurt you.

Isaac. No, no, I know you won't, my dear brother-in-law ; but that ill-looking thing there——

Don Ferd. What, then you won't tell me ?

Isaac. Yes, yes, I will ; I'll tell you all, upon my soul !—but why need you listen, sword in hand ?

Don Ferd. Why, there.—[*Puts up.*] Now.

Isaac. Why, then, I believe they are gone to—that is, my friend Carlos told me, he had left Donna Clara—dear Ferdinand, keep your hands off—at the convent of St. Catharine.

Don Ferd. St. Catharine !

Isaac. Yes ; and that Antonio was to come to her there.

Don Ferd. Is this the truth ?

Isaac. It is indeed ; and all I know, as I hope for life !

Don Ferd. Well, coward, take your life ; 'tis that false, dishonourable Antonio, who shall feel my vengeance.

Isaac. Ay, ay, kill him ; cut his throat, and welcome.

Don Ferd. But, for Clara ! infamy on her ! she is not worth my resentment.

Isaac. No more she is, my dear brother-in-law. I' faith, I would not be angry about her ; she is not worth it, indeed.

Don Ferd. 'Tis false ! she is worth the enmity of princes !

Isaac. True, true, so she is ; and I pity you exceedingly for having lost her.

Don Ferd. 'Sdeath, you rascal ! how durst you talk of pitying me ?

Isaac. Oh, dear brother-in-law, I beg pardon ! I don't pity you in the least, upon my soul !

Don Ferd. Get hence, fool, and provoke me no further ; nothing but your insignificance saves you !

Isaac. [*Aside.*] I'faith, then, my insignificance is the best friend I have.—[*Aloud.*] I'm going, dear Ferdinand.—[*Aside.*] What a curst hot hot-headed bully it is ! [*Exeunt severally.*

SCENE III.—*The Garden of the Convent.*

Enter DONNA LOUISA *and* DONNA CLARA.

Don. Louisa. And you really wish my brother may not find you out?

Don. Clara. Why else have I concealed myself under this disguise?

Don. Louisa. Why, perhaps, because the dress becomes you: for you certainly don't intend to be a nun for life.

Don. Clara. If, indeed, Ferdinand had not offended me so last night——

Don Louisa. Come, come, it was his fear of losing you made him so rash.

Don. Clara. Well, you may think me cruel, but I swear, if he were here this instant, I believe I should forgive him.

SONG.

By him we love offended,
　How soon our anger flies!
One day apart, 'tis ended;
　Behold him, and it dies.
Last night, your roving brother,
　Enraged, I bade depart;
And sure his rude presumption
　Deserved to lose my heart.
Yet, were he now before me,
　In spite of injured pride,
I fear my eyes would pardon
　Before my tongue could chide.

Don. Louisa. I protest, Clara, I shall begin to think you are seriously resolved to enter on your probation.

Don. Clara. And, seriously, I very much doubt whether the character of a nun would not become me best.

Don. Louisa. Why, to be sure, the character of a nun is a very becoming one at a masquerade: but no pretty woman, in her senses, ever thought of taking the veil for above a night.

Don. Clara. Yonder I see your Antonio is returned—I shall only interrupt you; ah, Louisa, with what happy eagerness you turn to look for him! [*Exit.*

Enter DON ANTHONIO.

Don Ant. Well, my Louisa, any news since I left you?

Don. Louisa. None. The messenger is not yet returned from my father.

Don Ant. Well, I confess, I do not perceive what we are to expect from him.

Don. Louisa. I shall be easier, however, in having made the trial: I do not doubt your sincerity, Antonio; but there is a chilling air around poverty, that often kills affection, that was not nursed in it. If we would make love our household god, we had best secure him a comfortable roof.

SONG.—*Don Antonio.*

How oft, Louisa, hast thou told,
 (Nor wilt thou the fond boast disown,)
Thou wouldst not lose Antonio's love
 To reign the partner of a throne !
And by those lips that spoke so kind,
 And by that hand I 've press'd to mine,
To be the lord of wealth and power,
 By heavens, I would not part with thine !
Then how, my soul, can we be poor,
 Who own what kingdoms could not buy ?
Of this true heart thou shalt be queen,
 In serving thee, a monarch I.
Thus uncontroll'd, in mutual bliss,
 I rich in love's exhaustless mine,
Do thou snatch treasures from my lips,
 And I 'll take kingdoms back from thine !

Enter MAID *with a letter.*

Don. Louisa. My father's answer, I suppose.

Don Ant. My dearest Louisa, you may be assured that it contains nothing but threats and reproaches.

Don. Louisa. Let us see, however.—[Reads]. *Dearest daughter, make your lover happy: you have my full consent to marry as your whim has chosen, but be sure come home and sup with your affectionate father.*

Don Ant. You jest, Louisa !

Don. Louisa. [*Gives him the letter.*] Read ! read !

Don Ant. 'Tis so, by heavens ! Sure there must be some mistake; but that's none of our business.——Now, Louisa, you have no excuse for delay.

Don. Louisa. Shall we not then return and thank my father ?

Don Ant. But first let the priest put it out of his power to recall his word.—I 'll fly to procure one.

Don. Louisa. Nay, if you part with me again, perhaps you may lose me.

Don Ant. Come, then—there is a friar of a neighbouring convent is my friend ; you have already been diverted by the manners of a nunnery ; let us see whether there is less hypocrisy among the holy fathers.

Don. Louisa. I 'm afraid not, Antonio—for in religion, as in friendship, they who profess most are the least sincere.   [*Exeunt.*

Re-enter DONNA CLARA.

Don. Clara. So, yonder they go, as happy as a mutual and confessed affection can make them, while I am left in solitude. Heigho! love may perhaps excuse the rashness of an elopement from one's friend, but I am sure nothing but the presence of the man we love can support it. Ha! what do I see! Ferdinand, as I live! How could he gain admission? By potent gold, I suppose, as Anthonio did. How eager and disturbed he seems! He shall not know me as yet.

[*Lets down her veil.*

Enter DON FERDINAND.

Don Ferd. Yes, those were certainly they—my information was right. [*Going.*

Don. Clara. [*Stops him.*] Pray, signor, what is your business here?

Don Ferd. No matter—no matter! Oh! they stop.—[*Looks out.*]
Yes, that is the perfidious Clara indeed!

Don. Clara. So, a jealous error—I'm glad to see him so moved.

[*Aside.*

Don Ferd. Her disguise can't conceal her—no, no, I know her too well.

Don. Clara. [*Aside.*] Wonderful discernment!—[*Aloud.*] But, signor——

Don Ferd. Be quiet, good nun; don't tease me!—By heavens, she leans upon his arm, hangs fondly on it! O woman, woman!

Don. Clara. But, signor, who is it you want?

Don Ferd. Not you, not you, so prythee don't tease me. Yet pray stay—gentle nun, was it not Donna Clara d'Almanza just parted from you?

Don. Clara. Clara d'Almanza, signor, is not yet out of the garden.

Don Ferd. Ay, ay, I knew I was right! And pray is not that gentleman, now at the porch with her, Antonio d'Ercilla?

Don. Clara. It is indeed, signor.

Don Ferd. So, so; but now one question more—can you inform me for what purpose they have gone away?

Don. Clara. They are gone to be married, I believe.

Don Ferd. Very well—enough. Now if I don't mar their wedding!

[*Exit.*

Don Clara. [*Unveils.*] I thought jealousy had made lovers quick-sighted, but it has made mine blind. Louisa's story accounts to me for this error, and I am glad to find I have power enough over him to make him so unhappy. But why should not I be present at his surprise when undeceived? When he's through the porch, I'll follow him; and, perhaps, Louisa shall not singly be a bride.

Song.

Adieu, thou dreary pile, where never dies
The sullen echo of repentant sighs!
Ye sister mourners of each lonely cell
Inured to hymns and sorrow, fare ye well!
For happier scenes I fly this darksome grove,
To saints a prison, but a tomb to love! [*Exit.*

SCENE IV.—*A Court before the Priory.*

Enter ISAAC, *crossing the stage,* DON ANTONIO *following.*

Don Ant. What, my friend Isaac!

Isaac. What, Antonio! wish me joy! I have Louisa safe.

Don Ant. Have you? I wish you joy with all my soul.

Isaac. Yes, I come here to procure a priest to marry us.

Don Ant. So, then, we are both on the same errand; I am come to look for Father Paul.

Isaac. Ha! I'm glad on't—but, i' faith, he must tack me; first my love is waiting.

Don Ant. So is mine—I left her in the porch.

Isaac. Ay, but I'm in haste to go back to Don Jerome.

Don Ant. And so am I too.

Isaac. Well, perhaps he'll save time, and marry us both together—or I'll be your father, and you shall be mine. Come along—but you are obliged to me for all this.

Don Ant. Yes, yes. [*Exeunt.*

SCENE V.—*A Room in the Priory.*

FATHER PAUL, FATHER FRANCIS, FATHER AUGUSTINE, *and other* FRIARS, *discovered at a table drinking.*

GLEE AND CHORUS.

This bottle's the sun of our table,
His beams are rosy wine:
We, planets, that are not able
Without his help to shine.

Let mirth and glee abound!
You'll soon grow bright
With borrow'd light,
And shine as he goes round.

Paul. Brother Francis, toss the bottle about, and give me your toast.

Fran. Have we drunk the Abbess of St. Ursuline?

Paul. Yes, yes; she was the last.

Fran. Then I'll give you the blue-eyed nun of St. Catherine's.

Paul. With all my heart.—[*Drinks.*] Pray, brother Augustine, were there any benefactions left in my absence?

Aug. Don Juan Corduba has left a hundred ducats, to remember him in our masses.

Paul. Has he? let them be paid to our wine merchant, and we'll remember him in our cups, which will do just as well. Anything more?

Aug. Yes; Baptista, the rich miser, who died last week, has bequeathed us a thousand pistoles, and the silver lamp he used in his own chamber, to burn before the image of St. Anthony.

Paul. 'Twas well meant, but we'll employ his money better—Baptista's bounty shall light the living, not the dead. St. Anthony is not afraid to be left in the dark, though he was.—[*Knocking.*] See who's there. [FATHER FRANCIS *goes to the door and opens it.*

Enter PORTER.

Port. Here's one without, in pressing haste to speak with Father Paul.

Fran. Brother Paul!

[FATHER PAUL *comes from behind a curtain, with a glass of wine, and in his hand a piece of cake.*

Paul. Here! how durst you, fellow, thus abruptly break in upon our devotions?

Port. I thought they were finished.

Paul. No, they were not—were they, brother Francis?

Fran. Not by a bottle each.

Paul. But neither you nor your fellows mark how the hours go; no, you mind nothing but the gratifying of your appetites; ye eat, and swill, and sleep, and gourmandise, and thrive, while we are wasting in mortification.

Port. We ask no more than nature craves.

Paul. 'Tis false, ye have more appetites than hairs! and your flushed, sleek, and pampered appearance is the disgrace of our order—out on't! If you are hungry, can't you be content with the wholesome roots of the earth? and if you are dry, isn't there the crystal spring?—[*Drinks.*] Put this away.—[*Gives the glass*] and show me where I'm wanted.—[PORTER *drains the glass.*—PAUL, *going, turns.*] So you would have drunk it if there had been any left! Ah, glutton! glutton! [*Exeunt.*

THE DUENNA.

Scene VI.—*The Court before the Priory.*

Enter Isaac *and* Don Antonio.

Isaac. A plaguey while coming, this same father Paul.—He's detained at vespers, I suppose, poor fellow.

Don Ant. No, here he comes.

Enter Father Paul.

Good father Paul, I crave your blessing.

Isaac. Yes, good father Paul, we are come to beg a favour.

Paul. What is it, pray?

Isaac. To marry us, good father Paul; and in truth thou dost look like the priest of Hymen.

Paul. In short, I may be called so; for I deal in repentance and mortification.

Isaac. No, no, thou seemest an officer of Hymen, because thy presence speaks content and good humour.

Paul. Alas, my appearance is deceitful. Bloated I am, indeed! for fasting is a windy recreation, and it hath swollen me like a bladder.

Don Ant. But thou hast a good fresh colour in thy face, father; rosy, i' faith!

Paul. Yes, I have blushed for mankind, till the hue of my shame is as fixed as their vices.

Isaac. Good man!

Paul. And I have laboured, too, but to what purpose? they continue to sin under my very nose.

Isaac. Efecks, father, I should have guessed as much, for your nose seems to be put to the blush more than any other part of your face.

Paul. Go, you're a wag.

Don Ant. But to the purpose, father—will you officiate for us?

Paul. To join young people thus clandestinely is not safe: and, indeed, I have in my heart many weighty reasons against it.

Don Ant. And I have in my hand many weighty reasons for it. Isaac, haven't you an argument or two in our favour about you?

Isaac. Yes, yes; here is a most unanswerable purse.

Paul. For shame! you make me angry: you forget who I am, and when importunate people have forced their trash—ay, into this pocket here—or into this—why, then the sin was theirs.—[*They put money into his pockets.*] Fie, now how you distress me! I would return it, but that I must touch it that way, and so wrong my oath.

Don Ant. Now, then come with us.

Isaac. Ay, now give us our title to joy and rapture.

Paul. Well, when your hour of repentance comes, don't blame me.

Don Ant. [*Aside.*] No bad caution to my friend Isaac.—[*Aloud.*] Well, well, father, do you do your part, and I'll abide the consequence.

Isaac. Ay, and so will I.

Enter DONNA LOUISA, *running.*

Don. Louisa. O Antonio, Ferdinand is at the porch, and inquiring for us.

Isaac. Who? Don Ferdinand! he's not inquiring for me, I hope.

Don Ant. Fear not, my love; I'll soon pacify him.

Isaac. Egad, you won't. Antonio, take my advice, and run away; this Ferdinand is the most unmerciful dog, and has the cursedest long sword! and, upon my soul, he comes on purpose to cut your throat.

Don Ant. Never fear, never fear.

Isaac. Well, you may stay if you will; but I'll get some one to marry me: for by St. Iago, he shall never meet me again, while I am master of a pair of heels.

[*Runs out.*—DONNA LOUISA *lets down her veil.*

Enter DON FERDINAND.

Don Ferd. So, sir, I have met with you at last.

Don Ant. Well, sir.

Don Ferd. Base, treacherous man! whence can a false, deceitful soul, like yours, borrow confidence, to look so steadily on the man you've injured!

Don Ant. Ferdinand, you are too warm: 'tis true you find me on the point of wedding one I loved beyond my life; but no argument of mine prevailed on her to elope.—I scorn deceit, as much as you. By heaven I knew not that she had left her father's till I saw her!

Don Ferd. What a mean excuse! You have wronged your friend, then, for one, whose wanton forwardness anticipated your treachery— of this, indeed, your Jew pander informed me; but let your conduct be consistent, and since you have dared to do a wrong, follow me, and show you have a spirit to avow it.

Don. Louisa. Antonio, I perceive his mistake—leave him to me.

Paul. Friend, you are rude, to interrupt the union of two willing hearts.

Don Ferd. No, meddling priest! the hand he seeks is mine.

Paul. If so, I'll proceed no further. Lady, did you ever promise this youth your hand? [*To* DONNA LOUISA, *who shakes her head.*

Don Ferd. Clara, I thank you for your silence—I would not have heard your tongue avow such falsity; be't your punishment to remember I have not reproached you.

Enter DONNA CLARA, *veiled.*

Don. Clara. What mockery is this?

Don Ferd. Antonio, you are protected now, but we shall meet.

[*Going,* DONNA CLARA *holds one arm, and* DONNA LOUISA *the other.*]

DUET.

Don. Louisa. Turn thee round, I pray thee,
    Calm awhile thy rage.
Don. Clara. I must help to stay thee,
    And thy wrath assuage.
Don. Louisa. Couldst thou not discover
    One so dear to thee?
Don. Clara. Canst thou be a lover,
    And thus fly from me?   [*Both unveil.*

Ferd. How's this? My Sister? Clara too—I'm confounded.

Louisa. 'Tis even so good brother.

Ferd. How! what—Impiety—did the man want to marry his own sister?

Louisa. And an't you ashamed of yourself to have come hither and behaved so rashly.

Clara. And arn't you ashamed of your own sagacity—

Louisa. Not to know your own sister—

Clara. And to turn away your own Mistress—

Louisa. Don't you see when jealousy blinds People?

Clara. Aye, and will you ever be jealous again?

Ferd. Never—never!—You—Sister I know will forgive me—but how, Clara, shall I presume——

Don. Clara. No, no; just now you told me not to tieze you—"Who do you want, good signor?" "Not you, not you!" Oh you blind wretch! but swear never to be jealous again and I'll forgive you.

Ferd. By all——

Clara. There that will do—you'll keep the oath just as well.
                                  [*Gives her Hand.*

Louisa. But Brother—Here is one whom some apology is due to.

Ferd. Anthonio, I am ashamed to think——

Anth. Not a word of excuse—Ferdinand—I have not been in Love myself without learning that a Lover's Anger should never be resented—but come let us retire, with this good Father, and we'll explain to you the cause of your error.

GLEE AND CHORUS.

Oft does Hymen smile to hear
    Wordy vows of feign'd regard;
Well he knows when they're sincere,
    Never slow to give reward:
For his glory is to prove
Kind to those who wed for love.   [*Exeunt.*

SCENE VII.—*A Grand Saloon in* DON JEROME'S *House.*

Enter DON JEROME, LOPEZ, *and* SERVANTS.

Don Jer. Be sure, now, let everything be in the best order—let all my servants have on their merriest faces: but tell them to get as little drunk as possible, till after supper.—[*Exeunt* SERVANTS] So, Lopez, where's your master? shan't we have him at supper?

Lop. Indeed, I believe not, sir—he's mad, I doubt! I'm sure he has frighted me from him.

Don Jer. Ay, ay, he's after some wench, I suppose: a young rake! Well, well, we'll be merry without him. [*Exit* LOPEZ.

Enter a SERVANT.

Ser. Sir, here is Signor Isaac. [*Exit.*

Enter ISAAC.

Don Jer. So, my dear son-in-law—there, take my blessing and forgiveness. But where's my daughter? where's Louisa?

Isaac. She's without, impatient for a blessing, but almost afraid to enter.

Don Jer. Oh, fly and bring her in.—[*Exit* ISAAC.] Poor girl, I long to see her pretty face.

Isaac. [*Without.*] Come, my charmer! my trembling angel!

Re-enter ISAAC *with* DUENNA; DON JEROME *runs to meet them; she kneels.*

Don Jer. Come to my arms, my—[*Starts back.*] Why, who the devil have we here?

Isaac. Nay, Don Jerome, you promised her forgiveness; see how the dear creature droops!

Don Jer. Droops indeed! Why, Gad take me, this is old Margaret! But where's my daughter? where's Louisa?

Isaac. Why, here, before your eyes—nay, don't be abashed, my sweet wife!

Don Jer. Wife with a vengeance! Why, zounds! you have not married the Duenna!

Duen. [*Kneeling.*] Oh, dear papa! you'll not disown me, sure!

Don Jer. Papa! papa! Why, zounds! your impudence is as great as your ugliness!

Isaac. Rise, my charmer, go throw your snowy arms about his neck, and convince him you are——

Duen. Oh, sir, forgive me! [*Embraces him.*

Don Jer. Help! murder!

Enter SERVANTS.

Ser. What's the matter, sir?

Don Jer. Why, here, this damned Jew has brought an old harridan to strangle me.

Isaac. Lord, it is his own daughter, and he is so hard-hearted he won't forgive her!

Enter DON ANTONIO *and* DUENNA LOUISA; *they kneel.*

Don Jer. Zounds and fury! what's here now? who sent for you, sir, and who the devil are you?

Don Ant. This lady's husband, sir.

Isaac. Ay, that he is, I'll be sworn; for I left them with a priest, and was to have given her away.

Don Jer. You were?

Isaac. Ay; that's my honest friend, Antonio; and that's the little girl I told you I had hampered him with.

Don Jer. Why, you are either drunk or mad—this is my daughter.

Isaac. No, no; 'tis you are both drunk and mad, I think—here's your daughter.

Don Jer. Hark ye, old iniquity! will you explain all this, or not?

Duen. Come then, Don Jerome, I will—though our habits might inform you all. Look on your daughter, there, and on me.

Isaac. What's this I hear?

Duen. The truth is, that in your passion this morning you made a small mistake; for you turned your daughter out of doors, and locked up your humble servant.

Isaac. O Lud! O Lud! here's a pretty fellow, to turn his daughter out of doors, instead of an old Duenna!

Don Jer. And, O Lud! O Lud! here's a pretty fellow, to marry an old Duenna instead of my daughter! But how came the rest about?

Duen. I have only to add, that I remained in your daughter's place, and had the good fortune to engage the affections of my sweet husband here.

Isaac. Her husband! why, you old witch, do you think I'll be your husband now? This is a trick, a cheat! and you ought all to be ashamed of yourselves.

Don Ant. Hark ye, Isaac, do you dare to complain of tricking? Don Jerome, I give you my word, his cunning Portuguese has brought all this upon himself, by endeavouring to overreach you, by getting your daughter's fortune, without making any settlement in return.

Don Jer. Overreach me!

Don. Louisa. 'Tis so, indeed, sir, and we can prove it to you.

Don Jer. Why, Gad, take me, it must be so, or he never could put up with such a face as Margaret's—so, little, Solomon, I wish you joy of your wife, with all my soul.

Don. Louisa. Isaac, tricking is all fair in love—let you alone for the plot!

Don Ant. A cunning dog, arn't you? A sly little villain, eh?

Don. Louisa. Roguish, perhaps; but keen, devilish keen!

Don Jer. Yes, yes; his aunt always called him little Solomon.

Isaac. Why, the plagues of Egypt upon you all! but do you think I'll submit to such an imposition?

Don Ant. Isaac, one serious word—you'd better be content as you are; for, believe me, you will find that, in the opinion of the world, there is not a fairer subject for contempt and ridicule than a knave become the dupe of his own art.

Isaac. I don't care—I'll not endure this. Don Jerome, 'tis you have done this—you would be so cursed positive about the beauty of her you locked up, and all the time I told you she was as old as my mother, and as ugly as the devil.

Duen. Why, you little insignificant reptile!——

Don Jer. That's right!—attack him, Margaret.

Duen. Dare such a thing as you pretend to talk of beauty?—A walking rouleau?—a body that seems to owe all its consequence to the dropsy! a pair of eyes like two dead beetles in a wad of brown dough! a beard like an artichoke, with dry shrivelled jaws that would disgrace the mummy of a monkey?

Don Jer. Well done, Margaret!

Duen. But you shall know that I have a brother who wears a sword —and, if you don't do me justice——

Isaac. Fire seize your brother, and you too! I'll fly to Jerusalem to avoid you?

Duen. Fly where you will, I'll follow you.

Don Jer. Throw your snowy arms about him, Margaret.—[*Exeunt* ISAAC *and* DUENNA.] But here, Louisa, are you really married to this modest Gentleman?

Louisa. Sir, in obedience to your commands I gave him my hand within this hour.

Don Jer. My commands!

Don Ant. Yes, Sir—here is your consent, under your own hand, and I thank you sincerely for your kindness.

Don Jer. How! would you rob me of my child by a trick, a false pretence? and do you think to get her fortune by the same means? Why, 'slife! you are as great a rogue as Isaac!

Don Ant. No, Don Jerome; though I have profited by this paper in gaining your daughter's hand, I scorn to obtain her fortune by deceit. There, sir—[*Gives a letter.*] Now give her your blessing for a dower, and all the little I possess shall be settled on her in return. Had you wedded her to a prince, he could do no more.

Don Jer. Why, Gad, take me, but you are a very extraordinary fellow! But have you the impudence to suppose no one can do a generous action but yourself? Here, Louisa, tell this proud fool of yours that he's the only man I know that would renounce your fortune; and, by my soul! he's the only man in Spain that's worthy of it. There, bless you both: I'm an obstinate old fellow when I'm in the wrong; but you shall now find me as steady in the right.

Enter Don Ferdinand *and* Donna Clara.

Another wonder still! Why, sirrah! Ferdinand, you have not stole a nun, have you?

Don Ferd. She is a nun in nothing but her habit, sir—look nearer, and you will perceive 'tis Clara d'Almanza, Don Guzman's daughter; and, with pardon for stealing a wedding, she is also my wife.

Don Jer. Gadsbud, and a great fortune! Ferdinand, you are a prudent young rogue, and I forgive you: and, ifecks, you are a pretty little damsel. Give your father-in-law a kiss, you smiling rogue!

Don. Clara. There, old gentleman; and now mind you behave well to us.

Don Jer. Ifecks, those lips ha'n't been chilled by kissing beads! Egad, I believe I shall grow the best-humoured fellow in Spain. Lewis! Sancho! Carlos! d'ye hear? are all my doors thrown open? Our children's weddings are the only holidays our age can boast; and then we drain, with pleasure, the little stock of spirits time has left us.—[*Music within.*] But, see, here come our friends and neighbours!

Enter Masqueraders.

And, i' faith, we'll make a night on't, with wine, and dance, and catches—then old and young shall join us.

Finale.

Don Jer. . . .   Come now for jest and smiling,
            Both old and young beguiling,
              Let us laugh and play, so blithe and gay,
              Till we banish care away.

Don. Louisa. Thus crown'd with dance and song,
            The hours shall glide along,
              With a heart at ease, merry, merry glees
              Can never fail to please.

L

Don Ferd.	Each bride with blushes glowing,
	Our wine as rosy flowing,
	Let us laugh and play, so blithe and gay,
	Till we banish care away.
Don Ant.	Then healths to every friend
	The night's repast shall end,
	With a heart at ease, merry, merry glees
	Can never fail to please.
Don. Clar.	Nor, while we are so joyous,
	Shall anxious fear annoy us;
	Let us laugh and play, so blithe and gay,
	Till we banish care away.
Don Jer.	For generous guests like these
	Accept the wish to please,
	So we'll laugh and play, so blithe and gay,
	Your smiles drive care away. [*Exeunt omnes.*

THE SCHOOL FOR SCANDAL.

A COMEDY.

DRAMATIS PERSONÆ.

SIR PETER TEAZLE	. *Mr. King.*	MOSES	. . . . .
SIR OLIVER SURFACE	*Mr. Yates.*	SNAKE	. . . . .
YOUNG SURFACE	. *Mr. Palmer.*	CARELESS—and other	
CHARLES		companions to CHARLES.	
(his *Brothev*)	. *Mr. Smith.*		
CRABTREE	. . *Mr. Parsons.*	LADY TEAZLE	. .
SIR BENJAMIN		MARIA	. . . . .
BACKBITE	. . *Mr. Dodd.*	LADY SNEERWELL	.
ROWLEY	. . . *Mr. Aikin.*	MRS. CANDOUR	. .
SPUNGE	. . . .	MISS VERJUICE	.

ACT 1:st.—SCENE 1:st.

LADY SNEERWELL'S *House.*

LADY SNEERWELL *at her dressing table with* LAPPET; MISS VERJUICE *drinking chocolate.*

Lady Sneerwell. The Paragraphs you say were all inserted:

Verj. They were Madam—and as I copied them myself in a feigned Hand there can be no suspicion whence they came.

Lady Sneer. Did you circulate the Report of Lady Brittle's Intrigue with Captain Boastall?

Verj. Madam by this Time Lady Brittle is the Talk of half the Town—and I doubt not in a week the Men will toast her as a Demirep.

Lady Sn. What have you done as to the insinuation as to a certain Baronet's Lady and a certain Cook.

Verj. That is in as fine a Train as your Ladyship could wish. I told the story yesterday to my own maid with directions to communicate it directly to my Hairdresser. He I am informed has a Brother who courts a Milliners' Prentice in Pallmall whose mistress has a first cousin whose sister is Feme de Chambre to Mrs. Clackit—so that in the common course of Things it must reach Mrs. Clackit's Ears within four-and-twenty hours and then you know the Business is as good as done.

L 2

Lady Sneer. Why truly Mrs. Clackit has a very pretty Talent—a great deal of industry—yet—yes—been tolerably successful in her way —To my knowledge she has been the cause of breaking off six matches of three sons being disinherited and four Daughters being turned out of Doors. Of three several Elopements, as many close confinements— nine separate maintenances and two Divorces.—nay I have more than once traced her causing a *Tête-à-Tête* in the Town and Country Magazine—when the Parties perhaps had never seen each other's Faces before in the course of their Lives.

Verj. She certainly has Talents.

Lady S. But her manner is gross.

Verj. 'Tis very true. She generally designs well has a free tongue and a bold invention—but her colouring is too dark and her outline often extravagant—She wants that delicacy of Tint—and mellowness of sneer—which distinguish your Ladyship's Scandal.

Lady Sneer. Ah you are Partial Verjuice.

Verj. Not in the least—everybody allows that Lady Sneerwell can do more with a word or a Look than many can with the most laboured Detail even when they happen to have a little truth on their side to support it.

Lady Sneer. Yes my dear Verjuice. I am no Hypocrite to deny the satisfaction I reap from the Success of my Efforts. [Wounded myself, in the early part of my Life by the envenomed Tongue of Slander I confess I have since known no Pleasure equal to the reducing others to the Level of my own injured Reputation.]

Verj. Nothing can be more natural—But my dear Lady Sneerwell There is one affair in which you have lately employed me, wherein, I confess I am at a Loss to guess your motives.

Lady Sneer. I conceive you mean with respect to my neighbour, Sir Peter Teazle, and his Family—Lappet.—-And has my conduct in this matter really appeared to you so mysterious ? ~~Exit Maid~~. —

Verj. Entirely so.

Lady Sneer. An old Batchelor as Sir Peter was having taken a young wife from out of the Country—as Lady Teazle is—are certainly fair subjects for a little mischievous raillery—but here are two young men— to whom Sir Peter has acted as a kind of Guardian since their Father's death, the eldest possessing the most amiable Character and universally well spoken of, the youngest the most dissipated and extravagant young Fellow in the Kingdom, without Friends or caracter—the former one an avowed admirer of yours and apparently your Favourite, the latter attached to Maria Sir Peter's ward—and confessedly beloved by her. Now on the face of these circumstances it is utterly unaccountable to me why you a young Widow with no great jointure—should not close with the passion of a man of such character and expectations as Mr. Surface—and more so why you should be so uncommonly earnest to destroy the mutual Attachment subsisting between his Brother Charles and Maria.

Lady Sneer. Then at once to unravel this mistery—I must inform you that Love has no share whatever in the intercourse between Mr. Surface and me.

Verj. No!

Lady Sneer. His real attachment is to Maria or her Fortune—but finding in his Brother a favoured Rival, He has been obliged to mask his Pretensions—and profit by my Assistance.

Verj. Yet still I am more puzzled why you should interest yourself in his success.

Lady Sneer. Heavens! how dull you are! cannot you surmise the weakness which I hitherto, thro' shame have concealed even from you—must I confess that Charles—that Libertine, that extravagant, that Bankrupt in Fortune and Reputation—that He it is for whom I am thus anxious and malicious and to gain whom I would sacrifice—everything——

Verj. Now indeed—your conduct appears consistent and I no longer wonder at your enmity to Maria, but how came you and Surface so confidential?

Lady Sneer. For our mutual interest—but I have found out him a long time since altho' He has contrived to deceive everybody beside—I know him to be artful, selfish and malicious—while with Sir Peter, and indeed with all his acquaintance, He passes for a youthful Miracle of Prudence—good sense and Benevolence.

Verj. Yes, yes—I know, Sir Peter vows He has not his equal in England; and, above all, He praises him as a *man of sentiment.*

Lady Sneer. True and with the assistance of his sentiments and hypocrisy he has brought Sir Peter entirely in his interests with respect to Maria and is now, I believe, attempting to flatter Lady Teazle into the same good opinion towards him—while poor Charles has no Friend in the House—though I fear he has a powerful one in Maria's Heart, against whom we must direct our schemes.

Ser. Mr. Surface.

Lady Sneer. Shew him up. He generally calls about this Time. I don't wonder at People's giving him to me for a Lover.

Enter SURFACE.

Surface. My dear Lady Sneerwell, how do you do to-day—your most obedient.

Lady Sneer. Miss Verjuice has just been arraigning me on our mutual attachment now ; but I have informed her of our real views and the Purposes for which our Geniuses at present co-operate. You know how useful she has been to us—and believe me the confidence is not ill-placed.

Surf. Madam, it is impossible for me to suspect that a Lady of Miss Verjuice's sensibility and discernment——

Lady Sneer. Well—well—no compliments now—but tell me when you saw your mistress or what is more material to me your Brother.

Surf. I have not seen either since I saw you—but I can inform you that they are at present at Variance—some of your stories have taken good effect on Maria.

Lady Sneer. Ah ! my dear Verjuice, the merit of this belongs to you. But do your Brother's Distresses encrease ?

Surf. Every hour. I am told He had another execution in his house yesterday—in short, his Dissipation and extravagance exceed anything I have ever heard of.

Lady Sneer. Poor Charles !

Surf. True, Madam—notwithstanding his Vices one can't help feeling for him—ah poor Charles ! I 'm sure I wish it was in my Power to be of any essential Service to him—for the man who does not share in the Distresses of a Brother—even though merited by his own misconduct—deserves——

Lady Sneer. O Lud, you are going to be moral, and forget that you are among Friends.

Surf. Egad, that 's true—I 'll keep that sentiment till I see Sir Peter. However it is certainly a charity to rescue Maria from such a Libertine who—if He is to be reclaim'd, can be so only by a Person of your Ladyship's superior accomplishments and understanding.

Verj. 'Twould be a Hazardous experiment.

Surface. But—Madam—let me caution you to place no more confidence in our Friend Snake the Libeller—I have lately detected him in frequent conference with old Rowland [Rowley] who was formerly my Father's Steward and has never been a friend of mine.

Lady Sneer. I 'm not disappointed in Snake, I never suspected the fellow to have virtue enough to be faithful even to his own Villany.

Enter MARIA.

Maria, my dear —how do you do—what 's the matter ?

Mar. O there is that disagreeable lover of mine, Sir Benjamin Backbite, has just call'd at my guardian's with his odious Uncle Crabtree—so I slipt out and ran hither to avoid them.

THE SCHOOL FOR SCANDAL.

Lady Sneer. Is that all?

Verj. Lady Sneerwell—I'll go and write the Letter I mention'd to you.

Surf. If my Brother Charles had been of the Party, madam, perhaps you would not have been so much alarmed.

Lady Sneer. Nay now—you are severe, for I dare swear the Truth of the matter is Maria heard *you* were here—but my dear—what has Sir Benjamin done that you should avoid him so——

Mar. Oh He has done nothing—but his conversation is a perpetual Libel on all his Acquaintance.

Surf. Aye and the worst of it is there is no advantage in not knowing Them, for He'll abuse a stranger just as soon as his best Friend—and Crabtree is as bad.

Lady Sneer. Nay but we should make allowance; Sir Benjamin is a wit and a poet.

Mar. For my Part—I own, madam—wit loses its respect with me, when I see it in company with malice.—What do you think, Mr. Surface?

Surf. Certainly, Madam, to smile at the jest which plants a Thorn on another's Breast is to become a principal in the mischief.

Lady Sneer. Pshaw—there's no possibility of being witty without a little nature—the malice of a good thing is the Barb that makes it stick.—What's your opinion, Mr. Surface?

Surf. Certainly madam—that conversation where the Spirit of Raillery is suppressed will ever appear tedious and insipid—

Mar. Well I'll not debate how far Scandal may be allowable—but in a man I am sure it is always contemtable.—We have Pride, envy, Rivalship, and a Thousand motives to depreciate each other—but the male-slanderer must have the cowardice of a woman before He can traduce one.

Lady Sneer. I wish my Cousin Verjuice hadn't left us—she should embrace you.

Surf. Ah! she's an old maid and is privileged of course.

Enter SERV.

Madam Mrs. Candour is below and, if your Ladyship's at leisure, will leave her carriage.

Lady Sneer. Beg her to walk in. Now, Maria, however here is a Character to your Taste, for tho' Mrs. Candour is a little talkative everybody allows her to be the best-natured and best sort of woman.

Mar. Yes, with a very gross affectation of good Nature and Benevolence—she does more mischief than the Direct malice of old Crabtree.

Surf. Efaith 'tis very true Lady Sneerwell—Whenever I hear the current running again the characters of my Friends, I never think them in such Danger as when Candour undertakes their Defence.

Lady Sneer. Hush here she is—

Enter Mrs. Candour.

Mrs. Can. My dear Lady Sneerwell, how have you been this Century? I have never seen you tho' I have heard of you very often.—Mr. Surface—the World says scandalous things of you—but indeed it is no matter what the world says, for I think one hears nothing else but scandal.

Surf. Just so, indeed, Ma'am.

Mrs. Can. Ah Maria, Child—what is the whole affair off between you and Charles? His extravagance, I presume—The Town talks of nothing else—

Mar. I am very sorry, Ma'am, the Town has so little to do.

Mrs. Can. True, true, Child; but there's no stopping people's Tongues. I own I was hurt to hear it—as I indeed was to learn from the same quarter that your guardian, Sir Peter, and Lady Teazle have not agreed lately so well as could be wish'd.

Mar. 'Tis strangely impertinent for people to busy themselves so.

Mrs. Can. Very true, Child; but what's to be done? People will talk—there's no preventing it.—why it was but yesterday I was told that Miss Gadabout had eloped with Sir Filagree Flirt. But, Lord! there is no minding what one hears; tho' to be sure I had this from very good authority.

Mar. Such reports are highly scandalous.

Mrs. Can. So they are Child—shameful! shameful! but the world is so censorious no character escapes. Lord, now! who would have suspected your friend, Miss Prim, of an indiscretion? Yet such is the ill-nature of people, that they say her unkle stopped her last week just as she was stepping into a Postchaise with her Dancing-master.

Mar. I'll answer for't: there are no grounds for the Report.

Mrs. Can. Oh, no foundation in the world, I dare swear, no more probably than for the story circulated last month, of Mrs. Festino's affair with Colonel Cassino—tho' to be sure that matter was never rightly clear'd up.

Surf. The license of invention some people take is monstrous indeed.

Mar. 'Tis so, but in my opinion, those who report such things are equally culpaple.

Mrs. Can. To be sure they are; Tale Bearers are as bad as the Tale makers—'tis an old observation and a very true one—but what's to be done, as I said before—how will you prevent People from talking—to-day, Mrs. Clackitt assured me, Mr. and Mrs. Honeymoon were at last become mere man and wife—like acquaintance—she likewise hinted that a certain widow in the next street had got rid of her Dropsy and recovered her shape in a most surprising manner—at the same Miss Tattle, who was by, affirm'd, that Lord Boffalo had discover'd his Lady at a house of no extraordinary Fame—and that Sir Harry Bouquet and Tom Saunter were to measure swords on a similar Provocation. but—Lord! do you think I would report these Things—No, no, Tale Bearers, as I said before, are just as bad as the tale-makers.

Surf. Ah! Mrs. Candour, if everybody had your Forbearance and good nature—

Mrs. Can. I confess, Mr. Surface, I cannot bear to hear People traduced behind their Backs, and when ugly circumstances come out against our acquaintances I own I always love to think the best—by the bye, I hope 'tis not true that your Brother is absolutely ruin'd—

Surf. I am afraid his circumstances are very bad indeed, Ma'am—

Mrs. Can. Ah! I heard so—but you must tell him to keep up his Spirits—everybody, almost, is in the same way—Lord Spindle, Sir Thomas Splint, Captain Quinze, and Mr. Nickit—all up, I hear, within this week; so, if Charles is undone, He'll find half his Acquaintance ruin'd too, and that, you know, is a consolation—

Surf. Doubtless, Ma'am—a very great one.

Enter SERV.

Ser. Mr. Crabtree and Sir Benjamin Backbite.

Lady Sneer. Soh! Maria, you see your lover pursues you—Positively, you shan't escape.

Enter CRABTREE and SIR BENJAMIN BACKBITE.

Crab. Lady Sneerwell, I kiss your hand. Mrs. Candour I don't believe you are acquainted with my Nephew Sir Benjamin Backbite—Egad, Ma'am, He has a pretty wit—and is a pretty Poet, too, isn't He Lady Sneerwell?

Sir Ben. O fie, Uncle!

Crab. Nay, egad, it's true—I back him at a Rebus or a Charade against the best Rhymer in the Kingdom—has your Ladyship heard the Epigram he wrote last week on Lady Frizzle's Feather catching Fire?—Do, Benjamin, repeat it—or the Charade you made last Night extempore at Mrs. Drowzie's conversazione—Come now your first is the Name of a Fish, your second a great naval commander—and

Sir Ben. Dear Uncle—now—prithee——

Crab. Efaith, Ma'am—'twould surprise you to hear how ready he is at all these Things.

Lady Sneer. I wonder Sir Benjamin you never publish anything.

Sir Ben. To say truth, Ma'am, 'tis very vulgar to Print and as my little Productions are mostly Satires and Lampoons I find they circulate more by giving copies in confidence to the Friends of the Parties—however, I have some love-Elegies, which, when favoured with this lady's smile, I mean to give to the Public.

[*Pointing to* MARIA.

Crab. 'Fore Heaven, ma'am, they'll immortalize you—you'll be handed down to Posterity, like Petrarch's Laura, or Waller's Sacharissa.

Sir Ben. Yes Madam, I think you will like them—when you shall see in a beautiful Quarto Page how a neat rivulet of Text shall meander thro' a meadow of margin—'fore Gad, they will be the most elegant Things of their kind—

Crab. But Ladies, have you heard the news?

Mrs. Can. What, Sir, do you mean the Report of——

Crab. No ma'am that's not it.—Miss Nicely is going to be married to her own Footman.

Mrs. Can. Impossible!

Crab. Ask Sir Benjamin.

Sir Ben. 'Tis very true, Ma'am—everything is fixed and the wedding Livery bespoke.

Crab. Yes and they say there were pressing reasons for 't.

Mrs. Can. It cannot be—and I wonder any one should believe such a story of so prudent a Lady as Miss Nicely.

Sir Ben. O Lud! ma'am, that's the very reason 'twas believed at once. She has always been so cautious and so reserved, that everybody was sure there was some reason for it at bottom.

Lady Sneer. Yes, a Tale of Scandal is as fatal to the Reputation of a prudent Lady of her stamp as a Fever is generally to those of the strongest Constitutions, but there is a sort of puny sickly Reputation, that is always ailing yet will outlive the robuster characters of a hundred Prudes.

Sir Ben. True Madam, there are Valetudinarians in Reputation as well as constitution—who being conscious of their weak Part, avoid the least breath of air, and supply their want of Stamina by care and circumspection—

Mrs. Can. Well, but this may be all mistake—You know, Sir Benjamin, very trifling circumstances often give rise to the most injurious Tales.

Crab. That they do, I'll be sworn Ma'am—did you ever hear how Miss Shepherd came to lose her Lover and her Character last summer at Tunbridge—Sir Benjamin you remember it—

Sir Ben. O to be sure the most whimsical circumstance—

Lady Sneer. How was it Pray—

Crab. Why, one evening at Mrs. Ponto's Assembly—the conversation happened to turn on the difficulty of breeding Nova-Scotia Sheep in this country—says a young Lady in company, I have known instances of it for Miss Letitia Shepherd, a first cousin of mine, had a Nova-Scotia Sheep that produced her Twins!"—"What!" cries the old Dowager Lady Dundizzy (who you know is as deaf as a Post), "has Miss Letitia Shepherd had twins?"—This Mistake—as you may imagine, threw the whole company into a fit of Laughing—However, 'twas the next morning everywhere reported, and in a few Days believed by the whole Town, that Miss Letitia Shepherd had actually been brought to Bed of a fine Boy and Girl—and in less than a week there were People who could name the Father, and the Farm House where the Babies were put out to Nurse.

Lady Sneer. Strange indeed!

Crab. Matter of Fact, I assure you—O Lud! Mr. Surface, pray, is it true that your uncle Sir Oliver is coming home—

Surf. Not that I know of indeed Sir.

Crab. He has been in the East Indies a long time—you can scarcely remember him—I believe—sad comfort on his arrival to hear how your Brother has gone on!

Surf. Charles has been imprudent, Sir, to be sure, but I hope no Busy people have already prejudiced Sir Oliver against him—He may reform—

Sir Ben. To be sure He may—for my Part I never believed him to be so utterly void of Principle as People say—and, tho' he has lost all his Friends, I am told nobody is better spoken of—by the Jews.

Crab. That's true, egad, nephew—if the Old Jewry was a Ward I believe Charles would be an alderman—no man more popular there, 'fore Gad, I hear He pays as many annuities as the Irish Tontine, and that whenever He's sick they have Prayers for the recovery of his Health in the synagogue—

Sir Ben. Yet no man lives in greater Splendour :—they tell me when He entertains his Friends—He can sit down to dinner with a dozen of his own Securities, have a score Tradesmen waiting in the Anti-Chamber, and an officer behind every guest's Chair.

Surf. This may be entertainment to you, Gentlemen, but you pay very little regard to the Feelings of a Brother.

Mar. Their malice is intolerable—Lady Sneerwell I must wish you a good morning——I'm not very well. [*Ex.* MAR.

Mrs. Can. O dear, she chang'd colour very much!

Lady Sneer. Do, Mrs. Candour, follow her—she may want assistance.

Mrs. Can. That I will with all my soul ma'am.—Poor dear Girl—who knows—what her situation may be! [*Ex.* Mrs. CAN.

Lady Sneer. 'Twas nothing but that she could not bear to hear Charles reflected on notwithstanding their difference.

Sir Ben. The young Lady's Penchant is obvious.

Crab. But Benjamin—you mustn't give up the Pursuit for that—follow her and put her into good humour—repeat her some of your verses—come, I'll assist you—

Sir Ben. Mr. Surface, I did not mean to hurt you—but depend on't your Brother is utterly undone—(*going*).

Crab. O Lud! aye—undone—as ever man was—can't raise a guinea.

Sir Ben. And everything sold—I'm told—that was movable—(*going*).

Crab. I was at his house—not a thing left but some empty Bottles that were overlooked and the Family Pictures, which I believe are framed in the Wainscot. (*Going.*)

Sir Ben. And I'm very sorry to hear also some bad stories against him. (*Going.*)

Crab. O, He has done many mean things—that's certain!

Sir Ben. But however as He is your Brother—— (*Going.*)

Crab. We'll tell you all another opportunity. [*Exe.*

Lady Sneer. Ha! ha! ha! 'tis very hard for them to leave a subject they have not quite run down.

Surf. And I believe the Abuse was no more acceptable to your Ladyship than Maria.

Lady Sneer. I doubt her Affections are farther engaged than we imagin'd, but the Family are to be here this Evening, so you may as well dine where you are and we shall have an opportunity of observing farther—in the meantime, I'll go and plot Mischief and you shall study Sentiments. [*Exe.*

SCENE II.—SIR PETER's House.

Enter SIR PETER.

Sir Pet. When an old Bachelor takes a young Wife—what is He to expect.—'Tis now six months since Lady Teazle made me the happiest of men—and I have been the most miserable Dog ever since that ever committed wedlock. We tift a little going to church—and came to a Quarrel before the Bells had done ringing—I was more than once nearly chok'd with gall during the Honeymoon—and had lost all comfort in Life before my Friends had done wishing me Joy—yet I chose with caution—a girl bred wholly in the country—who never knew luxury beyond one silk gown—nor dissipation above the annual Gala of a Race-Ball—Yet she now plays her Part in all the extravagant Fopperies of the Fashion and the Town, with as ready a Grace as if she had never seen a Bush nor a grass Plot out of Grosvenor-Square ! I am sneered at by my old acquaintance—paragraphed—in the news Papers—She dissipates my Fortune, and contradicts all my Humours—yet the worst of it is, I doubt I love her or I should never bear all this. However, I'll never be weak enough to own it.

Enter ROWLEY.

Row. Sir Peter, your servant :—how is 't with you Sir—

Sir Pet. Very bad—Master Rowley—very bad; I meet with nothing but crosses and vexations—

Row. What can have happened to trouble you since yesterday ?

Sir Pet. A good—question to a married man—

Row. Nay I'm sure your Lady Sir Peter can't be the cause of your uneasiness.

Sir Pet. Why, has anybody told you she was dead?

Row. Come, come, Sir Peter, you love her, notwithstanding your tempers do not exactly agree.

Sir Pet. But the Fault is entirely hers, Master Rowley—I am myself, the sweetest temper'd man alive, and hate a teasing temper ; and so I tell her a hundred Times a day—

Row. Indeed !

Sir Pet. Aye, and, what is very extraordinary, in all our disputes she is always in the wrong ! But Lady Sneerwell, and the Set she meets at her House, encourage the perverseness of her Disposition—then to complete my vexations—Maria—my Ward—whom I ought to have the Power of a Father over, is determined to turn Rebel, too, and absolutely refuses the man whom I have long resolved on for her husband— meaning I suppose, to bestow herself on his profligate Brother.

Row. You know, Sir Peter, I have always taken the Liberty to differ with you on the subject of these two young Gentlemen—I only wish you may not be deceived in your opinion of the elder. For Charles, my life on 't ! He will retrieve his errors yet—their worthy Father, once my honour'd master, was at his years nearly as wild a spark.

Sir Pet. You are wrong, Master Rowley—on their Father's Death you know I acted as a kind of Guardian to them both—till their uncle

Sir Oliver's Eastern Bounty gave them an early independence. Of course no person could have more opportunities of judging of their Hearts—and I was never mistaken in my life. Joseph is indeed a model for the young men of the Age—He is a man of Sentiment—and acts up to the Sentiments he professes—but for the other, take my word for 't [if] he had any grain of Virtue by descent—he has dissipated it with the rest of his inheritance. Ah! my old Friend, Sir Oliver will be deeply mortified when he finds how Part of his Bounty has been misapplied.

Row. I am sorry to find you so violent against the young man, because this may be the most critical Period of his Fortune. I came hither with news that will surprise you.

Sir Pet. What! let me hear—

Row. Sir Oliver is arrived and at this moment in Town.

Sir Pet. How!—you astonish me—I thought you did not expect him this month!—

Row. I did not—but his Passage has been remarkably quick.

Sir Pet. Egad, I shall rejoice to see my old Friend—'Tis sixteen years since we met—We have had many a Day together—but does he still enjoin us not to inform his Nephews of his Arrival?

Row. Most strictly—He means, before He makes it known to make some trial of their Dispositions and we have already planned something for the purpose.

Sir Pet. Ah, there needs no art to discover their merits—however he shall have his way—but pray, does he know I am married!

Row. Yes and will soon wish you joy.

Sir Pet. You may tell him 'tis too late—ah, Oliver, will laugh at me—we used to rail at matrimony together—but He has been steady to his Text—well, He must be at my house tho'—I'll instantly give orders for his Reception—but, Master Rowley—don't drop a word that Lady Teazle and I ever disagree.

Row. By no means.

Sir Pet. For I should never be able to stand Noll's jokes; so I'd have him think that we are a very happy couple.

Row. I understand you—but then you must be very careful not to differ while He's in the House with you.

Sir Pet. Egad—and so we must—that's impossible. Ah! Master Rowley when an old Batchelor marries a young wife—He deserves—no, the crime carries the Punishment along with it. [*Exe.*

End of Act 1st.

ACT 2d—SCENE 1st.

SIR PETER and LADY TEAZLE.

Sir Pet. Lady Teazle—Lady Teazle I'll not bear it.

Lady Teaz. Sir Peter—Sir Peter, you—may scold or smile, according to your Humour but I ought to have my own way in everything, and what's more, I will too—what! tho' I was educated in the country I know very well that women of Fashion in London are accountable to nobody after they are married.

Sir Pet. Very well! ma'am very well! so a husband is to have no influence, no authority?

Lady Teaz. Authority! no, to be sure—if you wanted authority over me, you should have adopted me and not married me; I am sure you were old enough.

Sir Pet. Old enough—aye there it is—well—well—Lady Teazle, tho' my life may be made unhappy by your Temper—I'll not be ruined by your extravagance—

Lady Teaz. My extravagance! I'm sure I'm not more extravagant than a woman of Fashion ought to be.

Sir Pet. No, no, Madam, you shall throw away no more sums on such unmeaning Luxury—'Slife, to spend as much to furnish your Dressing Room with Flowers in winter as would suffice to turn the Pantheon into a Greenhouse, and give a *Fête Champêtre* at Christmas.

Lady Teaz. Lord! Sir Peter, am I to blame because Flowers are dear in cold weather? You should find fault with the Climate, and not with me. For my Part I'm sure I wish it was spring all the year round—and that Roses grew under one's Feet!

Sir Pet. Oons! Madam—if you had been born to those Fopperies I shouldn't wonder at your talking thus;—but you forget what your situation was when I married you—

Lady Teaz. No, no, I don't—'twas a very disagreeable one or I should never have married you.

Sir Pet. Yes, yes, madam, you were then in somewhat a humbler Style—the daughter of a plain country Squire. Recollect, Lady Teazle, when I saw you first—sitting at your tambour in a pretty figured linen gown—with a Bunch of Keys at your side, and your apartment hung round with Fruits in worsted, of your own working—

Lady Teaz. O horrible!—horrible!—don't put me in mind of it!

Sir Pet. Yes, yes, Madam, and your daily occupation to inspect the Dairy, superintend the Poultry, make extracts from the Family Receipt-book, and comb your aunt Deborah's Lap Dog.

Lady Teaz. Abominable!

Sir Pet. Yes Madam—and what were your evening amusements? to draw Patterns for Ruffles, which you hadn't the materials to make—play Pope Joan with the Curate—to read a sermon to your Aunt—or be stuck down to an old Spinet to strum your father to sleep after a Fox Chase.

Lady Teaz. Scandalous—Sir Peter not a word of it true—

Sir Pet. Yes, Madam—These were the recreations I took you from—and now—no one more extravagantly in the Fashion—Every Fopery adopted—a head-dress to o'er top Lady Pagoda, with feathers pendant horizontal and perpendicular—you forget, Lady Teazle—when a little wired gauze with a few Beads made you a fly Cap not much bigger than a blew-bottle, and your Hair was comb'd smooth over a Roll—

Lady Teaz. Shocking! horrible Roll!!

Sir Pet. But now—you must have your coach—*Vis-à-vis*, and three powder'd Footmen before your Chair—and in the summer a pair of white cobs to draw you to Kensington Gardens—no recollection when you were content to ride double, behind the Butler, on a docked Coach-Horse?

Lady Teaz. Horrid!—I swear I never did.

Sir Pet. This, madam, was your situation—and what have I not done for you? I have made you woman of Fashion, of Fortune, of Rank—in short I have made you my wife.

Lady Teaz. Well then, and there is but one thing more you can make me to add to the obligation.

Sir Pet. What's that pray?

Lady Teaz. Your widow.—

Sir Pet. Thank you Madam—but don't flatter yourself, for though your ill-conduct may disturb my Peace it shall never break my Heart, I promise you—however, I am equally obliged to you for the Hint.

Lady Teaz. Then why will you endeavour to make yourself so disagreeable to me—and thwart me in every little elegant expense?

Sir Pet. 'Slife—Madam I pray, had you any of these elegant expenses when you married me?

Lady Teaz. Lud, Sir Peter, would you have me be out of the Fashion?

Sir Pet. The Fashion indeed!—what had you to do with the Fashion before you married me?

Lady Teaz. For my Part—I should think you would like to have your wife thought a woman of Taste—

Sir Pet. Aye there again—Taste! Zounds, Madam, you had no Taste when you married me—

Lady Teaz. That's very true indeed, Sir Peter! after having married you I should never pretend to Taste again, I allow.

Sir Pet. So—so then—Madam—if these are your Sentiments pray how came I to be honour'd with your Hand?

Lady Teaz. Shall I tell you the Truth?

Sir Pet. If it's not too great a Favour.

Lady Teaz. Why the Fact is I was tired of all those agreeable Recreations which you have so good naturally Described—and having a Spirit to spend and enjoy a Fortune—I determined to marry the first rich man that would have me.

Sir Pet. A very honest confession—truly—but pray, madam, was there no one else you might have tried to ensnare but me?

Lady Teaz. O lud—I drew my net at several but you were the only one I could catch.

Sir Pet. This is plain dealing indeed—

Lady Teaz. But now, Sir Peter, if we have finish'd our daily Jangle I presume I may go to my engagement at Lady Sneerwell's?

Sir Pet. Aye—there's another Precious circumstance—a charming set of acquaintance—you have made there!

Lady Teaz. Nay Sir Peter they are People of Rank and Fortune—and remarkably tenacious of reputation.

Sir Pet. Yes egad they are tenacious of Reputation with a vengeance, for they don't chuse anybody should have a Character but themselves! Such a crew! Ah! many a wretch has rid on hurdles who has done less mischief than these utterers of forged Tales, coiners of Scandal, and clippers of Reputation.

Lady Teaz. What would you restrain the freedom of speech?

Sir Pet. Aye they have made you just as bad [as] any one of the Society.

Lady Teaz. Why—I believe I do bear a Part with a tolerable Grace—But I vow I bear no malice against the People I abuse, when I say an ill-natured thing, 'tis out of pure Good Humour—and I take it for granted they deal exactly in the same manner with me, but Sir Peter you know you promised to come to Lady Sneerwell's too.

Sir Pet. Well well I'll call in, just to look after my own character.

Lady Teaz. Then, indeed, you must make Haste after me, or you'll be too late—so good bye to ye.

Sir Pet. So—I have gain'd much by my intended expostulation—yet with what a charming air she contradicts everything I say—and how pleasingly she shows her contempt of my authority—Well tho' I can't make her love me, there is certainly a great satisfaction in quarrelling with her; and I think she never appears to such advantage as when she is doing everything in her Power to plague me.   [*Exit.*

Scene 2nd

At LADY SNEERWELL'S.

LADY SNEERWELL, MRS. CANDOUR, CRABTREE, SIR BENJAMIN BACKBITE, and SURFACE.

Lady Sneer. Nay, positively, we will hear it.
Jos. Surf. Yes—yes the Epigram by all means.
Sir Ben. O plague on't unkle—'tis mere nonsense—
Crab. No no; 'fore gad very clever for an extempore!
Sir Ben. But ladies you should be acquainted with the circumstances. You must know that one day last week as Lady Betty Curricle was taking the Dust in High Park, in a sort of duodecimo Phaeton—she desired me to write some verses on her Ponies—upon which I took out my Pocket-Book—and in one moment produced—the following:—

> 'Sure never were seen two such beautiful Ponies;
> Other Horses are Clowns—and these macaronies,
> Nay to give 'em this Title, I'm sure isn't wrong,
> Their Legs are so slim—and their Tails are so long.

Crab. There Ladies—done in the smack of a whip and on Horseback too.
Jos. Surf. A very Phœbus, mounted—indeed Sir Benjamin.
Sir Ben. Oh dear Sir—Trifles—Trifles.

Enter LADY TEAZLE and MARIA.

Mrs. Can. I must have a Copy—
Lady Sneer. Lady Teazle—I hope we shall see Sir Peter?
Lady Teaz. I believe He'll wait on your Ladyship presently.
Lady Sneer. Maria my love you look grave. Come, you shall sit down to Piquet with Mr. Surface.
Mar. I take very little Pleasure in cards—however, I'll do as you Please.
Lady Teaz. I am surprised Mr. Surface should sit down with her—I thought He would have embraced this opportunity of speaking to me before Sir Peter came— [*Aside.*]
Mrs. Can. Now, I'll die but you are so scandalous I'll forswear your society.
Lady Teaz. What's the matter, Mrs. Candour?
Mrs. Can. They'll not allow our friend Miss Vermillion to be handsome.
Lady Sneer. Oh, surely she is a pretty woman......
[*Crab.*] I am very glad you think so ma'am.

Mrs. Can. She has a charming fresh Colour.

Crab. Yes when it is fresh put on—

Lady Teaz. O fie! I'll swear her colour is natural—I have seen it come and go—

Crab. I dare swear you have, ma'am: it goes of a Night, and comes again in the morning.

Sir Ben. True, uncle, it not only comes and goes but what's more egad her maid can fetch and carry it—

Mrs. Can. Ha! ha! ha! how I hate to hear you talk so! But surely, now, her Sister, is or was very handsome.

Crab. Who? Mrs. Stucco? O lud! she's six-and-fifty if she's an hour!

Mrs. Can. Now positively you wrong her fifty-two, or fifty-three is the utmost—and I don't think she looks more.

Sir Ben. Ah! there's no judging by her looks, unless one was to see her Face.

Lady Sneer. Well—well—if she does take some pains to repair the ravages of Time—you must allow she effects it with great ingenuity—and surely that's better than the careless manner in which the widow Ocre chaulks her wrinkles.

Sir Ben. Nay now—you are severe upon the widow—come—come, it isn't that she paints so ill—but when she has finished her Face she joins it on so badly to her Neck, that she looks like a mended Statue, in which the Connoisseur sees at once that the Head's modern tho' the Trunk's antique——

Crab. Ha! ha! ha! well said, Nephew!

Mrs. Can. Ha! ha! ha! Well, you make me laugh but I vow I hate you for it—what do you think of Miss Simper?

Sir Ben. Why, she has very pretty Teeth.

Lady Teaz. Yes and on that account, when she is neither speaking nor laughing (which very seldom happens)—she never absolutely shuts her mouth, but leaves it always on a-Jar, as it were——

Mrs. Can. How can you be so ill-natured!

Lady Teaz. Nay, I allow even that's better than the Pains Mrs. Prim takes to conceal her losses in Front—she draws her mouth till it resembles the aperture of a Poor's-Box, and all her words appear to slide out edgewise.

Lady Sneer. Very well Lady Teazle I see you can be a little severe.

Lady Teaz. In defence of a Friend it is but justice, but here comes Sir Peter to spoil our Pleasantry.

Enter SIR PETER.

Sir Pet. Ladies, your obedient—Mercy on me—here is the whole set! a character's dead at every word, I suppose.

Mrs. Can. I am rejoiced you are come, Sir Peter—they have been so censorious and Lady Teazle as bad as any one.

Sir Pet. That must be very distressing to you, Mrs. Candour I dare swear.

Mrs. Can. O they will allow good Qualities to nobody—not even good nature to our Friend Mrs. Pursy.

Lady Teaz. What, the fat dowager who was at Mrs. Codrille's last Night?

Lady Sn. Nay—her bulk is her misfortune and when she takes such Pains to get rid of it you ought not to reflect on her.

Mrs. Can. 'Tis very true, indeed.

Lady Teaz. Yes, I know she almost lives on acids and small whey—laces herself by pulleys and often in the hottest noon of summer you may see her on a little squat Pony, with her hair plaited up behind like a Drummer's and puffing round the Ring on a full trot.

Mrs. Can. I thank you Lady Teazle for defending her.

Sir Pet. Yes, a good Defence, truly!

Mrs. Can. But for Sir Benjamin, He is as censorious as Miss Sallow.

Crab. Yes and she is a curious Being to pretend to be censorious—an awkward Gawky, without any one good Point under Heaven!

Lady Sneer. Positively you shall not be so very severe. Miss Sallow is a Relation of mine by marriage, and, as for her Person great allowance is to be made—for, let me tell you a woman labours under many disadvantages who tries to pass for a girl at six-and-thirty.

Mrs. Can. Tho', surely she is handsome still—and for the weakness in her eyes considering how much she reads by candle-light it is not to be wonder'd at.

Lady Sneer. True and then as to her manner—upon my word I think it is particularly graceful considering she never had the least Education for you know her Mother was a Welch milliner, and her Father a sugar-Baker at Bristow.—

Sir Ben. Ah! you are both of you too good-natured!

Sir Pet. Yes, damned good-natured! Her own relation! mercy on me! [*Aside.*

Mrs. Can. For my Part I own I cannot bear to hear a friend ill-spoken of?

Sir Pet. No, to be sure!

Sir Ben. Ah you are of a moral turn Mrs. Candour and can sit for an hour to hear Lady Stucco talk sentiments.

Lady Sneer. Nay I vow Lady Stucco is very well with the Dessert after Dinner for she's just like the Spanish Fruit one cracks for mottoes—made up of Paint and Proverb.

Mrs. Can. Well, I never will join in ridiculing a Friend—and so I constantly tell my cousin Ogle—and you all know what pretensions she has to be critical in Beauty.

Lady Teazle. O to be sure she has herself the oddest countenance that ever was seen—'tis a collection of Features from all the different Countries of the globe.

Sir Ben. So she has indeed—an Irish Front——

Crab. Caledonian Locks——

Sir Ben. Dutch Nose——

Crab. Austrian Lips——

Sir Ben. Complexion of a Spaniard——

Crab. And Teeth *à la Chinoise*——

Sir Ben. In short, her Face resembles a *table d'hôte* at Spa—where no two guests are of a nation——

Crab. Or a Congress at the close of a general War—wherein all the members even to her eyes appear to have a different interest and her Nose and Chin are the only Parties likely to join issue.

Mrs. Can. Ha! ha! ha!

Sir Pet. Mercy on my Life a Person they dine with twice a week!
[*Aside.*

Lady Sneer. Go—go—you are a couple of provoking Toads.

Mrs. Can. Nay but I vow you shall not carry the Laugh off so—for give me leave to say, that Mrs. Ogle——

Sir Pet. Madam—madam—I beg your Pardon—there's no stopping these good Gentlemen's Tongues—but when I tell you Mrs. Candour that the Lady they are abusing is a particular Friend of mine, I hope you'll not take her Part.

Lady Sneer. Ha! ha! ha! well said, Sir Peter—but you are a cruel creature—too Phlegmatic yourself for a jest and too peevish to allow wit in others.

Sir Pet. Ah Madam true wit is more nearly allow'd to good Nature than your Ladyship is aware of.

Lady Sneer. True Sir Peter—I believe they are so near akin that they can never be united.

Sir Ben. O rather Madam suppose them man and wife because one seldom sees them together.

Lady Teaz. but Sir Peter is such an Enemy to Scandal I believe He would have it put down by Parliament.

Sir Pet. 'Fore heaven! Madam, if they were to consider the Sporting with Reputation of as much importance as poaching on manors—and pass an Act for the Preservation of Fame—there are many would thank them for the Bill.

Lady Sneer. O Lud! Sir Peter would you deprive us of our Privileges—

Sir Pet. Aye Madam—and then no person should be permitted to kill characters or run down reputations, but qualified old Maids and disappointed Widows.—

Lady Sneer. Go, you monster—

Mrs. Can. But sure you would not be quite so severe on those who only report what they hear?

Sir Pet. Yes Madam, I would have Law Merchant for that too—and in all cases of slander currency, whenever the Drawer of the Lie was not to be found, the injured Party should have a right to come on any of the indorsers.

Crab. Well for my Part I believe there never was a Scandalous Tale without some foundation.*

Lady Sneer. Come Ladies shall we sit down to Cards in the next Room?

Enter SERVANT whispers SIR PETER.

Sir Pet. I'll be with them directly.—[*Exit* SERVANT]. I'll get away unperceived.

Lady Sneer. Sir Peter you are not leaving us?

Sir Pet. Your Ladyship must excuse me—I'm called away by particular Business—but I leave my Character behind me— *Ex.*

Sir Ben. Well certainly Lady Teazle that lord of yours is a strange being—I could tell you some stories of him would make you laugh heartily if He wern't your Husband.

Lady Teaz. O pray don't mind that—come do let's hear 'em.

[join the rest of the Company going into the Next Room.

Surf. Maria I see you have no satisfaction in this society.

Mar. How is it possible I should? If to raise malicious smiles at the infirmities or misfortunes of those who have never injured us be

---

* The story in Act I. Scene I., told by Crabtree about Miss Letitia Piper, is repeated here, the speaker being Sir Peter :

Sir Peter. O nine out of ten malicious inventions are founded on some ridiculous misrepresentation—Mrs. Candour you remember how poor Miss Shepherd lost her Lover and her Character one Summer at Tunbridge.

Mrs. C. To be sure that was a very ridiculous affair.

Crab. Pray tell us Sir Peter how it was.

Sir P. Why madam— [The story follows.]

Mrs. C. Ha ha strange indeed—

Sir P. Matter of Fact I assure you......

Lady T. As sure as can be—Sir Peter will grow scandalous himself—if you encourage him to tell stories.

the province of wit or Humour, Heaven grant me a double Portion of Dullness—]

Surf. Yet they appear more ill-natured than they are—they have no malice at heart—

Mar. Then is their conduct still more contemptible for in my opinion—nothing could excuse the intemperance of their tongues but a natural and ungovernable bitterness of Mind.

Surf. Undoubtedly Madam—and it has always been a sentiment of mine—that to propagate a malicious Truth wantonly—is more despicable than to falsify from Revenge, but can you Maria feel thus or others and be unkind to me alone—nay is hope to be denied the tenderest Passion.—

Mar. Why will you distress me by renewing this subject—

Surf. Ah! Maria! you would not treat me thus and oppose your guardian's Sir Peter's wishes—but that I see that my profligate Brother is still a favour'd Rival.

Mar. Ungenerously urged—but whatever my sentiments of that unfortunate young man are, be assured I shall not feel more bound to give him up because his Distresses have sunk him so low as to deprive him of the regard even of a Brother.

Surf. Nay but Maria do not leave me with a Frown—by all that's honest, I swear—— Gad's Life here's Lady Teazle—you must not—no you shall—for tho' I have the greatest Regard for Lady Teazle——

Mar. Lady Teazle!

Surf. Yet were Sir Peter to suspect——

Lady Teaz. What's this, Pray—do you take her for me!—Child you are wanted in the next Room.—What's all this, pray—

Surf. O the most unlucky circumstance in Nature. Maria has somehow suspected the tender concern I have for your happiness, and threaten'd to acquaint Sir Peter with her suspicions—and I was just endeavouring to reason with her when you came.

Lady Teaz. Indeed but you seem'd to adopt—a very tender mode of reasoning—do you usually argue on your knees?

Surf. O she's a Child—and I thought a little Bombast——but Lady Teazle when are you to give me your judgment on my Library as you promised——

Lady Teaz. No—no I begin to think it would be imprudent—and you know I admit you as a Lover no farther than Fashion requires.

Surf. True—a mere Platonic Cicisbeo, what every London wife is entitled to.

Lady Teaz. Certainly one must not be out of the Fashion—however, I have so much of my country Prejudices left—that—though Sir

Peter's ill humour may vex me ever so, it never shall provoke me to——

Surf. The only revenge in your Power—well I applaud your moderation.

Lady Teaz. Go—you are an insinuating Hypocrite—but we shall be miss'd—let us join the company.

Surf. True, but we had best not return together.

Lady Teaz. Well don't stay—for Maria shan't come to hear any more of your Reasoning, I promise you— *Ex.*

Surf. A curious Dilemma truly my Politics have run me into. I wanted at first only to ingratiate myself with Lady Teazle that she might not be my enemy with Maria—and I have I don't know how—become her serious Lover, so that I stand a chance of Committing a Crime I never meditated—and probably of losing Maria by the Pursuit !—Sincerely I begin to wish I had never made such a Point of gaining so very good a character, for it has led me into so many curst Rogueries that I doubt I shall be exposed at last. *Ex.*

SCENE 3rd.—AT SIR PETER'S.

—ROWLEY and SIR OLIVER.—

Sir Oliv. Ha ! ha ! ha ! and so my old Friend is married, hey ?—a young wife out of the country !—ha ! ha ! that he should have stood Bluff to old Bachelor so long and sink into a Husband at last !

Row. But you must not rally him on the subject Sir Oliver—'tis a tender Point I assure you though He has been married only seven months.

Sir Oliv. Ah then he has been just half a year on the stool of Repentance—Poor Peter ! But you say he has entirely given up Charles—never sees him, hey ?

Row. His Prejudice against him is astonishing—and I am sure greatly increased by a jealousy of him with Lady Teazle—which he has been industriously led into by a scandalous Society—in the neighbourhood—who have contributed not a little to Charles's ill name. Whereas the truth is I believe if the Lady is partial to either of them his Brother is the Favourite.

Sir Oliv. Aye—I know—there are a set of malicious prating prudent Gossips both male and Female, who murder characters to kill time, and will rob a young Fellow of his good name before He has years to know the value of it......but I am not to be prejudiced against my nephew by such I promise you! No! no—if Charles has done nothing false or mean, I shall compound for his extravagance.

Row. Then my life on 't, you will reclaim him. Ah, Sir, it gives me new vigour to find that your heart is not turned against him—and that the son of my good old master has one friend however left—

Sir Oliv. What! shall I forget Master Rowley—when I was at his house myself—egad my Brother and I were neither of us very prudent youths—and yet I believe you have not seen many better men than your old master was

Row. 'Tis this Reflection gives me assurance that Charles may yet be a credit to his Family—but here comes Sir Peter——

Sir Oliv. Egad so He does—mercy on me—He's greatly altered—and seems to have a settled married look—one may read Husband in his Face at this Distance.—

Enter SIR PETER.

Sir Pet. Ha! Sir Oliver—my old Friend—welcome to England—a thousand Times!

Sir Oliv. Thank you—thank you—Sir Peter—and Efaith I am as glad to find you well believe me—

Sir Pet. Ah! 'tis a long time since we met—sixteen year I doubt Sir Oliver—and many a cross accident in the Time—

Sir Oliv. Aye I have had my share—but, what I find you are married—hey my old Boy—well—well it can't be help'd—and so I wish you joy with all my heart—

Sir Pet. Thank you—thanks Sir Oliver.—Yes, I have entered into the happy state but we'll not talk of that now.

Sir Oliv. True true Sir Peter old Friends shouldn't begin on grievances at first meeting. No, no—

Row. Take care pray Sir——

Sir Oliv. Well—so one of my nephews I find is a wild Rogue—hey?

Sir Pet. Wild!—oh! my old Friend—I grieve for your disappointment there—He's a lost young man indeed—however his Brother will make you amends; Joseph is indeed what a youth should be—everybody in the world speaks well of him—

Sir Oliv. I am sorry to hear it—he has too good a character to be an honest Fellow. Everybody speaks well of him! Psha! then He has bow'd as low to Knaves and Fools as to the honest dignity of Virtue.

Sir Pet. What Sir Oliver do you blame him for not making Enemies?

Sir Oliv. Yes—if He has merit enough to deserve them.

Sir Pet. Well—well—you'll be convinced when you know him—'tis edification to hear him converse—he professes the noblest Sentiments.

Sir Oliv. Ah plague on his Sentiments—if he salutes me with a scrap sentence of morality in his mouth I shall be sick directly—but however don't mistake me Sir Peter I don't mean to defend Charles's Errors—but before I form my judgment of either of them, I intend to make a trial of their Hearts—and my Friend Rowley and I have planned something for the Purpose.

Row. And Sir Peter shall own he has been for once mistaken.

Sir Pet. My life on Joseph's Honour——

Sir Oliv. Well come give us a bottle of good wine—and we'll drink the Lads' Healths and tell you our scheme.

Sir Pet. Alons, then——

Sir Oliv. But don't Sir Peter be so severe against your old Friend's son.

Sir Pet. 'Tis his Vices and Follies have made me his Enemy.—

Row. Come—come—Sir Peter consider how early He was left to his own guidance.

Sir Oliv. Odds my Life—I am not sorry that He has run out of the course a little—for my Part, I hate to see dry Prudence clinging to the green Juices of youth—'tis like ivy round a sapling and spoils the growth of the Tree.

End of Act 2.

ACT 3d.

Scene 1st.—At Sir Peter's.

Sir Peter—Sir Oliver—and Rowley.

Sir Pet. Well, then, we will see the Fellows first and have our wine afterwards.—but how is this, Master Rowley.—I don't see the Jet of your scheme.

Row. Why Sir—this Mr. Stanley whom I was speaking of, is nearly related to them by their mother. He was once a merchant in Dublin—but has been ruined by a series of undeserved misfortunes—and now lately coming over to solicit the assistance of his friends here—has been flyng into prison by some of his Creditors—where he is now with two helpless Boys.—

Sir Oliv. Aye and a worthy Fellow too I remember him. But what is this to lead to—?

Row. You shall hear—He has applied by letter both to Mr. Surface and Charles—from the former he has received nothing but evasive promises of future service, while Charles has done all that his extravagance has left him power to do—and He is at this time endeavouring to raise a sum of money—part of which, in the midst of his own distresses, I know He intends for the service of poor Stanley.

Sir Oliv. Ah! he is my Brother's Son.

Sir Pet. Well, but how is Sir Oliver personally to——

Row. Why Sir I will inform Charles and his Brother that Stanley has obtain'd permission to apply in person to his Friends—and as they have neither of them ever seen him let Sir Oliver assume his character—and he will have a fair opportunity of judging at least of the Benevolence of their Dispositions.

Sir Pet. Pshaw! this will prove nothing—I make no doubt Charles is Coxcomb and thoughtless enough to give money to poor relations if he had it—

Sir Oliv. Then He shall never want it—. I have brought a few Rupees home with me Sir Peter—and I only want to be sure of bestowing them rightly.—

Row. Then Sir believe me you will find in the youngest Brother one who in the midst of Folly and dissipation—has still, as our immortal Bard expresses it,—

"a Tear for Pity and a Hand open as the day for melting Charity."

Sir Pet. Pish! What signifies his having an open Hand or Purse either when He has nothing left to give!—but if you talk of humane Sentiments—Joseph is the man—Well, well, make the trial, if you please. But where is the fellow whom you brought for Sir Oliver to examine, relative to Charles's affairs?

Row. Below waiting his commands, and no one can give him better intelligence—This, Sir Oliver, is a friendly Jew, who to do him justice, has done everything in his power to bring your nephew to a proper sense of his extravagance.

Sir Pet. Pray let us have him in.

Row. Desire Mr. Moses to walk upstairs. [*Calls to* SERVANT.

Sir Pet. But Pray why should you suppose he will speak the truth?

Row. Oh, I have convinced him that he has no chance of recovering certain Sums advanced to Charles but through the bounty of Sir Oliver, who He knows is arrived; so that you may depend on his Fidelity to his interest. I have also another evidence in my Power, one Snake, whom I shall shortly produce to remove some of *your* Prejudices Sir Peter relative to Charles and Lady Teazle.

Sir Pet. I have heard too much on that subject.

Row. Here comes the honest Israelite.

Enter MOSES.

—This is Sir Oliver.

Sir Oliv. Sir—I understand you have lately had great dealings with my Nephew Charles.

Mos. Yes Sir Oliver—I have done all I could for him, but He was ruined before He came to me for Assistance.

Sir Oliv. That was unlucky truly—for you have had no opportunity of showing your Talents.

Mos. None at all—I hadn't the Pleasure of knowing his Distresses till he was some thousands worse than nothing, till it was impossible to add to them.

Sir Oliv. Unfortunate indeed! but I suppose you have done all in your Power for him honest Moses?

Mos. Yes he knows that—This very evening I was to have brought him a gentleman from the city who does not know him and will I believe advance some money.

Sir Pet. What one Charles has never had money from before?

Mos. Yes Mr. Premium, of Crutched Friars.

Sir Pet. Egad, Sir Oliver a Thought strikes me!—Charles you say does'nt know Mr. Premium?

Mos. Not at all.

Sir Pet. Now then Sir Oliver you may have a better opportunity of satisfying yourself than by an old romancing tale of a poor Relation —go with my friend Moses and represent Mr. Premium and then I'll answer for't you'll see your Nephew in all his glory.

Sir Oliv. Egad I like this Idea better than the other, and I may visit Joseph afterwards as old Stanley.

Sir Pet. True so you may.

Row. Well this is taking Charles rather at a disadvantage, to be sure — however Moses — you understand Sir Peter and will be faithful——

Mos. You may depend upon me—and this is near the Time I was to have gone.

Sir Oliv. I'll accompany you as soon as you please, Moses——but hold—I have forgot one thing—how the plague shall I be able to pass for a Jew?

Mos. There's no need—the Principal is Christian.

Sir Oliv. Is He—I'm very sorry to hear it—but then again—an't I rather too smartly dressed to look like a money-Lender?

Sir Pet. Not at all ; 'twould not be out of character, if you went in your own carriage—would it, Moses!

Mos. Not in the least.

Sir Oliv. Well—but—how must I talk there's certainly some cant of usury and mode of treating that I ought to know.

Sir Pet. Oh, there's not much to learn—the great point as I take it is to be exorbitant enough in your Demands hey Moses?

Mos. Yes that's very great Point.

Sir Oliv. I'll answer for't I'll not be wanting in that—I'll ask him eight or ten per cent. on the loan—at least.

Mos. You'll be found out directly—if you ask him no more than that, you'll be discovered immediately.

Sir Oliv. Hey!—what the Plague!—how much then?

Mos. That depends upon the Circumstances—if he appears not very anxious for the supply, you should require only forty or fifty per cent. —but if you find him in great Distress, and want the monies very bad —you may ask double.

Sir Pet. A good—onest Trade you're learning, Sir Oliver—

Sir Oliv. Truly, I think so—and not unprofitable—

Mos. Then you know—you haven't the monies yourself, but are forced to borrow them for him of a Friend.

Sir Oliv. O I borrow it of a Friend do I?

Mos. And your friend is an unconscion'd Dog—but you can't help it.

Sir Oliv. My Friend's an unconscionable Dog, is he?

Mos. Yes—and He himself hasn't the monies by him—but is forced to sell stock —at a great loss—

Sir Oliv. He is forced to sell stock is he—at a great loss, is he—well that's very kind of him—

Sir Pet. Efaith, Sir Oliver—Mr. Premium I mean—you'll soon be master of the Trade—but, Moses would have him inquire if the borrower is a minor—

Mos. O yes—

Sir Pet. And in that case his Conscience will direct him—

Mos. To have the Bond in another Name to be sure.

Sir Oliv. Well—well I shall be perfect—

Sir Pet. But hearkee wouldn't you have him also run out a little against the annuity Bill—that would be in character I should think—

Mos. Very much—

Row. And lament that a young man now must be at years of discretion before He is suffered to ruin himself!

Mos. Aye, great Pity!

Sir Pet. And abuse the Public for allowing merit to an act whose only object is to snatch misfortune and imprudence from the rapacious Relief of usury! and give the minor a chance of inheriting his estate without being undone by coming into Possession.

Sir Oliv. So—so—Moses shall give me further instructions as we go together.

Sir Pet. You will not have much time for your Nephew lives hard bye—

Sir Oliv. Oh Never—fear my Tutor appears so able that tho' Charles lived in the next street it must be my own Fault if I am not a compleat Rogue before I turn the Corner— *Exe*

Sir Pet. So—now I think Sir Oliver will be convinced—you shan't follow them Rowley. You are partial and would have prepared Charles for 'tother plot.

Row. No upon my word Sir Peter—

Sir Pet. Well, go bring me this Snake, and I'll hear what he has to say presently. I see Maria, and want to speak with her.—*Exe R.* I should be glad to be convinced my suspicions of Lady Teazle and Charles were unjust—I have never yet opened my mind on this subject to my Friend Joseph...I am determined. I will do it—He will give me his opinion sincerely.—

Enter MARIA.

So Child—has Mr. Surface returned with you—

THE SCHOOL FOR SCANDAL. 175

Mar. No Sir—He was engaged.

Sir Pet. Well—Maria—do you not reflect the more you converse with that amiable young man what return his Partiality for you deserves?

Mar. Indeed Sir Peter—your frequent importunity on this subject distresses me extremely—you compell me to Declare that I know no man who has ever paid me a particular Attention whom I would not prefer to Mr. Surface—

Sir Pet. Soh! Here's Perverseness—no—no—Maria, 'tis Charles only whom you would prefer—'tis evident his Vices and Follies have won your Heart.

Mar. This is unkind Sir—You know I have obey'd you in neither seeing nor corresponding with him—I have heard enough to convince me that He is unworthy my regard—Yet I cannot think it culpable—if while my understanding severely condemns his Vices, my Heart suggests some Pity for his Distresses.

Sir Pet. Well well pity him as much as you please, but give your Heart and Hand to a worthier object.

Mar. Never to his Brother!

Sir Pet. Go—perverse and obstinate! but take care, Madam—you have never yet known what the authority of a Guardian is—don't compell me to inform you of it.—

Mar. I can only say, you shall not have just Reason—'tis true, by my Father's will I am for a short period bound to regard you as his substitute, but I must cease to think you so when you would compel me to be miserable. *exit.*

Sir Pet. Was ever man so crossed as I am everything conspiring to fret me! I had not been involved in matrimony a fortnight before her Father—a hale and hearty man, died on purpose, I believe—for the Pleasure of plaguing me with the care of his Daughter......but here comes my Helpmate!—She appears in great good humour——how happy I should be if I could teaze her into loving me tho' but a little——

Enter LADY TEAZLE.

Lady Teaz. Lud! Sir Peter I hope you haven't been quarrelling with Maria? It isn't using me well to be ill humour'd when I am not bye—!

Sir Pet. Ah! Lady Teazle you might have the Power to make me good humour'd at all times—

Lady Teaz. I am sure—I wish I had—for I want you to be in a charming sweet temper at this moment—do be good humour'd now—and let me have two hundred Pounds will you?

Sir Pet. Two hundred Pounds! what an't I to be in a good humour without paying for it—but speak to me thus—and Efaith there's nothing I could refuse you. You shall have it—but seal me a bond or the repayment.

Lady Teaz. O no—there—my Note of Hand will do as well—

Sir Pet. And you shall no longer reproach me with not giving you an independent settlement—I shall shortly surprise you—and you'll not call me ungenerous — but shall we always live thus — hey?

Lady Teaz. If you—please—I'm sure I don't care how soon we leave off quarrelling provided you'll own you were tired first—

Sir Pet. Well—then let our future contest be who shall be most obliging.

Lady Teaz. I assure you Sir Peter Good Nature becomes you—you look now as you did before we were married—when you used to walk with me under the Elms, and tell me stories of what a Gallant you were in your youth—and chuck me under the chin you would—and ask me if I thought I could love an old Fellow who would deny me nothing—didn't you?

Sir Pet. Yes—yes—and you were as kind and attentive——

Lady Teaz. Aye so I was—and would always take your Part, when my acquaintance used to abuse you and turn you into ridicule—

Sir Pet. Indeed!

Lady Teaz. Aye—and when my cousin Sophy has called you a stiff peevish old batchelor and laugh'd at me for thinking of marrying one who might be my Father—I have always defended you—and said I didn't think you so ugly by any means, and that you'd make a very good sort of a husband—

Sir Pet. And you prophesied right—and we shall certainly now be the happiest couple——

Lady Teaz. And never differ again.

Sir Pet. No never—tho' at the same time indeed—my dear Lady Teazle—you must watch your Temper very narrowly—for in all our little Quarrels—my dear—if you recollect my Love you always began first—

Lady Teaz. I beg your Pardon—my dear Sir Peter—indeed—you always gave the provocation.

Sir Pet. Now—see, my Love take care—contradicting isn't the way to keep Friends.

Lady Teaz. Then don't you begin it my Love!

Sir Pet. There now—you are going on—you don't perceive my Life, that you are just doing the very thing my Love which you know always makes me angry.

Lady Teaz. Nay—you know if you will be angry without any reason—my Dear——

Sir Pet. There now you want to quarrel again.

Lady Teaz. No—I am sure I don't—but if you will be so peevish——

Sir Pet. There—now who begins first?

Lady Teaz. Why you to be sure—I said nothing—but there's no bearing your Temper.

Sir Pet. No—no—my dear—the fault's in your own temper.

Lady Teaz. Aye you are just what my Cousin Sophy said you would be—

Sir Pet. Your Cousin Sophy—is a forward impertinent Gipsey—

Lady Teaz. Go you great Bear—how dare you abuse my Relations—

Sir Pet. Now may all the Plagues of marriage be doubled on me, if ever I try to be Friends with you any more——

Lady Teaz. So much the Better.

Sir Pet. No—no Madam 'tis evident you never cared a pin for me—I was a madman to marry you—

Lady Teaz. And I am sure I was a Fooll to marry you—an old dangling Batchelor, who was single of fifty—only because He never could meet with any one who would have him.

Sir Pet. Aye—aye—Madam—but you were pleased enough to listen to me—you never had such an offer before—

Lady Teaz. No—didn't I refuse Sir Jeremy Terrier—who everybody said would have been a better Match—for his estate is just as good as yours—and he has broke his Neck since we have been married!

Sir Pet. I have done with you Madam! You are an unfeeling—ungrateful—but there's an end of everything—I believe you capable of anything that's bad—Yes, Madam—I now believe the Reports relative to you and Charles—Madam—yes—Madam—you and Charles are—not without grounds——

Lady Teaz. Take—care Sir Peter—you had better not insinuate any such thing! I'll not be suspected without cause I promise you——

Sir Pet. Very—well—Madam—very well! a separate maintenance—as soon as you Please. Yes Madam or a Divorce—I'll make an example of myself for the Benefit of all old Batchelors—Let us eparate, Madam.

Lady Teaz. Agreed—agreed—and now—my dear Sir Peter we are of a mind again, we may be the happiest couple—and never differ again, you know—ha! ha!—Well you are going to be in a Passion I see—and I shall only interrupt you—so, bye! bye! hey—young Jockey try'd and countered.   *Exit*

Sir Pet. Plagues and tortures! She pretends to keep her temper, can't I make her angry neither! O! I am the miserable fellow! But I'll not bear her presuming to keep her Temper—No she may break my Heart—but she shan't keep her Temper. *Ex.*

Scene 2d.

At Charles's House.

Enter Trip—Moses, and Sir Oliver.

Trip. Here Master Moses—if you'll stay a moment—I'll try whether Mr.——what's the Gentleman's Name?

Sir Oliv. Mr.——Moses—what *is* my name——

Mos. Mr. Premium——

Trip. Premium—very well. *ex. Trip—taking snuff.*

Sir Oliv. To judge by the Servants—one wouldn't believe the master was ruin'd—but what—sure this was my Brother's House——

Mos. Yes Sir Mr. Charles bought it of Mr. Joseph with the Furniture, Pictures, &c—just as the old Gentleman left it—Sir Peter thought it a great peice of extravagance in him.

Oliv. In my mind the other's economy in selling it to him was more reprehensible by half.——

Enter Trip.

Trip. My Master Gentlemen says you must wait, he has company, and can't speak with you yet.

Sir Oliv. If he knew who it was wanted to see him, perhaps he wouldn't have sent such a Message.

Trip. Yes—yes—Sir—He knows you are here—I didn't forget little Premium—no—no——

Sir Oliv. Very well—and pray Sir what may be your Name?

Trip. Trip Sir—my Name is Trip, at your Service.

Sir Oliv. Well then Mr. Trip—I presume your master is seldom without company——

Trip. Very seldom Sir—the world says ill-natured things of him but 'tis all malice—no man was ever better beloved—Sir he seldom sits down to dinner without a dozen particular Friends——

Sir Oliv. He's very happy indeed—you have a pleasant sort of Place here I guess?

Trip. Why yes—here are three or four of us pass our time agreeably enough—but then our wages are sometimes a little in arrear—and not very great either—but fifty Pounds a year and find our own Bags and Bouquets——

Sir Oliv. Bags and Bouquets!—Halters and Bastinadoes! [*Aside.*

Trip. But *à propos* Moses—have you been able to get me that little Bill discounted?

Sir Oliv. Wants to raise money too!—mercy on me! has his distresses, I warrant like a Lord—and affects Creditors and Duns! [*Aside.*

Mos. 'Twas not be done, indeed——

Trip. Good lack—you surprise me—My Friend Brush has indorsed it and I thought when he put his name at the Back of a Bill 'twas as good as cash.

Mos. No 'twouldn't do.

Trip. A small sum—but twenty Pound—harkee, Moses do you think you could get it me by way of annuity?

Sir Oliv. An annuity! ha! ha! a Footman raise money by annuity— Well done Luxury egad! [*Aside.*

Mos. Who would you get to join with you?

Trip. You know my Lord Applice—you have seen him however——

Mos. Yes——

Trip. You must have observed what an appearance he makes— nobody dresses better, nobody throws off faster—very well this Gentleman will stand my security.

Mos. Well—but you must insure your Place.

Trip. O with all my Heart—I'll insure my Place, and my Life too, if you please.

Sir Oliv. It's more than I would your neck——

Mos. But is there nothing you could deposit?

Trip. Why nothing capital of my master's wardrobe has drop'd lately—but I could give you a mortgage on some of his winter Cloaths with equity of redemption before November or—you shall have the reversion—of the French velvet, or a post obit on the Blue and Silver— these I should think Moses—with a few Pair of Point Ruffles as a collateral security—hey, my little Fellow?

Mos. Well well—we'll talk presently—we detain the Gentlemen——

Sir Oliv. O pray don't let me interrupt Mr. Trip's Negotiation.

Trip. Harkee—I heard the Bell—I believe, Gentlemen I can now introduce you—don't forget the annuity little Moses.

Sir Oliv. If the man be a shadow of his Master this is the Temple of Dissipation indeed! [*Exe.*

Scene 3d.

CHARLES—CARELESS, &c., &c.

At Table with Wine.

Chas. 'Fore Heaven, 'tis true!—there is the great Degeneracy of the age—many of our acquaintance have Taste—Spirit, and Politeness—but plague on 't they won't drink——

Care. It is so indeed—Charles—they give into all the substantial Luxuries of the Table—and abstain from nothing but wine and wit— Oh, certainly society suffers by it intolerably—for now instead of the social spirit of Raillery that used to mantle over a glass of bright Burgundy their conversation is become just like the Spa water they drink which has all the Pertness and flatulence of champaine without its spirit or Flavour.

1 *Gent.* But what are they to do who love Play better than wine——

Care. True—there's Harry diets himself—for gaming and is now under a hazard Regimen.

Chas. Then He'll have the worst of it—what you wouldn't train a horse for the course by keeping him from corn—For my Part egad I am never so successful as when I'm a little—merry—let me throw on a Bottle of Champaine and I never lose—at least I never feel my losses which is exactly the same thing.

2 *Gent.* Aye that may be—but it is as impossible to follow wine and play as to unite Love and Politics.

Chas. Pshaw—you may do both—Caesar made Love and Laws in a Breath—and was liked by the Senate as well as the Ladies—but no man can pretend to be a Believer in Love, who is an abjurer of wine—'tis the Test by which a Lover knows his own Heart—fill a dozen Bumpers to a dozen Beauties, and she that floats atop is the maid that has bewitched you.

Care. Now then Charles—be honest and give us yours——

Chas. Why I have withheld her only in compassion to you—if I toast her you should give a round of her Peers, which is impossible! on earth!

Care. O, then we'll find some canonized Vestals or heathen Goddesses that will do I warrant——

Chas. Here then—Bumpers—you Rogues—Bumpers! Maria—Maria——

1*st Gent.* Maria who?

Chas. Oh, damn the Surname 'tis too formal to be register'd in Love's calendar—but now Careless beware—beware—we must have Beauty's superlative.

1*st Gent.* Nay Never study Careless—we'll stand to the Toast— tho' your mistress should want an eye—and you know you have a song will excuse you——

Care. Egad so I have—and I'll give him the song instead of the Lady.——

THE SCHOOL FOR SCANDAL.

SONG.—AND CHORUS—*

Here's to the maiden of bashful fifteen;
  Here's to the widow of fifty;
Here's to the flaunting extravagant quean,
  And here's to the housewife that's thrifty.

Chorus. Let the toast pass,—
  Drink to the lass,
I'll warrant she'll prove an excuse for a glass.

Here's to the charmer whose dimples we prize;
  Now to the maid who has none, sir;
Here's to the girl with a pair of blue eyes,
  And here's to the nymph with but one, sir.

Chorus. Let the toast pass, &c.

Here's to the maid with a bosom of snow:
  Now to her that's as brown as a berry:
Here's to the wife with a face full of woe,
  And now to the damsel that's merry.

Chorus. Let the toast pass, &c.

For let 'em be clumsy, or let 'em be slim,
  Young or ancient, I care not a feather;
So fill a pint bumper quite up to the brim,
So fill up your glasses, nay, fill to the brim,
  And let us e'en toast them together.

Chorus. Let the toast pass, &c.
          [*Enter Trip whispers Charles.*

2nd Gent. Bravo Careless—Ther's Toast and Sentiment too

1st Gent. E' faith there's infinite charity in that song.——

Chas. Gentlemen, you must excuse me a little.—Careless, take the Chair, will you?

Care. Nay prithee, Charles—what now—this is one of your Peerless Beauties I suppose—has dropped in by chance?

Chas. No—Faith—to tell you the Truth 'tis a Jew and a Broker who are come by appointment.

Care. O dam it let's have the Jew in.

1 Gent. Aye and the Broker too by all means——

2 Gent. Yes yes the Jew and the Broker.

Chas. Egad with all my Heart—Trip—bid the Gentlemen walk in—tho' there's one of them a Stranger I can tell you——

Trip. What Sir—would you chuse Mr. Premium to come up with——

1st Gent. Yes—yes Mr. Premium certainly.

Care. To be sure—Mr. Premium—by all means Charles, let us give them some generous Burgundy, and perhaps they'll grow conscientious———

---
* The words which follow this title are not inserted in the manuscript of the play.

THE SCHOOL FOR SCANDAL.

Chas. O, Hang 'em—no—wine does but draw forth a man's natural qualities; and to make them drink would only be to whet their Knavery.

Enter TRIP—SIR OLIVER *and* MOSES.

Chas. So—honest Moses—walk in—walk in pray Mr. Premium—that's the Gentleman's name isn't it Moses.

Mos. Yes Sir.

Chas. Surf. Set chairs—Trim.—Sit down, Mr. Premium.—Glasses Trim.—sit down Moses.—Come, Mr. Premium I'll give you a sentiment—Here's Success to Usury—Moses fill the Gentleman a bumper.

Mos. Success to Usury!

Care. Right Moses—Usury is Prudence and industry and deserves to succeed——

Sir Oliv. Then Here is—all the success it deserves! [*Drinks.*

Chas. Mr. Premium you and I are but strangers yet—but I hope we shall be better acquainted by and bye——

Sir Oliv. Yes Sir hope we shall—more intimately perhaps than you'll wish. [*Aside.**

Care. No, no, that won't do! Mr. Premium, you have demurred at the toast, and must drink it in a pint bumper.

1 *Gent.* A pint bumper, at least.

Mos. Oh, pray, sir, consider—Mr. Premium's a gentleman.

Care. And therefore loves good wine.

2 *Gent.* Give Moses a quart glass—this is mutiny, and a high contempt for the chair.

Care: Here, now for't! I'll see justice done, to the last drop of my bottle.

Sir Oliv. Nay, pray, gentlemen—I did not expect this usage.

Chas. No, hang it, you shan't; Mr. Premium's a stranger.

Sir Oliv. Odd! I wish I was well out of their company. [*Aside.*

Care. Plague on 'em then! if they won't drink, we'll not sit down with them. Come, Harry, the dice are in the next room.—Charles, you'll join us when you have finished your business with the gentlemen?

Chas. I will! I will!—[*Exeunt* SIR HARRY BUMPER *and* GENTLEMEN; CARELESS *following.*] Careless.

Care. [*Returning.*] Well!

Chas. Perhaps I may want you.

Care. Oh, you know I am always ready: word, note, or bond, 'tis all the same to me. [*Exit.*

* From this place to Scene ii. Act IV. p. 191 several sheets are missing.

Mos. Sir, this is Mr. Premium, a gentleman of the strictest honour and secrecy; and always performs what he undertakes. Mr. Premium, this is——

Chas. Psha! have done. Sir, my friend Moses is a very honest fellow, but a little slow at expression: he'll be an hour giving us our titles. Mr. Premium, the plain state of the matter is this: I am an extravagant young fellow who wants to borrow money; you I take to be a prudent old fellow, who have got money to lend. I am blockhead enough to give fifty per cent. sooner than not have it! and you, I presume, are rogue enough to take a hundred if you can get it. Now, sir, you see we are acquainted at once, and may proceed to business without further ceremony.

Sir Oliv. Exceeding frank, upon my word. I see, sir, you are not a man of many compliments.

Chas. Oh, no, sir! plain dealing in business I always think best.

Sir Oliv. Sir, I like you the better for it. However, you are mistaken in one thing; I have no money to lend, but I believe I could procure some of a friend; but then he's an unconscionable dog. Isn't he, Moses? And must sell stock to accommodate you. Mustn't he, Moses!

Mos. Yes, indeed! You know I always speak the truth, and scorn to tell a lie!

Chas. Right. People that speak truth generally do. But these are trifles, Mr. Premium. What! I know money is n't to be bought without paying for 't!

Sir Oliv. Well, but what security could you give? You have no land, I suppose?

Chas. Not a mole-hill, nor a twig, but what's in the bough-pots out of the window!

Sir Oliv. Nor any stock, I presume?

Chas. Nothing but live stock—and that's only a few pointers and ponies. But pray, Mr. Premium, are you acquainted at all with any of my connections?

Sir Oliv. Why, to say the truth, I am.

Chas. Then you must know that I have a devilish rich uncle in the East Indies, Sir Oliver Surface, from whom I have the greates expectations?

Sir Oliv. That you have a wealthy uncle, I have heard; but how your expectations will turn out is more, I believe, than you can tell.

Chas. Oh, no!—there can be no doubt. They tell me I'm a prodigious favourite, and that he talks of leaving me everything.

Sir Oliv. Indeed! this is the first I've heard of it.

Chas. Yes, yes, 'tis just so. Moses knows 'tis true; don't you, Moses?

Mos. Oh, yes! I'll swear to't.

Sir Oliv. Egad, they'll persuade me presently I'm at Bengal.

[*Aside.*

Chas. Now I propose, Mr. Premium, if it's agreeable to you, a post-obit on Sir Oliver's life: though at the same time the old fellow has been so liberal to me, that I give you my word, I should be very sorry to hear that anything had happened to him.

Sir Oliv. Not more than I should, I assure you. But the bond you mention happens to be just the worst security you could offer me —for I might live to a hundred and never see the principal.

Chas. Oh, yes, you would! the moment Sir Oliver dies, you know, you would come on me for the money.

Sir Oliv. Then I believe I should be the most unwelcome dun you ever had in your life.

Chas. What! I suppose you're afraid that Sir Oliver is too good a life?

Sir Oliv. No, indeed I am not; though I have heard he is as hale and healthy as any man of his years in Christendom.

Chas. There again, now, you are misinformed. No, no, the climate has hurt him considerably, poor uncle Oliver. Yes, yes, he breaks apace, I'm told—and is so much altered lately that his nearest relations would not know him.

Sir Oliv. No! Ha! ha! ha! so much altered lately that his nearest relations would not know him! Ha! ha! ha! egad—ha! ha! ha!

Chas. Ha! ha!—you're glad to hear that, little Premium?

Sir Oliv. No, no, I'm not.

Chas. Yes, yes, you are—ha! ha! ha!—you know that mends your chance.

Sir Oliv. But I'm told Sir Oliver is coming over; nay, some say he is actually arrived.

Chas. Psha! sure I must know better than you whether he's come or not. No, no, rely on't he's at this moment at Calcutta. Isn't he, Moses?

Mos. Oh, yes, certainly.

Sir Oliv. Very true, as you say, you must know better than I, though I have it from pretty good authority. Haven't I, Moses?

Mos. Yes, most undoubted!

Sir Oliv. But, sir, as I understand you want a few hundreds immediately, is there nothing you could dispose of?

Chas. How do you mean?

Sir Oliv. For instance, now, I have heard that your father left behind him a great quantity of massy old plate.

Chas. O Lud! that's gone long ago. Moses can tell you how better than I can.

Sir Oliv. [*Aside.*] Good lack! all the family race-cups and corporation-bowls!—[*Aloud.*] Then it was also supposed that his library was one of the most valuable and compact.

Chas. Yes, yes, so it was—vastly too much so for a private gentleman. For my part, I was always of a communicative disposition, so I thought it a shame to keep so much knowledge to myself.

Sir Oliv. [*Aside.*] Mercy upon me! learning that had run in the family like an heir-loom!—[*Aloud.*] Pray, what has become of the books?

Chas. You must inquire of the auctioneer, Master Premium, for I don't believe even Moses can direct you.

Mos. I know nothing of books.

Sir Oliv. So, so, nothing of the family property left, I suppose?

Chas. Not much, indeed; unless you have a mind to the family pictures. I have got a room full of ancestors above: and if you have a taste for old paintings, egad, you shall have 'em a bargain!

Sir Oliv. Hey! what the devil! sure, you wouldn't sell your forefathers, would you?

Chas. Every man of them, to the best bidder.

Sir Oliv. What! your great-uncles and aunts?

Chas. Ay, and my great-grandfathers and grandmothers too.

Sir Oliv. [*Aside.*] Now I give him up!—[*Aloud.*] What the plague, have you no bowels for your own kindred? Odd's life! do you take me for Shylock in the play, that you would raise money of me on your own flesh and blood?

Chas. Nay, my little broker, don't be angry: what need you care, if you have your money's worth?

Sir Oliv. Well, I'll be the purchaser: I think I can dispose of the family canvas.—[*Aside.*] Oh, I'll never forgive him this! never!

Re-enter CARELESS.

Care. Come, Charles, what keeps you?

Chas. I can't come yet. I' faith, we are going to have a sale above stairs; here's little Premium will buy all my ancestors!

Care. Oh, burn your ancestors!

Chas. No, he may do that afterwards, if he pleases. Stay, Careless, we want you: egad, you shall be auctioneer—so come along with us.

Care. Oh, have with you, if that's the case. I can handle a hammer as well as a dice box! Going! going!

Sir Oliv. Oh, the profligates! [*Aside.*

Chas. Come, Moses, you shall be appraiser, if we want one. Gad's life, little Premium, you don't seem to like the business?

Sir Oliv. Oh, yes, I do, vastly! Ha! ha! ha! yes, yes, I think it a rare joke to sell one's family by auction—ha! ha!—[*Aside.*] Oh, the prodigal!

Chas. To be sure! when a man wants money, where the plague should he get assistance, if he can't make free with his own relations?

[*Exeunt.*

Sir Oliv. I'll never forgive him; never! never!

ACT IV.

SCENE I.—*A Picture Room in* CHARLES SURFACE'S *House.*

Enter CHARLES, SIR OLIVER, MOSES, *and* CARELESS.

Chas. Surf. Walk in, gentlemen, pray walk in;—here they are, the family of the Surfaces, up to the Conquest.

Sir Oliv. And, in my opinion, a goodly collection.

Chas. Ay, ay, these are done in the true spirit of portrait-painting; no *volontière grace* or expression. Not like the works of your modern Raphaels, who give you the strongest resemblance, yet contrive to make your portrait independent of you; so that you may sink the original and not hurt the picture. No, no; the merit of these is the inveterate likeness—all stiff and awkard as the originals, and like nothing in human nature besides.

Sir Oliv. Ah! we shall never see such figures of men again.

Chas. I hope not. Well, you see, Master Premium, what a domestic character I am; here I sit of an evening surrounded by my family. But come, get to your pulpit, Mr. Auctioneer; here's an old gouty chair of my grandfather's will answer the purpose.

Care. Ay, ay, this will do. But, Charles, I haven't a hammer; and what's an auctioneer without his hammer?

Chas. Egad, that's true. What parchment have we here? Oh, our genealogy in full. [*Taking pedigree down.*] Here, Careless, you shall have no common bit of mahogany, here's the family tree for you, you rogue! This shall be your hammer, and now you may knock down my ancestors with their own pedigree.

Sir Oliv. What an unnatural rogue!—an *ex post facto* parricide!
[*Aside.*

Care. Yes, yes, here's a list of your generation indeed;— faith, Charles, this is the most convenient thing you could have found for the business, for 'twill not only serve as a hammer, but a catalogue into the bargain. Come, begin—A-going, a-going, a-going!

Chas. Bravo, Careless! Well, here's my great uncle, Sir Richard Ravelin, a marvellous good general in his day, I assure you. He served in all the Duke of Marlborough's wars, and got that cut over his eye at the battle of Malplaquet. What say you, Mr. Premium? look at him—there's a hero! not cut out of his feathers, as your modern clipped captains are, but enveloped in wig and regimentals, as a general should be. What do you bid?

Sir Oliv. [*Aside to Moses.*] Bid him speak.

Mos. Mr. Premium would have you speak.

Chas. Why, then, he shall have him for ten pounds, and I'm sure that's not dear for a staff-officer.

Sir Oliv. [*Aside.*] Heaven deliver me! his famous uncle Richard for ten pounds!—[*Aloud.*] Very well, sir, I take him at that.

Chas. Careless, knock down my uncle Richard.—Here, now, is a maiden sister of his, my great-aunt Deborah, done by Kneller, in his best manner, and esteemed a very formidable likeness. There she is, you see, a shepherdess feeding her flock. You shall have her for five pounds ten—the sheep are worth the money.

Sir Oliv. [*Aside.*] Ah! poor Deborah! a woman who set such a value on herself!—[*Aloud.*] Five pounds ten—she's mine.

Chas. Knock down my aunt Deborah! Here, now, are two that were a sort of cousins of theirs.—You see, Moses, these pictures were done some time ago, when beaux wore wigs, and the ladies their own hair.

Sir Oliv. Yes, truly, head-dresses appear to have been a little lower in those days.

Chas. Well, take that couple for the same.

Mos. 'Tis a good bargain.

Chas. Careless!—This, now, is a grandfather of my mother's, a learned judge, well known on the western circuit.—What do you rate him at, Moses?

Mos. Four guineas.

Chas. Four guineas! Gad's life, you don't bid me the price of his wig.—Mr. Premium, you have more respect for the woolsack; do let us knock his lordship down at fifteen.

Sir Oliv. By all means.

Care. Gone!

Chas. And there are two brothers of his, William and Walter Blunt, Esquires, both members of Parliament, and noted speakers; and, what's very extraordinary, I believe, this is the first time they were ever bought or sold.

Sir Oliv. That is very extraordinary, indeed! I'll take them at your own price, for the honour of Parliament.

Care. Well said, little Premium! I'll knock them down at forty.

Chas. Here's a jolly fellow—I don't know what relation, but he was mayor of Norwich: take him at eight pounds.

Sir Oliv. No, no; six will do for the mayor.

Chas. Come, make it guineas, and I'll throw you the two aldermen here into the bargain.

Sir Oliv. They're mine.

Chas. Careless, knock down the mayor and aldermen. But, plague on't! we shall be all day retailing in this manner; do let us deal wholesale: what say you, little Premium? Give me three hundred pounds for the rest of the family in the lump.

Care. Ay, ay, that will be the best way.

Sir Oliv. Well, well, anything to accommodate you; they are mine. But there is one portrait which you have always passed over.

Care. What, that ill-looking little fellow over the settee?

Sir Oliv. Yes, sir, I mean that; though I don't think him so ill-looking a little fellow, by any means.

Chas. What, that? Oh; that's my uncle Oliver! 'Twas done before he went to India.

Care. Your uncle Oliver! Gad, then you'll never be friends, Charles. That, now, to me, is as stern a looking rogue as ever I saw; an unforgiving eye, and a damned disinheriting countenance! an inveterate knave, depend on't. Don't you think so, little Premium?

Sir Oliv. Upon my soul, sir, I do not; I think it is as honest a looking face as any in the room, dead or alive. But I suppose uncle Oliver goes with the rest of the lumber?

Chas. No, hang it! I'll not part with poor Noll. The old fellow has been very good to me, and, egad, I'll keep his picture while I've a room to put it in.

Sir Oliv. [*Aside.*] The rogue's my nephew after all!—[*Aloud.*] But, sir, I have somehow taken a fancy to that picture.

Chas. I'm sorry for't, for you certainly will not have it. Oons, haven't you got enough of them?

Sir Oliv. [*Aside.*] I forgive him everything!—[*Aloud.*] But, sir, when I take a whim in my head, I don't value money. I'll give you as much for that as for all the rest.

Chas. Don't tease me, master broker; I tell you I'll not part with it, and there's an end of it.

Sir Oliv. [*Aside.*] How like his father the dog is.—[*Aloud.*] Well, well, I have done.—[*Aside.*] I did not perceive it before, but I think I never saw such a striking resemblance.—[*Aloud.*] Here is a draught for your sum.

Chas. Why, 'tis for eight hundred pounds!

Sir Oliv. You will not let Sir Oliver go?

Chas. Zounds! no! I tell you, once more.

Sir Oliv. Then never mind the difference, we'll balance that another time. But give me your hand on the bargain; you are an honest fellow, Charles—I beg pardon, sir, for being so free.—Come, Moses.

Chas. Egad, this is a whimsical old fellow!—But hark'ee, Premium, you'll prepare lodgings for these gentlemen.

Sir Oliv. Yes, yes, I'll send for them in a day or two.

Chas. But, hold; do now send a genteel conveyance for them, for, assure you, they were most of them used to ride in their own carriages.

Sir Oliv. I will, I will—for all but Oliver.

Chas. Ay, all but the little nabob.

Sir Oliv. You're fixed on that?

Chas. Peremptorily.

Sir Oliv. [*Aside.*] A dear extravagant rogue!—[*Aloud.*] Good day! Come, Moses.—[*Aside.*] Let me hear now who dares call him profligate! [*Exit with* MOSES.

Care. Why, this is the oddest genius of the sort I ever met with!

Chas. Egad, he's the prince of brokers, I think. I wonder how the devil Moses got acquainted with so honest a fellow.—Ha! here's Rowley.—Do, Careless, say I'll join the company in a few moments.

Care. I will—but don't let that old blockhead persuade you to squander any of that money on old musty debts, or any such nonsense; for tradesmen, Charles, are the most exorbitant fellows.

Chas. Very true, and paying them is only encouraging them.

Care. Nothing else.

Chas. Ay, ay, never fear.—[*Exit* CARELESS.] So! this was an odd old fellow, indeed. Let me see, two-thirds of these five hundred and thirty odd pounds are mine by right. Fore Heaven! I find one's ancestors are more valuable relations than I took them for!—Ladies and gentlemen, your most obedient and very grateful servant.

[*Bows ceremoniously to the pictures.*

Enter ROWLEY.

Ha! old Rowley! egad, you are just come in time to take leave of your old acquaintance.

Row. Yes, I heard they were a-going. But I wonder you can have such spirits under so many distresses.

Chas. Why, there's the point! my distresses are so many, that I can't afford to part with my spirits; but I shall be rich and splenetic, all in good time. However, I suppose you are surprised that I am not more sorrowful at parting with so many near relations; to be sure, 'tis very affecting; but you see they never move a muscle, so why should I?

Row. There's no making you serious a moment.

Chas. Yes, faith, I am so now. Here, my honest Rowley, here, get me this changed directly, and take a hundred pounds of it immediately to old Stanley.

Row. A hundred pounds! Consider only——

Chas. Gad's life, don't talk about it! poor Stanley's wants are pressing, and, if you don't make haste, we shall have some one call that has a better right to the money.

Row. Ah! there's the point! I never will cease dunning you with the old proverb——

Chas. Be just before you're generous.—Why, so I would if I could; but Justice is an old hobbling beldame, and I can't get her to keep pace with Generosity, for the soul of me.

Row. Yet, Charles, believe me, one hour's reflection——

Chas. Ay, ay, it's very true; but, hark'ee, Rowley, while I have, by Heaven I'll give; so, damn your economy! and now for hazard.

[*Exeunt.*

Scene 2ᵈ: the Parlour.

Enter SIR OLIVER—MOSES——

Mos. Well sir, I think as Sir Peter said you have seen Mr. Charles in high Glory—'tis great Pity He's so extravagant.

Sir Oliv. True—but he would not sell my Picture—

Mos. And loves wine and women so much—

Sir Oliv. But He wouldn't sell my Picture.

Mos. And game so deep—

Sir Oliv. But He wouldn't sell my Picture. O—here's Rowley!

Enter ROWLEY.

Row. So—Sir Oliver—I find you have made a Purchase——

Sir Oliv. Yes—yes—our young Rake has parted with his Ancestors like old Tapestry—sold Judges and Generals by the foot—and maiden Aunts as cheap as broken China.—

Row. And here has he commissioned me to re-deliver you Part of the purchase-money—I mean tho' in your necessitous character of old Stanley——

Mos. Ah! there is the Pity of all! He is so damned charitable.

Row. And I left a Hosier and two Tailors in the Hall—who I'm sure won't be paid, and this hundred would satisfy 'em.

Sir Oliv. Well—well—I'll pay his debts and his Benevolences too—I'll take care of old Stanley—myself— But now I am no more a Broker, and you shall introduce me to the elder Brother as Stanley——

Row. Not yet awhile—Sir Peter I know means to call there about this time.

Enter TRIP.

Trip. O Gentlemen—I beg Pardon for not showing you out—this way—Moses, a word. [*Ex.* TRIP with MOSES.

Sir Oliv. There's a Fellow for you— Would you believe it that Puppy intercepted the Jew, on our coming, and wanted to raise money before he got to his master!

Row. Indeed!

Sir Oliv. Yes—they are now planning an annuity Business— Ah Master Rowley in my Day Servants were content with the Follies of their Masters when they were worn a little Thread Bare but now they have their Vices like their Birth Day cloaths with the gloss on. [*Exe.*

Scene—3:ᵈ A Library.

SURFACE and SERVANT.

Surf. No Letter from Lady Teazle?

Ser. No Sir—

Surf. I am surprised she hasn't sent if she is prevented from coming—! Sir Peter certainly does not suspect me—yet I wish I may not lose the Heiress, thro' the scrape I have drawn myself in with the wife—However, Charles's imprudence and bad character are great Points in my Favour.

Ser. Sir—I believe that must be Lady Teazle—

Surf. Hold see—whether it is or not before you go to the Door—I have a particular Message for you if it should be my Brother.

Ser. 'Tis her ladyship Sir—She always leaves her Chair at the milliner's in the next Street.

Surf. Stay—stay—draw that Screen before the Window—that will do—my opposite Neighbour is a maiden Lady of so curious a temper!—[SERVANT draws the screen and exit.] I have a difficult Hand to play in this Affair—Lady Teazle has lately suspected my Views on Maria—but She must by no means be let into that secret, at least till I have her more in my Power.

Enter LADY TEAZLE—

Lady Teaz. What Sentiment in soliloquy—have you been very impatient now?—O Lud! don't pretend to look grave—I vow I couldn't come before——

Surf. O Madam Punctuality is a species of Constancy, a very unfashionable quality in a Lady.

Lady Teaz. Upon my word you ought to pity me, do you know Sir Peter is grown so ill-tempered to me of Late! and so jealous! of Charles too that's the best of the story isn't it?

Surf. I am glad my scandalous Friends keep that up. (Aside.)

Lady Teaz. I am sure I wish He would let Maria marry him—and then perhaps He would be convinced—don't you—Mr. Surface?

Surf. Indeed I do not.—[Aside.] O certainly I do—for then my dear Lady Teazle would also be convinced how wrong her suspicions were of my having any design on the silly Girl——

Lady Teaz. Well—well I'm inclined to believe you—besides I really never could perceive why she should have so many admirers.

Surf. O for her Fortune—nothing else—

Lady Teaz. I believe so for tho' she is certainly very pretty—yet she has no conversation in the world—and is so grave and reserved—that I declare I think she'd have made an excellent wife for Sir Peter.—

Surf. So she would.

Lad. Teaz. Then—one never hears her speak ill of anybody—which you know is mighty dull—

Sur. Yet she doesn't want understanding—

Lad Teaz. No more she does—yet one is always disappointed when one hears [her] speak—For though her Eyes have no kind of meaning in them—she very seldom talks Nonsense.

Sur. Nay—nay surely—she has very fine eyes—

Lad. Teaz. Why so she has—tho' sometimes one fancies there's a little sort of a squint—

Sur. A squint—O fie—Lady Teazle.

Lad. Teaz. Yes yes—I vow now—come there is a left-handed Cupid in one eye—that's the Truth on't.

Sur. Well—his aim is very direct however—but Lady Sneerwell has quite corrupted you.

Lad. Teaz. No indeed—I have not opinion enough of her to be taught by her, and I know that she has lately rais'd many scandalous hints of me—which you know one always hears from one common Friend, or other.

Surf. Why to say truth I believe you are not more obliged to her than others of her acquaintance.

Lad. Teaz. But isn't [it] provoking to hear the most ill-natured Things said to one and there's my friend Lady Sneerwell has circulated I don't know how many scandalous tales of me, and all without any foundation, too; that's what vexes me.

Surf. Aye Madam to be sure that is the Provoking circumstance—without Foundation—yes yes—there's the mortification indeed—for when a slanderous story is believed against one—there certainly is no comfort like the consciousness of having deserved it——

Lady Teaz. No to be sure—then I'd forgive their malice—but to attack me, who am really so innocent—and who never say an ill-natured thing of anybody—that is, of any Friend—! and then Sir Peter too—to have him so peevish—and so suspicious—when I know the integrity of my own Heart—indeed 'tis monstrous.

Surf. But my dear Lady Teazle 'tis your own fault if you suffer it—when a Husband entertains a groundless suspicion of his Wife and withdraws his confidence from her—the original compact is broke and she owes it to the Honour of her sex to endeavour to outwit him—

Lady Teaz. Indeed—So that if He suspects me without cause it follows that the best way of curing his Jealousy is to give him reason for 't—

Surf. Undoubtedly—for your Husband [should] never be deceived in you—and in that case it becomes you to be frail in compliment to his discernment—

Lady Teaz. To be sure what you say is very reasonable—and when the consciousness of my own Innocence——

Surf. Ah : my dear—Madam there is the great mistake—'tis this very conscious Innocence that is of the greatest Prejudice to you—what is it makes you negligent of Forms and careless of the world's opinion—why the consciousness of your Innocence—what makes you thoughtless in your Conduct and apt to run into a thousand little imprudences—why the consciousness of your Innocence—what makes you impatient of Sir Peter's temper, and outrageous at his suspicions—why the consciousness of your own Innocence—

Lady Teaz. 'Tis very true

Surf. Now my dear Lady Teazle if you but once make a trifling *Faux Pas* you can't conceive how cautious you would grow, and how ready to humour and agree with your Husband.

Lady Teaz. Do you think so—

Surf. O I'm sure on 't ; and then you'd find all scandal would cease at once—for in short your Character at Present is like a Person in a Plethora, absolutely dying of too much Health—

Lady Teaz. So—so—then I perceive your Prescription is that I must sin in my own Defence—and part with my virtue to preserve my Reputation.—

Surf. Exactly so upon my credit Ma'am

Lady Teaz. Well certainly this is the oddest Doctrine—and the newest Receipt for avoiding calumny.

Surf. An infallible one believe me—Prudence like experience must be paid for—

Lady Teaz. Why if my understanding were once convinced——

Surf. Oh, certainly Ma'lam, your understanding *should* be convinced—yes—yes—Heaven forbid I should persuade you to do anything you *thought* wrong—no—no—I have too much honor to desire it—

Lady Teaz. Don't—you think we may as well leave Honor out of the Argument? [*Rises.*

Surf. Ah—the ill effects of your country education I see still remain with you.

Lady Teaz. I doubt they do indeed—and I will fairly own to you, that If I could be persuaded to do wrong it would be by Sir Peter's ill-usage—sooner than your honourable Logic, after all.

Surf. Then by this Hand, which He is unworthy of——

Enter SERVANT.

Sdeath, you Blockhead—what do you want?

Ser. I beg your Pardon Sir, but I thought you wouldn't chuse Sir Peter to come up without announcing him?

Surf. Sir Peter—Oons—the Devil!

Lady Teaz. Sir Peter! O Lud! I'm ruined! I'm ruin'd!

Ser. Sir, 'twasn't I let him in.

Lady Teaz. O I'm undone—what will become of me now Mr. Logick. —Oh! mercy, He's on the Stairs—I'll get behind here—and if ever I'm so imprudent again—— [goes behind the screen—

Surf. Give me that—Book!——

[Sits down—SERV. pretends to adjust his Hair—

Enter SIR PETER—

Sir Pet. Aye—ever improving himself!—Mr. Surface—

Surf. Oh! my dear Sir Peter—I beg your Pardon—(Gaping and throws away the Book.) I have been dosing over a stupid Book! well—I am much obliged to you for this Call—You haven't been here I believe since I fitted up this Room—Books you know are the only Things I am a Coxcomb in—

Sir Pet. 'Tis very neat indeed—well well that's proper—and you make even your Screen a source of knowledge—hung I perceive with Maps—

Surf. O yes—I find great use in that Screen.

Sir Pet. I dare say you must—certainly—when you want to find out anything in a Hurry.

Surf. Aye or to hide anything in a Hurry either—

o 2

Sir Pet. Well I have a little private Business--if we were alone—

Surf. You needn't stay.

Ser. No—Sir—— (Ex. Serv.)

Surf. Here's a Chair—Sir Peter—I beg——

Sir Pet. Well—now we are alone—there *is* a subject—my dear Friend—on which I wish to unburthen my Mind to you—a Point of the greatest moment to my Peace—in short, my good Friend—Lady Teazle's conduct of late has made me very unhappy.

Surf. Indeed I'm very sorry to hear it—

Sir Pet. Yes 'tis but too plain she has not the least regard for me—but what's worse, I have pretty good Authority to suspect that she must have formed an attachment to another.

Surf. Indeed! you astonish me.

Sir Pet. Yes—and between ourselves—I think I have discover'd the Person.

Surf. How—you alarm me exceedingly!

Sir Pet. Ah: my dear Friend I knew you would sympathize with me.—

Surf. Yes—believe me Sir Peter—such a discovery would hurt me just as much as it would you—

Sir Pet. I am convinced of it—ah—it is a happiness to have a Friend whom one can trust even with one's Family secrets—but have you no guess who I mean?

Surf. I haven't the most distant Idea—it can't be Sir Benjamin Backbite.

Sir Pet. O—No. What say you to Charles?

Surf. My Brother--impossible!—O no Sir Peter you mustn't credit the scandalous insinuations you hear—no no—Charles to be sure has been charged with many things but I can never think He would meditate so gross an injury—

Sir Pet. Ah! my dear Friend—the goodness of your own Heart misleads you—you judge of others by yourself.

Surf. Certainly Sir Peter—the Heart that is conscious of its own integrity is ever slowest to credit another's Treachery.—

Sir Pet. True—but your Brother has no sentiment you never hear him talk so.—

Surf. Well there certainly is no knowing what men are capable of—no—there is no knowing—yet I can't but think Lady Teazle herself has too much Principle——

Sir Pet. Aye but what's Principle against the Flattery of a handsome—lively young Fellow—

Surf. That's very true—

Sir Pet. And then you know the difference of our ages makes it very improbable that she should have any great affection for me—and if she were to be frail and I were to make it Public—why the Town would only laugh at the foolish old Batchelor, who had married a girl——

Surf. That's true—to be sure People would laugh.

Sir Pet. Laugh—aye and make Ballads—and Paragraphs and the Devil knows what of me—

Surf. No—you must never make it public—

Sir Pet. But then again that the Nephew of my old Friend, Sir Oliver should be the Person to attempt such an injury—hurts me more nearly—

Surf. Undoubtedly—when Ingratitude barbs the Dart of Injury—the wound has double danger in it—

Sir Pet. Aye—I that was in a manner left his Guardian—in his House he had been so often entertain'd—who never in my Life denied him my advice—

Surf. O 'tis not to be credited—There may be a man capable of such Baseness, to be sure—but for my Part till you can give me positive Proofs you must excuse me withholding my Belief. However, if this should be proved on him He is no longer a brother of mine I disclaim kindred with him—for the man who can break thro' the Laws of Hospitality—and attempt the wife of his Friend deserves to be branded as the Pest of Society.

Sir Pet. What a difference there is between you—what noble sentiments!—

Surf. But I cannot suspect Lady Teazle's honor.

Sir Pet. I'm sure I wish to think well of her—and to remove all ground of Quarrel between us—She has lately reproach'd me more than once with having made no settlement on her—and, in our last Quarrel, she almost hinted that she should not break her Heart if I was dead.—now as we seem to differ in our Ideas of Expense I have resolved she shall be her own Mistress in that Respect for the future—and if I were to die—she shall find that I have not been inattentive to her Interests while living—Here my Friend are the Draughts of two Deeds which I wish to have your opinion on—by one she will enjoy eight hundred a year independent while I live—and by the other the bulk of my Fortune after my Death.

Surf. This conduct Sir Peter is indeed truly Generous! I wish it may not corrupt my pupil.—[Aside.]

Sir Pet. Yes I am determined she shall have no cause to complain—tho' I would not have her acquainted with the latter instance of my affection yet awhile.

Surf. Nor I—if I could help it.

Sir Pet. And now my dear Friend if you please we will talk over the situation of your Hopes with Maria.

Surf. No—no—Sir Peter—another Time if you Please—(*softly*).

Sir Pet. I am sensibly chagrined at the little Progress you seem to make in her affection.

Surf. I beg you will not mention it—What are my Disappointments when your Happiness is in Debate (*softly*). 'Sdeath I shall be ruined every way

Sir Pet. And tho' you are so averse to my acquainting Lady Teazle with *your* passion, I am sure she's not your Enemy in the Affair.

Surf. Pray Sir Peter, now oblige me.—I am really too much affected by the subject we have been speaking of to bestow a thought on my own concerns—The Man who is entrusted with his Friend's Distresses can never——

Enter SERVANT.

Well, Sir?

Ser. Your Brother Sir, is—speaking to a Gentleman in the Street, and says He knows you're within.

Surf. 'Sdeath, Blockhead—I'm *not* within—I'm out for the Day.

Sir Pet. Stay—hold—a thought has struck me—you shall be at home.

Surf. Well—well—let him up.—(*Ex.* Serv.). He'll interrupt Sir Peter, however. [*Aside.*

Sir Pet. Now, my good Friend—oblige me I Intreat you—before Charles comes—let me conceal myself somewhere—Then do you tax him on the Point we have been talking on—and his answers may satisfy me at once.—

Surf. O Fie—Sir Peter—would you have *me* join in so mean a Trick? to trepan my Brother too?

Sir Pet. Nay you tell me you are *sure* He is innocent—if so you do him the greatest service in giving him an opportunity to clear himself —and—you will set my Heart at rest—come you shall not refuse me —here behind this Screen will be—hey! what the Devil—there seems to be one listener here already—I'll swear I saw a Petticoat.—

Surf. Ha! ha! ha! Well this is ridiculous enough—I'll tell you, Sir Peter—tho' I hold a man of Intrigue to be a most despicable Character—yet you know it doesn't follow that a man is to be an absolute Joseph either—hark'ee—'tis a little French Milliner—a silly Rogue that plagues me—and having some character, on your coming she ran behind the Screen.—

Sir Pet. Ah a Rogue—but 'egad she has overheard all I have been saying of my Wife.

Surf. O 'twill never go any farther, you may depend on 't.

Sir Pet. No!—then efaith let her hear it out.—Here's a Closet will do as well.—

Surf. Well, go in there.—

Sir Pet. Sly rogue—sly Rogue.—

Surf. Gad's my Life what an Escape—! and a curious situation I'm in!—to part man and wife in this manner.—

Lady Teaz. [peeps out] Couldn't I steal off—

Surf. Keep close, my Angel!

Sir Pet. (peeping out) Joseph—tax him home.

Surf. Back—my dear Friend

Lady Teaz. (peeping out) Couldn't you lock Sir Peter in?—

Surf. Be still—my Life!

Sir Pet. [Peeping] You're sure the little Milliner won't blab?

Surf. In! in! my good Sir Peter—'Fore Gad, I wish I had a key to the Door.

Enter CHARLES.

Chas. Hollo! Brother—what has been the matter? your Fellow wouldn't let me up at first—What have you had a Jew or a wench with you.—

Surf. Neither Brother I assure you.

Chas. But—what has made Sir Peter steal off? I thought He had been with you—

Surf. He *was* Brother—but hearing you were coming He didn't chuse to stay—

Chas. What was the old Gentleman afraid I wanted to borrow money of him?

Surf. No Sir—but I am sorry to find Charles—you have lately given that worthy man grounds for great Uneasiness.

Chas. Yes they tell me I do that to a great many worthy men—but how so Pray?

Surf. To be plain with you Brother He thinks you are endeavouring to gain Lady Teazle's Affections from him.

Chas. Who I—O Lud! not I upon my word.—Ha! ha! ha! so the old Fellow has found out that He has got a young wife has He? or what's worse she has discover'd that she has an old Husband?

Surf. This is no subject to jest on Brother—He who can laugh——

Chas. True true as you were going to say—then seriously I never had the least idea of what you charge me with, upon my honour.

Surf. Well it will give Sir Peter great satisfaction to hear this.

Chas. (Aloud.) To be sure, I once thought the lady seemed to have taken a fancy—but upon my soul I never gave her the least encouragement.—Beside you know my Attachment to Maria—

Surf. But sure Brother even if Lady Teazle had betray'd the fondest Partiality for you——

Chas. Why—look'ee Joseph—I hope I shall never deliberately do a dishonourable Action—but if a pretty woman was purposely to throw herself in my way—and that pretty woman married to a man old enough to be her Father——

Surf. Well?

Chas. Why I believe I should be obliged to borrow a little of your Morality, that's all.—but, Brother do you know now that you surprize me exceeding by naming me with Lady Teazle—for faith I always understood *you* were her Favourite—

Surf. O for shame! Charles—This retort is Foolish.

Chas. Nay I swear I have seen you exchange such significant Glances——

Surf. Nay—nay—Sir—this is no jest—

Chas. Egad—I'm serious—Don't you remember—one Day, when I called here——

Surf. Nay—prithee—Charles

Chas. And found you together——

Surf. Zounds, Sir—I insist——

Chas. And another time when your Servant——

Surf. Brother—brother a word with you—Gad I must stop him—
(aside)

Chas. Informed—me that——

Surf. Hush!—I beg your Pardon but Sir Peter has overheard all we have been saying—I knew you would clear yourself, or I shouldn't have consented—

Chas. How Sir Peter—Where is He—

Surf. Softly, there! (Points to the closet.)

Chas. (In the Closet!) O 'fore Heaven I'll have him out—Sir Peter come forth!

Surf. No—no——

Chas. I say Sir Peter—come into court.—(Pulls in SIR PETER.) What—my old Guardian—what turn inquisitor and take evidence incog.—

Sir Pet. Give me your hand—Charles—I believe I have suspected you wrongfully; but you mustn't be angry with Joseph—'twas my Plan—

Chas. Indeed!—

Sir Pet. But I acquit you—I promise you I don't think near so ill of you as I did—what I have heard has given me great satisfaction.

Chas. Egad then 'twas lucky you didn't hear any more. Wasn't it Joseph?

Sir Pet. Ah! you would have retorted on him.

Chas. Aye—aye—that was a Joke.

Sir Pet. Yes, yes, I know his honor too well.

Chas. Yet you might as well have suspected him as me in this matter, for all that—mightn't He, Joseph?

Sir Pet. Well well I believe you—

Surf. Would they were both out of the Room!

Enter SERV. whispers SURFACE.

Sir Pet. And in future perhaps we may not be such Strangers.

Surf. Gentlemen—I beg Pardon—I must wait on you downstairs—Here is a Person come on particular Business——

Chas. Well you can see him in another Room—Sir Peter and I haven't met a long time and I have something to say [to] him.

Surf. They must not be left together.—I'll send this man away and return directly— (SURFACE goes out).

Sir Pet. Ah—Charles if you associated more with your Brother, one might indeed hope for your reformation—He is a man of Sentiment— Well! there is nothing in the world so noble as a man of Sentiment!

Chas. Pshaw! He is too moral by half—and so apprehensive of his good Name, as he calls it, that I suppose He would as soon let a Priest in his House as a Girl—

Sir Pet. No—no—come come,—you wrong him. No, no, Joseph is no Rake but he is no such Saint in that respect either. I have a great mind to tell him—we should have such a Laugh!

Chas. Oh, hang him? He's a very Anchorite—a young Hermit!

Sir Pet. Harkee—you must not abuse him, he may chance to hear of it again I promise you.

Chas. Why you won't tell him?

Sir Pet. No—but—this way. Egad, I'll tell him—Harkee, have you a mind to have a good laugh against Joseph?

Chas. I should like it of all things—

Sir Pet. Then, E'faith, we will—I'll be quit with him for discovering me.—He had a girl with him when I called. (Whispers.)

Chas. What Joseph you jest—

Sir Pet. Hush!—a little French Milliner—and the best of the Jest is—she's in the room now.

Chas. The devil she is—

Sir Pet. Hush! I tell you. (Points.)
Chas. Behind the screen! Odds Life, let's unveil her!
Sir Pet. No—no! He's coming—you shan't indeed!
Chas. Oh, egad, we'll have a peep at the little milliner!
Sir Pet. Not for the world—Joseph will never forgive me.
Chas. I'll stand by you——
Sir Pet. Odds Life! Here He's coming—

(Surface enters just as Charles throws down the Screen.)

Re-enter JOSEPH SURFACE.

Chas. Lady Teazle! by all that's wonderful!
Sir Pet. Lady Teazle! by all that's Horrible!
Chas. Sir Peter—This is one of the smartest French Milliners I ever saw!—Egad, you seem all to have been diverting yourselves here at Hide and Seek—and I don't see who is out of the Secret!—Shall I beg your Ladyship to inform me!—Not a word!—Brother!—will you please to explain this matter? What! is Honesty Dumb too?—Sir Peter, though I found you in the Dark—perhaps you are not so now—all mute! Well tho' I can make nothing of the Affair, I make no doubt but you perfectly understand one another—so I'll leave you to yourselves.—[Going.] Brother I'm sorry to find you have given that worthy man grounds for so much uneasiness!—Sir Peter—there's nothing in the world so noble as a man of Sentiment!—

(Stand for some time looking at one another. Ex.)

Surf. Sir Peter—notwithstanding I confess that appearances are against me. If you will afford me your Patience I make no doubt but I shall explain everything to your satisfaction.—

Sir Pet. If you please—Sir—

Surf. The Fact is Sir—that Lady Teazle knowing my Pretensions to your ward Maria—I say Sir Lady Teazle—being apprehensive of the Jealousy of your Temper—and knowing my Friendship to the Family. She Sir—I say call'd here—in order that I might explain those Pretensions—but on your coming being apprehensive—as I said of your Jealousy—she withdrew—and this, you may depend on't is the whole truth of the Matter.

Sir Pet. A very clear account upon the word and I dare swear the Lady will vouch for every article of it.

Lady Teaz. For not one word of it Sir Peter—

Sir Pet. How don't you think it worth while to agree in the lie.

Lady Teaz. There is not one Syllable of Truth in what that Gentleman has told you.

Sir Pet. I believe you upon my soul Ma'am—

Surf. 'Sdeath, madam, will you betray me! (Aside.

Lady Teaz. Good Mr. Hypocrite by your leave I will speak for) myself—

Sir Pet. Aye let her alone Sir—you'll find she'll make out a better story than you without Prompting.

Lady Teaz. Hear me Sir Peter—I came hither on no matter relating to your Ward and even ignorant of this Gentleman's pretensions to her—but I came—seduced by his insidious arguments—and pretended Passion at least to listen to his dishonourable Love if not to sacrifice your Honour to his Baseness.

Sir Pet. Now, I believe, the Truth is coming indeed

Surf. The Woman's mad—

Lady Teaz. No Sir—she has recovered her Senses. Your own Arts have furnished her with the means. Sir Peter—I do not expect you to credit me—but the Tenderness you express'd for me, when I am sure you could not think I was a witness to it, has penetrated so to my Heart, that had I left the Place without the Shame of this discovery— my future life should have spoken the sincerity of my Gratitude—as for that smooth-tongued Hypocrite—who would have seduced the wife of his too credulous Friend while he pretended honourable addresses to his ward—I behold him now in a light so truly despicable that I shall never again Respect myself for having Listened to him. Exit.

Surf. Notwithstanding all this Sir Peter—Heaven knows——

Sir Pet. That you are a Villain!—and so I leave you to your conscience—

Surf. You are too Rash Sir Peter—you *shall* hear me—The man who shuts out conviction by refusing to——

(Exe. Surface following and speaking.

ACT 5th, Scene 1st.

The Library.

Enter SURFACE—SERV.

Surf. Mr. Stanley! and why should you think I would see him?—you must know he came to ask something!

Ser. Sir—I shouldn't have let him in but that Mr. Rowley came to the Door with him.

Surf. Pshaw!—Blockhead to suppose that I should now be in a Temper to receive visits from poor Relations!—well why don't you show the Fellow up?

Ser. I will—Sir—Why, Sir—it was not my Fault that Sir Peter discover'd my Lady——

Surf. Go, fool!—(*Ex.* SERV.) Sure Fortune never play'd a man of my policy such a Trick before—my character with Sir Peter!—my Hopes with Maria!—destroy'd in a moment!—I'm in a rare Humour to listen to other People's Distresses!—I shan't be able to bestow even a benevolent sentiment on Stanley—So! here—He comes and Rowley with him—I *must* try to recover myself, and put a little Charity into my Face however.—— ex.

Enter SIR OL. and ROWLEY.

Sir Oliv. What! does He avoid us? that was He—was it not?

Row. It was Sir—but I doubt you are come a little too abruptly—his Nerves are so weak that the sight of a poor Relation may be too much for him—I should have gone first to break you to him.

Sir Oliv. A Plague of his Nerves—yet this is He whom Sir Peter extolls as a Man of the most Benevolent way of thinking!—

Row. As to his way of thinking—I can't pretend to decide for, to do him justice He appears to have as much speculative Benevolence as any private Gentleman in the Kingdom—though he is seldom so sensual as to indulge himself in the exercise of it——

Sir Oliv. Yet [he] has a string of charitable Sentiments I suppose at his Fingers' ends!—

Row. Or, rather at his Tongue's end Sir Oliver; for I believe there is no sentiment he has more faith in than that 'Charity begins at Home.'

Sir Oliv. And his I presume is of that domestic sort which never stirs abroad at all.

Row. I doubt you'll find it so—but He's coming—I mustn't seem to interrupt you—and you know immediately—as you leave him—I come in to announce—your arrival in your real Character.

Sir Oliv. True—and afterwards you'll meet me at Sir Peter's——

Row. Without losing a moment. ex.

Sir Oliv. So—I see he has premeditated a Denial by the Complaisance of his Features.

Enter Surf.

Surf. Sir—I beg you ten thousand Pardons for keeping—you a moment waiting—Mr. Stanley—I presume——

Sir Oliv. At your Service.

Surf. Sir—I beg you will do me the honour to sit down—I entreat you Sir.

Sir Oliv. Dear Sir there's no occasion—too civil by half!

Jos. Surf. I have not the Pleasure of knowing you, Mr. Stanley—but I am extremely happy to see you look so well—you were nearly related to my mother—I think Mr. Stanley——

Sir Oliv. I was Sir—so nearly that my present Poverty I fear may do discredit to her Wealthy Children—else I should not have presumed to trouble you.—

Surf. Dear Sir—there needs no apology—He that is in Distress tho' a stranger has a right to claim kindred with the wealthy—I am sure I wish I was of that class, and had it in my power to offer you even a small relief.

Sir Oliv. If your Unkle, Sir Oliver were here—I should have a Friend——

Surf. I wish He was Sir, with all my Heart—you should not want an advocate with him—believe me Sir.

Sir Oliv. I should not need one—my Distresses would recommend me.—but I imagined—his Bounty had enabled you to become the agent of his Charity.

Surf. My dear Sir—you are strangely misinformed—Sir Oliver is a worthy Man, a worthy man—a very worthy sort of Man—but avarice Mr. Stanley is the vice of age——I will tell you my good Sir in confidence :—what he has done for me has been a mere—nothing tho' People I know have thought otherwise and for my Part I never chose to contradict the Report.

Sir Oliv. What!—has he never transmitted—you—Bullion—Rupees —Pagodas!

Surf. O Dear Sir—Nothing of the kind—no—no—a few Presents now and then—china, shawls, congo Tea, Avadavats—and indian Crackers—little more, believe me.

Sir Oliv. Here's Gratitude for twelve thousand pounds !—Avadavats and indian Crackers.

Surf. Then my dear—Sir—you have heard, I doubt not, of the extravagance of my Brother—Sir—there are very few would credit what I have done for that unfortunate young man.

Sir Oliv. Not I for one !

Surf. The sums I have lent him ! indeed—I have been exceedingly to blame—it was an amiable weakness ! however I don't pretend to defend it—and now I feel it doubly culpable—since it has deprived me of the power of serving *you* Mr. Stanley as my Heart directs——

Sir Oliv. Dissembler ! Then Sir—you cannot assist me ?

Surf. At Present it grieves me to say I cannot—but whenever I have the ability, you may depend upon hearing from me.

Sir Oliv. I am extremely sorry——

Surf. Not more than I am believe me—to pity without the Power to relieve is still more painful than to ask and be denied——

Sir Oliv. Kind Sir—your most obedient humble servant.

Surf. You leave me deeply affected Mr. Stanley—William—be ready to open the door——

Sir Oliv. O, Dear Sir, no ceremony——

Surf. Your very obedient——

Sir Oliv. Your most obsequious——

Surf. You may depend on hearing from me whenever I can be of service——

Sir Oliv. Sweet Sir—you are too good——

Surf. In the mean time I wish you Health and Spirits——

Sir Oliv. Your ever grateful and perpetual humble Servant——

Surf. Sir—yours as sincerely——

Sir Oliv. Charles !—you are my Heir.   ex.

SURF. Sol.

Soh !—This is one bad effect of a good Character—it invites applications from the unfortunate and there needs no small degree of address to gain the reputation of Benevolence without incurring the expence.—The silver ore of pure Charity is an expensive article in the catalogue of a man's good Qualities—whereas the sentimental French Plate I use instead of it makes just as good a shew—and pays no tax.

Enter ROWLEY.

Row. Mr. Surface—your Servant : I was apprehensive of interrupting you, tho' my Business demands immediate attention—as this Note will inform you——

Surf. Always Happy to see Mr. Rowley—how—Oliver—Surface!—My Unkle arrived!

Row. He is indeed—we have just parted—quite well—after a speedy voyage—and impatient to embrace his worthy Nephew.

Surf. I am astonished!—William stop Mr. Stanley, if He's not gone——

Row. O—He's out of reach—I believe.

Surf. Why didn't you let me know this when you came in together.—

Row. I thought you had particular—Business—but I must be gone to inform your Brother, and appoint him here to meet his Uncle. He will be with you in a quarter of an hour——

Surf. So he says. Well—I am strangely overjoy'd at his coming—never to be sure was anything so damn'd unlucky!

Row. You will be delighted to see how well He looks.

Surf. O—I'm rejoiced to hear it—just at this time——

Row. I'll tell him how impatiently you expect him——

Surf. Do—do—pray—give my best duty and affection—indeed, I cannot express the sensations I feel at the thought of seeing him!—certainly his coming just at this Time is the cruellest piece of ill Fortune——   Exe.

SCENE 2d: *at* SIR PETER'S.—*House.*

Enter MRS. CANDOUR *and* MADAM—SERVANT.

Serv. Indeed Ma'am, my Lady will see nobody at Present.

Mrs. Can. Did you tell her it was her Friend Mrs. Candour——

Serv. Yes Ma'am but she begs you will excuse her——

Mrs. Can. Do go again—I shall be glad to see her if it be only for a moment—for I am sure she must be in great Distress ex. MAID—Dear Heart—how provoking!—I'm not mistress of half the circumstances!—We shall have the whole affair in the newspapers with the Names of the Parties at length before I have dropt the story at a dozen houses.

Enter SIR BENJAMIN.

Sir Benjamin you have heard, I suppose——

Sir Ben. Of Lady Teazle and Mr. Surface——

Mrs. Can. And Sir Peter's Discovery——

Sir Ben. O the strangest Piece of Business to be sure——

Mrs. Can. Well I never was so surprised in my life!—I am so sorry for all Parties—indeed,

Sir Ben. Now I don't Pity Sir Peter at all—he was so extravagant—partial to Mr. Surface——

Mrs. Can. Mr. Surface!—why 'twas with Charles Lady Teazle was detected.

Sir Ben. No such thing Mr. Surface is the gallant.

Mrs. Can. No—no—Charles is the man—'twas Mr. Surface brought Sir Peter on purpose to discover them——

Sir Ben. I tell you I have it from one——

Mrs. Can. And I have it from one——

Sir Ben. Who had it from one who had it——

Mrs. Can. From one immediately—but here comes Lady Sneerwell—perhaps she knows the whole affair.

Enter LADY SNEERWELL!—

Lady Sneer. So—my dear Mrs. Candour Here's a sad affair of our Friend Teazle——

Mrs Can. Aye my dear Friend, who could have thought it.

Lady Sneer. Well there is no trusting to appearances tho'—indeed she was always too lively for me.

Mrs. Can. To be sure, her manners were a little too—free—but she was very young——

Lady Sneer. And had indeed some good Qualities.

Mrs. Can. So she had indeed—but have you heard the Particulars?

Lady Sneer. No—but everybody says that Mr. Surface——

Sir Ben. Aye there I told you—Mr. Surface was the Man.

Mrs. Can. No—no—indeed the assignation was with Charles——

Lady Sneer. With Charles!—You alarm me Mrs. Candour!

Mrs. Can. Yes—yes He was the Lover—Mr. Surface—do him justice—was only the Informer.

Sir Ben. Well I'll not dispute with you Mrs. Candour—but be it which it may—I hope that Sir Peter's wound will not——

Mrs. Can. Sir Peter's wound! O mercy! I didn't hear a word of their Fighting——

Lady Sneer. Nor I a syllable!

Sir Ben. No—what no mention of the Duel——

Mrs. Can. Not a word——

Sir Ben. O, Lord—yes—yes—they fought before they left the Room.

Lady Sneer. Pray let us hear.

Mrs. Can. Aye—do oblige—us with the Duel——

Sir Ben. 'Sir'—says Sir Peter—immediately after the Discovery, 'you are a most ungrateful Fellow.'

Mrs. Can. Aye to Charles——

Sir Ben. No, no—to Mr. Surface—'a most ungrateful Fellow; and old as I am, Sir,' says He, 'I insist on immediate satisfaction.'

Mrs. Can. Aye that must have been to Charles for 'tis very unlikely Mr. Surface should go to fight in his own House.

Sir Ben. Gad's Life, Ma'am, not at all—giving me immediate satisfaction—on this, Madam—Lady Teazle seeing Sir Peter in such Danger—ran out of the Room in strong Hysterics—and Charles after her calling out for Hartshorn and Water! Then Madam—they began to fight with Swords——

Enter CRABTREE.

Crab. With Pistols—Nephew—I have it from undoubted authority.

Mrs. Can. Oh, Mr. Crabtree then it is all true——

Crab. Too true indeed Ma'am, and Sir Peter Dangerously wounded——

Sir Ben. By a thrust in second—quite thro' his left side

Crab. By a Bullet lodged in the Thorax——

Mrs. Can. Mercy—on me Poor Sir Peter——

Crab. Yes, ma'am tho' Charles would have avoided the matter if he could——

Mrs. Can. I knew Charles was the Person——

Sir Ben. O my Unkle I see knows nothing of the matter——

Crab. But Sir Peter tax'd him with the basest ingratitude——

Sir Ben. That I told you, you know——

Crab. Do Nephew let me speak—and insisted on immediate——

Sir Ben. Just as I said——

Crab. Odds life! Nephew allow others to know something too—A Pair of Pistols lay on the Bureau—for Mr. Surface—it seems, had come home the Night before late from Salt-Hill where He had been to see the Montem with a Friend, who has a Son at Eton—so unluckily the Pistols were left Charged——

Sir Ben. I heard nothing of this——

Crab. Sir Peter forced Charles to take one and they fired—it seems pretty nearly together—Charles's shot took Place as I tell you—and Sir Peter's miss'd—but what is very extraordinary the Ball struck against a little Bronze Pliny that stood over the Fire Place—grazed out of the window at a right angle—and wounded the Postman, who was just coming to the Door with a double letter from Northamptonshire.

Sir Ben. My Unkle's account is more circumstantial I must confess—but I believe mine is the true one for all that.

Lady Sneer. I am more interested in this Affair than they imagine—and must have better information.— Ex.

Sir Ben. Ah! Lady Sneerwell's alarm is very easily accounted for.--

Crab. Yes yes, they certainly *do* say—but that's neither here nor there.

Mrs. Can. But pray where is Sir Peter at present——

Crab. Oh! they—brought him home and He is now in the House, tho' the Servants are order'd to deny it——

Mrs. Can. I believe so—and Lady Teazle—I suppose attending him——

Crab. Yes yes—and I saw one of the Faculty enter just before me——

Sir Ben. Hey—who comes here——

Crab. Oh, this is He—the Physician depend on 't.

Mrs. Can. O certainly it must be the Physician and now we shall know——

Enter Sir Oliver.

Crab. Well, Doctor—what Hopes?

Mrs. Can. Aye Doctor how's your Patient?

Sir Ben. Now Doctor isn't it a wound with a small sword——

Crab. A bullet lodged in the Thorax—for a hundred!

Sir Oliv. Doctor!—a wound with a small sword! and a Bullet in the Thorax!—oon's are you mad, good People?

Sir Ben. Perhaps, Sir, you are not a Doctor

Sir Oliv. Truly Sir I am to thank you for my degree If I am.

Crab. Only a Friend of Sir Peter's then I presume—but, sir, you must have heard of his accident—

Sir Oliv. Not a word!

Crab. Not of his being dangerously wounded?

Sir Oliv. The Devil he is!

Sir Ben. Run thro' the Body ——

Crab. Shot in the breast——

Sir Ben. By one Mr. Surface——

Crab. Aye the younger.

Sir Oliv. Hey! what the plague! you seem to differ strangely in your accounts—however you agree that Sir Peter is dangerously wounded.

Sir Ben. Oh yes, we agree in that.

Crab. Yes, yes, I believe there can be no doubt in that.

Sir Oliv. Then, upon my word, for a person in that Situation, he is the most imprudent man alive—For here he comes walking as if nothing at all was the matter.

Enter Sir Peter.

Odd's heart, sir Peter! you are come in good time I promise you, for we had just given you over!

Sir Ben. 'Egad, Uncle this is the most sudden Recovery!

Sir Oliv. Why, man, what do you do out of Bed with a Small Sword through your Body, and a Bullet lodg'd in your Thorax?

Sir Pet. A Small Sword and a Bullet—

Sir Oliv. Aye these Gentlemen would have kill'd you without Law or Physic, and wanted to dub me a Doctor to make me an accomplice.

Sir Pet. Why! what is all this?

Sir Ben. We rejoice, Sir Peter, that the Story of the Duel is not true—and are sincerely sorry for your other Misfortune.

Sir Pet. So—so—all over the Town already! [*Aside*

Crab. Tho', Sir Peter, you were certainly vastly to blame to marry at all at your years.

Sir Pet. Sir, what Business is that of yours?

Mrs. Can. Tho' Indeed, as Sir Peter made so good a Husband, he's very much to be pitied.

Sir Pet. Plague on your pity, Ma'am, I desire none of it.

Sir Ben. However Sir Peter, you must not mind the Laughing and Jests you will meet with on the occasion.

Sir Pet. Sir, I desire to be master in my own house.

Crab. 'Tis no Uncommon Case, that's one comfort.

Sir Pet. I insist on being left to myself, without ceremony,—I insist on your leaving my house directly!

Mrs. Can. Well, well, we are going and depend on't, we'll make the best report of you we can.

Sir Pet. Leave my house!

Crab. And tell how hardly you have been treated.

Sir Pet. Leave my House—

Sir Ben. And how patiently you bear it.

Sir Pet. Friends! Vipers! Furies! Oh that their own Venom would choke them!

Sir Oliv. They are very provoking indeed, Sir Peter.

Enter ROWLEY.

Row. I heard high words: what has ruffled you Sir Peter—

Sir Pet. Pshaw what signifies asking—do I ever pass a Day without my Vexations?

Sir Oliv. Well I'm not Inquisitive—I come only to tell you, that I have seen both my Nephews in the manner we proposed.

Sir Pet. A Precious Couple they are!

Row. Yes and Sir Oliver—is convinced that your judgment was right Sir Peter.

Sir Oliv. Yes I find Joseph is Indeed the Man after all.

212   THE SCHOOL FOR SCANDAL.

Row. Aye as Sir Peter says, He's a man of Sentiment.

Sir Oliv. And acts up to the Sentiments he professes.

Row. It certainly is Edification to hear him talk.

Sir Oliv. Oh, He's a model for the young men of the age! But how's this, Sir Peter? you don't Join us in your Friend Joseph's Praise as I expected.

Sir Pet. Sir Oliver, we live in a damned wicked world, and the fewer we praise the better.

Row. What do *you* say so, Sir Peter—who were never mistaken in your Life?

Sir Pet. Pshaw—Plague on you both—I see by your sneering you have heard—the whole affair—I shall go mad among you!

Row. Then to fret you no longer Sir Peter—we are indeed acquainted with it all—I met Lady Teazle coming from Mr. Surface's so humbled, that she deigned to request *me* to be her advocate with you—

Sir Pet. And does Sir Oliver know all too?

Sir Oliv. Every circumstance!

Sir Pet. What of the closet and the screen—hey

Sir Oliv. Yes yes—and the little French Milliner. Oh, I have been vastly diverted with the story! ha! ha! ha!

Sir Pet. 'Twas very pleasant!

Sir Oliv. I never laugh'd more in my life, I assure you: ha! ha!

Sir Pet. O vastly diverting! ha! ha!

Row. To be sure Joseph with his Sentiments! ha! ha!

Sir Pet. Yes his sentiments! ha! ha! a hypocritical Villain!

Sir Oliv. Aye and that Rogue Charles—to pull Sir Peter out of the closet: ha! ha!

Sir Pet. Ha! ha! 'twas devilish entertaining to be sure—

Sir Oliv. Ha! ha! Egad, Sir Peter I should like to have seen your Face when the screen was thrown down—ha! ha!

Sir Pet. Yes, my face when the Screen was thrown down: ha! ha! ha! O I must never show my head again!

Sir Oliv. But come—come it isn't fair to laugh at you neither my old Friend—tho' upon my soul I can't help it—

Sir Pet. O pray don't restrain your mirth on my account: it does not hurt me at all—I laugh at the whole affair myself—Yes—yes—I think being a standing Jest for all one's acquaintance a very happy situation—O yes—and then of a morning to read the Paragraphs about Mr. S——, Lady T——, and Sir P——, will be so entertaining!—I shall certainly leave town tomorrow and never look mankind in the Face again!

Row. Without affectation Sir Peter, you may despise the ridicule of Fools—but I see Lady Teazle going towards the next Room—I am sure you must desire a Reconciliation as earnestly as she does.

Sir Oliv. Perhaps *my* being here prevents her coming to you—well I'll leave honest Rowley to mediate between you; but he must bring you all presently to Mr. Surface's—where I am now returning—if not to reclaim a Libertine, at least to expose Hypocrisy.

Sir Pet. Ah! I'll be present at your discovering yourself there with all my heart; though 'tis a vile unlucky Place for discoveries.

Sir Oliv. However it is very convenient to the carrying on of my Plot that you all live so near one another! Ex. SIR O.

Row. We'll follow—

Sir Pet. She is not coming here you see, Rowley—

Row. No but she has left the Door of that Room open you perceive.—see she is in Tears—!

Sir Pet. She seems indeed to wish I should go to her.—how dejected she appears—

Row And will you refrain from comforting her—

Sir Pet. Certainly a little mortification appears very becoming in a wife—don't you think it will do her good to let her Pine a little.

Row. O this is ungenerous in you—

Sir Pet. Well I know not what to think—you remember Rowley the Letter I found of her's—evidently intended for Charles?

Row. A mere forgery, Sir Peter—laid in your way on Purpose—this is one of the Points which I intend Snake shall give you conviction on—

Sir Pet. I wish I were once satisfied of that—She looks this way——what a remarkably elegant Turn of the Head she has! Rowley I'll go to her—

Row. Certainly—

Sir Pet. Tho' when it is known that we are reconciled, People will laugh at me ten times more!

Row. Let—them laugh—and retort their malice only by showing them you are happy in spite of it.

Sir Pet. Efaith so I will—and, if I'm not mistaken we may yet be the happiest couple in the country—

Row. Nay Sir Peter—He who once lays aside suspicion——

Sir Pet. Hold Master Rowley—if you have any Regard for me—never let me hear you utter anything like a Sentiment. I have had enough of *them* to serve me the rest of my Life. Exe.

Scene the Last.

The Library.

SURFACE and LADY SNEERWELL.

Lady Sneer. Impossible! will not Sir Peter immediately be reconciled to *Charles?* and of consequence no longer oppose his union with *Maria?* the thought is Distraction to me!

Surf. Can Passion—furnish a Remedy?

Lady Sneer. No—nor cunning either. O I was a Fool, an Ideot—to league with such a Blunderer!

Surf. Surely Lady Sneerwell I am the greatest Sufferer—yet you see I bear the accident with Calmness.

Lady Sneer. Because the Disappointment hasn't reached your *Heart*—your interest only attached you to Maria—had you felt for her—what I have for that ungrateful Libertine—neither your Temper nor Hypocrisy could prevent your showing the sharpness of your Vexation.

Surf. But why should your Reproaches fall on me for this Disappointment?

Lady Sneer. Are not you the cause of it? what had you to bate in your Pursuit of Maria to pervert Lady Teazle by the way.—had you not a sufficient field for your Roguery in blinding Sir Peter and supplanting your Brother—I hate such an avarice of crimes—'tis an unfair monopoly and never prospers.

Surf. Well I admit I have been to blame—I confess I deviated from the direct Road of wrong but I don't think we're so totally defeated neither.

Lady Sneer. No!

Surf. You tell me you have made a trial of Snake since we met—and that you still believe him faithful to us—

Lady Sneer. I do believe so.

Surf. And that he has undertaken should it be necessary—to swear and prove that Charles is at this Time contracted by vows and Honour to your Ladyship—which some of his former letters to you will serve to support—

Lady Sneer. This, indeed, might have assisted—

Surf. Come—come it is not too late yet—but hark! this is probably my Unkle Sir Oliver—retire to that Room—we'll consult further when He's gone.—

Lady Sneer. Well but if *He* should find you out to—

Surf. O I have no fear of that—Sir Peter will hold his tongue for his own credit sake—and you may depend on't I shall soon Discover Sir Oliver's weak side!—

Lady Sneer. I have no diffidence of your abilities—only be constant to one roguery at a time— (Ex.)

Surf. I will—I will—So 'tis confounded hard after such bad Fortune, to be baited by one's confederate in evil—well at all events my character is so much better than Charles's, that I certainly—hey—what!—this is not Sir Oliver—but old Stanley again!—Plague on't that He should return to teaze me just now—I shall have Sir Oliver come and find him here—and——

(Enter SIR OLIVER.)

Gad's life, Mr. Stanley—why have you come back to plague me at this time? you must not stay now upon my word!

Sir Oliv. Sir—I hear your Unkle Oliver is expected here—and tho' He has been so penurious to you, I'll try what He'll do for me—

Surf. Sir! 'tis impossible for you to stay now—so I must beg——come any other time and I promise you you shall be assisted.

Sir Oliv. No—Sir Oliver and I must be acquainted—

Jos. Surf. Zounds Sir then [I] insist on your quitting the—Room directly—

Sir Oliv. Nay Sir——

Jos. Surf. Sir—I insist on't—here William show this Gentleman out. Since you compel me Sir—not one moment—this is such insolence. [Going to push him out.

Enter CHARLES.

Chas. Heyday! what's the matter now?—what the Devil have you got hold of my little Broker here! Zounds—Brother, don't hurt little Premium. What's the matter—my little Fellow?

Surf. So! He has been with you, too, has He—

Chas. To be sure He has! Why, 'tis as honest a little——But sure Joseph you have not been borrowing money too have you?

Surf. Borrowing—no!—But, Brother—you know sure we expect Sir Oliver every——

Chas. O Gad, that's true—Noll mustn't find the little Broker here to be sure—

Surf. Yet Mr. Stanley insists——

Chas. Stanley—why his name's Premium—

Surf. No no Stanley.

Chas. No, no—Premium.

Surf. Well no matter which—but——

Chas. Aye aye Stanley or Premium, 'tis the same thing as you say—for I suppose He goes by half a hundred Names, besides A. B's at the Coffee-House. [Knock.

Surf. 'Sdeath—here's Sir Oliver at the Door——Now I beg— Mr. Stanley——

Chas. Aye aye and I beg Mr. Premium——

Sir Oliv. Gentlemen——

Surf. Sir, by Heaven you shall go—

Chas. Aye out with him certainly——

Sir Oliv. This violence——

Surf. 'Tis your own Fault.

Chas. Out with him to be sure.   (Both forcing SIR OLIVER out.)

(Enter SIR PETER TEAZLE, LADY TEAZLE, MARIA, and ROWLEY.)

Sir Pet. My old Friend, Sir Oliver!—hey! what in the name of wonder!—Here are dutiful Nephews!—assault their Unkle at his first Visit!

Lady Teaz. Indeed Sir Oliver 'twas well we came in to rescue you.

Row. Truly it was—for I perceive Sir Oliver the character of old Stanly was no Protection to you.

Sir Oliv. Nor of Premium either—the necessities of the former could not extort a shilling from that benevolent Gentleman; and with the other I stood a chance of faring worse than my Ancestors, and being knocked down without being bid for.

Surf. Charles!

Chas. Joseph!

Surf. 'Tis compleat!

Chas. Very!

Sir Oliv. Sir Peter—my Friend and Rowley too—look on that elder Nephew of mine—You know what He has already received from my Bounty and you know also how gladly I would have look'd on half my Fortune as held in trust for him—judge then my Disappointment in discovering him to be destitute of Truth—Charity—and Gratitude—

Sir Pet. Sir Oliver—I should be more surprized at this Declaration, if I had not myself found him to be selfish—treacherous and Hypocritical.

Lady Teaz. And if the Gentleman pleads not guilty to these pray let him call *me* to his Character.

Sir Pet. Then I believe we need add no more—if He knows himself He will consider it as the most perfect Punishment that He is known to the world—

Chas. If they talk this way to Honesty—what will they say to *me* by-and-bye!

Sir Oliv. As for that Prodigal—his Brother there——

Chas. Aye now comes my Turn—the damn'd Family Pictures will ruin me—

Surf. Sir Oliver—Unkle—will you honour me with a hearing—

Chas. I wish Joseph now would make one of his long speeches and I might recollect myself a little—

Sir Oliv. And I suppose you would undertake to vindicate yourself entirely—

Surf. I trust I could—

Sir Oliv. Nay—if you desert your Roguery in its Distress and try to be justified—you have even less principle than I thought you had.— [To CHARLES SURFACE,] Well, Sir—and *you* could *justify* yourself too I suppose—

Chas. Not that I know of, Sir Oliver.

Sir Oliv. What little Premium has been let too much into the secret I presume.

Chas. True—Sir—but they were Family Secrets, and should not be mentioned again you know.

Row. Come Sir Oliver I know you cannot speak of Charles's Follies with anger.

Sir Oliv. Odd's heart no more I can—nor with gravity either—Sir Peter do you know the Rogue bargain'd with me for all his Ancestors —sold me Judges and Generals by the Foot, and Maiden Aunts as cheap as broken China!

Chas. To be sure, Sir Oliver, I did make a little free with the Family Canvas that's the truth on't :—my Ancestors may certainly rise in judgment against me there's no denying it—but believe me sincere when I tell you, and upon my soul I would not say so if I was not—that if I do not appear mortified at the exposure of my Follies, it is because I feel at this moment the warmest satisfaction in seeing you, my liberal benefactor.

Sir Oliv. Charles—I believe you—give me your hand again : the ill-looking little fellow over the Couch has made your Peace.

Chas. Then Sir—my Gratitude to the original is still encreased.

Lady Teaz. [*Advancing.*] Yet I believe, Sir Oliver, here is one whom Charles is still more anxious to be reconciled to.

Sir Oliv. O I have heard of his Attachment there—and, with the young Lady's Pardon if I construe right that Blush——

Sir Pet. Well—Child—speak your sentiments—you know—we are going to be reconciled to Charles—

Mar. Sir—I have little to say—but that I shall rejoice to hear that He is happy—For me—whatever claim I had to his Affection—I willing resign to one who has a better title.

Chas. How Maria!

Sir Pet. Heyday—what's the mystery now ? while he appeared an incorrigible Rake, you would give your hand to no one else and now that He's likely to reform I'll warrant you won't have him!

Mar. His own Heart—and Lady Sneerwell know the cause.

[*Chas.*] Lady Sneerwell!

Surf. Brother it is with great concern—I am obliged to speak on this Point, but my Regard to Justice obliges me—and Lady Sneerwell's injuries can no longer—be concealed— (goes to the Door)

Enter LADY SNEERWELL.

Sir Pet. Soh! another French milliner egad! He has one in every Room in the House I suppose—

Lady Sneer. Ungrateful Charles! Well may you be surprised and feel for the indelicate situation which your Perfidy has forced me into.

Chas. Pray Unkle, is this another Plot of yours? for as I have Life I don't understand it.

Surf. I believe Sir there is but the evidence of one Person more necessary to make it extremely clear.

Sir Pet. And that Person—I imagine, is Mr. Snake—Rowley—you were perfectly right to bring him with us—and pray let him appear.

Row. Walk in, Mr. Snake—

Enter SNAKE.

I thought his Testimony might be wanted—however it happens unluckily that He comes to confront Lady Sneerwell and not to support her—

Lady Sneer. A Villain!—Treacherous to me at last! Speak, Fellow, have you too conspired against me?

Snake. I beg your Ladyship—ten thousand Pardons—you paid me extremely Liberally for the Lie in question—but I unfortunately have been offer'd double to speak the Truth.

Lady Sneer. The Torments of Shame and Disappointment on you all!

Lady Teaz. Hold—Lady Sneerwell—before you go let me thank you for the trouble you and that Gentleman have taken in writing Letters from me to Charles and answering them yourself—and let me also request you to make my Respects to the Scandalous College—of which you are President—and inform them that Lady Teazle, Licentiate, begs leave to return the diploma they granted her—as she leaves of[f] Practice and kills Characters no longer.

Lady Sneer. Provoking—insolent!—may your Husband live these fifty years! [*Exit.*

Sir Pet. Oons what a Fury——

Lady Teaz. A malicious Creature indeed!

Sir Pet. Hey—not for her last wish ?—

Lady Teaz. O No—

Sir Oliv. Well Sir, and what have you to say now ?

Surf. Sir, I am so confounded, to find that Lady Sneerwell could be guilty of suborning Mr. Snake in this manner to impose on us all that I know not what to say——however, lest her Revengeful Spirit should prompt her to injure my Brother I had certainly better follow her directly. Exit.

Sir Pet. Moral to the last drop !

Sir Oliv. Aye and marry her Joseph if you can.—Oil and Vinegar egad :—you'll do very well together.

Row. I believe we have no more occasion for Mr. Snake at Present—

Snake. Before I go—I beg Pardon once for all for whatever uneasiness I have been the humble instrument of causing to the Parties present.

Sir Pet. Well—well you have made atonement by a good Deed at last—

Snake. But I must Request of the Company that it shall never be known—

Sir Pet. Hey !—what the Plague—are you ashamed of having done a right thing once in your life ?

Snake. Ah : Sir—consider I live by the Badness of my Character ! —I have nothing but my Infamy to depend on !—and, if it were once known that I had been betray'd into an honest Action, I should lose every Friend I have in the world.

Sir Oliv. Well—well we'll not traduce you by saying anything to your Praise never fear. Ex. SNAKE.

Sir Pet. There's a precious Rogue—Yet that fellow is a Writer and a Critic.

Lady Teaz. See Sir Oliver there needs no persuasion now to reconcile your Nephew and Maria—

Sir Oliv. Aye—aye—that's as it should be and egad we'll have the wedding to-morrow morning—

Chas. Thank you, dear Unkle !

Sir Pet. What ! you rogue don't you ask the Girl's consent first—

Chas. Oh, I have done that a long time—above a minute ago—and She has look'd yes—

Mar. For Shame—Charles—I protest Sir Peter, there has not been a word———

Sir Oliv. Well then the fewer the Better—may your love for each other never know—abatement.

Sir Pet. And may you live as happily together as Lady Teazle and I—intend to do—

Chas. Rowley my old Friend—I am sure you congratulate me and I suspect too that I owe you much.

Sir Oliv. You do, indeed, Charles—

Rowley. If my Efforts to serve you had not succeeded you would have been in my debt for the attempt—but deserve to be happy—and you over-repay me.

Sir Pet. Aye honest Rowley always said you would reform.

Chas. Surf. Why as to reforming Sir Peter I'll make no promises— and that I take to be a proof that I intend to set about it—But here shall be my Monitor—my gentle Guide.—ah! can I leave the Virtuous path those Eyes illumine?

    Tho' thou, dear Maid, should'st wave thy Beauty's Sway,
    —Thou still must Rule—because I will obey:
    An humbled fugitive from Folly View,
    No sanctuary near but Love and *You*:
    You can indeed each anxious Fear remove,
    For even Scandal dies if you approve.   [*To the audience.*

EPILOGUE.

BY MR. COLMAN.

SPOKEN BY LADY TEAZLE.

I, who was late so volatile and gay,
Like a trade-wind must now blow all one way,
Bend all my cares, my studies, and my vows,
To one dull rusty weathercock—my spouse!
So wills our virtuous bard—the motley Bayes
Of crying epilogues and laughing plays!
Old bachelors, who marry smart young wives,
Learn from our play to regulate your lives:
Each bring his dear to town, all faults upon her—
London will prove the very source of honour.
Plunged fairly in, like a cold bath it serves,
When principles relax, to brace the nerves:
Such is my case; and yet I must deplore
That the gay dream of dissipation's o'er.
And say, ye fair! was ever lively wife,
Born with a genius for the highest life,

Like me untimely blasted in her bloom,
Like me condemn'd to such a dismal doom ?
Save money—when I just knew how to waste it !
Leave London—just as I began to taste it !
   Must I then watch the early crowing cock,
The melancholy ticking of a clock ;
In a lone rustic hall for ever pounded,
With dogs, cats, rats, and squalling brats surrounded ?
With humble curate can I now retire,
(While good Sir Peter boozes with the squire,)
And at backgammon mortify my soul,
That pants for loo, or flutters at a vole
Seven's the main ! Dear sound that must expire,
Lost at hot cockles round a Christmas fire ;
The transient hour of fashion too soon spent,
Farewell the tranquil mind, farewell content !
Farewell the plumèd head, the cushion'd tête,
That takes the cushion from its proper seat !
That spirit-stirring drum !—card drums I mean,
Spadille—odd trick—pam—basto—king and queen !
And you, ye knockers, that, with brazen throat,
The welcome visitors' approach denote ;
Farewell all quality of high renown,
Pride, pomp, and circumstance of glorious town !
Farewell ! your revels I partake no more,
And Lady Teazle's occupation 's o'er !
All this I told our bard ; he smiled, and said 'twas clear,
I ought to play deep tragedy next year.
Meanwhile he drew wise morals from his play,
And in these solemn periods stalk'd away :—
" Bless'd were the fair like you ; her faults who stopp'd,
And closed her follies when the curtain dropp'd !
No more in vice or error to engage,
Or play the fool at large on life's great stage."

THE CRITIC;

OR, A TRAGEDY REHEARSED.

A DRAMATIC PIECE IN THREE ACTS.

TO MRS. GREVILLE.

MADAM,—In requesting your permission to address the following pages to you, which, as they aim themselves to be critical, require every protection and allowance that approving taste or friendly prejudice can give them, I yet ventured to mention no other motive than the gratification of private friendship and esteem. Had I suggested a hope that your implied approbation would give a sanction to their defects, your particular reserve, and dislike to the reputation of critical taste, as well as of poetical talent, would have made you refuse the protection of your name to such a purpose. However, I am not so ungrateful as now to attempt to combat this disposition in you. I shall not here presume to argue that the present state of poetry claims and expects every assistance that taste and example can afford it; nor endeavour to prove that a fastidious concealment of the most elegant productions of judgment and fancy is an ill return for the possession of those endowments. Continue to deceive yourself in the idea that you are known only to be eminently admired and regarded for the valuable qualities that attach private friendships, and the graceful talents that adorn conversation. Enough of what you have written has stolen into full public notice to answer my purpose, and you will, perhaps, be the only person, conversant in elegant literature, who shall read this address and not perceive that by publishing your particular approbation of the following drama, I have a more interested object than to boast the true respect and regard with which I have the honour to be, Madam, your very sincere and obedient humble servant,   R. B. SHERIDAN.

DRAMATIS PERSONÆ.

AS ORIGINALLY ACTED AT DRURY LANE THEATRE IN 1779.

SIR FRETFUL PLAGIARY	} *Mr. Parsons.*
PUFF	*Mr. King.*
DANGLE	*Mr. Dodd.*
SNEER	*Mr. Palmer.*
SIGNOR PASTICCIO RITORNELLO	} *Mr. Delpini.*
INTERPRETER	*Mr. Baddeley.*
UNDER PROMPTER	*Mr. Phillimore*
MR. HOPKINS	*Mr. Hopkins.*
MRS. DANGLE	*Mrs Hopkins.*
SIGNORE PASTICCIO RITORNELLO	{ *Miss Field and the Miss Abrams.*

Scenemen, Musicians, and Servants.

CHARACTERS OF THE TRAGEDY.

Lord Burleigh .	*Mr. Moody.*	Justice . . .	*Mr. Packer.*
Governor of Tilbury Fort . .	*Mr. Wrighten.*	Son	*Mr. Lamash.*
		Constable . .	*Mr. Fawcett.*
Earl of Leicester	*Mr. Farren.*	Thames . . .	*Mr. Gawdry.*
Sir Walter Raleigh . . .	*Mr. Burton.*	Tilburina . .	*Miss Pope.*
		Confidant . .	*Mrs. Bradshaw.*
Sir Christopher Hatton . .	*Mr. Waldron.*	Justice's Lady	*Mrs. Johnston.*
		First Niece .	*Miss Collett.*
Master of the Horse . . .	*Mr. Kenny.*	Second Niece.	*Miss Kirby.*
Don Ferolo Whiskerandos . .	*Mr. Bannister, jun.*	Knights, Guards, Constables, Sentinels, Servants, Chorus, Rivers, Attendants, &c., &c.	
Beefeater . .	*Mr. Wright.*		

Scene,—London : *in* Dangle's *House during the First Act, and throughout the rest of the Play in* Drury Lane Theatre.

PROLOGUE.

BY THE HONOURABLE RICHARD FITZPATRICK.

The sister Muses, whom these realms obey,
Who o'er the drama hold divided sway,
Sometimes by evil counsellors, 'tis said,
Like earth-born potentates have been misled.
In those gay days of wickedness and wit,
When Villiers criticised what Dryden writ,
The tragic queen, to please a tasteless crowd,
Had learn'd to bellow, rant, and roar so loud,
That frighten'd Nature, her best friend before,
The blustering beldam's company foreswore ;
Her comic sister, who had wit 'tis true,
With all her merits, had her failings too :
And would sometimes in mirthful moments use
A style too flippant for a well-bred muse ;
Then female modesty abash'd began
To seek the friendly refuge of the fan,
Awhile behind that slight intrenchment stood,
Till driven from thence, she left the stage for good.
In our more pious, and far chaster times,
These sure no longer are the Muse's crimes !
But some complain that, former faults to shun,
The reformation to extremes has run.
The frantic hero's wild delirium past,
Now insipidity succeeds bombast :

So slow Melpomene's cold numbers creep,
Here dulness seems her drowsy court to keep,
And we are scarce awake, whilst you are fast asleep.
Thalia, once so ill-behaved and rude,
Reform'd, is now become an arrant prude ;
Retailing nightly to the yawning pit
The purest morals, undefiled by wit !
Our author offers, in these motley scenes,
A slight remonstrance to the drama's queens :
Nor let the goddesses be over nice ;
Free-spoken subjects give the best advice.
Although not quite a novice in his trade,
His cause to-night requires no common aid.
To this, a friendly, just, and powerful court,
I come ambassador to beg support.
Can he undaunted brave the critic's rage ?
In civil broils with brother bards engage ?
Hold forth their errors to the public eye,
Nay more, e'en newspapers themselves defy ?
Say, must his single arm encounter all ?
By number vanquish'd, e'en the brave may fall ;
And though no leader should success distrust,
Whose troops are willing, and whose cause is just ;
To bid such hosts of angry foes defiance,
His chief dependence must be, your alliance.

ACT I.

Scene I.—*A Room in* Dangle's *House.*

Mr. *and* Mrs. Dangle *discovered at breakfast, and reading newspapers.*

Dang. [*Reading.*] *Brutus to Lord North.—Letter the second on the State of the Army*—Psha! *To the first L dash D of the A dash Y.—Genuine extract of a Letter from St. Kitt's.—Coxheath Intelligence.—It is now confidently asserted that Sir Charles Hardy*—Psha! nothing but about the fleet and the nation!—and I hate all politics but theatrical politics.—Where's the Morning Chronicle?

Mrs. Dang. Yes, that's your Gazette,

Dang. So, here we have it.—[*Reads.*] *Theatrical intelligence extraordinary.—We hear there is a new tragedy in rehearsal at Drury Lane Theatre, called the Spanish Armada, said to be written by Mr. Puff, a gentleman well known in the theatrical world. If we may allow ourselves to give credit to the report of the performers, who, truth to say, are in general but indifferent judges, this piece abounds with the most striking and received beauties of modern composition.*—So! I am very glad my friend Puff's tragedy is in such forwardness.—Mrs. Dangle, my dear, you will be very glad to hear that Puff's tragedy——

Mrs. Dang. Lord, Mr. Dangle, why will you plague me about such nonsense?—Now the plays are begun I shall have no peace.—Isn't it sufficient to make yourself ridiculous by your passion for the theatre, without continually teasing me to join you? Why can't you ride your hobby-horse without desiring to place me on a pillion behind you, Mr. Dangle?

Dang. Nay, my dear, I was only going to read——

Mrs. Dang. No, no; you will never read anything that's worth listening to. You hate to hear about your country; there are letters every day with Roman signatures, demonstrating the certainty of an invasion, and proving that the nation is utterly undone. But you never will read anything to entertain one.

Dang. What has a woman to do with politics, Mrs. Dangle?

Mrs. Dang. And what have you to do with the theatre, Mr. Dangle? Why should you affect the character of a critic? I have no patience with you!—haven't you made yourself the jest of all your acquaintance by your interference in matters where you have no business? Are you not called a theatrical Quidnunc, and a mock Mæcenas to second-hand authors?

Dang. True; my power with the managers is pretty notorious.

Q

But is it no credit to have applications from all quarters for my interest—from lords to recommend fiddlers, from ladies to get boxes, from authors to get answers, and from actors to get engagements?

Mrs. Dang. Yes, truly; you have contrived to get a share in all the plague and trouble of theatrical property, without the profit, or even the credit of the abuse that attends it.

Dang. I am sure, Mrs. Dangle, you are no loser by it, however; you have all the advantages of it. Mightn't you, last winter, have had the reading of the new pantomime a fortnight previous to its performance? And doesn't Mr. Fosbrook let you take places for a play before it is advertised, and set you down for a box for every new piece through the season? And didn't my friend, Mr. Smatter, dedicate his last farce to you at my particular request, Mrs. Dangle?

Mrs. Dang. Yes; but wasn't the farce damned, Mr. Dangle? And to be sure it is extremely pleasant to have one's house made the motley rendezvous of all the lackeys of literature; the very high 'Change of trading authors and jobbing critics!—Yes, my drawing-room is an absolute register-office for candidate actors, and poets without character.—Then to be continually alarmed with misses and ma'ams piping hysteric changes on Juliets and Dorindas, Pollys and Ophelias; and the very furniture trembling at the probationary starts and unprovoked rants of would-be Richards and Hamlets!—And what is worse than all, now that the manager has monopolized the Opera House, haven't we the signors and signoras calling here, sliding their smooth semibreves, and gargling glib divisions in their outlandish throats—with foreign emissaries and French spies, for aught I know, disguised like fiddlers and figure dancers?

Dang. Mercy! Mrs. Dangle!

Mrs. Dang. And to employ yourself so idly at such an alarming crisis as this too—when, if you had the least spirit, you would have been at the head of one of the Westminster associations—or trailing a volunteer pike in the Artillery Ground! But you—o' my conscience, I believe, if the French were landed to-morrow, your first inquiry would be, whether they had brought a theatrical troop with them.

Dang. Mrs. Dangle, it does not signify—I say the stage is *the mirror of Nature,* and the actors are *the Abstract and brief Chronicles of the Time:* and pray what can a man of sense study better?— Besides, you will not easily persuade me that there is no credit or importance in being at the head of a band of critics, who take upon them to decide for the whole town, whose opinion and patronage all writers solicit, and whose recommendation no manager dares refuse.

Mrs. Dang. Ridiculous!—Both managers and authors of the least merit laugh at your pretensions.—The public is their critic—without whose fair approbation they know no play can rest on the stage, and with whose applause they welcome such attacks as yours, and laugh at the malice of them, where they can't at the wit.

Dang. Very well, madam—very well!

Enter SERVANT.

Ser. Mr. Sneer, sir, to wait on you.

Dang. Oh, show Mr. Sneer up.—[*Exit* SERVANT.]—Plague on 't, now we must appear loving and affectionate, or Sneer will hitch us into a story.

Mrs. Dang. With all my heart; you can't be more ridiculous than you are.

Dang. You are enough to provoke——

Enter SNEER.

Ha! my dear Sneer, I am vastly glad to see you.—My dear, here's Mr. Sneer.

Mrs. Dang. Good-morning to you, sir.

Dang. Mrs. Dangle and I have been diverting ourselves with the papers. Pray, Sneer, won't you go to Drury Lane Theatre the first night of Puff's tragedy?

Sneer. Yes; but I suppose one shan't be able to get in, for on the first night of a new piece they always fill the house with orders to support it. But here, Dangle, I have brought you two pieces, one of which you must exert yourself to make the managers accept, I can tell you that; for 'tis written by a person of consequence.

Dang. So! now my plagues are beginning.

Sneer. Ay, I am glad of it, for now you'll be happy. Why, my dear Dangle, it is a pleasure to see how you enjoy your volunteer fatigue, and your solicited solicitations.

Dang. It's a great trouble—yet, egad, it's pleasant too.—Why, sometimes of a morning I have a dozen people call on me at breakfast-time, whose faces I never saw before, nor ever desire to see again.

Sneer. That must be very pleasant indeed!

Dang. And not a week but I receive fifty letters, and not a line in them about any business of my own.

Sneer. An amusing correspondence!

Dang. [*Reading.*] *Bursts into tears and exit.*—What, is this a tragedy?

Sneer. No, that's a genteel comedy, not a translation—only taken from the French: it is written in a style which they have lately tried to run down; the true sentimental, and nothing ridiculous in it from the beginning to the end.

Mrs. Dang. Well, if they had kept to that, I should not have been such an enemy to the stage; there was some edification to be got from those pieces, Mr. Sneer!

Sneer. I am quite of your opinion, Mrs. Dangle: the theatre, in proper hands, might certainly be made the school of morality; but now, I am sorry to say it, people seem to go there principally for their entertainment!

Mrs. Dang. It would have been more to the credit of the managers to have kept it in the other line.

Sneer. Undoubtedly, madam; and hereafter perhaps to have had it recorded, that in the midst of a luxurious and dissipated age, they preserved two houses in the capital, where the conversation was always moral at least, if not entertaining!

Dang. Now, egad, I think the worst alteration is in the nicety of the audience!—No *double-entendre*, no smart innuendo admitted; even Vanbrugh and Congreve obliged to undergo a bungling reformation!

Sneer. Yes, and our prudery in this respect is just on a par with the artificial bashfulness of a courtesan, who increases the blush upon her cheek in an exact proportion to the diminution of her modesty.

Dang. Sneer can't even give the public a good word! But what have we here?—This seems a very odd——

Sneer. Oh, that's a comedy, on a very new plan; replete with wit and mirth, yet of a most serious moral! You see it is called *The Reformed House-breaker;* where, by the mere force of humour, house-breaking is put in so ridiculous a light, that if the piece has its proper run, I have no doubt but that bolts and bars will be entirely useless by the end of the season.

Dang. Egad, this is new indeed!

Sneer. Yes; it is written by a particular friend of mine, who has discovered that the follies and foibles of society are subjects unworthy the notice of the comic muse, who should be taught to stoop only to the greater vices and blacker crimes of humanity—gibbeting capital offences in five acts, and pillorying petty larcenies in two.—In short, his idea is to dramatize the penal laws, and make the stage a court of ease to the Old Bailey.

Dang. It is truly moral.

Re-enter SERVANT.

Ser. Sir Fretful Plagiary, sir.

Dang. Beg him to walk up.—[*Exit* SERVANT.] Now, Mrs. Dangle, Sir Fretful Plagiary is an author to your own taste.

Mrs. Dang. I confess he is a favourite of mine, because everybody else abuses him.

Sneer. Very much to the credit of your charity, madam, if not of your judgment.

Dang. But, egad, he allows no merit to any author but himself, that's the truth on 't—though he's my friend.

Sneer. Never.—He is as envious as an old maid verging on the desperation of six and thirty; and then the insidious humility with which he seduces you to give a free opinion on any of his works, can be exceeded only by the petulant arrogance with which he is sure to reject your observations.

Dang. Very true, egad—though he's my friend.

Sneer. Then his affected contempt of all newspaper strictures; though, at the same time, he is the sorest man alive, and shrinks like scorched parchment from the fiery ordeal of true criticism: yet is he so covetous of popularity, that he had rather be abused than not mentioned at all.

Dang. There's no denying it—though he is my friend.

Sneer. You have read the tragedy he has just finished, haven't you?

Dang. Oh, yes; he sent it to me yesterday.

Sneer. Well, and you think it execrable, don't you?

Dang. Why, between ourselves, egad, I must own—though he is my friend—that it is one of the most—He's here——[*Aside.*]—finished and most admirable perform——

Sir Fret. [*Without.*] Mr. Sneer with him did you say?

Enter SIR FRETFUL PLAGIARY.

Dang. Ah, my dear friend!—Egad, we were just speaking of your tragedy.—Admirable, Sir Fretful, admirable!

Sneer. You never did anything beyond it, Sir Fretful—never in your life.

Sir Fret. You make me extremely happy; for without a compliment, my dear Sneer, there isn't a man in the world whose judgment I value as I do yours and Mr. Dangle's.

Mrs. Dang. They are only laughing at you, Sir Fretful; for it was but just now that——

Dang. Mrs. Dangle!—Ah, Sir Fretful, you know Mrs. Dangle.— My friend Sneer was rallying just now:—he knows how she admires you, and——

Sir Fret. O Lord, I am sure Mr. Sneer has more taste and sincerity than to——[*Aside.*] A damned double-faced fellow!

Dang. Yes, yes—Sneer will jest—but a better humoured——

Sir Fret. Oh, I know——

Dang. He has a ready turn for ridicule—his wit costs him nothing.

Sir Fret. No, egad—or I should wonder how he came by it. [*Aside.*

Mrs. Dang. Because his jest is always at the expense of his friend.

[*Aside.*

Dang. But, Sir Fretful, have you sent your play to the managers yet?—or can I be of any service to you?

Sir Fret. No, no, I thank you: I believe the piece had sufficient recommendation with it.—I thank you though.—I sent it to the manager of Covent Garden Theatre this morning.

Sneer. I should have thought now, that it might have been cast (as the actors call it) better at Drury Lane.

Sir Fret. O 'Lud! no—never send a play there while I live—hark'ee! [*Whispers* SNEER.

Sneer. Writes himself!—I know he does.

Sir Fret. I say nothing—I take away from no man's merit—am hurt at no man's good fortune—I say nothing.—But this I will say—through all my knowledge of life, I have observed—that there is not a passion so strongly rooted in the human heart as envy.

Sneer. I believe you have reason for what you say, indeed.

Sir Fret. Besides—I can tell you it is not always so safe to leave a play in the hands of those who write themselves.

Sneer. What, they may steal from them, hey, my dear Plagiary?

Sir Fret. Steal!—to be sure they may; and, egad, serve your best thoughts as gypsies do stolen children, disfigure them to make 'em pass for their own.

Sneer. But your present work is a sacrifice to Melpomene, and he, you know, never——

Sir Fret. That's no security: a dexterous plagiarist may do anything. Why, sir, for aught I know, he might take out some of the best things in my tragedy, and put them into his own comedy.

Sneer. That might be done, I dare be sworn.

Sir Fret. And then, if such a person gives you the least hint or assistance, he is devilish apt to take the merit of the whole——

Dang. If it succeeds

Sir Fret. Ay, but with regard to this piece, I think I can hit that gentleman, for I can safely swear he never read it.

Sneer. I'll tell you how you may hurt him more.

Sir Fret. How?

THE CRITIC.

Sneer. Swear he wrote it.

Sir Fret. Plague on't now, Sneer, I shall take it ill!—I believe you want to take away my character as an author.

Sneer. Then I am sure you ought to be very much obliged to me.

Sir Fret. Hey!—sir!——

Dang. Oh, you know, he never means what he says.

Sir Fret. Sincerely then—do you like the piece?

Sneer. Wonderfully!

Sir Fret. But come, now, there must be something that you think might be mended, hey?—Mr. Dangle, has nothing struck you?

Dang. Why, faith, it is but an ungracious thing, for the most part, to——

Sir Fret. With most authors it is just so, indeed; they are in general strangely tenacious! But, for my part, I am never so well pleased as when a judicious critic points out any defect to me; for what is the purpose of showing a work to a friend, if you don't mean to profit by his opinion?

Sneer. Very true.—*Why then though I seriously admire the piece upon the whole—yet there is one small objection which if you'll give me leave, I'll mention—

Sir Fret. You can't oblige me more.

Sneer. I think it wants Incident.

Sir Fret. Good God! you surprise me—wants Incident—

Sneer. Yes I own I think the Incidents are too few.

Sir Fret. Believe me there is no Person for whose Judgment I have a more implicit Deference. But I protest to you I am only apprehensive myself that the Incidents are too crowded—Mr. Dangle how does it strike you?

Dang. Really I cannot agree with Mr. Sneer—I think the Plot quite sufficient—and the four first Acts by many Degrees the best I ever read or saw in my Life—If I might venture to suggest anything it is that the interest rather falls off in the Fifth Act.

Sir Fret. Rises I believe you mean Sir.

Dang. No I don't, upon my word.

Sir Fret. Yes yes you do—it certainly don't fall off—I assure you—no no it don't fall off.

Dang. Now Mrs. Dangle did you say it struck you in the same light?†

Mrs. Dang. No, indeed, I did not.—I did not see a fault in any part of the play, from the beginning to the end.

* The sheets of manuscript which are preserved begin here.
† End of this part of the manuscript.

Sir Fret. Upon my soul, the women are the best judges after all!

Mrs. Dang. Or, if I made any objection, I am sure it was to nothing in the piece; but that I was afraid it was on the whole, a little too long.

Sir Fret. Pray, madam do you speak as to duration of time; or do you mean that the story is tediously spun out?

Mrs. Dang. O Lud! no.—I speak only with reference to the usual length of acting plays.

Sir Fret. Then I am very happy—very happy indeed—because the play is a short play, a remarkably short play. I should not venture to differ with a lady on a point of taste; but on these occasions, the watch, you know, is the critic.

Mrs. Dang. Then, I suppose, it must have been Mr. Dangle's drawling manner of reading it to me.

Sir Fret. Oh, if Mr. Dangle read it, that's quite another affair!—But I assure you, Mrs. Dangle, the first evening you can spare me three hours and a half, I'll undertake to read you the whole, from beginning to end, with the prologue and epilogue, and allow time for the music between the acts.

Mrs. Dang. I hope to see it on the stage next.

Dang. Well, Sir Fretful, I wish you may be able to get rid as easily of the newspaper criticisms as you do of ours.

Sir Fret. The newspapers! Sir, they are the most villainous—licentious—abominable—infernal—Not that I ever read them—no—I make it a rule never to look into a newspaper.

Dang. You are quite right; for it certainly must hurt an author of delicate feelings to see the liberties they take.

Sir Fret. No, quite the contrary! their abuse is, in fact, the best panegyric—I like it of all things. An author's reputation is only in danger from their support.

Sneer. Why, that's true—and that attack, now, on you the other day——

Sir Fret. What? where?

Dang. Ay, you mean in a paper of Thursday: it was completely ill-natured, to be sure.

Sir Fret. Oh, so much the better.—Ha! ha! ha! I wouldn't have it otherwise.

Dang. Certainly it is only to be laughed at; for——

Sir Fret. You don't happen to recollect what the fellow said, do you?

Sneer. Pray, Dangle—Sir Fretful seems a little anxious——

Sir Fret. O Lud, no!—anxious!—not I—not the least.—I—but one may as well hear, you know.

Dang. Sneer, do you recollect ?—[*Aside to* SNEER.] Make out something.

Sneer. [*Aside to* DANGLE.] I will.—[*Aloud.*] Yes, yes, I remember perfectly.

Sir Fret. Well, and pray now—not that it signifies—what might the gentleman say ?

Sneer. Why, he roundly asserts that you have not the slightest invention or original genius whatever ; though you are the greatest traducer of all other authors living.

Sir Fret. Ha ! ha ! ha !—very good !

Sneer. That as to comedy, you have not one idea of your own, he believes, even in your commonplace-book—where stray jokes and pilfered witticisms are kept with as much method as the ledger of the lost and stolen office.

Sir Fret. Ha ! ha ! ha !—very pleasant !

Sneer. Nay, that you are so unlucky as not to have the skill even to steal with taste :—but that you glean from the refuse of obscure volumes, where more judicious plagiarists have been before you ; so that the body of your work is a composition of dregs and sentiments—like a bad tavern's worst wine.

Sir Fret. Ha ! ha !

Sneer. In your more serious efforts, he says, your bombast would be less intolerable, if the thoughts were ever suited to the expression : but the homeliness of the sentiment stares through the fantastic encumbrance of its fine language, like a clown in one of the new uniforms !

Sir Fret. Ha ! ha !

Sneer. That your occasional tropes and flowers suit the general coarseness of your style, as tambour sprigs would a ground of linsey-woolsey ; while your imitations of Shakspeare resemble the mimicry of Falstaff's page, and are about as near the standard of the original.

Sir Fret. Ha !

Sneer. In short, that even the finest passages you steal are of no service to you ; for the poverty of your own language prevents their assimilating ; so that they lie on the surface like lumps of marl on a barren moor, encumbering what it is not in their power to fertilize !

Sir Fret. [*After great agitation.*] Now, another person would be vexed at this !

Sneer. Oh ! but I wouldn't have told you—only to divert you.

Sir Fret. I know it—I am diverted.—Ha ! ha ! ha !—not the least invention !—Ha ! ha ! ha !—very good !—very good !

Sneer. Yes—no genius ! ha ! ha ! ha !

Dang. A severe rogue! ha! ha! ha! But you are quite right, Sir Fretful, never to read such nonsense.

Sir Fret. To be sure—for if there is anything to one's praise, it is a foolish vanity to be gratified at it; and, if it is abuse—why one is always sure to hear of it from one damned good-natured friend or other!

Enter SERVANT.

Ser. Sir, there is an Italian gentleman, with a French interpreter, and three young ladies, and a dozen musicians, who say they are sent by Lady Rondeau and Mrs. Fugue.

Dang. Gadso! they come by appointment!—Dear Mrs. Dangle, do let them know I'll see them directly.

Mrs. Dang. You know, Mr. Dangle, I shan't understand a word they say.

Dang. But you hear there's an interpreter.

Mrs. Dang. Well, I'll try to endure their complaisance till you come. [*Exit.*

Ser. And Mr. Puff, sir, has sent word that the last rehearsal is to be this morning, and that he'll call on you presently.

Dang. That's true—I shall certainly be at home.—[*Exit* SERVANT.] —Now, Sir Fretful, if you have a mind to have justice done you in the way of answer, egad, Mr. Puff's your man.

Sir Fret. Psha! sir, why should I wish to have it answered, when I tell you I am pleased at it?

Dang. True, I had forgot that. But I hope you are not fretted at what Mr. Sneer——

Sir Fret. Zounds! no, Mr. Dangle; don't I tell you these things never fret me in the least?

Dang. Nay, I only thought——

Sir Fret. And let me tell you, Mr. Dangle, 'tis damned affronting in you to suppose that I am hurt when I tell you I am not.

Sneer. But why so warm, Sir Fretful?

Sir Fret. Gad's life! Mr. Sneer, you are as absurd as Dangle: how often must I repeat it to you, that nothing can vex me but your supposing it possible for me to mind the damned nonsense you have been repeating to me!—and, let me tell you, if you continue to believe this, you must mean to insult me, gentlemen—and, then, your disrespect will affect me no more than the newspaper criticisms—and I shall treat it with exactly the same calm indifference and philosophic contempt—and so your servant. [*Exit.*

Sneer. Ha! ha! ha! poor Sir Fretful! Now will he go and vent his philosophy in anonymous abuse of all modern critics and authors.

—But, Dangle, you must get your friend Puff to take me to the rehearsal of his tragedy.

Dang. I'll answer for 't, he'll thank you for desiring it. But come and help me to judge of this musical family: they are recommended by people of consequence, I assure you.

Sneer. I am at your disposal the whole morning!—but I thought you had been a decided critic in music as well as in literature.

Dang. So I am—but I have a bad ear. I' faith, Sneer, though, I am afraid we were a little too severe on Sir Fretful—though he is my friend.

Sneer. Why, 'tis certain, that unnecessarily to mortify the vanity of any writer is a cruelty which mere dulness never can deserve; but where a base and personal malignity usurps the place of literary emulation, the aggressor deserves neither quarter nor pity.

Dang. That's true, egad!—though he's my friend!

SCENE II.—*A Drawing-room in* DANGLE'S *House.*

MRS. DANGLE, SIGNOR PASTICCIO RITORNELLO, SIGNORE PASTICCIO RITORNELLO, INTERPRETER, *and* MUSICIANS *discovered.*

Interp. Je dis, madame, j'ai l'honneur to introduce et de vous demander votre protection pour le Signor Pasticcio Ritornello et pour sa charmante famille.

Signor Past. Ah! vosignoria, noi vi preghiamo di favoritevi colla vostra protezione.

1 *Signora Past.* Vosignoria fatevi questi grazie.

2 *Signora Past.* Si, signora.

Interp. Madame—me interpret.—C'est à dire—in English—qu'ils vous prient de leur faire l'honneur——

Mrs. Dang. I say again, gentlemen, I don't understand a word you say.

Signor Past. Questo signore spiegherò——

Interp. Oui—me interpret.—Nous avons les lettres de recommandation pour Monsieur Dangle de——

Mrs. Dang. Upon my word, sir, I don't understand you.

Signor Past. La Contessa Rondeau è nostra padrona.

3 *Signora Past.* Si, padre, et Miladi Fugue.

Interp. O!—me interpret.—Madame, ils disent—in English—Qu'ils ont l'honneur d'être protégés de ces dames.—You understand?

Mrs. Dang. No, sir,—no understand!

Enter DANGLE *and* SNEER.

Interp. Ah, voici, Monsieur Dangle !

All Italians Ah ! Signor Dangle !

Mrs. Dang. Mr. Dangle, here are two very civil gentlemen trying to make themselves understood, and I don't know which is the interpreter.

Dang. Eh, bien !

[*The* INTERPRETER *and* SIGNOR PASTICCIO *here speak at the same time.*]

Interp. Monsieur Dangle, le grand bruit de vos talens pour la critique, et de votre intérêt avec messieurs les directeurs à tous les théâtres——

Signor Past. Vosignoria siete si famoso par la vostra conoscenza, e vostra interessa colla le direttore da——

Dang. Egad, I think the interpreter is the hardest to be understood of the two !

Sneer. Why, I thought, Dangle, you had been an admirable linguist !

Dang. So I am, if they would not talk so damned fast.

Sneer. Well, I'll explain that — the less time we lose in hearing them the better—for that, I suppose, is what they are brought here for.

[*Speaks to* SIGNOR PASTICCIO—*they sing trios, &c.,* DANGLE *beating out of time.*]

Enter SERVANT *and whispers* DANGLE.

Dang. Show him up.—[*Exit* SERVANT.] Bravo ! admirable ! bravissimo ! admirablissimo !—Ah ! Sneer ! where will you find voices such as these in England ?

Sneer. Not easily.

Dang. But Puff is coming.—Signor and little signoras obligatissimo !—Sposa Signora Danglena—Mrs. Dangle, shall I beg you to offer them some refreshments, and take their address in the next room.

[*Exit* MRS. DANGLE *with* SIGNOR PASTICCIO, SIGNORE PASTICCIO, MUSICIANS, *and* INTERPRETER, *ceremoniously.*]

Re-enter SERVANT.

Ser. Mr. Puff, sir. [*Exit.*

Enter Puff.*

Dang. My dear Puff !

Puff. My dear Dangle, how is't with you ?

Dang. Mr. Sneer give me leave to introduce Mr. Puff to you.

---

* From this place to the end the manuscript has been followed.

Puff. Mr. Sneer! Sir he is a Gentleman whom I have long panted for the Honor of knowing—a Gentleman whose critical Talents and transcendent Judgment——

Sneer. Dear sir——

Dang. Nay don't be modest Sneer—my Friend Puff only talks to you in the style of his Profession.

Sneer. Of his profession!

Puff. Yes Sir—I make no Secret of the trade I follow—among Friends and Brother Authors—Dangle knows I love to be Frank on the subject—and to advertise my self vivâ voce.—I am Sir—a Practitioner in Panegyric—or to speak more Plainly—a Professor of the Art of Puffing, at your service or anybody else's.

Sneer. Sir, you are very Obliging—I fancy Mr. Puff I have often admired your Talents in the daily Prints.

Puff. Yes I flatter myself I do as much Business in that way as any six of the Fraternity in Town.—devilish hard work all the summer, friend Dangle,—never worked harder! But, hark 'ee,—the winter managers were a little sore I believe.

Dang. O no I believe they took it all in good part.

Puff. Ah! then that must have been affectation in them—for egad there were some of the Attacks which there was no laughing at.

Sneer. Aye the humourous ones.—But I should think, Mr. Puff, that Authors would in general be able to do this sort of work for themselves.

Puff. Aye but in a clumsy way—besides we look on that as an encroachment—and so take the opposite side. I dare say now you conceive half the very civil Paragraphs and advertisements you see are written by the Parties concerned or their Friends—no such thing —nine out of ten [are] manufactured by me in the way of Business.

Sneer. Indeed!

Puff. Even the auctioneers now—the auctioneers I say—tho' the rogues have lately got some credit for their Language—not an article of the merit [is] theirs—take 'em out of their pulpits, and they are as dull as catalogues!—No Sir; 'twas I first enrich'd their style—'twas I first taught them to crowd their Advertisements with panegyrical superlatives, each epithet rising above the other like the Bidders in their own auction Rooms! From me they learned to inlay their Phraseology with variegated Chips of Exotic metaphor: By me too their inventive faculties were called forth—yes Sir by me they were instructed to clothe ideal walls with gratuitous fruits—to insinuate obsequious Rivulets into visionary Groves—to teach courteous shrubs to nod their approbation of the grateful soil—or on emergencies to raise upstart oaks where there never had been an Acorn—to create a delightful Vicinage without the assistance of a Neighbour—waft salubrious Gales or fix the temple of Hygeia in the fens of Lincolnshire!

Dang. I am sure you have done them infinite Service—for now when a Gentleman's ruined, He parts with his House with some credit.

Sneer. Service! egad if they had any gratitude they would erect a statue to him—they would figure you as a presiding Mercury, the God of traffic and Fiction, with a Hammer in his Hand instead of a Caduceus.—But pray Mr. Puff what first put you on exercising your Talents in this way?

Puff. Egad Sir—sheer Necessity—the proper Parent of an art so nearly allied to Invention—You must know Mr. Sneer that from the first Time I tried my hand at an Advertisement my success was such that for some time after I led a most extraordinary Life indeed!

Sneer. How Pray—

Puff. Sir I supported myself two years entirely by my misfortunes.

Sneer. By your misfortunes!

Puff. Yes Sir assisted by long sickness and other occasional Disorders! and a very comfortable Living I had of it.

Sneer. From Sickness and misfortunes! You practised as a Doctor and an Attorney at once?

Puff. No egad both maladies and miseries were my own.

Sneer. Hey—what the Plague!

Dang. 'Tis true, efaith.

Puff. Hark'ee!— By Advertisements — *To the charitable and Humane! and to those whom Providence hath blessed with Affluence!*

Sneer. Oh! I understand you.

Puff. And, in truth, I deserved what I got! for, I suppose never man went thro such a series of Calamities in the same space of time. Sir—I was five times made a bankrupt, and *reduced from a state of Affluence by a train of unavoidable misfortunes*—then Sir, tho a very *industrious Tradesman I was twice burned out and lost my little all both Times*—I lived upon those Fires a month—I soon after was confined by a most excruciating Disorder and *lost the use of my Limbs*—that told very well for I had the case strongly attested and went about to collect the subscriptions myself.

Dang. Egad—I believe that was when you first call'd on me.

Puff. In November last—O no—I was at that Time *a close prisoner in the Marshalsea for a Debt benevolently contracted to serve a friend.* I was afterwards twice *tapp'd for a Dropsy* which declined into a very profitable *consumption.* I was then *reduced to*—O no—then I became *a widow with six helpless children*—after having had *eleven Husbands press'd and being left every time eight months gone with child, and without money to get me into an Hospital*—

Dang. Mercy on me—

Sneer. And you bore all with Patience, I make no Doubt—

Puff. Why yes—tho' I made some judicious attempts at Felo de se—but as [I] did not find them answer, I left off killing myself very soon—Well Sir at last what with Bankruptcies, Fires, Gout, Dropsies, Imprisonments and other valuable calamities having got together a pretty handsome sum I determined to quit a Business which had always gone rather against my conscience—and in a more liberal way still to indulge my Talent for Fiction and embellishment thro my favourite Channels of Diurnal Communication—and so Sir you have my History.

Sneer. Most obligingly communicative indeed—but surely Mr. Puff there is no great mystery in your Present Profession?

Puff. Mystery! Sir—I will take upon me to say the matter was never scientifically treated nor reduced to Rule before.

Sneer. Reduced to Rule!

Puff. O Lud Sir, you are very ignorant, I am afraid—Yes Sir—Puffing is of various Sorts—the Principal are, *the Puff direct—the Puff oblique—the Puff collateral, the Puff Preliminary,* and *the Puff Collusive.* These all as circumstances require assume the varied Forms of Letter to the Editor—occasional Anecdote—impartial Critique—observation from Correspondent, or Advertisement from the Party.

Sneer. The Puff direct, I can conceive——

Puff. O yes that's simple enough—for instance,—A new comedy or Farce is to be produced at one of the Theatres (though by-the-by they don't bring out half what they ought to do)—the author, suppose Mr. Smatter, or Mr. Flimsey—or any particular Friend of mine—very well—the **Day** before it is performed I write an account of the manner in which it was received—I have the Plot from the Author—and only add—"characters strongly drawn—highly colour'd—hand of a master—fund of genuine humour—mine of Invention—neat Dialogue—Attic salt." Then for the performance—"Mr. Dodd was astonishingly great in the Character of young Mr. Something—that universal and judicious Actor Mr. Palmer perhaps never appeared to more advantage—but it is impossible for language to do justice to Mr. King—indeed he more than merited those repeated Bursts of applause which he drew from a most brilliant and judicious Audience —as to the scenery—the miraculous Powers of Mr. Loutherbourg's

Pencil are universally acknowledged—in short we are at a loss which to admire most, the unrivall'd Genius of the Author—the great attention and Liberality of the Managers—The wonderful abilities of the Painter, or the incredible exertions of all the Performers."

Sneer. That's pretty well indeed—Sir.

Puff. O cool—quite cool—to what I sometimes do.

Sneer. And you think there are any who are influenced by this?

Puff. O Lud yes Sir—the number of those who go thro' the fatigue of judging for themselves is very small indeed.

Sneer. Well Sir the Puff Preliminary?

Puff. O that Sir does well in the Form of a caution—in a matter of Gallantry now—Sir Flimsy Gossimer wishes to be well with Lady Fanny Fete—he applies to me—I open trenches for him with a Paragraph in the Morning Post.—" It is recommended to the beautiful and accomplished Lady F four stars F dash E to be on her guard against that dangerous character, Sir F dash G ; who, however pleasing and insinuating his manners may be, is certainly not remarkable for the *constancy of his Attachments!*"—in italics. Here you see Sir Flimsy Gossimer is introduced to the particular notice of Lady Fanny—who perhaps never thought of him before—she finds herself publicly cautioned to avoid him which naturally makes her desirous to see him—the observation of their Acquaintance causes a pretty kind of mutual embarrassment—this produces a sort of sympathy of interest, which if Sir Flimsy is unable to improve effectually He at least gains the credit of having their names mention'd together by a particular set, and in a particular way—which nine times out of ten is the full accomplishment of modern Gallantry.

Dang. Egad, Sneer, you will be quite an adept in the Business.

Puff. Now Sir the *Puff Collateral* is much used as an appendage to advertisements, and may take the Form of Anecdote.—" Yesterday, as the celebrated George Bonmot was sauntering down St. James's Street, He met the lively Lady Mary Myrtle coming out of the Park : —' Good God, Lady Mary,' said George, ' I'm surprised to meet you in a white Jacket,—for I expected never to have seen you but in a full-trimmed uniform and a Light Horseman's Cap !'—' Heavens, George, where could you have learned that?'—' Why,' replied the wit, ' I just saw a Print of you in a new Publication called the Camp Magazine ; which, by the bye, is a devilish clever thing and is sold at No. 3, on the right hand of the way two Doors from the Printing Office, the corner of Ivy Lane, Paternoster Row."

Sneer. Ah ! that's very ingenious indeed—

Puff. But the *puff collusive* is the newest of any—for it acts in the disguise of determined Hostility—it is much used by Bold booksellers and enterprizing Poets.—" An indignant correspondent observes —that the New Poem call'd *Beelzebub's Cotillon, or Proserpine's Fête Champêtre*, is one of the most unjustifiable Performances He ever read. The severity with which certain characters are handled is quite shocking—and as there are many descriptions in it too warmly colour'd for female Delicacy the shameful avidity with which this Piece is bought by all People of Fashion is a reproach on the taste of the Times, and a disgrace to the Delicacy of the Age." Here you see the two strongest inducements are held forth—1st, that nobody ought to read it—and secondly, that everybody buys it—on the strength of which the Publisher boldly prints the tenth Edition, before he had sold ten of the first—and then establishes it by threatening himself with the Pillory, or absolutely indicting himself for *Scan. Mag.*

Dang. Ha! ha! gad, I know it's so—

Puff. As to the Puff oblique, or Puff by Implication it is too various and extensive to be illustrated by an Instance—it attracts in Titles and Presumes in Patents—it lurks in the Limitation of a Subscription —and invites in the assurance of crowd and incommodation at Public Places, it delights to draw forth conceal'd merit, with a most disinterested assiduity—and often wears a countenance of smiling censure and tender Reproach—it has a wonderful memory for Parliamentary Debates and will often give the whole speech of a favoured member with the most flattering accuracy. But above all it is a great Dealer in Reports and Suppositions—it has the earliest intelligence of intended Preferments that will reflect honour on the Patrons and embryo Promotions of modest Gentlemen who know nothing of the matter themselves—it can hint a Ribband for implied services in the air of a common Report—and with the carelessness of a casual Paragraph suggest officers into commands to which they have no pretension but their wishes. This—Sir is the last Principal Class of the Art of Puffing—a Practice which I hope you will now agree with me is of the highest Dignity—yielding a Tablature of Benevolence and Public Spirit ; befriending equally Trade Gallantry Criticism and Politics— The applause of Genius—The Register of Charity—The Triumph of Heroism—the self Defence of Contractors—the Fame of Patriots— and the Gazette of Ministers.

Sneer. Sir, I am completely a convert both to the importance and ingenuity of your profession ; and now, sir, there is but one thing which can possibly increase my respect for you, and that is, your permitting me to be present this morning at the rehearsal of your new trage——

R

Puff. Hush, for heaven's sake!—*My* tragedy!—Egad, Dangle, I take this very ill: you know how apprehensive I am of being known to be the author.

Dang. I' faith I would not have told—but it's in the papers, and your name at length in the Morning Chronicle.

Puff. Ah! those damned editors never can keep a secret!—Well, Mr. Sneer, no doubt you will do me great honour—I shall be infinitely happy—highly flattered——

Dang. I believe it must be near the time—shall we go together?

Puff. No; it will not be yet this hour, for they are always late at that theatre: besides, I must meet you there, for I have some little matters here to send to the papers, and a few paragraphs to scribble before I go.—[*Looking at memorandums.*] Here is *A conscientious Baker, on the subject of the Army Bread;* and *a Detester of visible Brickwork, in favour of the new-invented Stucco;* both in the style of Junius, and promised for to-morrow. The Thames navigation too is at a stand. Misomud or Anti-shoal must go to work again directly.—Here too are some political memorandums—I see; ay—*To take Paul Jones, and get the Indiamen out of the Shannon—reinforce Byron—compel the Dutch—to—*so!—I must do that in the evening papers, or reserve it for the Morning Herald; for I know that I have undertaken to-morrow, besides, to establish the unanimity of the fleet in the Public Advertiser, and to shoot Charles Fox in the Morning Post.—So, egad, I ha'n't a moment to lose.

Dang. Well, we'll meet in the Green Room. [*Exeunt severally.*

ACT II.

Scene I.

Dangle, Puff, *and* Sneer.

Puff. I say that what Shakspeare says of the Actors may be better applied to the Purpose of Plays—*They* ought to be "the Abstract and brief Chronicle of the Times." Therefore when History, and particularly the History of our own country furnishes anything like a case in Point to the time in which an Author writes if he knows his own Interest, he'll take advantage of it—so Sir—I call my Tragedy *The Spanish Armada*; and have laid the scene before Tilbury Fort.

Sneer. A most Happy Thought certainly!

Dang. Egad it was—I told you so—but pray now I don't understand how you have contrived to introduce any Love into it? and that you know is as necessary to a modern Tragedy as—to a Simile, and therefore you had better not try to make one on the subject.

Puff. Love! O nothing so easy—for it is a received Point among Poets, that where History gives you a good heroic out Line for a Play, you may fill up with a little love at your own Discretion: in doing which nine times out of Ten you only make up a Deficiency in the private History of the Times. Now I rather think I have done this with some Address.

Sneer. No scandal about Queen Elizabeth I hope—

Puff. O Lud no—no—I only suppose the Governor of Tilbury Fort's Daughter to be in Love with the son of the Spanish Admiral.

Sneer. O is that all

Dang. Excellent efaith—I see it at once—But won't this appear rather improbable?

Puff. To be sure it will—but what the Plague! a Play is not to show occurrences that happen every Day—but things just so strange, that tho' they never did they might happen.

Sneer. Certainly nothing is unnatural that is not Physically impossible.

Puff. Very true and for that matter Don, for that's the Lover's Name, might have been over here in the train of the Spanish ambassador; or Tilburnia, for that is the lady's name, might have been in Love with him from having heard his character, or seen his Picture; or from knowing that he was the last man in the world she ought to be in Love or for any other good female Reason—however Sir the Fact is that tho' she's but a Knight's Daughter egad she is in Love like any Princess!

Dang. Poor young Lady—I feel for her already! for I can conceive how great the conflict must be between her Passion and her Duty—her Love for her country and her Love for Don.

Puff. O amazing—her poor susceptible Heart is swayed to and fro by contending Passions like——

Enter UNDER PROMPTER.

Und. Promp. Sir the scene is set and everything is ready to begin if you please.

Puff. Egad then we'll lose no Time.

Und. Promp. Tho, I believe Sir you will find it very short for all the Performers have profited by the kind Permission you granted them.

Puff. Hey what!

Und. Promp. You know Sir you gave them leave to cut out or omit whatever they found heavy or unnecessary to the Plot—and I must own they have taken very liberal advantage of your Indulgence.

Puff. Well well they are in general very good Judges and I know I am luxuriant.—Now, Mr. Hopkins as soon as you please—

Und. Promp. [*To the* Orchestra.] Gentlemen will you play a few Bars of something to——

Puff. Aye that's right—for as we have the Scenes and dresses egad, we'll go to't as if it was the first Night's Performance—but you need not mind stopping between the acts—Orchestra *Play.* Soh stand clear Gentlemen—now you know there will be a cry of Down! Down!—Hats off!—Silence!—Then up curtain, and let us see what our Painters have done for us. [*Curtain rises.*

SCENE II.—Before Tilbury Fort.

"SENTINELS asleep.

Dang. Tilbury Fort!—very fine indeed!

Puff. Now what do you think I open with—

Sneer. Faith I can't guess.

Puff. A clock.—Hark!—[*Clock strikes.*] I open with a clock striking to beget an awful attention in the Audience—it also marks the time, which is four o'clock in the morning and saves a Description of the rising Sun and a great deal about gilding the eastern Hemisphere.

Dang. But pray are the Centinels to be asleep?

Puff. Fast as Watchmen.

Sneer. Isn't that odd though at such an alarming crisis?

Puff. Aye, but smaller things must give way to a striking scene at the opening. And the case is that two great men are coming to this very spot to begin the Piece—it is not to be supposed now they would open their Lips if these Fellows were watching them—so egad I must either have sent them off their Posts—or set them asleep.

Sneer. O that accounts for it—but tell us who are these coming ?

Puff. Those are they—Sir Walter Raleigh, and Sir Christopher Hatton—you'll know Sir Christopher by his turning out his Toes—famous you know for his Dancing—I like to preserve all the little Traits of Character—now observe—

"*Enter* Sir Walter Raleigh *and* Sir Christopher Hatton.
Sir Christ. True, gallant Raleigh ! "—

Dang. What they had been talking before

Puff. O yes all the way as they came along.—I beg Pardon Gentlemen but these are Particular Friends of mine whose Remarks may be of great service to us.—don't mind interrupting them whenever anything strikes you.

"*Sir Christ.* True, gallant Raleigh !
    But O, thou champion of thy Country's fame,
    There is a Question which I yet must ask :
    A Question which I never ask'd before—
    What mean these mighty Armaments ?
    This general muster and this Throng of Chiefs ?

Sneer. Pray Mr. Puff, how came Sir Christopher Hatton never to ask that question before ?

Puff. What before the Play began !—how the plague could he ?

Dang. That's true, efaith !

Puff. But you will hear what he thinks of the Matter.

"*Sir Christ.* Alas, my noble Friend, when I behold
    Yon tented Plains in martial Symmetry
    Array'd ; when I count o'er yon glittering lines
    Of crested warriors, where the Proud Steeds Neigh,
    And valour-breathing Trumpet's shrill Appeal,
    Responsive vibrate on my listening ear ;
    When virgin Majesty herself I view,
    Like her Protecting Pallas, veil'd in steel,
    With graceful Confidence exhort to Arms !
    When briefly all I hear—or see bears stamp
    Of martial preparation and of stern defence,
    I cannot but surmise—forgive, my Friend,
    If the Conjecture's rash—I cannot but
    Surmise—the State some Danger apprehends ! "

Sneer. A very cautious Conjecture that.

Puff. Yes that's his Character—not to give an opinion but on good Grounds.—now then.

"*Sir Walt.* O most accomplish'd Christopher!"——

Puff. He calls him by his Christian Name, to show that they are on the most familiar Terms.

"*Sir Walt.* O most accomplish'd Christopher—I find
    Thy staunch Sagacity still tracks the future,
    In the fresh Print of the o'ertaken Past."

Puff. Figurative!

"*Sir Walt.* Thy Fears are just—
Sir Christ. But where? whence? when? and what
    The Danger is—meth'nks I fain wou'd learn.
Sir Walt. You know, my Friend, scarce two revolving suns,
    And three revolving moons, have closed their course
    Since Haughty Philip, in despight of Peace,
    With hostile hand hath struck at England's Trade.
Sir Christ. I know it well.
Sir Walt. Philip, you know, is proud Iberia's king!
Sir Christ. He is—
Sir Walt.   His subjects in base Bigotry
    And Catholic Oppression held—while we
    You know the Protestant Persuasion own—
Sir Christ. We do—
Sir Walt. You know beside—his boasted Armament,
    The famed Armada, by the Pope Baptized,
    With Purpose to invade these Realms——
Sir Christ.   Is sailed—
    Our last advices so advise—
Sir Walt. While the Spanish Admiral's chief hope,
    his darling son——
Sir Christ.   Don——
Sir Walt. The same—by chance a Prisoner hath been ta'en,
    And in this fort of Tilbury——
Sir Christ.   Is now
    Confined—'tis true, and oft from yon tall turret's top
    I've mark'd the youthful Spaniard's haughty mien—
    Unconquer'd, tho' in chains.
Sir Walt.   You also know——"

Dang. Mr. Puff, as he knows all this, why does Sir Walter go on telling him?

Puff. But the Audience are'nt supposed to know anything of the matter, are they?

Sneer. True; but I think you manage ill — for there certainly appears no reason why Sir Walter should be so communicative.

Puff. Fore Gad now that's one of the most *ungrateful* observations I ever heard—for the less inducement *he* has to tell all this, the more I think you ought to be obliged to him—for I'm sure you'd know nothing of the Plot without it—

Dang. That's very true, upon my word!

Puff. But you'll find He was not going on.

"*Sir Christ.* Enough, enough—'tis plain—
   And I no more am in Amazement lost!"——

Puff. Here now you see Sir Christopher didn't in Fact ask any one Question for his own Information.

Sneer. No, indeed his has been a most disinterested curiosity!

Dang. Really I find that we are very much obliged to them both.

Puff. To be sure you are. Now then for the commander-in-chief, the Earl of Leicester, who, you know, was no favourite but of the queen's.—We left off—*in amazement lost!*

"*Sir Christ.*   Am in amazement lost.
  But see—where noble Leicester comes—supreme
  In Honours and Command.
Sir Walt. . .   And yet, methinks,
  At such a time, so perilous, so fear'd,
  That Staff might well become an abler Grasp.
Sir Christ. And so, by Heaven think I—but, soft He's Here!"

Puff. Aye they envy him!—

Sneer. But who are these with him?

Puff. O very valiant knights! one's the Governor of the Fort, the other the master of the horse. And now, I think, you shall hear some better Language. I was obliged to be plain and intelligible in the first Scene, because there was so much matter of Fact in it; but now faith! you have trope, Figure and Metaphor, as Plenty as noun substantives.

"*Enter* EARL OF LEICESTER, GOVERNOR, MASTER OF THE HORSE, KNIGHTS, &c.

Leic. . . How's this, my friends! is't thus your new-fledged zeal,
  And plumèd valour moulds in roosted sloth?
  Why dimly glimmers that Heroic Flame,
  Whose reddening Blaze, by patriot Spirit fed,
  Should be the beacon of a kindling Realm?
  Can the quick current of a Patriot Heart
  Thus stagnate in a cold and pond-like converse,
  Or freeze in Tideless Inactivity?
  No rather let the Fountain of your Valour
  Spring through each stream of enterprise,
  Each petty channel of conducive Daring,
  Till the full torrent of your foaming Wrath
  O'erwhelm the Flats of sunk Hostility!"

Puff. There it is—followed up!

"Sir Walt.   No more the freshening Breath of thy Rebuke
    Hath fill'd the swelling canvas of our Souls
    And thus tho' fate should cut the cable of
                    [*All take hands.*
    Our Hopes—in Friendship's closing line
    We'll grapple with despair, and if we fall,
    We'll fall in glory's Wake!
Leic. . . There spoke old England's Genius!
    Then, are we all resolved?
All. . . We are—all resolved.
Leic. . . To conquer—or be free?
All. . . To conquer, or be free.
Leic. . . All?
All. . . All."

Dang. Nem. con! egad!

Puff. O yes!—where they do agree on the Stage their unanimity is wonderful!

" Leic. . . Then let's embrace—and now——   [*Kneels.*"

Sneer. What the Plague, is he going to Pray?

Puff. Yes—hush:—in great emergencies, there is nothing like a **Prayer.**

" Leic. . . O mighty Mars!"

Dang. But why should he pray to Mars?

Puff. Hush!

" Leic. . .   If in thy Homage bred,
    Each Point of Discipline I've still observed;
    Nor but by due Promotion and the right
    Of Service to the Rank of major General
    Have risen assist thy Votary now!
Gov. . . . Yet do not rise—hear me!
Knight. . . And me!
Sir Walt. . And me!
Sir Christ. . And me!
All. . Behold thy votaries submissive beg,
    That thou wilt deign to grant them, all they ask!
    Assist them to accomplish all their ends,
    And sanctify whatever means they use
    To gain them!"

Sneer. A very orthodox Quintetto!

Puff. Vastly well gentlemen—is that well managed or not? Have you such a prayer as that on the stage?

Sneer. Not exactly.

Leic. [*To* Puff.] But Sir—you haven't settled how we are to get off here.

Puff. You couldn't go off kneeling, could ye?

Sir Walt. [*To* Puff.] O no Sir impossible!

Puff. It would have a good effect efaith! if you could exeunt praying!—Yes, and would vary the establish'd mode of springing off with a glance at the Pit.

Sneer. Oh, never mind—so as you get them off!—I'll answer for't the Audience won't care how.

Puff. Well then repeat the last Line standing and go off the old way.

"*All.* . . And sanctify whatever means we use
        To gain them.   [*Exeunt.*"

Dang. Bravo—a fine exit.

Sneer. Well really Mr. Puff——

Puff. Stay a moment!

"*The* Centinels *get up.*

1 *Sent.* . . All this shall to Lord Burleigh's ear.

2 *Sent.* . . 'Tis meet it should—The General it seems is disaproved.
                                  [*Exeunt.*"

Dang. Hey!—why, I thought those Fellows had been asleep?

Puff. Only a pretence there's the Art of it—I mean it to mark Lord Burleigh's Character who you know was famous for his skill in procuring Intelligence and employ'd all sorts of People as spies.

Sneer. But isn't it odd they never were taken Notice of—not even by the commander-in-chief?

Puff. O Lud Sir—if people who want to listen or overhear were not always connived at in a Tragedy, there would be no carrying on any Plot in the World.

Dang. That's certain!

Puff. But take care—my dear Dangle—the morning-gun is going to fire.   [*Cannon fires.*

Dang. Hey—Well, that will have a fine effect!

Puff. I think so, and helps to realize the scene. There are more cannon to fire.

Und. Promp. [*Within.*] No Sir.

Puff. Now Then for soft music. (musick)

Sneer. Pray what's that for?

Puff. It shows that Tilburina is coming—nothing introduces you a Heroine like soft music. Here she comes—all in tune to the minuet in Ariadne.

Dang. And her confidant, I suppose?
Puff. To be sure!

"*Enter* TILBURINA *and* CONFIDANT.

Tilb. . . . Now has the whispering breath of gentle morn
Bid Nature's voice and Nature's beauty rise;
While orient Phœbus, with unborrow'd hues,
Clothes the waked loveliness which all night slept
In heavenly drapery! Darkness is fled.
   Now Flowers unfold their Beauties to the Sun,
   And blushing kiss the Beam he sends to wake them—
   The strip'd Carnation, and the guarded Rose,
   The vulgar Wall Flower, and smart Gillyflower,
   The Polyanthus mean—the dapper Daisy,
   Sweet William, and sweet Marjory—and all
   The Tribe of single and of double Pinks!
   Now too the feather'd Warblers tune their Notes—
   Around, and charm the listening Grove. The Lark!
   The Linnet, Chaffinch, Bullfinch, Goldfinch, Greenfinch!
   —But O to me no joy can they afford
   Nor Rose, nor Wallflower, nor smart Gillyflow'r,
   Nor Polyanthus mean, nor dapper Daisy,
   Nor William sweet, nor marjory—nor Lark,
   Linnet, nor all the finches of the grove!

Puff. Your white Handkerchief, Ma'am!——
Tilb. I thought, sir, I wasn't to use that till *heart-rending woe.*
Puff. O yes, madam, at 'the Finches of the Grove,' if you please.

"*Tilb.* . . . Nor all the finches of the grove! [*Weeps.*"

Puff. Vastly well, Ma'am!
Dang. Vastly well Indeed!

"*Tilb.* . . For, O, too sure, Heart-rending woe is now
   The Lot of wretched Tilburina!"

Dang. Oh!
Sneer. Oh!

"*Con.* . . Be comforted, sweet Lady—who knows,
   But Heaven has yet some milk-white Day in store?
Tilb. . . . Alas! my gentle Nora,
   Thy tender youth as yet hath never mourn'd
   Love's fatal Dart—else wouldst thou know that when
   The soul is sunk in comfortless Despair,
   It cannot taste of merriment."

Dang. That's certain—

"*Con.* . . But—see where your stern father comes:
   It is not meet that he should find you thus."

Puff. Hey, what the Plague!—what a cut is here? Why, what's become of the description of her first meeting with Don—his gallant behaviour in the sea-fight—and the simile of the Canary Bird?

Tilb. Indeed Sir, you'll find they will not be miss'd.

Puff. Very well—very well!

Tilb. [*To* CONFIDANT.] The cue, ma'am, if you please.

"*Con.* . . It is not meet that he should find you thus.
Tilb. . . . Thou counsel'st right—but 'tis no easy task
    For barefaced Grief to wear a Mask of Joy.
      Enter GOVERNOR.
Gov. . . . How's this—in Tears?—O Tilburina shame!
    Is this a Time for maudling tenderness,
    And Cupid's baby woes—hast thou not heard
    That Haughty Spain's Pope—consecrated fleet
    Advances to our Shores, while England's fate,
    Like a clipp'd Guinea, trembles in the scale?
Tilb. . . . Then is the crisis of *my* Fate at hand!
    I see the fleets approach—I see——'

Puff. Now pray Gentlemen, mind. This is one of the most useful Figures we Tragedy writers have by which a Hero or Heroine, in consideration of their being often obliged to overlook Things that *are* on the Stage, is allowed to hear and see a number of things that are not.

Sneer. Yes—a kind of Poetical Second-sight!

Puff. Yes.—Now then, ma'am.

"*Tilb.* . .   I see their Decks
    Are clear'd—I see the signal made
    The Line is form'd—a cable's length asunder!
    I see the frigates station'd in the rear;
    And now I hear the Thunder of the guns!
    I hear the victor's shouts—I also hear
    The vanquish'd groan!—and now 'tis smoke—and now
    I see the loose sails shiver in the wind
    I see—I see—what soon you'll see——
Gov. . . . Hold Daughter Peace—this love hath turn'd thy Brain:
    The Spanish Fleet thou *canst* not see—because
    —It is not yet in Sight!"

Dang. Egad tho', the Governor seems to make no Allowance for this poetical Figure you talk of.

Puff. No—a plain matter of Fact man—that's his Character.

"*Tilb.* . . But will you then refuse his offer?
Gov. . . . I must I will I can I ought I do.
Tilb. . . . Think what a noble Price.
Gov. . . . No more you urge in vain—
Tilb. . . . His Liberty is all he asks."

Sneer. All who asks Mr. Puff?

Puff. Egad Sir, I can't tell—Here has been such cutting and slashing I don't know where they have got to myself.

Tilb. Indeed Sir, you will find it will connect very well.

"—And your reward secure."

Puff. O—if they hadn't been so devilish free with their cutting here, you 'd [have] found that Don has been tampering for his Liberty—and has persuaded Tilburina to make this Proposal to her Father—and now pray observe the conciseness with which the Argument is conducted—egad, the pro and con goes as smart as Hits in a Fencing-match. It is indeed a sort of small-sword-logic, which we have borrowed from the French.

" *Tilb.* . . A Retreat in Spain!
Gov. . . . Outlawry here!
Tilb. . . . Your Daughter's Prayer!
Gov. . . . Your Father's Oath!
Tilb. . . . My Lover!
Gov. . . . My Country!
Tilb. . . . Tilburina!
Gov. . . . England!
Tilb. . . . A Title!
Gov. . . . Honour!
Tilb. . . . A Pension!
Gov. . . . Conscience!
Tilb. . . . A Thousand Pounds!
Gov. . . . Ha! thou hast touch'd me nearly——"

Puff. There you see—she threw in Tilburina. Quick parry Carte with England! thrust in tierce a Title!—parried by Honour. Ha! a Pension over the arm!—put by by conscience. Then flankonade with a thousand pounds—and a palpable Hit egad!

Sneer. Well Push'd indeed.

" *Tilb.* . . Canst thou—
 Reject the suppliant, and the Daughter too?
Gov. . . . No More—I would not hear thee plead in Vain:
 The Father softens—but the Governor's resolved. [*Exit.*"

Dang. Aye that Antithesis of Persons, is a most established Figure.

" *Tilb.* . . 'Tis well—hence then fond Hopes,—fond Passion hence;
 Duty behold I am all over thine——
Whisk. . . [*Without.*] Where is my love—my Tilb...Ha!
Tilb. . . . Ha!
Don. . . [*Without.*] Where is my Love—my——
Tilb. . . Ha!
Whisk. . . My beauteous Enemy!——"

Puff. O dear Ma'am, you must start a great deal more than that—

Consider you had just determined in favour of Duty—when in a moment, the sound of his Voice revives your Passion—overthrows your resolution—destroys your obedience—if you don't express all that in your start—you do nothing at all.

Tilb. Well—we'll try again.

Dang. Speaking from within has always a fine effect.

Sneer. Very.

" *Tilb.* . . . Behold I am all—over thine.
Don. . . . Where is my Love? my——
Tilb. . . . Ha!
Don. . . . My beauteous Enemy!
    My conquering Tilburina! (enter) ha! is't thus
    We meet—why are thy looks averse? what means—

Puff. Heyday—Here's a cut!—What are all the mutual Protestations out?

Tilb. Now pray Sir, don't interrupt us here—you ruin one's feelings.

Sneer. No, pray don't interrupt them.

" *Whisk.* . One last embrace.
Tilb. . . . Now farewell—for ever.
Whisk. . . For ever!
Tilb. . . . Aye for ever!   [*Going.*"

Puff. Gad's life!—Sir! Ma'am! if you go out without the Parting look, you might as well dance out. Here—here!—

Con. But pray Sir—How am I to get off here?

Puff. Pshaw! what the Devil signifies how *you* get off! edge away at the Top or where you will. Now, Ma'am—you see——

Tilb. We understand you Sir.

" *Both.* . . Oh! [*Turning back, and exeunt.—Scene closes.*"

Dang. O charming—

Puff. Hey!—'tis pretty well I believe—you see I don't attempt to strike out anything new—but I take it I improve on the establish'd modes.

Sneer. You do indeed—but pray isn't Queen Elizabeth to appear?

Puff. No—not once—but she is to be talked of for ever—so that egad you'll think a hundred Times that she is on the point of coming in.

Sneer. Hang it I think it's a pity to keep her in the Green-Room all the Night.

Puff. O no, that always has a fine Effect—it keeps up Expectation.

Dang. But aren't we to have a Battle neither?

Puff. Yes yes, you will have a Battle at last but egad it's not to be by Land—but by Sea—and that's the only quite new thing in the Piece.

Dang. O—ho—what Drake at the Armada hey.

Puff. Yes efaith—Fire-Ships and all—then we shall end with a Procession. Hey that will do I think?

Sneer. No doubt on 't.

Puff. But come we must not lose Time—so now for the Underplot.

Sneer. Hey what the Plague, have you another Plot?

Puff. O Lud yes—ever while you live have two Plots to your Tragedy. The grand Point in managing them is only to let your Under Plot have as little connection with your chief Plot as possible. —I flatter myself nothing can be more distinct than mine, for as in my chief Plot the characters are all great People, I have laid my under Plot in low Life and—as the former is to end in deep Distress, I make the other end as happy as a Farce—Now Mr. Hopkins as soon as you please.

Enter UNDER PROMPTER.

Under Promp. Sir—the Carpenters say it is impossible you can go to the Park Scene yet.

Puff. The Park Scene! no—I mean the Description scene here in the wood.

Under Promp. Sir the Performers have cut it out.

Puff. Cut it out!

Under Promp. Yes Sir.

Puff. What! the whole account of Queen Elizabeth?

Under Promp. Yes Sir.

Puff. And the Description of her Horse and Side-Saddle?

Under Promp. Yes Sir.

Puff. So—so—this is very fine indeed!—Mr. Hopkins how the Devil could you suffer this?

Mr. Hop. [*From within.*] Sir indeed the Pruning Knife——

Puff. The Pruning Knife—zounds!—the Axe!—why here has been such lopping and topping—I shan't have the bare Trunk of my Play left presently!—Very well Sir—the performers must do as they please—but upon my soul I'll print it every word.

Sneer. That I would indeed.

Puff. Very well Sir—then we must go on.—Zounds I wouldn't have parted with the Description of the Horse!—Well Sir go on.— Sir it was one of the finest and most laboured Things.—Very well, sir; let them go on.—There you had him and his accoutrements, from the Bit to the Crupper.—Very well Sir; we must go to the Park Scene.

Under Promp. Sir—there's the point—the Carpenters say that unless there is some Business put in here before the Drop they sha'n't have time to clear away the Fort—

Puff. So! this is a pretty Dilemma, indeed—Do call the Head Carpenter to me.

Under Promp. Mr. Butler—(enter Carpenter dress'd) Here he is Sir.

Puff. Hey—this is the Head Carpenter!

U. P. Yes—Sir—He was to have walked as one of the Generals at the Review—For the truth is your Tragedy employs everybody in the company.

P. O—then pray Mr. General-Carpenter what is all this?

Mr. Carp. Why Sir, you only consider what my men have to do—they have to remove Tilbury Fort with the Cannon and to sink Gravesend and the River and I only desire three minutes to do it in.

P. Hah! and they've cut the Scene.

Carp. Besides if I could manage in less, I question if the Lamplighter could clear away the Sun in the time.

Puff. Do call one of them here.

Carp. Master Lamplighter! (Without) Mr. Langley! Here (enter Lamplighter as a River God and a Page holding up his train.)

Puff. Sir—your most obedient servant—Who the Devil's this!

U. P. The master Lamplighter, Sir. He does one of the River Gods in the Procession.

Puff. O, a River God is he—well Sir you won't have time I understand—

L. Three minutes at least Sir—unless you have a mind to burn the Fort.

P. Hah! and they've cut out the Scene!

Carp. Lord Sir, there only wants a little business to be put in here —just as long as while we have been speaking will do it—

Puff. What then are you all ready now? (from behind) Yes all clear.

Puff. O then I shall easily manage it—

U. P. Clear the Stage.

Puff. And do General keep a sharp look out and beg the River God not to spare his Oyl in the last scene—it must be brilliant. Gentlemen I beg a thousand Pardons.

Sneer. O dear Sir—these little things will happen. [*Exeunt.*

ACT III.

Scene I.—*The Theatre, before the curtain.*

Enter Puff, Sneer, *and* Dangle.

Puff. Well, we are ready; now then for the justices.
[*Curtain rises.*
"Justices, Constables, &c., *discovered.*"

Sneer. This I suppose is a sort of Senate Scene.

Dang. It is the Under-Plot, isn't it?

Puff. Yes.—What, gentlemen, do you mean to go at once to the Discovery Scene?

Just. If you please, sir.

Puff. Oh, very well!—Hark'ee, I don't chuse to say anything more but efaith they have mangled my play in a most Shocking Manner.

Dang. It's a great pity!

Puff. Now then Mr. Justice if you please.

"*Just.* . . Are all the Volunteers without?
Const. . .   They are.
         Some ten in Fetters, and some twenty Drunk.
Just. . . . Attends the youth—whose most opprobrious Fame
         And clear convicted Crimes have stamp'd for soldier?
Const. . . He waits your Pleasure—eager to repay
         The best Reprieve that sends him to the Fields
         Of Glory, there to raise his branded Hand
         In Honour's cause.
Just. . . .   'Tis well—'tis Justice arms him!
         Oh! may he now defend his Country's Laws
         With half the Spirit he has broke them all!
         If 'tis your Worship's Pleasure—bid him enter.
Const. . I fly—the Herald of your will.   [*Exit.*"

Puff. Quick, sir.

Sneer. But, Mr. Puff, I think not only the Justice, but the Clown seems to talk in as high a style as the first Hero among them.

Puff. Heaven forbid they shouldnt in a free country—Sir I'm not for making slavish Distinctions—and giving all the fine Language to the upper Sort of People.

Dang. That's very noble in you indeed!

"Enter the Justice's Lady."

Puff. Now, pray mark this Scene.

"*Lady* . . Forgive this interruption, good my Love ;
       But as I just now pass'd a handcuff'd youth,
       Whom rude Hands hither lead—strange bodings seized
       My flutt'ring Heart—and to myself I said,
       An' if our Jack had lived he'd surely been
       This Stripling's Height !
Just. . . . Ha ! sure some Powerful sympathy directs
       Us both——for this youth.
              Enter SON and CONSTABLE.
              What is thy name?
Son . . . My Name's John Wilkins—*Alias* have I none—
       Though orphan'd, and without a Friend
Just. . .   Thy Parents ?
Son . . . My Father dwelt in Rochester—and was,
       As I have heard—a Fishmonger—no more."

Puff. What Sir do you leave out the account of your Birth, Parentage, and Education ?

Son. They have settled it so Sir.

Puff. O !

"*Lady* . . How loudly Nature whispers to my Heart
       Had He no other Name ?
Son . . .   I've seen a Bill
       Of his sign'd Tomkins, creditor.
Jus. Ha ! by Heavens ! Our Boy is now before us.
Lady. Has he his Ears?
Son. Lady—for three long winters have I mourned their Loss.
Lady. It is ! it is !
Just. . . . This does indeed confirm
       Each circumstance the Gipsy told quick loose
       Those ignominious [bonds ?] prepare
Son . . .   I do.
       Just. . . . No Orphan, nor without a Friend art thou—
       I am thy Father; here's thy Mother; there
       Your uncle—this thy first cousin, and Those
       Are all your near Relations !
Lady . . . O ecstasy of Bliss !
Son . . . O most unlook'd for Happiness !
Lady . . . O wonderful event ! (Faints.)"

Puff. There, you see Relationship like murder will out.

"*Just.* . . . See she revives—this joy's too much !
       But come—and we'll unfold the rest within ;
       And thou must needs want rest and food.
       Hence may each orphan hope, as Chance directs,
       To find a Father where he least expects !   [*Exeunt.*'

Puff. What do you think of that ?

Dang. One of the finest Discovery scenes I ever saw!—Why this Under Plot would have made a Tragedy in itself.

Sneer. Aye or a Comedy either.

Puff. And keeps quite clear you see of the other.

"*Enter* SCENEMEN, *taking away the seats.*"

Puff. The scene remains does it?

Sceneman. Yes Sir.

Puff. You are to leave one chair, you know.—But it's always awkward in a Tragedy you Fellows coming in in your Playhouse Liveries to remove things. I wish that could be managed better.

"Enter BEEFEATER.

Beef. . . . Perdition catch my soul but I *do* love thee!"

Sneer. Haven't I heard that line before?

Puff. No, I fancy not.—Where, pray?

Dang. Yes, I think there's something like it in Othello.

Puff. Gad! now you put me in mind on't, I believe there is—but that's no consequence—all that can be said is that two People happen'd o hit upon the same thought—and Shakespeare made use of it first, that's all.

Sneer. Very true.

Puff. Now Sir, your Soliloquy—but speak more to the Pit if you please——

"*Beef.* . . Though hopeless Love finds comfort in Despair,
   It never can endure a Rival's Bliss!
   But soft—I am observed.   [*Exit.*"

Dang. That's a very short Soliloquy.

Puff. Yes—but it would have been a great deal longer if He had not been observed.

Sneer. A most sentimental Beefeater That Mr. Puff!

Puff. Hark'ee—I wouldn't have you be too sure that He is a Beefeater.

Sneer. O what, a Hero in Disguise?

Puff. No Matter—I only give you a hint—but now for my principal character. Here He comes—Lord Burleigh in Person! Pray Gentlemen, step this way—softly—I only hope He's perfect—if He is but perfect!—

"Enter LORD BURLEIGH, goes slowly to a chair and sits."

Sneer. Mr. Puff!

Puff. Hush!—Vastly well!

Dang. What isn't he to speak at all?

Puff. Egad I thought you'd ask me that—yes it is a very likely thing—that a minister in his situation with the whole affairs of the Nation on his Head, should have time to talk !—but hush ! or you'll put him out.

Sneer. Put him out ! how the Plague can that be if He's not going to say anything ?

Puff. There's a reason ! why his Part is to *think*—and how the plague do you imagine he can *think*—if you keep talking—

Dang. That's very true, upon my word !

"LORD BURLEIGH *comes forward,* "*Shakes his head, and exit.*"

Puff. Now—hush !—close !

Sneer. He is very perfect indeed ! Now, pray what did he mean that——

Puff. You don't take it—

Sneer. No I don't upon my soul.

Puff. Why, by that shake of his Head, he gave you to Understand that even tho' everything was to be hoped from the Justice of their cause and wisdom of their measures—yet, if there was not a greater spirit shown on the Part of the People, the country would at last fall a sacrifice to the hostile ambition of the Spanish monarchy.

Sneer. The Devil ! did He mean all that by shaking his Head ?

Puff. Every word of it—if He shook his Head as I taught him.

Dang. Ah ! there certainly is a vast deal to be done on the Stage by dumb show and expression of Face !

Sneer. Oh, here are some of our old acquaintance.

"*Enter* SIR CHRISTOPHER HATTON *and* SIR WALTER RALEIGH.

Sir Christ.   My niece and your niece too !
    By Heaven ! there's witchcraft in 't.—He could not else
    Have gain'd their hearts.—But see where they approach :
    Some horrid purpose lowering on their brows !

Sir Walt.   Let us withdraw and mark them.   [*They withdraw.*"

Sneer. What is all this ?

Puff. Ah ! here has been more pruning !—but the fact is, these two young ladies are also in love with Don Whiskerandos. Now, Gentlemen—this scene goes entirely for what we call situation and *Stage Effect*, by which the greatest applause may be obtain'd, without the assistance of Language, Sentiment, or Character : pray mark !

" Enter two NIECES.

1st Niece.   Ellena here !
    She is his Scorn as much—that is
    Some comfort still ! "

Puff. O dear—Ma'am you are not to say that to her face !—Aside—Ma'am—aside.—The whole scene is to be aside. Very true Sir.

"1st Niece. She is his scorn as much as I—
That is some comfort still. [Aside.
2nd Niece. He scorns I know Ellena's love;
But Tilburina lords it o'er his Heart. [Aside.
1st Niece. . But see the proud Destroyer of my Peace—In freedom too
Revenge is all the good I've left. [Aside.
2nd Niece. He comes the false Disturber of my Quiet.
By Tilburina feared
Now Vengeance do thy worst. [Aside.

            Enter DON FEROLO WHISKERANDOS.

Whisk. . O hateful Liberty—if thus
In vain I seek my Tilburina !
Both Nieces.   And ever shalt !

    SIR CHRISTOPHER HATTON *and* SIR WALTER RALEIGH *come forward.*
Sir Christ. and Sir Walt. Hold ! we will avenge you.
Whisk. . . Hold you—or see your Nieces bleed !

Puff. There's situation for you ! there's an heroic Group !—You see I have them all at a dead Lock. The Ladies can't stab Whiskerandos—he durst not strike them, for fear of their unkles—the unkles durst not kill him because of their Nieces. — and every one of them is afraid to let go first.

Sneer. Why, then they must stand there for ever !

Puff. So they would, if I hadn't a good contrivance for 't.—Now mind——

          "*Enter* BEEFEATER *with his halbert,*
Beef. . . In the Queen's Name I charge you all to drop
Your Swords and Daggers !
              [*They drop their swords and daggers.*"

Sneer. That is a contrivance indeed !

Puff. Aye—in the queen's name.

" Sir Christ. Come, niece !
Sir Walt. . Come, niece !   [*Exeunt with the two* NIECES.
Whisk. . . What's he, who bids us thus renounce our guard?
Beef. . . Thou must do more—renounce thy love !
Whisk. . . Thou liest—base Beefeater !
Beef. . •   Ha ! hell ! the lie !
By Heaven thou'st roused the lion in my heart !
Off, yeoman's habit !—base disguise ! off ! off !
    [*Discovers himself by throwing off his upper dress, and
    appearing in a very fine waistcoat.*
Am I a Beefeater now ?
Or beams my crest as terrible as when
In Biscay's Bay I took thy captive sloop ? "

Puff. There, egad ! he comes out to be the very captain of the privateer who had taken Whiskerandos prisoner—and was himself an old lover of Tilburina's.

Dang. **Admirably managed indeed!**

Puff. **Now stand out of their way.**

Whisk. . . I thank thee Fortune, that hast thus bestowed
A weapon to chastise this Insolent. [*Takes up one of the swords.*

Beef. . . . I take thy challenge, Spaniard, and I thank thee,
Fortune, too! [*Takes up one of the swords."*

Dang. That's excellently contrived!—It seems as if the two uncles had left their swords on purpose for them.

Puff. No, egad, they could not help leaving them.

" *Whisk.* . Vengeance and Tilburina!
Beef. . . . Exactly so——
[*They fight—and after the usual number of wounds given,* WHISKERANDOS *falls.*

Whisk. . . O cursed parry!—that last thrust in tierce
Was fatal.—Captain, thou hast fenced well!
And Whiskerandos quits this bustling scene
For all eter——
Beef. . . ——nity—he would have added, but stern death
Cut short his being, and the noun at once!"

Puff. O my dear sir, you are too slow: now mind me.—Sir, shall I trouble you to die again?

" *Whisk.* . And Whiskerandos quits this bustling scene
For all eter——
Beef. . . . ——nity—he would have added,——

Puff. No Sir—that's not it—once more, if you please Don Whiskerandos.

Whisk. I wish Sir, you would Practise this without me—I can't stay dying here all Night.

Puff. Very well—we'll go it over by-and-bye—[*Exit* WHISKERANDOS.] I must humour these gentlemen!

" *Beef.* . . Farewell—brave Spaniard!"

Puff. Dear sir, you needn't speak that speech, as the Body's walked off.

Beef. That's true, sir—then I'll join the Fleet.

Puff. If you please.—[*Exit* BEEFEATER.] Now, who comes on?

"Enter GOVERNOR.

Gov. . . . A Hemisphere of Evil Planets reign!
And every planet sheds contagious frenzy!
My Spanish prisoner is slain! my Daughter,
Meeting the dead corse Borne along, has gone
Distract! *Trumpets.*
But Hark! I am summon'd to the Fort:
Perhaps the Fleets have met! amazing crisis!
O Tilburina! from thy aged father's beard
Thou'st pluck'd the few black hairs which time had left! [*Exit."*

Puff. True.—Now enter Tilburina !

Sneer. Egad the Business comes on quick here.

Puff. Yes Sir—now she comes in stark mad in white satin.

Sneer. Why in white satin ?

Puff. O Lud Sir—when a Heroine goes mad she always goes into white Satin.—don't she, Dangle ?

Dang. Always—

Enter TILBURINA *and her* CONFIDANT *mad.*

Sneer. But, what the Deuce ! is the confidante to be mad too ?

Puff. To be sure she is—the Confidante is always to do whatever her mistress does—weep when she weeps—smile when she smiles—go mad when she goes mad.—Now, Ma'am—but keep your madness in the background.

"*Tilb.* . . The wind whistles—the moon rises—see, they have kill'd my squirrel in his cage—is this a Grasshopper?—Ah no; it is my Friend—you shall not keep him—I know you have him in your Pocket—An oyster may be cross'd in Love !—who says A whale's a Bird?—ha ! did you call my Love ?—He's here ! He's there !—He's everywhere ! Ah me ! he's nowhere. [*Exit.*"

Puff. There, do you ever desire to see anybody madder than that ?

Sneer. Never, while I live.

Puff. Now then for my magnificence—my Battle—and my procession !—You are all ready ?

Und. Promp. Yes, Sir.

Puff. Is the Thames dressed ?

Thames. Here I am Sir.

Puff. Very well, indeed !—See—Gentlemen, there's a River for you !—

Sneer. But pray who are these Gentlemen in green with him—

Puff. Those—those are his Banks.

Sneer. His banks—

Puff. Yes—but hey what the Plague you have got both your Banks on one side.—Here here—Ever while you live, Thames, go between your banks.—[*Bell rings.*] Now but !—Away !

[*Exit* THAMES *between his banks.*
[*Curtain drops.*

A JOURNEY TO BATH.

A COMEDY.

BY MRS. FRANCES SHERIDAN.

Men.	*Women.*
LORD STEWKLY.	LADY FILMOT.
SIR JEREMY BULL, Bar^t	LADY BELL AIRCASTLE.
SIR JONATHAN BULL, his brother, a City K^t	MRS. TRYFORT, a citizens widow.
EDWARD, son to Sir JONATHAN.	LUCY, her daughter.
CHAMPIGNION.	MRS. SURFACE, one who keeps a lodging house at Bath.
STAPLETON.	

Scene—Bath.

ACT the 1st

SCENE THE FIRST.—The Parade at Bath.

Enter STAPLETON *at one side,* MRS. SURFACE *at the other meeting him, stops short.*

Mrs. Surface. Well,—let me dye if at a little distance I knew you!—I declare you trip along as brisk as eighteen, and look as fresh this morning! but my dear Sir where are you going in such haste?

Stapleton. To look for an other lodging.

Mrs. Sur. Marry heaven forbid! I'd rather lose every lodger in my house than you.

Stap. Your house! Why your house is like a fair, what betwixt my lady Filmot's visitors, my Lord Stewkly's hair-dressers, and that roystering Westindian and his drunken Negroes, a man cant enjoy an hours repose.

Mrs. Sur. I know it my good Sir, I know it, and it grieves me to the very heart—That same Lord Stewkly is no better than he should be, (between ourselves) as for my lady Filmot, she is—a fine lady, thats all—I speak ill of nobody behind their backs; and for Mr. Champignion, he is a Fool poor man; but take no notice that I told you so.

Stap. Then there's that fat woman, that lyes abed one half of the day, and laughs the other half; she and her daughter come thundering to the door at all hours of the night.

Mrs. Sur. Ha ha ha, Mrs. Tryfort—and yet she is here for her health—Oh these citizens Mr. Stapleton! Her daughter is going to be married you must know, and the lover and his father, and Uncle are coming into my house to day.

Stap. Then I will go out of your house to night.

Mrs. Sur. I'd part with my two eyes sooner, you se[e] now I would. No, I'll tell you what I'll do for you; you shall just step another flight of stairs, and then you will have no body over your head but Lady Bell Aircastle.

Stap. What, is that she that's all way sweeping a flimzy train of scoured silk up and down stairs?

Mrs. Sur. The very same, ha ha ha, lord help her she is as proud as lucifer and as poor as Lazarus; lives mostly upon tea breakfast, dinner, and supper poor Soul! but she is of a great family—if you will take her own word for it—not over young neither, for all she looks so well; but I would't tell this to everybody.

Stap. Oh I know you are wonderfully tender of reputations, you hate scandal.

Mrs. Sur. Ay, as I do poison; I do, as I would be done by, Mr. Stapleton. Well now, what pritty nice things shall I get you for your dinner, for I am going to market.

Stap. Psha—I dont care.

Mrs. Sur. Oh I know your taste, there is nobody can please you like myself.

Stap. Well, well get you gone, I must make out my walk and then go home to write letters. (*Aside*, a cajoling baggage.)

[*Exit* STAP.

Mrs. Sur. Good morning to you good Sir, and a pleasant walk to you, dear Sir—A peevish Cur, but I had rather have him than an empty room. [*Exit* MRS. SURFACE.

SCENE CONTINUES.

2nd SCENE.—*Enter* LADY FILMOT *and* LORD STEWKLY.

Lady Filmot. Poh, poh my Lord this Jealousy's all affectation.

Lord Stewkly. Affectation Madam! Why dont you think you give me cause for it?

Lady F. Yes—if you loved me I grant you; but those days are over.

Lord. Upon my word Ma'am, I dont know how it may be on your side; but for my part I assure you very solemnly that my heart is—

Lady F. As much devoted to you as ever—ha ha ha! You think perhaps that I expect such a declaration from you; but I will spare you the pain of dissimulation, by telling you at once, that I know your heart is as much at ease about me as—

Lord. As what pray Ma'am?

Lady F. As mine is about your lordship.

Lord. Very well ma'am, then I suppose our acquaintance is to be at an end.

Lady F. By no means; why shoud our being no longer lovers, hinder us from being friends?

Lord. The transition I own is not difficult; but to tell you my mind freely, I believe you never did *really* love me.

Lady F. I protest I *liked* you vastly; but for *love*, oh lud! a woman, who at sixteen, consented to a match of interest, is not likely at almost double that age, to be a slave to softer passions.

Lord. That circumstance might have convinced me that your heart was never capable of tenderness: So fine a woman, with your understanding and education, to sacrifice herself in the bloom of youth for money!

Lady F. Nay, the sacrifice was not voluntary neither: I was only passive on the occasion, and suffered myself to be persuaded by a Mother, to marry a man for whom I did not care a pinch of snuff, because he was heir to a rich old miser. She piqued herself on her dexterity in making the match, and I made a merit of my obedience in accepting it.

Lord. And the fruits of your meritorious obedience was—

Lady F. Ruin—I grant you; but that was not my fault: the inexorable old cit turned his son out of doors and declared he would disinherit him. We found ourselves both undone. He indeed woud have kindly persuaded me to starve with him; but not being quite fond enough of him for that, I prudently bid him good by, and returned back to my mother. He was unreasonable enough to be offended at this—threw himself into the service of the East India Company, and went abroad in a pet, swearing we should never hear of him more; and thus ended my matrimonial scheme of felicity, which lasted just two months and eleven days.

Lord. A good pleasant history. But one woud think ma'am that such an adventure might deter you from making an interested marriage a second time.

Lady F. Not in the least—one may make a shift to enjoy life with tolerable tranquility with taking *love* into the bargain; but there is no one comfort to be procured without riches: and your lordship may remember I made that my objection, when on our first acquaintance, you seemed disposed to take me for life.

Lord. Tis true; but yet you hinted at a kinder reason, for you told me that you knew not but that your husband was then living.

Lady F. Why at that time I really was uncertain about his fate; but there is now no room to doubt of it, as in consequence of his death, you find his niece, Miss Tryfort is her grandfather's heir, for it seems the stubborn old fellow dyed at last without a will.—Come come my lord, take my word for it, we are both now much better qualified to see, and to promote our mutual interest, than when we were foolish enough to be fond of each other.—Your business is to marry a fortune,—so is mine.

Lord. And I think I can guess where *your* shafts are aimed; young Edward Bull is your mark.

Lady F. The very same, and if you will give me leave to point *your* artillery, I will direct it to—

Lord. Miss Lucy Tryfort, I presume.

Lady F. Right—and now can you have the face to say you had not resolved on this before?

Lord. Why no faith, I'll take example by your frankness, and tell you honestly that I had; but dont you know that the young people are destined for each other?

Lady F. I know their *parents* intend it; but I hope their stars will dispose of them better. As Lucy's estate woud have been my poor dear spouse's, had he lived, I think I have a sort of right in the disposal of it, and woud not wish to bestow it better than on your lordship.

Lord. Oh ma'am your most obedient. I suppose neither the girl nor her mother suspect in the least [substituted for "have the least suspicion of "] who you are?

Lady F. How should they? I never saw either of them till they came hither. They never heard of me by my present name, and I have a little too much spirit to acknowledge myself the widow of a man whom his purse-proud relations abandoned for marrying. let them e'en enjoy his fortune, for my stripling will inherit all his fathers wealth.

Lord. Oh then you are *sure* of him?

Lady F. Why—not absolutely, I must totally rout the present sovereign of his heart, before I even let him suspect my design of filling her throne—I have persuaded his Uncle Sir Jeremy, (who by the way admires me prodigiously) to change their former lodgings and come into our house.

Lord. Sir Jonathan and his son, I suppose, follow of course?

Lady F. Oh to be sure; poor Sir Jonathan you know is to be led by a hair, and looks up to his brother as to an oracle. This you will see gives me more frequent opportunities—

Lord. Yes, yes I see, and approve of your design—I suppose Edward breakfasts with me this morning—tho' faith I don't remember whether I askd him or not,

Lady F. For shame my lord! but I'll soon rectify that omission — I fancy 'tis almost the hour. I must just step home and adjust myself a little, and then—but where is it we are to be?

Lord. Oh at Spring gardens—I'll go before you, for I suppose you reserve for your swain the honour of squiring you thither.

Lady F. Oh certainly.

Lord. Ma'am I submit

Lady F. With a most exemplary patience ha ha ha! Is not this better than being in love now? [*Exit severally.*

Scene 3ᵈ

Stapleton's appartment.

Enter Sir Jonathan *followed by two or three servants with trunks.*

Sir Jonathan. There there, set them down and go for the rest. lack a day I am so weary!

[*He throws himself into an armed chair.*

Enter Stapleton *with a pen in his hand.*

Stap. Why what the plague is all this noise about?

Sir Jo. Sir!

Stap. Whats all this lumber here?

Sir Jo. Lumber do you call it? I hope I may bring my baggage into my own lodgings Sir without offence to anybody

Stap. Your own lodgings Sir why these are my lodgings

Sir Jo. Hey! introth I believe I am wrong sure enough. Well thats comical! now I think of it my brother Jeremy told me it was up *one* pair of stairs, and I have come up two, ha ha ha I beg your pardon Sir; sit down, pray dont let me be your hindrance.

Stap. Pray Sir let these things be taken away.

Sir Jo. Presently when my servants come back; but I protest I am so tired with going to and fro that I must needs rest a while; pray be seated Sir and let us have a little chat, for I dont love ceremony.

Stap. Nor I dont love intrusion Sir.

Sir Jo. No, nor I neither when a man does it designedly; but I like now to stumble on an acquaintance by chance; one often gets good friends in that way. May I be so bold Sir as to ask you your name? *My* name's Bull, Sir Jonathan they call me; but a knight batchelor.

Stap. (*aside* This mans simplicity almost tempts me to excuse his impertinence) Stapleton's my name Sir.

Sir Jo. Ha, Stapleton; married or single, if I may be so free?

Stap. Single, thank my stars.

Sir Jo. One shoud be thankful for everything to be sure. I buried a very good wife; but I have a son a fine pritty youth as you shoud see; and I have an elder brother, he's a baronet, a fine man too in his own way.

Stap. Well Sir I am glad of it; but if you please, I'll call my servant to remove your trunks.

Sir Jo. No, no Sir, dont trouble yourself, I am in no hurry; but I wish you knew this brother of mine, you woud like him I believe. He has had a fine education. I was only bred to business; but faith it has turned out better than all his learning; for he, poor gentleman, spent what estate there was in the family upon an election, and lost it too; that was the worst of it, for it almost turned his brain.

Stap. Ay, that was bad indeed, to lose his election and his wits too.

Sir Jo. Oh I dont mean that neither, no, no, no God forbid! Wit, he has more wit than I have, for that matter; but it vexd him grievously, for you must know he is a little haughty, being the elder branch of the family as he calls it, and a man of learning: Yet we differ sometimes in opinion; but I durstn't always speak my mind to him, for he has the gift of speech better than I have, and will harangue you so, that he won't leave you a word to say.

Stap. Why you dont seem wanting in fluency of speech yourself Sir Jonathan.

Sir Jo. No, no no, in my own way; but then he was a famous speaker in Parliament once; he is a scholar too, and I have bred my son one. I had him at a grammar school, and he understands latin almost as well as his Uncle. I am going to marry him soon to a young lady that lodges in this house: I don't know whether you know Miss Tryfort?

Stap. Tryfort! I have heard the name. Pray who is she Sir?

Sir Jo. Why one of those that has had good luck. Her grandfather dyed some time ago and his whole fortune comes to her; for her fathers dead, and an uncle she had, that married foolishly and ran away, and so she is the only heir in the family.

Stap. And she is to be married to your son?

Sir Jo. And she is to be married to my son, the affair is settled between—lack-a-day theres my brother Jeremy! [SIR JEREMY *calls without* Sr Jonathan! Why where are you?] now will he be as angry with me for this little mistake—I am coming brother. Sir your humble servant. I shall be proud to be better acquainted with you.

Stap. Sir I am yours [*exit* SIR JONATHAN] tho I hate to mix with the world I can be entertained with a recital of its follies at a distance. This man seems to be thrown in my way on purpose: I'll cultivate his acquaintance. The communicativeness of his temper will be a means to gratify my curiosity—who's there? [*Enter a* SERVANT.] Remove these things and set the chamber to rights. [*Exit* STAPLETON.

SCENE 4th—A parlour.

Enter SIR JONATHAN *and* Sʳ JEREMY.

Sir Jeremy. Fy, fy Sir Jonathan, I am ashamed of your blundering thus eternally.

Sir Jo. Well, well brother dont be angry there is no great harm done.

Sir Jer. Sir Jonathan!

Sir Jo. Brother!

Sir Jer. I want some conference with you.

Sir Jo. I am very willing to hear you, brother.

Sir Jer. You know I never gave my assent to this junction (for I cant call it an alliance) between my nephew and this girl.

Sir Jo. Gazooks! brother why didn't we come hither to solemnize the wedding?

Sir Jer. No.

Sir Jo. No! why wasn't it agreed that they shoud be married the day that Ned was to be one and twenty, and wont that be next Saturday, and woud he let me rest till he made me come down hither after Mrs. Tryfort?

Sir Jer. I grant you, I grant you all that Sir Jonathan; yet there are sudden events which sometimes require as sudden a change of measures, and he is a deplorable politician that is not prepared for exigencies.

Sir Jo. I cant for my life see what Politicks has to do with my son's marriage.

Sir Jer. Ha ha, I know *you* cant; but I can.

Sir Jo. Why. What fresh objection have you started now?

Sir Jer. Ph—uph—no blood, no family, no connections, fy, fy! I'd rather see the boy married to a woman of consequence, tho he did n't get sixpence with her.

Sir Jo. By my faith and so woudn't I. Put forty thousand pound into one scale, and consequence as you call it into tother, and see which will weigh heaviest?

Sir Jer. Theres the case! tho' you are of an antient family yourself yet having had the misfortune to be thrown early into trade it has abased your ideas: now for my part tho I have somewhat abridged the inheritance of my ancestors in reducing it from twelve hundred, to about two I believe hundred pounds a year,—yet I did it in a cause I am not ashamed of. I am the first eldest son of the family for these seven generations that have been out of the Senate house, I can tell you that.

Sir Jo. Oh brother you spent a world of money about that same business.

Sir Jer. And woud spend another world again tomorrow, on the same occasion; and if it shoud ever be Ned's great happiness to get into Parliament—

Sir Jo. Ned into Parliament. Oh lord oh lord; lookee brother with submission, I woud not give sixpence, no not sixpence—

Sir Jer. I know it, yet tis fit notwithstanding as Edward is the only representative of the family, that the name shoud be revived with some degree of splendor; but instead of that, you want irretrievably to mix the bloud with the puddle of City.

Sir Jo. Dont abuse the City, brother, I dont know what we shoud do without it.

Sir Jer. I dont, the City may have its use; but dont let us confound all order, all distinction, and fancy trade's people are upon a footing with legislators. I have no object in view for myself, (they have thought proper to leave *me* out) but I own it woud please me to reflect, that my posterity, even in the collateral line, were to be guardians of the liberty of their country, instead of being doomd to the drudgery of making money.

Sir Jo. Dont abuse money neither, brother, I can assure you it is a very good thing.

Sir Jer. It appears so to *you* no doubt, who have been used to buy and sell, and thank the people that you gained by; but I who have been brought up with a Spirit of independence, woud sooner be reduced to eat my own shoe leather, than be obliged to e'en a man alive.

Sir Jo. I dont understand such fine-spun notions, not I.

Sir Jer. I know you dont, and for that reason have often suspected your legitimacy; for excepting yourself, I never knew any one of the family that had not those notions.

Sir Jo. May be so, brother; have you anything more to say to me, for I have a good deal of business to do.

Sir Jer. The old way! When ever *I* was disposed to inform you a little, *you* had always business; havn't I known you, rather than miss your hour of going to Change, refuse to hear me repeat a speech on which perhaps the welfare of the whole nation depended?

Sir Jo. (hastily). You dont want to speak a speech now brother, do you?

Sir Jer. No Sir, not at present; but if you were fit to be trusted with the conduct of your own affairs, I coud tell you that there is something now on the tapis that perhaps may be the making of a certain young man.

Sir Jo. What is it brother, I shall be very glad to hearken to any thing for the good of my son.

Sir Jer. Matters are not yet come to that maturity that I could wish; but I had a mind to sound you, to feel your pulse a little on the occasion, Sir Jonathan; so I shall for the present, only throw out to you at large, that there is a certain person of condition here, that possibly woudn't be averse to entering into a treaty of marriage with us.

Sir Jo. With *us!* I dont very well take your meaning brother.

Sir Jer. I dont intend you shoud brother; this is not the juncture for explanations. At a proper time perhaps I may let you a little more behind the curtain; in the meanwhile I have given you a *hint* just to play with, Sir Jonathan; and so now you may go about your *business* as you call it, for I am engaged to breakfast with my lord Stewkly this morning.

Sir Jo. Very well, when you come back I shall be glad of a little further discourse with you, so brother your humble servant.

Sir Jer. Good morning to you Sir Jonathan [*exit* SIR JONATHAN]. A weak man; but he means well. [*Exit* SIR JEREMY.

SCENE THE 5th—Spring Gardens.

Enter LORD STEWKLY *and* LADY FILMOT.

Lord. And so you coudn't persuade the stripling?

Lady F. He coloured, and said he must ask his fathers leave.

Lord. I wish my damsel were *capable* of blushing; but she is too ignorant even for that; for when I asked her, she only stared, made me half a dozen curtisies, and then said she was laced so tight, it had given her a pain in the stomach, and asked me if I knew what was good for the cholic ha ha ha.

Lady F. Oh you must get the mother of your side; she wants of all things to be taken notice of by the *quality*, as she phrases it.—You ought to visit her, tis the vainest poor creature, and the fondest of hard words, which without *mis*calling, she always takes care to misapply.—She perfectly adores me, because I always speak to her, whenever I meet her.

Lord. Lady Bell I think cant prevail on herself to shew her the least civility.

Lady F. No; and the poor woman does take such pains to get into her good graces! and then Lady Bell draws up her long neck, gives her a supercilious stare, and turning to me, 'shall we walk Lady Filmot' for you see there's *no*body here: and then poor Mrs Tryfort finding herself *nobody*, looks *so* mortified, and follows us *so* close, in order to appear one of our company, that I talk to her out of mere compassion.

Lord. Ha ha ha poor woman!

Lady F. But how in the name of wonder can you afford to treat such an intolerable crowd as you have collected here this morning?

Lord. To let you into a secret, Champignion pays, tho I have the credit of it. You must know he is *ambitious*, as he calls it, of being galant. [He is] immensely rich, ostentatious and never easy but in devising the means to squander.

Lady F. And I suppose you are kind enough to assist him.

T

Lord. Oh he has taken me for his pattern; and upon his consulting me what handsome thing he ought to do, I told him I intended giving an entertainment here this morning; but to oblige him, would let him do it in my stead, and as he is a stranger, undertook to ask the company in his name.

Lady F. That was very kind of you; but wont he discover that you have asked them in your own?

Lord. No, for I told him it would be the height of good breeding not to appear till the company were seated, and to slip away before they rose, to avoid the usual ceremony of bowing and curtsying; so that as he will be fidgetting about all the morning, he will only have the appearance of my deputy.

Lady F. Very well contrived, I declare.

Lord. Oh I have laid such a train for mirth—you must know he is immoderately vain of his person; and as he wants of all things to captivate some woman of quality, I have told him that Lady Bell Aircastle is in love with him.

Lady F. Gracious! why she would not condescend to look at him.

Lord. I know it; but I shall give her to understand that he is in *love* with *her*, which I think may afford us some pleasant scenes. Besides this will lead the profuse coxcomb into a thousand schemes of expensive pleasure, which will serve for entertainment, in our intervals of more serious business.

Lady F. Ay there you say something—and here comes your fool with all his busy consequence about him.

6 SCENE.

Enter CHAMPIGNION.

Lord. Well, Mr Champignion are any of your company come yet?

Cham. A few my lord, but I steppd out of the way to avoid being impolite you know; tho I deprive myself of the pleasure of gazing at the ladies; there are abundance of your sex ma'am, are to do me the honour to breakfast with me this morning.

Lady F. So I hear Sir, and you seem to have prepared a very elegant entertainment for us.

Cham. I have endeavoured to make it as grand ma'am as the place would afford; for you know ma'am how can we batchelors employ our time better, than in shewing our respect to the ladies ma'am?

Lady F. Very true, Sir.

Cham. It wont cost me above fifty guineas, and you know ma'am that's but a trifle to a single fellow like me, to purchase the favour of the fair sex, especially ladies of quality.

Lady F. Oh certainly; lady Bell Aircastle is to do the honours of your table, I think Sir?

Cham. She is of a prodigious great family! Her father was the seventeenth earl in a direct line; and blood you know ma'am entitles people—but apropos, my lord, a word with you.—Your ladyship will excuse me for a minute. [*he takes* LORD STEWKLY *aside*] I am told she is so monstrously proud that she will not marry any man that can't produce a pedigree, (of *gentry* at least) up to the flood, and split me if I can tell who my grandfather was!

Lord. Thats a little unlucky; but as you are not known here, you can easily make a pedigree for yourself.

Cham. Ay; but who can I get to vouch for the truth of it my lord?

Lord. Nay, that indeed I cant tell.

Cham. If I could but find some poor devil (with the appearance of a gentleman tho') who woudn't scruple to assert an innocent lye, you know my lord, Id pay him handsomely for his pains.

Lord. Why I fancy such a one may be easily found.

Cham. Egad I have hit, my lord! that shabby knight thats just come into our house—the poor dog has beggard himself they tell me, yet sets up for something, and knows everybody.

Lord. Who, Sir Jeremy Bull do you mean?

Cham. Ay, he, my lord, Ill give him a hundred guineas for a handsome lye, provided he'll swear to it.

Lord. Have a care how you make such a proposal to him!

Cham. Nay nay, hang it, my lord I'll give him two hundred for that matter rather than fail.

Lord. But I tell you Sir he is a man that—

Cham. I declare here's lady Bell just come into the garden. I had best slip aside till she joins you, you know, my lord.

[*He skips nimbly a little way from* LORD S.

7 Scene

Enter LADY BELL

Lord. Good morning to your ladyship

Lady Bell. Why my lord Stewkley, you have certainly invited the whole corporation of Bath with their wives and children; the place wont contain them, its quite a mob, dont you think so lady Filmot?

Cham. (advancing). A mob ma'am? heres none but people of quality, and the best gentry, I can assure your ladyship.

Lady Bell (aside). Who is this person my Lord?

Lord. I thought your ladyship knew Mr. Champignion!

Lady Bell. Do you know anything of him lady Filmot

Lady F. Oh yes ma'am, he is a friend of my lord's.

Lady Bell (as if observing company at a distance). An absolute Mob I declare, I scarce know any of them.

Cham. I hope your ladyship will excuse my taking the liberty of requesting the honour of—

Lord (aside). Hush! you'll spoil all!

Cham. Egad my lord I must make her know than I am no more company for Mob than her ladyship.

Lady Bell. What does the young man say my lord?

Lord. That there has been scarce any one asked ma'am but people of fashion.

Cham. That was my design, ma'am, or I shoud not have had the ambition to desire the favour of your ladyships presiding; but we poor unmarried fellows you know ma'am, that are so unfortunate as not to have ladies of our own, you know ma'am—

Lady Bell. What does He mean, lady Filmot?

Lady F. (aside to LORD*).* It will all come out—I fancy ma'am my lord emploied him to invite some of the company.

[*Aside to* LADY BELL.

Lady Bell. Oh, is it that? and so Sir you have asked all your own acquaintance I suppose?

Cham. To be sure Ma'am, and woud if there had been more of them; I did not come here to *save* I can assure your ladyship.

Lord (aside). Fy! you'll disgrace yourself. Ay ay ma'am, my friend Champignion is as generous as a Prince, and would have me to be so too—Come Sir will you walk ?

Cham. Faith my lord I am no niggard when ladies are in the question: we squandering puppies begrudge nothing on our pleasures. I have ordered that no expence shall be spared, I can tell you ma'am.

Lady Bell. Pray my lord what has he to do with this entertainment ?

Cham. I have the honour of giving it as I take it ma'am

Lady Bell. I understood it had been yours, my lord Stewkly ?

Lord. (So!) Why to tell you the truth ma'am I intended it so; but my friend here is so munificent he has taken it upon himself. I thought I had told your ladyship so.

Lady Bell. Then I hope I shall be excused from presiding, there are some people here possibly that may like such a thing.

Cham (aside to LADY FILMOT). She is prodigeously proud, and yet for all that— [*He talks apart to* LADY FIL.

Lord. A word with you lady Bell—I dont know whether you suspect it or not, but the man's in love with you over head and ears, and it is intirely on your account that he has done all this.

Lady Bell. In love with *me!* Why prithee my lord who *is* the Creter ?

Lord. He is worth above a hundred thousand pound

Lady Bell. Ay; but did he get it by *doing* anything, I suppose he is a trading fellow ?

Lord. Why I own he is *but* a private gentleman.

Lady Bell. But are you sure he is *even* a gentleman ?

Lord. Of a considerable family at Antigua

Lady Bell. He he ha I think I'll speak to him; one woudn't be rude you know even to one's inferior.—Mr. a—I think these gardens are pretty enough

Cham. Oh quite pretty ma'am; but nothing to what we have abroad. I have such gardens ma'am, it woud delight your ladyship to see them. I have a prodigious taste that way ma'am.

Lord (aside). Mark that.

Lady F. And then you have such fine fruits Mr. Champignion!

Cham. Oh lord ma'am you have nothing like them here; if we had but such fine *ladies* our Island would be a perfect paradise ma'am.

Lord (aside). Do you observe?

Lady Bell. Lord Mr. — I didn't think you West-indians had been so well bred

Cham. Nobody more so, I assure you ma'am; we are remarkable for it. I had a good mind to have brought my six fellows to have waited this morning, only my lord told me, some of the fair sex are a little timerous of negroes.

Lady Bell. I dont dislike them for my part.

Cham. If I had known that ma'am, I should have tried to have collected twenty or thirty to have attended your ladyship ma'am.

Lord. Come ladies, I fancy most of the company are assembled by this time; suppose we were to go to them.

Cham. Will your ladyship favour me with your hand?

Lady Bell. I can find my way Sir—Come lady Filmot, my Lord Stewkly, your arm if you please.

Lady F. I'll follow your ladyship.

Exit all but LADY FILMOT

8 SCENE.

Enter EDWARD,

who runs behind a tree making signs to Lady F. not to discover him.

Enter LUCY *running,*

and looking about. lady Filmot points to the opposite side and Lucy runs out.

Lady F. Mr. Edward! Mr. Edward! what you have been at play? (EDWARD *comes out*

Ed. Yes ma'am just to pass away the time till breakfast

Lady Fil. Is that young girl any relation of yours

Ed. Does your ladyship think she favours me?

Lady F. I dare say she favours you Sir; but I dont think she resembles you in the least, she doesn't appear to me to be at all handsome, that is she is not at all like you—I mean she is not—

in short she is not like you.—but I was going to say, if she were one of your family, I shoud be glad to introduce her into some of the best company here.

Ed. She would be vastly obliged to you I am sure ma'am

Lady F. Ay, but if she is no relation of yours you know—

Ed. She is not at present; but one of these days perhaps, who knows?

Lady F. Oh, I understand you; she's a mistress then?

Ed. Ah, you found me out by my colouring; but don't you tell now lady Filmot

Lady F. Poor girl, I pity her.

Ed. Pity her! lord ma'am for what? She likes me as well as I do her.

Lady F. No doubt ont; and she has no rivals to be sure.

Ed. No, upon my credit; we have been in love since we were children no higher than this

Lady F. And are likely to continue so! Ah thou little Coquette!

Ed. *I* a coquette! Oh heavens, you dont take me for a lady I hope ma'am

Lady F. Oh there are *male* coquets, and you are one or I am mistaken.

Ed. Ha ha ha; you are very comical I do declare lady Filmot. Why I protest I don't well know what a coquet is.

Lady F. No, no, not you, you poor innocent! You don't know how to make yourself agreeable, and to say a thousand things with your eyes.

Ed. With my eyes. I say things with my eyes ha ha ha!

ACT 2d.

Scene *the* 1st, Lady Filmot's *appartment*.

Lady Filmot *and* Edward. *A chess board before them.*

Lady F. This lesson is sufficient for to day; we must'nt tire young beginners.

Ed. I never can remember that Knight's move; I believe your ladyship thinks me very dull.

Lady F. I should not judge so by looking at you.—Come we'll have done, I can play no more.

Ed. I hope you are not ill lady Filmot, you look so grave!

Lady F. I am not very well.

Ed. I am vastly sorry upon my word.

Lady F. Are you? Why then I wish I were well for your sake.

Ed. So do I too, I declare.—How did you like Miss Tryforts dancing this morning, ma'am?

Lady F. I did n't mind her.

Ed. Oh dear, why did'nt you see me dancing with her after Lord Stewkly?

Lady F. Yes certainly, I saw *you* dance, and observed something moving along with you.

Ed. That was shee; she is reckoned a charming dancer.

Lady F. She might pass at a City ball.

Ed. Why ma'am dont *you* like her?

Lady F. If *you* like her, she, she needn't be solicitous about the opinion of others.

Ed. Ay; but your approbation ma'am, who are so good a judge—

Lady F. Agreeable flatterer!

Ed. You who are so genteel yourself—

Lady F. Polished creature!

Ed. Now tell me on upon your honour which dances best, she or *I*?

Lady F. What signify *my* thoughts?

Ed. I'd give the universe to know them.

Lady F. Why, then, beyond comparison you are the best, and she is the very awkwardest dancer I ever beheld.

Ed. Absolutely? ha ha ha, how she'd be vexed to hear you had said so!

Lady F. Oh you must'nt tell her, it woud mortify the poor thing; for you may suppose that WE *must* understand better what is called grace and elegance than—you'll pardon me; but I really think it a great pity that your lot hadn't thrown you amongst people of fashion.

Ed. So it is upon my reputation, and so my Uncle Jeremy always said; I shoud like it of all things, their ways are so different from ours in the City. I dont know how it is, but they are always in good humour I think

Lady F. Oh, ever, ever, tis a characteristic mark of quality never to be out of temper. Why you are of a good family yourself Mr. Edward.

Ed. And I am of a good family myself as you say ma'am, thats of *one* side.—and then they are so obliging and kind to strangers!

Lady F. And so sentimental! do you understand sentiments?

Ed. Oh yes ma'am, I have drunk sentiments very often, we give them for toasts.

Lady F. Those are but commonplace things; but some day or other I'll give you a lecture on the subject of sentiments; I am sure you'll like it.

*Ed. Any*thing from your *ladyship*

Lady F. Really. Why you begin to grow dangerous Child.

Ed. I dangerous! I declare Lady Filmot you talk strangely! Why you have more danger in your little finger than ten such as me.

Lady F. Captivating little rogue! hush! here's company.

2ᵈ SCENE.—*Enter* MRS. TRYFORT.

Mrs. T. How does your ladyship do to-day? So Mr. Edward?

Lady F. Dear Mrs. Tryfort, how came it you were not at the breakfast this morning?

Mrs. T. It was not for want of being *askd* I assure your ladyship; but I was so ill! ha ha ha! lord it isn't long since I got out of bed.—I declare this is a fatiguing life one leads, and exhilerates one's spirits so much, that I have scarce strength to rise in a morning; but then one keeps such good company ha ha that it makes amends for the bad hours.

Lady F. Ay, as you observe; but I hope you will be able to go to the rooms tonight, Mr. Champignion gives tea.

Mrs. T. Why if I find myself tolerably well; but I am so low every morning, ha ha ha, I protest I use almost an ounce of salvolatile constantly in my tea—your ladyship I suppose will be there, and Lady Bell, and Lord Stewkly.—To be sure he is one of *the* best bred, most polite, good humourd charming men living! and takes as much pains to teach my Lucy, and make her illiterate, as if he were absolutely her master.

Ed. Pray what is he teaching her ma'am?

Lady F. Oh a song I suppose.

Mrs. T. I left them together practising, and he has such a genteel manner, and keeps time so finely with his head, and says Piano; with such an air! and then takes Lucy by the hand, and is so much the gentleman, lord what difference there is between folks.

Ed. Shall we go and hear the Pianoing lady Filmot?

Lady F. No, we wont disturb them now, it will improve Miss, my lord has a very pritty taste in singing.

Mrs. T. Oh in everything ma'am he is a progeny! a perfect progeny lady Filmot!—In the first place he is a most prodigious wit, and then he speaks all the languages in the world, and is so full of compliments, and such a charming poet!

Lady F. He is very accomplished I know.

Ed. But how came you to find out all this Mrs. Tryfort?

Mrs. T. Why I have had him above an hour with me to day: your ladyship must know he desired leave to come to my toilet, that was polite! its the way he says in France.

Lady F. Ay and here too, you know amongst people of fashion.

Ed. I am sure it is not the way in the City, for Lucy woud never let me in when she was putting on her cloaths.

Mrs. T. How *can* you be so vulgar Mr. Edward! Can't you say dressing? I wish you woud learn of my lord.

Lady F. Oh very soon he'll want no instructions.

Mrs. T. And my lord dresses so prodigiously, and understands the fashions so well, and has such pritty names for things, and praises everything up to the skies! but *never* flatters: no, *that* he declares he's above.

Ed. And you believe him?

Lady F. No body can doubt my lords veracity.

Mrs. T. And Lucy says he dances wonderfully.

Ed. Did Lucy say so?

Mrs. T. Miss Tryfort said so sir

Lady F. There I differ with her a little, I have seen *some* whose dancing pleased me better.

[LADY F. *looks at* EDWARD *and he winks at her.*

Mrs. T. Well I know he is a terrestrial man altogether and so free, and comprehensive; he told me all about himself, just as if we had been old acquaintance: and what do you think the comical creature wanted me to do?

Lady F. What?

Mrs. T. I declare to put on a little red, ha ha ha! Oh fy my lord, says I, I never did such a thing in all the days of my life. But my dear ma'am says he, (stroking my cheek with his hand so agreably) do but *try;* let *me* just touch it for you, only to heighten your bloom a little; you want but that to be the very image of the Marquise de Rouge (who was but eighteen) that I used to visit at Paris. Wasnt that vastly witty and clever?

Ed. I hope you wont advise Lucy to paint; but *she* doesn't want it indeed.

Lady F. No, nor Mrs. Tryfort neither in my opinion.

Mrs. T. Your ladyship's so obliging to say so. To be sure when I am well I have a pritty good complexion; my lord said it was only my illness that made it not quite so brilliant as my daughters.

Ed. Ha ha ha, My lord's above flattery you know ma'am.

Mrs. T. I declare you are so unbred, I wonder her ladyship can bear to talk with you.

Lady F. Oh I like his plain natural manner of all things.

Mrs. T. But so vulgar you know ma'am. Dear I wish I coud remember the verses my lord made on Lucy.

Ed. Verses! did he make verses on her?

Mrs. T. Just offhand now, I forget what he called them

Ed. Extempore may be.

Mrs. T. No, none of your nonsensical extemprys, it was some charming French word.

Lady F. Impromtu.

Mrs. T. Ay that was the very title of them

Ed. I have a good mind to go and spoil their impromtu.

Lady F. Indeed you shan't, for I intend you shall gallant me to the pump room.

Ed. Well I'll just leave you there; but I must run back tho.

Mrs. T. There's politeness for you!

Lady F. Nothing but easy freedom.

Mrs. T. Shall I beg the favour of your ladyship to allow Lucy to practise a little on your Harpsichord, just when you are abroad?

Lady F. Whenever she pleases ma'am

Mrs. T. Your ladyships immensely good,—I wish I coud recollect my lords verses.—they begin

>When Lucia sings we bless th' inchanting sound
>And bless the notes that do—

lord I forget what comes next—

Ed. Ha ha ha Are those what my lord gave you for his own poetry? Why the song's as old as yourself.

Mrs. T. Sir you are a little too pert let me tell you, and so much taciturnity doesn't become a young man.—your ladyship woud be charmd with the verses if I coud think of them.

Lady F. Come ma'am you may recover them as we walk!

Mrs. T. I'll just step and tell my daughter that she may practise a little here, now your ladyship is going out, and I will wait on you again directly   [*Exit* Mrs. Tryfort.

Ed. Why Mrs. Tryfort seems to be quite in love with my lord Stewkly, I shoud be sorry Lucy saw with her mother's eyes

Lady F. There's no accounting for peoples ridiculous tastes; now to *me*, the artless, unaffected manners of one who has seen less of the world, has ten thousand times the charms of all lord Stewkly's studied address.

Ed. And I am sure your ladyship has ten thousand times more sense than Mrs. Tryfort, with all her airs.

Lady F. Come then we'll not wait for her; but slip out, and have our own little chat to ourselves. You shall be my cissisbey

Ed. What maam?

Lady F. I'll tell you as we go along, tis' the prettyest thing in the world.

[*Exit* LADY F. *and* ED.

3ᵈ SCENE.

Enter MRS. TRYFORT, LUCY, *and* LORD STEWKLY.

Mrs. T. Bless me, her ladyship's gone! I must follow her, or she'll think me monstrously ill bred. Be sure now Miss, mind, and do all that my lord bids you. There child sit down to the harpsichord, your lordship will excuse me for leaving you so deliberately

Lord. Oh ma'am there needs no apology [*Exit* MRS. TRYFORT] Come my sweet little pupil: just that single passage over again that charmed me so in the next room.

Lu. Shan't I play, my lord?

Lord. I had rather hear your voice without the instrument. [LU. *sings*] ravishing upon my soul! You have the finest ear in Nature, and your voice is absolutely angelic.

Lu. And my master used always to say I sung out of tune.

Lord. He was a blockhead, and didn't understand his business.

Lu. And what vexed me more, Mr. Edward used to join with him and say so too.

Lord. And what need you mind what Mr. Edward says?

Lu. Oh I must mind him because——

Lord. Because what? [*She puts her hands before her face*] Oh heavens not a lover I hope! Why sure that raw stripling has not the assurance to pretend to you!

Lu. He is but young to be sure my lord; but as my mama says, thats a fault that will mend

Lord. You cant *like* him! thats morally impossible

Lu. Why they used to say in town he was a very pritty young man.

Lord. Oh my dear Miss Tryfort there never was such a mistake, the lad might be well enough behind a counter.

Lu. He keeps no shop I can assure you my lord.

Lord. And so you'd be content to sit down for life in Cornhill?

Lu. Why pray my lord mayn't one be as happy there as any where else?

Lord. Happy! what happy in Cornhill! Oh for shame. I must speak to your mama about it.

Lu. She knows it already my lord, so you needn't think to make mischief.

Lord. [*aside*] So, I find my difficulty will be *here*) But ma'am hadn't you rather be my lady, than plain Mrs. Any body?

Lu. I *shoud* like to be a lady, that I own; I *may* come to be lady Mayoress you know my lord.

Lord. Oh paltry! we laugh at those titles at our end of the town: No, no ma'am, a coronets the thing for you.

Lu. I woud not give a pin for a coronet I assure you my lord.

Lord. (*aside*) that won't do I see) No? thats surprising! Shoudn't you like to take the place of Lady Filmot, and Lady Bell Aircastle?

Lu. Yes, that I shoud vastly; for I don't love either of them, lady Bell is so proud she'll never speak to me, and lady Filmot is always whispering with Mr. Edward.

Lord. That you must know she does to teaze me, for she is the arrentest coquet in nature; but I have thought of a way to be even with her, if you woud assist me in a little piece of innocent revenge that I have plotted against her.

Lu. Oh with all my heart, I love mightily to be in plots, I am always plotting when I am at home.

Lord. Well, I'll tell you then; You must know I made some slight addresses to lady Filmot, and was at first, as you may imagine, very well received: not that I was absolutely in love with her, only I thought her the prettyest woman here, before your arrival, madam.

Lu. Oh my lord, she is a great deal handsomer than I am.

Lord. You are the only person, herself excepted, that thinks so I believe: but, however, fancying herself secure of me, she has a mind to try her power, and giggles with your lover merely to make me uneasy; but I'll let her see I despise her little arts, by making love to another woman before her face.

Lu. Indeed you'll serve her right.

Lord. Now as you are incontestably the object of every ones admiration here, I have made choice of you for the person, if you will allow me the honour of addressing you.

Lu. Ay,—but not in Earnest tho' my lord.

Lord. No, no its to be all in jest; but then you must *seem* to receive me kindly, and that will vex her to the heart.

Lu. Very well; but then mus'nt I tell Edward the truth?

Lord. Not for the world; for He'd tell *her*, and then the Joke would be lost; we shall have time enough to let him into the secret. I only want to pique her pride for a day or two

Lu. Well, I own I shoud like to vex her a little. When shall we begin?

Lord. The very first time we happen to see her. Suppose we were to go now and meet her in her walks—and be sure you smile and look pleased at what I say.

Lu. Oh never fear my lord; but remember I am not in earnest

Lord. No, by no means—Come then. (*aside*) Her love of *mischief*, may probably effect that, to which even her *vanity* Coud'nt prompt her! [*Exit* LORD S. and LUCY.

SCENE 4th CHANGES TO THE PARADE.

Enter SIR JONATHAN *meeting* STAPLETON.

Sir Jo. Ha! Mr Stapleton, well met, have you been taking a walk by yourself? thats melancholy like; now I love company and chearfulness, and I'd have you do the same.

Stap. But I love solitude Sir

Sir Jo. You are not troubled in mind I hope Sir. If you have any thing that disturbs you the best way is to tell it; theres great comfort in opening ones mind to a friend.

Stap. But suppose a man has no friend Sir?

Sir Jo. Nay, faith that would be hard in a Christian country; for my part I am always ready to listen to every body's story; and I am as ready to tell my own.

Stap. I thank you Sir; but at present I am not in a humour either to hear your story or to tell my own, so good by to you [*going*]

Sir Jo. Harkee, Mr. Stapleton, pray did you meet my son any where?

Stap. Your son Sir, why I don't know him!

Sir Jo. Ha ha ha, how shoud you, faith; now I think of it I believe you never saw him. He is a pritty slender youth, with his own curld hair.

Stap. And a light colourd frock?

Sir Jo. Ay, ay the same, thats Ned.

Stap. Then I can tell you he is got into very bad hands.

Sir Jo. Bad hands, Sir! how, how, which way?

Stap. A ladys Sir, a *fine* lady's.

Sir Jo. A fine lady, why you dont call that bad hands I hope Mr. Stapleton? Neds fit company I can tell you for the finest lady in the land; why he'll make you as handsome a bow, and pen you as pretty a letter, and compose you as moving a love speech too, out of his own head, as e'er a fine beau of them all. No, no I don't fear Neds behaviour.

Stap. Nor don't you fear his morals neither?

Sir Jo. Oh, thats another thing, Sir, quite and clear.

Stap. Why then Sir, I tell you as a friend, your son is in danger; I saw him just now enter the Pump room, a fine sprightly female leaning on his arm. Her modish dress, and a certain air of levity which I observed in her countenance, opposed to the plain garb, and modest deportment of the youth struck me.

Sir Jo. Ay, isn't he a pretty modest youth?

Stap. A mixture of pity and curiosity, excited me to observe them; and as there was no other company in the room (for thats the time I chuse) I took out a paper and pretended to read, to leave them more at liberty.

Sir Jo. Well Sir?

Stap. Without minding me, she drew him into a corner, and enterd into a conversation—

Sir Jo. Ha ha ha, good, I warrant Ned found enough to say to her.

Stap. Ay; but Sir she said enough to him to have alarmd a parent, had I been one.

Sir Jo. Ha ha ha I'll be hang'd if this wasn't lady Filmot, the pleasantest good humourd woman in the world. She takes great notice of *my* boy and of me to[o] indeed, and of my brother Sir Jeremy—ha ha ha I can't but laugh at your thinking my son in danger; why she says any thing that comes uppermost man.

Stap. Well Sir, remember I have warnd you.

Sir Jo. Oh I thank you Mr. Stapleton; its kindly done of you, tho you may be a little out in your judgment. That same lady Filmot is a mighty civil woman, and very Jocose too.— Oh here comes my brother, heres Sir Jeremy, will you let me introduce you to him Sir?

Stap. No Sir—fare you well.   *Exit* STAP.

Sir Jo. Short enough in troth; but he seems melancholy poor man.

5th SCENE.

Enter SIR JEREMY.

Sir Jer. Who is that you were talking to, Sir Jonathan?

Sir Jo. Who that gentleman? Why truly I don't know much of him brother. He is a little crazy I believe, or vapourish; but I take him to be a very good sort of a man. Well but now brother if you are at leisure, I should be glad to know what you meant by the hint you were pleased to give me this morning?

Sir Jer. There is a time for all things Sir Jonathan, I am not at leisure at present; I am going to see if there are any letters for me to day. [*going*]

Sir Jo. I'll save you the trouble then, for I am just come from the post office, and can tell you there are not.

Sir Jer. No! thats pretty extraordinary!

Sir Jo. But Brother, will you do me the favour just to tell me—

Sir Jer. Why if I were *just* to tell you as you call it, ten to one if you coud comprehend one word of what I shoud say

Sir Jo. That will be *your* fault brother, not mine; do you speak plain, and I'll warrant I'll understand you.

Sir Jer. I'll be hang'd if I do, tho I shall put the thing as clear as that two and two make four. Well then Sir, you are to know, with regard to the subject of our last conference that after having maturely deliberated, weighd, considerd, and laid all circumstances together (touching the affair in debate) I apprehend that it is wholly inconsistent, (upon a general view of things) that it is inconsistent I say with our true interest to ratify the proposed treaty; therefore without entering into further preliminaries, in my humble opinion according to the maxims of sound policy, I take it to be the wiser measure to prevent, rather than to remedy; as it is more easy to anticipate than to cure an evil—you apprehend?

Sir Jo. N—ot very clearly brother.

Sir Jer. You dont take my meaning then?

Sir Jo. No, by my troth

Sir Jer. Ho, ho, I thought you were to understand me if I spoke plain

Sir Jo. But you have *not* spoke plain brother Jeremy

Sir Jer. I havn't—O mighty well Sir, mighty fine! I honour you extremely.

Sir Jo. I dont understand mysteries for my part, nor I can't abide concealments.

Enter CHAMPIGNION.

6th SCENE.

Sir Jer. Silence, Sir Jonathan.

Cham. Whats your argument gentlemen, for I love dearly to be in secrets?

Sir Jo. Then my brother Jeremy's your man Sir, for he makes a secret of every thing.

Sir Jer. Or rather Sr Jonathans your man Sir, for he makes a secret of nothing.

Cham. Prithee gentleman let's have the secret between you?

Sir Jo. Why my brother Jeremy here—

Sir Jer. So, you will shoot your bolt in spite of me!

Sir Jo. Well, tell it yourself then

Cham. Let me beseech you Sir Jeremy, I am inclined to think beforehand that I shall be of your side of the question (*aside*) I'll coax him a little)

Sir Jer. There may be something in that—you may inform the gentleman.

Sir Jo. By my troth I dont know well what to inform him of, for I dont know myself what youd be at; but you talkd something to me this morning about marrying my son to a great lady—

Cham. Oh if that be the case you are quite right Sir Jeremy.

Sir Jer. You are of that opinion Sir?

Cham. I am clear in the thing: and I assure you the young gentleman is beginning to be taken great notice of by the ladies; if I were you Sir Jonathan, I woud'nt let him look lower than a viscounts daughter at least. We handsome rogues can set just what price we please on our persons.

Sir Jo. Ned is a handsome youth to be sure; but I dont want to sell him Mr. Champignion

Cham. Oh fy, fy Sir Jonathan, hang it, no I don't mean a money bargain.

Sir Jer. Ay; but Sir Jonathan understands no other.

Cham. Oh filthy! I have no notion of that; here your son has his pockets full of money, and is a very pretty figure. This, (if I don't flatter myself) is just my own case. What do we want then but the distinction of ingrafting our families upon nobility? I declare I woud rather have my wife calld my lady, than be married to a cherubim.

Sir Jo. Oh heaven forgive you Mr. Champignion!

Sir Jer. And Sir Jonathan woud rather add a few dirty thousands to his sons heap, than enrich his grand childrens veins with the first blood in the realm.

Sir Jo. And so I woud Sir Jeremy, for I never knew good come of those matches. When a plain man marries a lady of quality, he is master of nothing that belongs to him, it is my lady such a ones *house*, my lady such a ones *liveries*, and my lady such a ones *children;* and e'gad he's nobody but my lady such a ones husband himself.

Cham. Now, that would be *my* pride Sir, to have people say, there's Mr. Champignion—what of such a place? No he that married my lady—no matter who; but perhaps I may have the honour of giving my name to a certain lady of quality before it be long.

Sir Jer. Oh we can guess who—Lady Bell!

Cham. I name no names Sir Jeremy; but with regard to the fair sex I am the luckiest dog in the universe.

Sir Jo. Lady Bell! Why if it be Lady Bell Aircastle they say she is not worth a souse.

Cham. The very reason, why I woud chuse her ladyship Sir.

Sir Jo. And I suppose thats the very reason why her ladyship chuses you Sir, ha ha ha.

Cham. Ha ha ha, I declare, that only wants the circumstance of being true, to be a pretty good thing; but the lady has *Eyes* Sir Jonathan, and without vanity I take it my *money* is not my only recommendation.

Sir Jer. But it is his criterion of merit Mr. Champignion, he thinks there can be no good quality without it.

Cham. The rascallyest thing in nature; I declare I am never so happy as when I'm a throwing it away. I have been looking out these two or three days for some honest gentleman that may have occasion for a small sum that I may give it to him, for you must know I pique myself upon doing generous things.

Sir Jer. I fancy Sir there may be such honest gentlemen found in the world.

Cham (*aside*). Oh he takes my meaning I see; I'll make him the offer). I have a hundred guineas loose in my pocket at this present moment which are at your service Sir Jeremy, I came on purpose to look for you.

Sir Jer. At my service Sir! for what?

Cham. apart to SIR JER.] I tell you that another time, you may do me a good turn; but mum: (*speaking aloud*) Oh dear Sir I have only a mind to oblige you with a trifle.

Sir Jo. (*aside to* CHAM.) Gadso Sir, you'll make him angry.

Sir Jer. Oblige me with a trifle!

Cham. (*aside*) I'll double it if you'll swallow an oath—not a word more—

Sir Jer. advances to him laying his hand upon his sword]. Look in my face Sir! and tell me if you see anything there that coud encourage you to presume—

Cham. No faith Sir it was not your face that encouraged me; but—but to tell you the truth—

Sir Jer. My garb perhaps! I am not an embroiderd puppy; but Sir I despise dress, and Sir you are an illiberal coxcomb, and I am inclined to think are sprung from the dregs of the people!

Sir Jo. There—there! I told you so, Oh he has a very high spirit

Cham. I declare Sir Jonathan that I am very glad there are no ladies present to hear him treat me so very ungenteely, and hang me if I know what its for either.—May I perish if here isn't lady Bell herself! for heavens sake gentlemen dont be familiar with me before her, for she cant endure any thing but a beau.

7th SCENE.

Enter LADY BELL.

Oh ma'am isn't your ladyship tired with walking? But I protest your ladyships presence is as necessary as the Suns, to give light and warmth to everything.

Lady Bell. Ha ha ha, well enough imagined; but I really am fatigued, and am now going home. lord who are those ordinary people that you were talking to?

Cham. half-aside) Only tradesmen of mine ma'am to whom I have been giving orders.

Sir Jer. advancing] Whom do you call tradesmen Coxcomb?

Sir Jo. Ay whom do you call tradesmen, Mr. Coxcomb, as my brother Jeremy says? Why *I* am not a *trades*man, much less this gentleman, who is a baronet by birth, and a man of learning too.

Lady B. What is the meaning of all this?

Cham. Oh ma'am they are a couple of very uncivilized persons I assure your ladyship. Will you allow me to wait on your ladyship home ma'am?

Sir Jer. Ay you do well to put yourself under a lady's protection, or I should teach you how to treat men of lineage.

Lady B. Lineage! I must enquire into this, if he be really a man of lineage!

Sir Jo. Of as antient a one as any in England I can assure your ladyship, tho' I say it that am but his brother.

Sir Jer. That I shoud think beneath me to mention, if this plantation fop here, this vender of molossus hadn't dared to offer me a bribe, for what ends he best can tell.

Lady B. Oh insufferable, and have I been acquainted with a fellow that deals in sugar! Sir I desire you will never presume to approach me again!

Cham. Oh heavens ma'am your ladyship cant be so hard hearted sure! I declare I was only offering him a little of my bounty, for every body knows I have the spirit of an Emperor, and the poor gentleman I really apprehended was one that had met with misfortunes.

Sir Jer. I have met with disappointments I grant, such perhaps as dont happen every day.

Cham. Faith Sir I only heard you had spent a good Estate, and that happens every day in the year as I take it.

Lady B. You are not the only person of condition Sir that has suffered in that particular; but thank my stars, it is not in the power of fortune to rob us of our illustrious birth.

Sir Jer. Madam you seem to have a just estimate of things; but for this paltry fellow here, who has been emploied to offer me money—

Lady B. Why he must be ignorance itself, Sir Jeremy!

Sir Jer. I question if he be so ignorant as he appears Madam. If I ben't mistaken a certain person that shall be nameless is at the bottom of this; but I'll let them all see that my integrity is as unshaken as when—I wont name Æra—This fellow may be a spy too, for what I know

Lady B. M^r I shall dispense with your attendance, this gentleman will wait on me home.

Sir Jer. With all my heart Madam, for to tell you the truth I dont much admire that young man's looks.

Lady B. Nor I neither, I assure you Sir Jeremy.

> *He gives his hand to* LADY BELL, *who casting a disdainful look at* CHAMPIGNION, *she and* SIR JEREMY *strut out together.*

Cham. Do you understand the meaning of all this Sir Jonathan? for perish me if I do!

Sir Jo. Egad they are both too high flown for me or you either, so you had best leave them to one another.

Cham. Let me dye if I am not the most unlucky dog in the universe; I must go and look for my lord Stewkly, that he may make up this breach between her Ladyship and me. I wish you and your antient blood were at the Antipodes, as I hope for mercy Sir. *Exit* CHAM.

Sir Jo. Heaven forbid, Mr Champignion, what would my poor boy do for me then? I must go and see whats become of him tho, I believe he is lost. *Exit* SIR JONATHAN.

END OF THE 2nd ACT.

ACT THE 3ᵈ SCENE 1ˢᵗ

PARADE

Enter LADY FILMOT *and* EDWARD.

Ed. But wasn't your ladyship surpriz'd to see with what attention she seemd to listen to my lord?

Lady F. Nay, she absolutely flirted with him! but I woudn't have you be alarmd, there *may* be nothing in it, at least I hope so for your sake.

Ed. You are very good Madam, to say so; perhaps I have taken the thing more seriously than I ought to have done.

Lady F. I dare say you have.—and yet we women are very fantastical; and *dress*, often does more than person, especially with young people, who haven't been used to the beau monde. If you were to appear as gay as Lord Stewkly, the difference between you woud then be so apparent!

Ed. I'd give the world to make the experiment, and go to the rooms to night dressed as fine as him.

Lady F. Oh you little tyrant, what a thought is that! and yet I like it so well, that I am resolved you shall put it in execution.

Ed. Lord ma'am, which way! My father never lets me wear any thing but these nasty plain cloaths.

Lady F. That's nothing—Champignion's wardrobe shall supply us, as it might half the town. A trifling alteration will make a suit of his cloaths fit you. I'll borrow one which he has never worn just for the Jokes sake, and my frizeur shall dress your hair in the very height of the mode.

Ed. Oh my dear lady Filmot, that will be charming; but I'll let nobody know a word of my design.

Lady F. Not a syllable, till you flash upon them all at once, and for that reason you shall dress in my appartment; you know you are my Cicisbey, and those little liberties are always allowable.

Ed. Thats true I protest, I had like to have forgot that I was your Cicisbey.—What's this that I am to do? let me con it over now that I may remember it. In the first place, I may come into your room in a morning before you are up, in the next—

Lady F. Hold, hold not that *yet*, you are only to be admitted to my toilet for the first week.

Ed. Oh, ay, that's true; I may come in when you are dressing. I am to put essence into your handkerchief, reach you your combs, your pins, and y^r powder as you want them, and if your woman shoud not be in the way, I am to tye your necklace string and adjust your Tucker.

Lady F. Very right, and by way of reward I am to—

Ed. Oh I remember, you are to let me stick a patch on just where I think it will become you best.

Lady F. Good.

Ed. I am never to be from your elbow all day if you command me. I am to help you tea, coffee, and fruit before any other lady in the company, and give it you on my knee.

Lady F. I shall dispense with that part of the ceremony, except when we are alone. Well what next?

Ed. I am to read to you when you dont chuse to see company at home, and to carry your knotting bag in my pocket when you go to make a morning visit. I am to attend you to all publick places and home again, and to see you up to your chamber door.— Is there anything else?

Lady F. Those are the most material articles, the rest are but trifles, such as never paying attention to any lady in my presence—

Ed. What not to Lucy?

Lady F. No, not even to *her* without my leave; but I shan't be strict. Never to approve of any thing that I have not first commended. To be always ready to smile when I seem pleased, and to look melancholy if I shoud happen to frown.—Thats all I think.

Ed. I declare its mighty pretty.

Lady F. Oh amazingly, and I dare say you'll acquit yourself very well

Ed. And when I am *dressed*, I fancy your ladyship wont dislike me.

Lady F. Insinuating creature! I shall be almost afraid to trust myself with you.—But come, you shall go home with me, and I'll transform you into a beau in a trice.

Ed. I think I shall be even with Miss Lucy for her airs.

Lady F. Isn't that she, and her mother, just turned the corner? We'll not let them see us.

[*She takes him by the hand and ex^t.*

SCENE 2^d.

Enter MRS. TRYFORT *and* LUCY.

Mrs. T. You see what it is child to circulate with people of quality, when would you have heard such language in the City?

Lu. But indeed mama its only a Joke, just a little plot between my lord Stewkly and me, he is not in earnest.

Mrs. T. But I can tell you he *is* in earnest Miss, and to let you into a secret, ever since the agitation of your fortune, I resolved that you shoud marry a lord.

Lu. A lord, Madam! and whats to become of poor Mr. Edward?

Mrs. T. Dont tell me of Mr. Edward, a little insignificant mechanic. I hope we may look over his head now, for if you must know the truth, I left London on purpose that you might abdicate him.

Lu. But madam you know he has your promise, and indeed I like him better than I do lord Stewkly.

Mrs. T. I declare you are so inarticulate in your notions, that I believe you are a changling. You haven't a grain of your mothers spirit! Ha ha ha I vow I wish his lordship had chosen *me* instead of you; and perhaps if I had encouraged the thing— but no matter—oh heres Mrs. Surface, I'll ask her judgment on the affair.

SCENE 3^d.

Enter MRS. SURFACE.

Mrs. S. What walking still ladies? Oh I have news to tell you, we are to have a masquerade tomorrow night: I have been at a wax house to enquire after some habits.

Mrs. Tr. And can they be done here? I'll certainly go to it.

Mrs. S. Ay that they can. Some fine gay sparks had such a design about a month ago, and engaged a shop keeper here in town to bring down a great parcel of dresses; but they dropd the frolic, and the cloaths were never used, so the man has them still.

Mrs. Tr. Oh I'll infallibly go, and so shall you too Miss Lucy. I suppose this is my lord Stewkly's thought, he is so ingenious and full of his artifices.

Mrs. S. Ay, that he is, as e'er a man in England.

Mrs. Tr. Mind that Lucy.

Mrs. S. Between ourselves he has more art than honesty; but I woudn't say that to every body.

Lu. Mind that mama!

Mrs. Tr. What do you mean by every body, Mrs. Surface? Why isn't he a prodigeous fine gentleman?

Mrs. S. (*aside*) Oh sits the wind there) Fine! nay for that matter there isn't a *finer* gentleman in Europe. Ay, ay, no body can deny that. I warrant you can distinguish a *fine* gentleman with half an eye.

Mrs. Tr. What do you think now Miss Lucy?

Lu. Nothing Madam; but I still prefer Edward to him.

Mrs. S. Why then by my truly thats a *pretty* young man, so modest, so bashful!—

Mrs. Tr. Lord Mrs. Surface where's your taste? I thought you were a woman of more speculation.

Mrs. S. Oh he's but a sorry strippling to be sure my dear Ma'am; but then considering you know—

Mrs. Tr. But my lord Stewkly is so embelished, Mrs. Surface! No body can be embelished that has not been abroad you know. Oh if you were to hear him describe contagious countries as I have done, it woud astonish you. He is a perfect map of geography.

Lu. I dare say Edward understands geography as well as *he* does.

Mrs. S. I'll lay my life a sensible lad, and well-disposed. If I were as young and as handsome as some body he shoudn't be long without a wife

Mrs. Tr. Oh monstrous! I declare Mrs. Surface you are enough to give one the vapours.

Mrs. S. But I dont compare him to my lord Stewkly tho; no no, no, hold you there, they are not to be named in a day, no not in the same day

Lu. I wish Sir Jonathan were to hear you Mrs. Surface.

Mrs. S. My sweet creature you wont tell him I hope. You know I am as fond of Mr. Edward as if he were my own child, I dont know his fellow!

Mrs. Tr. But Mrs. Surface!

Mrs. S. My lord Stewkly to be sure is the very perfection of a man—

Lu. But Mrs. Surface!

Mrs. S. (*aside*) Lord what shall I say between these two fools) Well my beauty, what were you going to say?

Lu. Why only that you may praise one man without undervaluing another.

Mrs. S. Now blessings on your pretty constant heart! Mr. Edward must be the man then.

Mrs. Tr. Was there ever anything so satyrical? Silly chit that might be a Countess if she had the grace to deserve it.

Lu. But madam I dont desire it

Mrs. Tr. There's for you Mrs. Surface, a foolish metamorphosis

Mrs. S. A countess! I'll lay all the money in my purse, you'll be a Countess yet; I saw it in your cup when you drank coffee with me 'tother day.

Mrs Tr. Do you observe that Miss?

Mrs. S. (*aside to Lucy*] I dreamt last night that you were married to Mr. Edward, and my dreams always come to pass! — But good Madam hadnt you better step home and take something comfortable? I'm afraid you'll be sick I declare. A glass of Jelly, or a little chicken broth, I have both ready made.

Mrs. Tr. I don't care if I do, Mrs. Surface.—Come child, I wish you coud persuade this low minded girl to be a countess.

Mrs. S. Leave it to me, I'll warrant you.   *ex*[t] M<small>RS</small>. T<small>R</small>.

Lu. Dear Mrs. Surface I beg you will try to reason my mama out of this notion about lord Stewkly; indeed he has no thought of me.

Mrs. S. (*aside*) Oh ho is that the case) Give yourself no trouble about it, Mr. Edwards the man, mark what I say to you.

Ex[t] M<small>RS</small>. S. *and* L<small>UCY</small>.

4ᵗʰ Scene continues.

Enter LORD STEWKLY *and* CHAMPIGNION.

Cham. A barbarous old dog to talk of plantations before her ladyship. And my looks too, to find fault with them, when all the world allows no body ever lookd better!

Lord. It was horribly unlucky thats certain; and *I* shall be in disgrace too, for having introduced you, for I know as fond as she is of you, it will be hard to reconcile her to the thoughts of a man who has ever defiled his hands with trade.

Cham. Gads mercy my lord what shall I do? if I coud purchase nobility for fifty thousand pounds I woud let out every drop of blood in my veins, so I coud fill them again with your lordships; poison me if I woud not.

Lord. Why, *blood* you know my dear friend is not to be purchased; but a little may, and I have been casting about how to assist you a little in that way.

Cham. Have you? My dear dear lord you will make me the happiest dog in Nature; for what signifies person and fortune, if a man's discarded by the fair sex for want of a title, you know my lord?

Lord. True; but yet I am afraid at present we can't well procure more than Knighthood for you.

Cham. Well, well hang it my lord, Sir Christopher's better than nothing, you know, just to make a beginning with.

Lord. Why if that will content you, I think I have interest enough to recommend you to a red ribbon, *that* you know will be an additional honour!

Cham. Oh my lord! the thing of the universe that I sigh for; for then you know every body *sees* that a man's somebody. Besides, it sets off the figure so charmingly!

Lord. Oh, nothing more becoming—the fees tho on these occasions are pretty high.

Cham. Your lordship cant recommend the thing more to me than by saying so; *I* who can make ducks and drakes with doubloons!

Lord. Nay its no very great matter, five or six hundred pound I believe.

Cham. Oh paltry, my lord, I was in hopes it had been five or six thousand. I detest everything that is cheap,—besides I always give double the worth of a thing.

Lord. Well, I believe I have influence enough to get this done for you, if it is not already disposed of.—That indeed—

Cham. Oh heavens my lord send an express off directly, and if you will be so good as to negotiate the affair for me I shall be everlastingly obliged to your lordship.

Lord. There is no time to be lost as you observe. I'll write about it immediately. If we are not too late I am sure of it; and in that case the fees of office will be necessary.

Cham. Here's my pocket book for you my dear lord; you will find that paltry sum in it, for I never carry less about me; and if your lordship will but inform Lady Bell of the honour which is intended me, I think I may face her boldly.

Lord. Doubtless; but take no notice of it to any one else, till the thing is done. I suppose lady Bell will be at the Masquerade to morrow night?

Cham. Duce take me if I have the courage to invite her ladyship as yet; but now I think I'll venture.

Lord. By all means; but come, I had best go and dispatch my letters, so I'll bid you good by.

Cham. Your lordship's most devoted, you will do me the honour to remember I give a little supper to night after the ball!

Lord. I shall attend you Sir—thou art the very prince of Planters!

Cham. I am no *miser*, as you lordship shall find.

Ex^t severally.

SCENE 5th *changes to* MRS. SURFACES *parlour.* STAPLETON *and* MRS. SURFACE.

Stap. This parlour of yours is the very Mart of Scandal. I always know when you pull me in here, that you have some scurrilous anecdote to communicate, and ten to one a lye into the bargain.

Mrs. S. Did you ever know me tell you an untruth? Me!

No not for all I am worth, I woud not tell you an untruth Mr. Stapleton.

Stap. The only circumstance that makes me doubt, is, that the *girl* you say is not as fond of the match as the mother is.

Mrs. S. Poor foolish thing she fancys herself in love with that raw Cub young Bull. Not but he'd be a better match; for my Lord isn't worth a groat; but thats between ourselves.

Stap. And why didn't you hint that to Mrs. Tryfort?

Mrs. S. My dear Sir its no business of mine! What is it to me you know? They are none of them good for anything. And as for Sir Jonathan, he is such a troublesome, inquisitive, meddling old blockhead that—

bless us! 6th S: *Enter* Sir Jonathan

talk of — you know who, they say and he'll appear! Oh Sir Jonathan, I was just speaking of you; if you had come in but a little sooner, you woud have heard—

Stap. Such enconiums on you Sir Jonathan! as woud have made you blush, our landlady here has been saying *such* things!

Mrs. S. Thats my foolish way; I can't for the life of me help praising people when I take a fancy to them, both to their faces and behind their backs, 'tis all one to *me*.

Sir Jo. Ay, ay theres nothing like being plain and downright, Mrs. Surface, always speak as you think.

Mrs. S. In troth I am a little too blunt sometimes, for I told Mr. Edward this morning that he didn't hold up his head, and I gave him a chuck under the chin, just this way; I hope I dont make too free with *you* good Sir—(*curtsying to* Sir Jonathan)

Sir Jo. No, no, no, you are heartily welcome Mrs. Surface.

Mrs. S. And the pretty Soul, smiled in my face, and said thank you Mrs. Surface, Oh you are happy to be father to such a son.

Stap. But I am told that Mrs. Tryfort wants to marry her daughter to this lord Stewkly; do you know anything of that Sir Jonathan?

Sir Jo. Whu–ph! As soon as she'd marry her to the great Mogul! No, no Mr. Stapleton, dont believe a word of it.

Stap. Mrs. Surface is my Author.

Mrs. S. Lord Sir how shoud *I* know? (*aside to* Stap.) Why woud you bring *me* in? I only gave you the hint as a friend.

Mr. Stap. But you ought in justice to tell Sir Jonathan what you know.

Sir Jo. An *honest* woman! I'll be sworn she woud; but theres nothing in it, nothing in it Mrs. Surface, depend upon it. —Thats just like my friend Stapleton here, who fancy'd lady Filmot had designs upon *my* son, ha ha ha do you remember Mr. Stapleton?

Stap. I do Sir Jonathan, and you will find both the one, and the other true.

Sir Jo. You are a very good man, I believe Mr. Stapleton; but I woudn't be suspicious for all the money in the Bank. A man has no comfort that doubts this, and believes that, and fears t'other: now I never suspect any body; but take the world as it comes.

Stap. And were you never deceivd Sir Jonathan?

Sir Jo. Not that I remember; I always dealt with honest people, and believe every man and woman so till I find them otherwise.

Stap. Well Sir repentance is often the fruits of credulity. I wish you ma'yn't find it so.—fare you well.

Mrs. S. Dont you drink coffee with us Mr. Stapleton?

Stap. No—I drink it by myself. [*Ex^t* STAPLE.

Mrs. S. A whimsical captious fellow as ever came into a house! I wish I was well rid of him.

7th S. *Enter* SIR JEREMY.

Sir Jer. But Mrs. Surface, I thought our coffee had been ready.

Sir Jo. And so did I too, that was what I came in for.

Mrs. S. I'll go and order it in the next parlour directly good Sir Jeremy. [*Ex^t* MRS. SURFACE.

Sir Jo. Why then I'll go and take another turn on the Parade till its ready—Will you walk Brother?

Sir Jer. No, Sir Jonathan, I have had walking enough.

Ex^t SIR JOHN.

8th S.

Enter LADY FILMOT.

Lady F. Oh Sir Jeremy, I have been loooking for you, I have a request to make.

Sir Jer. Your ladyship may always command me.

Lady F. You must know I have been endeavouring to make your nephew look a little more like one of us: I have left him to dress in my apartment, but as I intend to surprise Sir Jonathan and the ladies, I want you to make some excuse for his not attending them to the rooms, as I purpose taking him with *me*.

Sir Jer. With all my heart madam; and I shoud be very glad your ladyship woud take him intirely under your tuition, for Sir Jonathan will absolutely undo the young man.

Lady F. I protest I am afraid so too, Sir Jeremy, for the youth is amazingly confined in his notions I am surprized Sir, that you, who to the advantages of great parts, have joined those of a learned education—

Sir Jer. Oh your humble servant madam.

Lady F. That you, I say, have not had influence enough to get him out of the hands of *poor* Sr Jonathan, in order to train him your way.

Sir Jer. I have endeavoured at it madam; but *poor* Sir Jonathan, as you very justly and emphatically call him, has the misfortune to think his *own* head as wise as other peoples.

Lady F. Lud what an incredible difference there is between you and your brother! *He* a plodding, simple, plain creature; humble to a fault, ignorant of everything but traffic, and fond of nothing but wealth.—

Sir Jer. A very just description, madam.

Lady F. You on the other hand, active, and enterprizing, profoundly versed in *men* as well as books; and from a consciousness of the dignity of your character, joyned to a noble spirit of freedom, shew a manly pride in everything you do, and a thorough contempt for riches.

Sir Jer. Your ladyship has a very discerning Eye!

Lady F. I have been told Sir Jeremy that you were a most incomparable speaker in Parliament.

Sir Jer. Why—I was generally pretty well heard Madam—tho I fancy there were some who now and then wished me silent.

Lady F. I dont in the least doubt it, Sr Jeremy.

Sir Jer. I have said such things! Oh lady Filmot there *was* a time! if you were but to have heard me when my indignation was rouzed! but that's all over with me—

Lady F. Lord it must have been amazingly fine! so animated! so patriotic!

Sir Jer. Oh Madam, I coud thunder like Jupiter in those days; but—heaven knows what they are doing now! I was willing to have lent them my assistance; but let that matter rest.—

Lady F. Dear what a loss it is to your country that you are not in Parliament!

Sir Jer. Oh Madam—I *hope* not. To be sure every man is not blessed with equal talents; yet I flatter myself we have some pretty good men—very decent I dare say,—I should hope that *my* loss is not *considerably* felt.

Lady F. Ah, Sir Jeremy, I very much fear it is.

Sir Jer. Your ladyships regard to the good of the common-weal may make you apprehensive; tho, without vanity I *was* considered as somebody in my day.

Lady F. If you have any of your speeches written Sir Jeremy, I shoud take it as an infinite favour, if you woud lend one or two of them to me.

Sir Jer. Why Madam I did make a few that I believe I can recite from memory—pretty strong they were—ticklers i'faith!

Lady F. And you'll repeat them to me some day?

Sir Jer. Your ladyship has a taste for Orations I presume?

Lady F. Oh I doat on an Oration!

Sir Jer. You dont like flimzy flowery stuff do you?

Lady F. Oh by no means

Sir Jer. You like nerve?

Lady F. Of all things

Sir Jer. I *think* I shall please you

Lady F. You are always manly, I dare say

Sir Jer. I was no chicken Lady Filmot.

Lady F. Bold sentiments delivered in bold words, I'll answer for it.

Sir Jer. Yes—I fancy I can please you—I have one speech that I think is a chef d'œuvre, a two-edged sword i'faith. Away I flashed, down with them by dozens egad like ninepins.—none of your water gruel Oratory for me.—What do you think my crest is?

Lady F. I dont know, a Lyon perhaps.

Sir Jer. An Oak, and my motto is—you understand latin?

Lady F. No, Sir Jeremy.

Sir Jer. Thats a pity; I'll tell you in English then, *Sooner break than bend*—a whim of my own, it wasn't the family device.

Lady F. Sooner break than bend! vastly expressive I declare.

Sir Jer. Sooner break than bend, Iron and Steel, Iron and Steel—

Lady F. What a charming preceptor you woud make to your Nephew!—

Sir Jer. Oh lord Madam, why that fool his father has no more ambition than a Dervice of four-score. I own my utmost wish is to see the boy in Parliament.—That's the sphere of action Lady Filmot. My sun is set; but I shoud like to see a little star of my family twinkle there.

Lady F. Certainly, Sir Jeremy.—My lord Stewkly has a borough in his gift, and the present representative is extremely old; but I dont know how it is, my lord has such a strange partiality to his kindred, that he will give it to none but a relation; he has often told me, if I were a man I should have it.

Sir Jer. Ha ha, your ladyship is akin to him then I presume?

Lady F. Very nearly.

Sir Jer. Why then Madam, tho' your ladyship can't accept of it in propria persona, you may give him a relation who may you know?

Lady F. Oh lord, Sir Jeremy, do you think I'd marry again?

Sir Jer. Why not Madam?

Lady F. Oh dear! Well we wont talk of that now.—I fancy by this time your nephew is dressed. Suppose you were to come up stairs with me to see him, and who knows but you may oblige me with one of your speeches!

Sir Jer. I can refuse your ladyship nothing. But first I'll go and make apology for my nephew's not attending his father, and some other idle company here that perhaps expect he shoud go with them.—I 'll wait on your ladyship again immediately.

[*Ex^t* Sir Jer.

Lady F. So, this same borough has made Sir Jeremy my fast friend and ally; I dare say he will beg my acceptance both of his nephew's person and fortune.—If he shoud, I think I shan't refuse the poor thing. [*Ex^t* Lady F.

9th Scene. The Rooms.

Different parties at cards. One table filled with children at lottery Tickets. Mrs. Tryfort *has just done playing with* Lord Stewkly *and* Champignion. Lady Bell *looking on.*

Lord. Do you *always* play with such good success Ma'am? I never saw anything like it!

Mrs. T. Ha ha ha I am generally prodigious lucky indeed my lord; but this evening I contribute it intirely to your lordship's skill.

Lord. Oh dear Ma'am you play infinitely better than I do.

Mrs. T. I am sorry Mr. Champignion I am to carry away so many of your guineas ha ha ha—does your ladyship *never* play?

Lady B. Never in such mixed companies.

Mrs. T. I believe you are to give me thirty Sir.

Cham. Lord Ma'am I am quite ashamed of paying you such a *trifle*, when I play with ladies I always deprecate good fortune; for you must know ma'am tis death to me to win of them.

Lord. In that case Mr. Champignion I shoud think myself rather unfortunate to have you for a partner: what do *you* think lady Bell?

Lady B. I think my lord that in those sort of places, one is often forced to take up with strange sort of creters for partners: I wish people of fashion coud make it a rule never to play with any below themselves.

Mrs. T. Perhaps madam that might oblige them to play lower than they woud chuse ha ha ha.

Lady B. And one is so shock'd by ill breeding some times, my lord, that I shall forswear coming for my part.

Cham. Then Madam your ladyship will make an absolute desert of the rooms, for I am sure *I*'ll never come.

Lady B. And *you* are all the world, you know Mr.—the man however has some manners [*aside to* LORD S.

Cham. aside to LORD S.) I am glad her ladyship vouchsafes to speak to me again.

Lord. aside to CHAM.] Oh, I told her the honour you were to receive.

10th S. *Enter* LUCY.

Mrs. T. Lord child where have you been?

Lu. I was only getting a dish of tea mama. Have you done playing?

Lady B. Heavens above! what Company! my lord shall we saunter about a little?

Lord. My dear lady Bell how can you be so severe? Why you'll break this poor fellows heart if you discard him.

Lady B. Oh ridiculous, you cant imagine how unfeeling the common people are!

Lord. Upon my life tho, he hasn't been himself since you forbid him your presence.

Lady B. You may tell him I dont forbid him to follow me.

[*She goes to the other end of the room* LORD S. *whispers* CHAM. *and he follows her.*

Lord. Why Miss Tryfort you look so enchantingly, that both the ladies and the men will consider you as a common enemy tonight.

Lu. I am sure my lord I dont want to inchant anybody, I have no desire of being taken for a witch.

Lord. A lady may possess natural magic madam without a crime; besides tis evident that the charms you deal in are celestial!

Lu. I dont understand you my Lord.

Mrs. T. My lord she has so little alacrity, that your lordships fine language is thrown away upon her. Your lordship must speak, in the vulgar tongue for her to comprehend you.—I think I'll go and see what the company are doing in the next room.— Miss you needn't come, it looks so odd to have such a great girl dangling after one. *Ex*^t MRS. TRYFORT.

Lord. My dear madam you are not afraid I hope of trusting yourself a little while with me?

Lu. I am not afraid my lord; but I dont know that we have anything to talk of.

Lord. If I had your permission I coud soon find a very agreeable subject.

Lu. I had rather sit and look at the company, my lord.

Scene 11th.

Enter LADY FILMOT *and* EDWARD *dressd like a beau,* SIR JEREMY *following.*

Lady F. I knew we shoud be full early; but you were so impatient Mr. Edward! and I'll swear Sir Jeremy you had me fast by the ear that I coud have listend till tomorrow morning!

Sir Jer. Ha ha, persons of your ladyships taste—but my *best* speech I have reserved for the last: it was made on occasion of a bill that was brought in—

[LADY F. *and* SIR JER. *talk in dumb shew*]

Lu. Good stars! why sure that can't be Mr. Edward that is with lady Filmot? as I live and breathe it is he—look my lord!

Lord. Mercy on us what a figure she has made of the boy! ha ha ha thats good, faith.

Lu. I *will* go and ask the meaning of it.

Lord. My dear creature what are you about? Woud you go to be laugh'd at by lady Filmot? You see the things done on purpose.

Lu. I thought he had some design in his head by his keeping so much out of my sight today

Lord. Lady Filmot's designs with regard to *me*, you find are now apparent; but I beg you'll help me to disappoint them.—remember our plot as soon as she observes us.

Lu. Yes, yes, I see well enough what she woud be at; but I wonder Edward woud be so silly as to joyn her in her contrivance without telling me of it!

Lord. For the same reason I suppose that you have not told him of ours. [*they talk in dumb shew*]

Lady F. Oh I long to hear it! what fire, what enthusiasm you must have exerted!

Sir Jer. The subject, you see, demanded my whole force.

Lady F. Aside to EDWARD] Bless me, that cant be Miss Tryfort sure in such familiar chat with my lord Stewkly!

Sir Jer. And faith when once I was up, *out* it pourd like a torrent.

Lady F. A very inundation I dare say Sir Jeremy [*aside to* EDWARD]. Why the girl's coquetting I declare!

Sir Jer. And then hear him, hear him, hear him, was the word!

Lady F. Ay Sir Jeremy, hear him (*aside to* EDWARD) why this is astonishing Mr. Edward, do you observe?

Ed. I'll go and interrupt them, upon my reputation!

Lady F. By no means Sir, no interruptions.

Sir Jer. Interruptions! if any man dared to interrupt *me* he was soon called to order.

Lady F. No doubt of it Sir Jeremy—[*to* EDW.] Don't you know that it is one article of your duty not to speak to any lady without my leave?

Ed. Ay; but you know ma'am you said you woud not be strict.

Lady F. At present I will; for I see my lord Stewkly wants to nettle me, you know what I told you today?

Ed. Oh that's true, upon my credit I had forgot. How Lucy and I shall laugh when we come to explain!

Lady F. Oh it will be an inexhaustible source of mirth when you two are at your fireside next winter, so comfortably with your City neighbours.

Sir Jer. What does your ladyship say of the City, for I was in a sort of a revery?

Lady F. I was saying Sir Jeremy, how happy your Nephew and Miss Tryfort will be when they are married.

Sir Jer. Between ourselves Madam, I hope that will never be.

Lady F. You dont like the match then Sir Jeremy?

Sir Jer. Oh shameful, degrading to the last degree. If I had your ladyship at Bull-hall, I coud shew you a line of ancestry, that woud convince you we are not a people of yesterday.

Ed. Pray Uncle how came it, you never shewd them to me?

Sir Jer. Why the land and the Mansion house has slippd thro' our finger's boy; but thank heaven the family pictures are still extant.

Lady F. That's a great consolation Sir Jeremy!

Sir Jer. Why so it is madam; this stripling is not a mushroom, I can tell you lady Filmot.

Lady F. I knew it well Sir.

Sir Jer. Edward!

Ed. Uncle!

Sir Jer. Do you think you have courage enough to make love to this lady here?

Ed. Who *me* uncle! Why my lady Filmot woud laugh at me if I shoud.

Sir Jer. Try, my child; if I were at your age I shoud hardly be deterred by the fear of a fine woman's laughing at me.

Lady F. Oh Sir, my respect for Sir Jeremy, as well as my good opinion of you, will secure you against that.

Sir Jer. Lookee there! harkee Edward, if you have any of my blood in your veins [*He whispers him*] I leave you to give you the opportunity.

> [SIR JER. *retires to the other end of the room. Seems to enter into conversation with* LADY BELL *who is sitting with* CHAMPIGNION; *but keeps his eye on his nephew and* LADY FILMER.]

Lady F. What does Sir Jeremy say?

Ed. That he will go away madam to give me the opportunity.

Lady F. Oh he has a mind to divert himself; suppose we were to humour him now and pretend to carry on a little courtship, just for his entertainment—he is observing us you see.

Ed. If I were capable ma'am of saying such handsome things as your ladyship deserves—

Lady F. Everything you say Sir, receives such a grace from your manner!—

Ed. I must be very dull, *indeed* ma'am, if your ladyship didn't inspire me; you are the Iphegenia in the fable.

Lady F. Oh that thou didst but resemble Cimon in the *real* as well as the assumed passion!

Ed. (*aside*) Ha, I vow I believe she likes me in down right earnest] If I were sure of being as successful ma'am!

Lady F. (*aside*) How solemn the young rogue looks! I declare I think he is half serious] I should not else desire the resemblance. You are wrapt Mr. Edward! [EDWARD *muses*] What are you thinking of? I shall be jealous.

Ed. Then your ladyship must be jealous of yourself; for I assure you I was thinking of you.

Lady F. (*aside*) Oh, he improves apace! Lucy thy throne begins to totter!] Oh you must think of *me* when I am absent.

Ed. Does your ladyship ever think of *me* when I am absent?

Lady F. Come and sit down with me yonder, and I will tell you. [*they retire a little and sit down*

SCENE 12th.

Enter SIR JONATHAN *looking curiously about at all the Company.*

Sir Jo. Where can this boy of mine be?

SCENE: 13th.

As he is peeping about, MRS. TRYFORT *enters and meets him.*

Ha Mrs. Tryfort! I am glad I have met you. A mans in a wilderness here! do you know where Ned is? in some corner with Miss Lucy I'll lay my life!

Mrs. T. I know nothing of him, Sir Jonathan; do you think Miss Tryfort doesnt understand punctuality better than to go into corners with young fellows?

[*She goes and joyns* LORD STEWKLY *and* LUCY

Sir Jo. Heighty toity! whats the meaning of this? Oh, yonder's lady Filmot, I'll go and ask her.

Lady F. What, Sir Jonathan! [*He goes to her and* EDWARD] then you have ventured amongst us I see.

Sir Jo. To look for a stray son of mine an't please your ladyship, that's all.

Lady F. And can't you find him Sir Jonathan?

Sir Jo. No introth, I enquired for him of Mrs. Tryfort just now, and I thought she answerd me a little short or so.

Lady F. May be this gentleman can inform you.

Sir Jo. Can he? pray Sir do you know—mercy upon me! Why sure—pray Sir—this cant be 'Ned?—Yes faith it is too—and I not to know him! not to know my own son! ha ha ha a good joke faith.

Lady F. Ha ha ha, Well Sir Jonathan how do you like him?

Sir Jo. Like him! introth I think he is not to be *dis*liked (You sly young varlet to play me such a trick,) but how come you by all these trappings Ned?

Lady F. Tis only my livery, Sir Jonathan.

Sir Jo. Your livery, Madam?

Ed. Oh yes Sir I am her ladyships Cicesbey

Sir Jo. Her ladyships what Edward?

Ed. Her Cicesbey Sir

Sir Jo. Pray Madam what may that be?

Lady F. Tis only a title that a lady bestows on a galant young man, who for a time devotes himself to her service.

Sir Jo. Ha, I never heard of the title before. Does your uncle know that you are a Cicesbey? He is very fond of those out o' the way conceits.

Lady F. Oh Sir Jeremy is quite delighted with it.

Sir Jo. Ay, I knew it would please him; but what does Lucy say to it?

Lady F. Why really Sir Jonathan, she has been so taken up with lord Stewkly that she doesn't seem to take the least notice of anything else.

Sir Jo. What I suppose his lordship is *her* Cicesby? I have a mind to go and join them; perhaps Mrs. Tryfort may be in a better humour now.

[SIR JONATHAN *goes up to them.*

LADY BELL *and* CHAM. *advance;* SIR JEREMY, LADY FIL. *and*
EDWARD.

Lady B. It's true; and then the honours you are to receive may be a step to nobility. Pray what were those services that you did the Government abroad?

Cham. Services Ma'am?

Lady B. Ay, my lord Stewkly told me it was upon that account you were to have the compliment paid you.

Cham. aside Gadszooks what shall I say? he shoud have prepared for this.] Oh dear Ma'am; trifles, not worth entertaining your ladyship with; but we lucky fellows often have our services overpaid especially when the ladies do us the favour to smile on us.

Lady B. (*aside*) modest enough and not ungenteel). Well I wont press you.

Cham. (*aside*) Egad I am glad of it!

Lady B. to *lady Fil.* A'n't you tired of being so long in one place Lady Filmot? Suppose we were to go and look at them dancing in the next room.

Lady F. (*aside*) pish, how unreasonable!—I'll wait on you. Come Mr. Edward I command you to attend me, you are not weary of your service already I hope?

Ed. If your ladyships commands are always so obliging, you will not hear me complain.

Lady B. (*aside to* CHAM.) I'll swear he is not ill bred!

Cham. Oh ma'am theres nothing like the conversation of the fair sex, for polishing a man.

Lady B. Provided they are of quality!

Cham. I never give that apellation to any other, Ma'am.

Lady B. I declare your notions are rather above the vulgar.

Cham. Lord Ma'am I detest the Vulgar.

Lady B. U—gh so do I! Come Sir.

  Ext LADY B. *and* CHAM. LADY FIL. EDWARD *and* SIR JEREMY.

Sir Jo. Why you are not to mind those things Miss Lucy; he is her Cicesbey I tell you, ha ha ha tis the pleasantest frolic!

Lu. With all my heart Sir Jonathan.

Mrs. T. I dare say Miss's mind is in the greatest agility about it.

Sir Jo. Tis but a joke you know, you will have him again with you presently.

Mrs. T. Dear Sir you needn't incommode yourself, we dont in the least want his company.

Sir Jo. Come, come I know you are angry with Ned; but I'll go and bring him to you, the quarels of lovers you know—ha ha ha.   [*Ex^t* SIR JONATHAN

Lord. If I were you now, I woudn't gratify the boy's vanity, nor lady Filmot's ill nature, by letting them see they had made you uneasy; poor Sir Jonathan's awkward zeal will be for making up the quarel as he calls it, in the face of the company.

Mrs. T. I'll disappoint him then my lord, for Miss and I will quit the rooms directly, to let him see we dont want to come to any embarrassment.

Lord. Oh the very thing Ma'am, you have hit on the nicest expedient! [*Re-enter* SIR JONATHAN.

Sir Jo. Ned will be with you in a minute, I gave him a whisper, and he said he woud steal out to you presently.

Lord. Steal out Sir Jonathan! Why of whom is he afraid?

Lu. Of lady Filmot I suppose.

Sir Jo. True, thats true, in troth I had forgot how the thing was.

Mrs. T. Come Miss, my lord, will you be so kind as to put her into her chair—give my lord your hand Lucy—Your servant Sir Jonathan.

Exit MRS. *and* MISS TRYFORT *and* LORD S.

Sir Jo. Your servant Sir Jonathan! and your servant Mrs. *Tryfort* you go to that! by my faith I think these quality notions have turned the woman's head. I'll talk with my lady Filmot about it, and my brother Jeremy, they'll advise me between them; for I dont know what to make of all this for my part.

Ext. SIR JO. *as returning again to ye company in ye other room.*

SCENE 14th.

re-enter LORD STEWKLY, LADY FILMOT *enters as from the other room, meets, and stops him.*

Lord. What have you quitted your Adonis?

Lady F. I have engaged him in the dance merely to detain him, and slippd out on purpose intercept you; for I woud have him think that you are gone home with Lucy, which Sir Jonathan this minute whisperd me you were.

Lord. And so I shoud; but that they are engaged to sup abroad.

Lady F. I know it, and for that reason concluded you woud return.—Matters are now in the finest train you can imagine. You woud have been amazed if you had heard him talk; he began to say pritty things I assure you, his new cloaths inspired him.

Lord. Why as lightly as you treat it, there is more in that than you imagine. I have seen many a young fellow who in a plain coat and a bob wig, wouldn't open his mouth amongst ladies when dressd in a birth-day suit, become the very bel esprit of the company.

Lady F. I know it, and it was upon that experience I founded the success of my hopes. I wanted to give my stripling courage to speak his mind to me.

Lord. I wonder you weren't afraid of creating to yourself rivals, for the lad really lookd handsome.

Lady F. Oh my lord you are a mere novice; my first view was to make my Narcissus fall in love with himself and no transition more natural from that, than to fall in love with the woman, who *next* to himself he supposed his greatest admirer.

Lord. You ladies are better versed in those mysteries than we are; but I believe you are right.

Lady F. Infallibly—for raise but a mans vanity, and who will he think so worthy of him as the first discoverer of his extraordinary merits?

Lord. Ha ha ha what a fool you have made of the poor boy.

Lady F. You mistake, I have only made a *Coxcomb* of him; *any* woman (provided she has influence) can make a *fool* of any *man*, (as far I mean as it regards herself) but to make a coxcomb pro bono publico, requires parts, and that I think I have effected. —Do you know that we are to meet at [the] Spa tomorrow? I proposed the assignation, he bowed, and said he wouldn't fail, for the tender creature really begins to pity me.

Lord. Ha ha ha How you bring him to do that with so utter an insensibility on your side astonishes me!

Lady F. Lud, my lord one woud imagine you had stepd into the world but yesterday; why thats the very thing! take it for granted, a woman never plays the coquet well with a man she really loves. *I* acknowledge myself one, intended so by Nature;

who the better to enable me to act my part, never incommoded me with those troublesome companions calld *tender feelings:* women who *have* those; sometimes affect our character; but it never sits easy on them.

Lord. Well—from this meeting of yours, do I hope to make a total separation between the lovers. Lucy is already piqued and not so averse to me as she was. Her mother doats on me. I am to breakfast with her tomorrow, and if I can contrive to get them both to your place of rendesvous where they may have an opportunity of seeing you, I think the business may be done effectually.

Lady F. It was the very thing I meant to have proposed to you, as it will forward both of our schemes together. Sir Jeremy is already my fast friend, and Sir Jonathan you know is everybody's friend—so, get you away my lord for I woudn't have any of the family see you here.

Lord. Well, I'll go somewhere and kill an hour at picquet; so wishing your ladyship success I leave you to return to your love.

Lady F. Adieu, cruel indifferent! *Ex^t severally*

END OF THE 3^d ACT.

Belief in the devil as a pathological problem is discussed in "The Devil," a historical, medical and critical study by two French psychologists, Maurice Garcon and Jean Vinchon. The book, translated from the French by Hader Guest, will be published early in February by E. P. Dutton & Co.